WARRANT IN
CONTEMPORARY
EPISTEMOLOGY

Studies in Epistemology and Cognitive Theory
General Editor: Paul K. Moser, Loyola University of Chicago

WARRANT IN CONTEMPORARY EPISTEMOLOGY

Essays in Honor of Plantinga's Theory of Knowledge

Edited by
Jonathan L. Kvanvig

ROWMAN & LITTLEFIELD PUBLISHERS, INC.
Lanham • Boulder • New York • London

ROWMAN & LITTLEFIELD PUBLISHERS, INC.

Published in the United States of America
by Rowman & Littlefield Publishers, Inc.
4720 Boston Way, Lanham, Maryland 20706

3 Henrietta Street
London WC2E 8LU, England

British Cataloging in Publication Information Available

Library of Congress Cataloging-in-Publication Data

Warrant in contemporary epistemology : essays in honor of Plantinga's
theory of knowledge / edited by Jonathan L. Kvanvig.
p.   cm.
Includes bibliographical references and index.
1. Plantinga, Alvin.   Warrant.   2. Plantinga, Alvin.   Warrant and
proper function.   3. Plantinga, Alvin—Contributions in theory of
knowledge.   4. Knowledge, Theory of.   5. Belief and doubt.
I. Plantinga, Alvin.   II. Kvanvig, Jonathan L.
BD161.P58   1996   121'.6—dc20   95-52079   CIP

ISBN 0-8476-8158-0 (cloth: alk. paper)
ISBN 0-8476-8159-9 (pbk.: alk. paper)

Printed in the United States of America

♾ ™ The paper used in this publication meets the minimum requirements of
American National Standard for Information Sciences—Permanence of Paper
for Printed Library Materials, ANSI Z39.48—1984.

Contents

Part IV. Warrant, Justification, and Expert Knowledge

Part V. Virtue Epistemology

Part VI. Alvin Plantinga Replies

Introduction

The concept of warrant is of one of a group of concepts (including rationality and justification) that are thought by many to make a crucial difference in explaining the difference between true belief and knowledge. According to such views, knowledge requires not only true belief, but also justified or rational or warranted belief. Of sustained attempts to understand these concepts, Alvin Plantinga's two-volume work on the nature of warrant[1] stands out as the most recent and among the very best. The present volume of essays is prompted by Plantinga's work on the nature of warrant. In some cases, the contributors critically assess features of Plantinga's account of warrant, and in other cases they compare Plantinga's views with the standard alternatives found in the past half-century or so of work in epistemology. Plantinga's work also includes brief excursions about the connections between epistemology and metaphysics, and some of the essays explore that territory as well. The purpose of the volume is thus to explore further some of the central topics in epistemology in light of the new and penetrating work on the subject offered by Plantinga. As such, it is intended both to further research in epistemology and to honor the work Plantinga has done.

Plantinga's two volumes on the nature of warrant cover the range of controversial issues in contemporary epistemology, assessing the current state of research in this central area of philosophical thought and presenting a new account of the nature of warrant. The crucial element in this new account is that for a belief to be warranted it must be the result of cognitive equipment that is functioning properly. There are other requirements as well: the equipment must be functioning in an environment appropriate to that kind of equipment, the statistical probability of truth in such an environment must be high, and the purpose of the equipment must be to produce true belief. The heart of the theory is nonetheless found in the claim that warrant requires properly functioning cognitive equipment. According to Plantinga, talk about properly functioning cognitive equipment commits us to some claim about the design plan for that equipment. For the equipment to be functioning properly is for it to be operating as it was designed to operate. Such an account, Plantinga claims, helps us understand not only the concept of warrant but also the concept of knowledge, for warrant is that property, enough of which, that is sufficient for knowledge in conjunction with true belief. Warrant is thus that elusive property sought by epistemologists for centuries that distinguishes true belief from knowledge.

Such a viewpoint puts Plantinga at odds with many approaches within contemporary epistemology, approaches represented in this collection. First, it puts Plantinga at odds with coherentists and other internalists about the normative character of warrant. Coherentists typically think of warrant or justification as the property a belief has when it coheres best with other beliefs of the same person, and internalists think of the property of warrant or justification as a property that one can tell by introspection alone whether it is present. Plantinga disagrees with both of these claims, arguing that coherence is neither necessary nor sufficient for warrant, and that only beliefs objectively likely to be true can be warranted and hence warrant cannot be a property internally accessible by reflection alone. These issues are addressed in essays in Part I.

Second, Plantinga's views conflict with one of the dominant trends over the past thirty years in understanding the nature of knowledge. According to that approach, what fills the gap between true belief and knowledge is *undefeated* justification or warrant. What it is for warrant to be undefeated is a very complex issue, but what is crucial to the view is that a person can know even though that person lacks complete information about the issue in question. The difference between a case where one has both warrant and knowledge and a case where one has only warrant has to do with the *fragility* of the warrant. When you lack knowledge, your warrant is fragile enough that it disappears upon acquiring some of the information you lack; when you have knowledge, your warrant can withstand such further learning. Such an account makes crucial use of concepts such as information and evidential support between beliefs and information, concepts that play no role whatsoever in Plantinga's account of the nature of knowledge. Plantinga thereby commits himself to the view that the nature of knowledge can be explicated without any need to develop an account of what it is to have a warrant that is undefeated by information one does not possess; the crucial work in understanding the nature of knowledge is only that of clarifying what it is for cognition to be functioning properly. These issues are addressed in Part II.

Plantinga's epistemological theory has implications for other areas of philosophy as well. Because it appeals to the notion of a design plan, metaphysical issues arise for the theory. Plantinga claims that his theory is a naturalistic one, compatible with the dominant materialist/physicalist/naturalist sentiment among contemporary philosophers, but he also claims that the theory of proper function best flourishes within a theistic metaphysics. He also thinks that evolutionary naturalist accounts of cognition inevitably undermine themselves by giving us reason to doubt the reliability of the very equipment by which some arrive at such conclusions. These ties between epistemology and metaphysics are explored in Part III.

Other issues arise as well, issues about whether Plantinga's account is compatible with the kind of knowledge experts have, whether Plantinga's account of warrant can be extended in the way he suggests to give an account of *degrees* of warrant, and the extent to which Plantinga's approach to knowledge is appropriately compared with the tradition of understanding knowledge in terms of normatively appropriate true belief of the sort immune from Gettier-like counterexamples. These issues occupy Part IV of this collection.

A new development in the past decade or so has been the rise of virtue epistemology, modeled on virtue theories in ethics. Plantinga's view can be seen as a version of virtue epistemology, for properly functioning features of cognition are excellent candidates for cognitive or intellectual virtues of a person. One may question, however, whether virtue epistemology can be successful, and also question whether Plantinga's variation of the view is the best one. Part V discusses these questions.

In the final essay, Plantinga responds to the variety of discussions and criticism, sometimes defending and sometimes amending his views in light of these essays. The result is a collection which both honors Plantinga's contribution to epistemology and deepens and extends our understanding of these crucial issues in contemporary epistemology and related areas.

Notes

1. Alvin Plantinga, *Warrant: The Current Debate* and *Warrant and Proper Function* (New York: Oxford University Press, 1993).

Part I

Coherentism and Internalism

1

Plantinga and Coherentisms

William G. Lycan

When I was a graduate student in the 1960s, the pantheon of American philosophy enshrined just four *theoi*: in alphabetical order, Roderick Chisholm, Nelson Goodman, W. V. Quine, and Wilfrid Sellars. Of these, the last three (allowing a bit of interpretation in Goodman's case) defended coherentist epistemologies that have had enormous influence. But only Chisholm is cited by Alvin Plantinga in *Warrant: The Current Debate*[1]—despite his concern to show that "[c]oherentism is clearly mistaken" (p. 80) and that even "an impure (contaminated?)" or "chastened" coherentism (p. 87, Laurence BonJour's[2] coherentism taken as an example) is false. More generally, Plantinga acknowledges not a single contribution of *explanatory* coherentism, or "explanationism" as it is often portmanteau'd, to "the current debate."[3] Why is that?

I

One reason, no doubt, is epistemology's enduring taxonomic confusion over the definition of "coherentism" (usually complicated by the concern to oppose coherentism with "foundationalism").[4] It is almost never easily determined whether someone's theory of doxastic justification counts as "coherentist." So we should look first at Plantinga's own legitimately stipulative definition (pp. 78–79):

[Coherentism is the thesis that] a belief *B* is properly basic for a person *S* if and only if *B* appropriately coheres with the rest of *S*'s noetic structure

3

(or with some part of it, or with an appropriately purified version of it, or some part of *that*). . . . If a proposition *B* coheres with my noetic structure, then *B* is warranted for me; its warrant does not arise, however, by virtue of my believing it *on the basis of* the rest of my noetic structure, so that those other propositions are my *evidence*—deductive, inductive, or abductive—for *B*. . . . A *pure* coherentist resolutely rejects warrant transmission [equivalent to, I think, "warrant transfer," a belief's inheriting of warrant from another belief on which it is based] altogether; for her, all propositions that enjoy warrant in a noetic structure are basic in that structure.

(A subject's "noetic structure" is "the set of propositions he believes, together with certain epistemic relations that hold between him and them" (p. 72); a belief is "basic" if it is accepted but "not on the evidential basis of other beliefs" (p. 68), and "properly" basic as sanctioned by this epistemology or that one (p. 70). For a "pure" coherentist, every proposition is basic and none inherits warrant from any other particular belief or small set of beliefs. An impure coherentist grants that some warrant is transferred or transmitted—hence that some beliefs are not basic—but insists that some beliefs are basic and properly so.)

Typically an explanationist is not a pure coherentist. For she or he holds that a hypothesis is warranted by its ability to explain a particular set of data better than any other available hypothesis, and so seems to allow that the best hypothesis inherits its warrant from the data set, and so does not reject warrant transfer entirely. But just as typically, the explanationist maintains that the data propositions themselves are warranted by *being explained*, and/but they are not initially based on the hypothesis that does the explaining and so do not inherit their warrant in the manner of transfer/transmission.[5] So our "typical" explanationist is an impure coherentist in Plantinga's sense, and does seem to be saying that many beliefs are properly basic in virtue of (explanatorily) cohering with their subjects' noetic structures. If all this is right, then such an explanationist does qualify as a coherentist according to Plantinga's own definition, for (p. 79) impure coherentists are coherentists.

II

But there is a powerful argument against the "typical" position, one which both resonates with Plantinga's original objection to pure coherentism—(that "[w]arrant cannot magically arise just by virtue of a large evidential circle" (p. 78)—and might help to explain his ignoring of the position. It arises from the problem of what Keith Lehrer has called "explained unexplainers"[6]: Some data propositions that justify explanatory hypotheses are themselves justified by explaining more primitive data in their turn. But many other data propositions are not so justified, because they do not explain anything else.[7] Yet (a) an explanatory hypothesis is justified by the data it explains only if the data propositions are themselves justified, and presumably (b) the data propositions are justified "by being explained" only if the explanatory hypotheses are themselves justified; and so on the "typical" view there is nowhere for justification to get an initial foothold. Since an explanans presupposes an explanandum, how does the whole explanatory enterprise get started in the first place? It seems the explanationist must appeal to something besides coherence entirely, and hence does no longer qualify as even an impure coherentist.

An explanationist who truly loves coherence might resist either or both of the foregoing two conditional premises (a) and (b), holding the explanatory relation itself to have an epistemic kind of intrinsic value. I do not think such a view is stupid, silly, easily refuted, or even (in Plantinga's phrase, p. 78) "miserably implausible." But I agree it is not wildly attractive and I am not eager to defend it.[8] I would rather advance a version of explanationism that grants the two conditional premises.

III

Indeed, I have defended an explanationist view of that sort in my own epistemology book, *Judgement and Justification*.[9] Accepting the two conditionals, I had to confront the problem of the explained unexplainers head on, and find an independent entry into the circle of being-justified-by-explaining and being-justified-by-being-explained. I found it in a particular application of what I called the Principle of Credulity, which is: "Accept at the outset each of those things that seems to be true."

At any given time we involuntarily find ourselves holding any number of beliefs—at least those produced by perception and by memory, though I shall not yet make any appeal to those faculties as justifying. Call such unconsidered beliefs "spontaneous" beliefs.[10] They are mostly about our immediate environment, about past events, perhaps about our own mental states, and probably more. Now, since all their contents are things that seem true to us, the Principle of Credulity tacks those propositions in place long enough for them to serve as data for explanation. And once they are justly available for explaining, they soon acquire the kinds of coherence that are constituted by a proposition's being explained (on which more shortly).

But why should anyone accept the Principle of Credulity? It seems to fly in the face of the best lessons that philosophy has tried to teach us since Socrates, notably that no belief should go unexamined or be accepted uncritically. And never mind the lofty ideals of Athens: As Lehrer has observed,[11] any Reidian "innocent until proven guilty" principle of this kind stops sounding like just plain good sense as soon as one considers cases in which large utilities—very good consequences or very bad ones—hang on whether the belief in question is true or false.

IV

Nonetheless the Principle is defensible. For it is a consequence of the more general characteristically explanationist claim that *conservativeness*, as W. V. Quine and J. S. Ullian call it and as they argue,[12] is a theoretical virtue: T_1 will and should be preferred to T_2 if T_1 fits better with what we already believe. (If this in its turn sounds dogmatic or bigoted, notice that, *inescapably*, we never even consider competing hypotheses that would strike us as grossly implausible. For example, no homicide detective addresses the hypothesis that the crime was committed by invisible alien invaders from the planet Mongo; often real detectives do not even consider the proverbial and less outlandish "passing tramp" theory.)

Granted, epistemic conservatism is itself controversial and in need of defense against those who find it unmotivated, arbitrary, immoral, and the like. I have argued for it at considerable length in Chapters 7 and 8 of my book aforementioned,[13] but I can hardly even sketch the whole business here. The key contention is that whatever epistemic or justifying status inheres in the other standard pragmatic theoretical virtues (simplicity, testability, fruitfulness, power, and the like), conservativeness shares that same status. Many philosophers have doubted whether any of the pragmatic virtues *eo ipso* justifies beliefs at all,[14] but the present point is that whether or not the other virtues have that power, conservativeness stands or falls with the rest of them.

That comparative claim can be made good so long as (i) any plausible defense of the other pragmatic virtues as justifying applies to conservativeness as well, and (ii) there is no special objection to conservatism that does not also impugn the other virtues. So far as I know, both these conditions hold. My own defense of each of the pragmatic virtues is a kind of epistemic rule-utilitarian argument, an appeal to cognitive efficiency and good design.[15] That defense applies to conservativeness in particular, as I argue specifically, and so does every other defense that occurs to me. Nor have I heard a special objection directed against conservatism that lacks force against the other virtues.[16]

Against the philosophers who for whatever reason scorn the pragmatic virtues generally, I can say nothing here that would turn their hearts. I do urge them to think hard about the paradoxes of confirmation, particularly the Raven, and about the problems of induction and statistical inference, particularly Goodman's "Grue paradox." I urge them even more strongly to read my book.[17]

V

A further word of mitigation about conservatism is needed. The claim that conservativeness is a theoretical virtue is not to be taken in a Gothic, Prussian, Republican, New Democrat, or even more than the most fainthearted way. For in any given case it is easily overridden by any other explanatory advantage; we readily modify our existing beliefs in exchange for gains in simplicity or power, not to mention under pressure from new data. Conservatism is and ought to be the slave of our other pragmatic cognitive interests. A belief is justified by the bare fact of our holding it, I maintain, but only to the smallest degree. For justification in the fuller sense that we normally ask of beliefs, considerably more coherence is required.

There are at least three further kinds of coherence that make for justification of a spontaneous belief. One is consistency with other spontaneous beliefs. (Of course, which of two mutually incompatible such beliefs should be dropped is a question that drags in wider explanatory considerations.) A second and more testing kind of coherence is consistency, and perhaps looser explanatory fit, with one's larger belief structure having to do with one's current environment, recent past, and mode of access to those. Some spontaneous beliefs will be nearly instantaneously rejected as misperceptions, miscalculations, inaccurate memories, and the like because of their failure to square with the empirical predictions proceeding from other, firmer bodies of perceptual and memory data under logical pressure from fairly low-level justified explainers. But when a spontaneous belief does cohere in each of the two ways just mentioned, it may be called "tenable."[18]

A third and still more demanding kind of coherence is, of course, being explained. (Many of our beliefs are tenable in the sense just defined, but are unexplained; some will never be explained.) The more throughly explained a proposition is for the subject, to that extent the higher its degree of coherence, and so the higher its degree of warrant. Fourth,[19] the subject's total belief system may yield at least a tacit metabelief as to how the first-order belief in question was produced in her or him and that its source is generally reliable. (As in my book, p. 168, I understand this phenomenon in a very undemanding way; it is exemplified not just by professional philosophers and adult laypersons, but by most young children.) N.B.: Such metabeliefs *need not be true*.[20]

So it is that a spontaneous belief gets swept up into a large coherent explanatory structure. The belief is incorporated into a system of beliefs connected by logical and explanatory relations and (typically) containing metabeliefs about the sources of beliefs.

It is the third and fourth kinds of coherence that are not exhibited by what I call "wild" spontaneous beliefs—superstitious forebodings, *déjà vu*, mild hallucinations, and the like. Such beliefs may be tenable in my sense, but normally they are soon ruled out by their failure to be explained and/or by our having reason to think that they have no reliable source.

VI

There is a critical idea that some people have about coherence theories and perception. It worries even some professed coherentists: As BonJour puts it (*op. cit.*, p. 108), calling it the "input objection,"

> Coherence is purely a matter of the *internal* relations between the components of the belief system; it depends in no way on any sort of relation between the system of beliefs and anything external to that system. . . . Nothing about any requirement of coherence dictates that a coherent system of beliefs need receive any sort of *input* from the world

or be in any way causally influenced by the world. But this is surely an absurd result.

More generally, it has seemed to some critics that no coherentist can explain the special role played by experience in the maintenance and warranting of our belief systems.

I believe the importance of input and experience, though overwhelming, is contingent. As a matter of fact, given the kind of creature we are and the way in which we are embedded in our environments, sensory experience provides our most voluminous and richest flow of data for explanation. (I daresay that is true for any biological creature in any normal environment, but it is still contingent.) And data are *per se* of crucial importance, not only for the trivial reason that an explanans requires an explanandum. An explanatory system is more powerful, hence better warranted, to the extent that it has more data to explain, and as Karl Popper emphasized, a theory that has risked falsification and survived is to that extent better warranted than one which has risked falsification less.

Moreover, as a matter of fact, our perceptual data give rise *rather automatically* to a highly coherent view of our immediate environmental surrounds: It is in 3-D, it comes already broken up into objects that fall under various useful classifications, etc. This is because our perceptual modules evolved to work in that informationally efficient way, which is no accident but is still contingent.

Nor do I grant that the idea of inputless justification is "absurd," much less "surely" so. An organism that is systematically sensorily deprived (however far-fetched it is to imagine such a thing) might still form some justified beliefs—about the workings of its own mind, for example. Or imagine the fortuitous equivalent of a brain in a vat, that is, a brain kept alive but unconnected to the rest of the world, that just happens to have the sequence of experiences that a competent mad scientist would have fed it; such a being, I maintain, would be as well justified in its beliefs as you or I.

The latter claim is not uncontroversial. Also, perhaps the input objection is really pointing toward the deeper worry that any system of beliefs *might* be made as coherent as anyone could wish, but still be completely nuts. I shall take up those issues further in Part X.

VII

Now that I have briefly expounded my explanationist solution to the problem of explained unexplainers, let us check to see whether my overall view resists Plantinga's main objections to coherence theories. He begins by offering several alleged counterexamples to the necessity of coherence, which if sound would, he says (p. 83, 83n), work against either pure or impure theories.

First (p. 82), Plantinga says he might be warranted in believing a necessary falsehood, say by reasonably taking the word of an expert mathematician whose arithmetical proof is impressive but, unbeknownst to anyone, subtly fallacious. But presumably a contradiction cannot cohere with the rest of his belief set.[21]

I am not among those who see incoherence in every inconsistency. There are at least two real-world ways in which a belief system can be inconsistent while still exhibiting a high degree of coherence, say a considerably higher degree than is possessed by your belief system or mine right now. One is by being compartmentalized: Perhaps there is a side to the subject's life that is comparatively self-contained, whose characteristic data do not interact with the rest of the subject's data and which has its own fairly modular explanatory structure. Somewhere in that structure is a proposition that distantly or not so distantly contradicts something the subject believes back in the mainstream of her or his cognitive life. (For a scientific analogue, consider someone who accepts both general relativity and quantum mechanics.) But the subject never has occasion to conjoin the two conflicting beliefs— hence never believes a contradiction itself—and each of the two explanatory structures, the mainstream one and the compartmentalized one, is highly coherent in itself. In such a case, I think the subject may be very well justified in believing each of the two conflicting propositions.

The other sort of nondamaging inconsistency that occurs to me is the one to which most normal natural-language speakers are subject throughout their lives: They believe the axioms of a Tarskian truth definition for their native languages, and those languages contain ordinary unrestricted truth predicates. This matters hardly at all. And similar points can be based on epistemic paradoxes, such as the Lottery and the Preface.[22]

For that matter, departing briefly from the real world, a person might start with a highly coherent belief system, say vastly better than yours or mine, and for whatever reason add to it a single contradictory proposition, say that aliens from the planet Werdna are both round and square in shape. If this person has also internalized a paraconsistent logic[23] (a prudent policy), he or she will infer nothing from the contradiction. The contradiction is itself a horrible anomaly, demanding yet defying explanation, but we may suppose that, standing alone, it is outweighed by the sum of the noncoherencies in your noetic structure or mine; thus, most of the subject's beliefs are still better justified than ours.

But what about Plantinga's arithmetical falsehood? I am less sure how to approach that case, in part because the whole business of believing necessary truths and necessary falsehoods is vexed in each of several ways. One important thing to note is that, like any other proposition, a necessary falsehood is believed or disbelieved only under a propositional mode of presentation,[24] and may be believed under one such guise but not under another. Under one mode of presentation, the necessary falsehood may not be recognizable (perhaps by anyone) as such, and it may have inferential connections to other beliefs that are in every psychological way like those which relate consistent beliefs.

Consider Lois Lane's belief that Superman is better looking than Clark Kent. Though necessarily false, her belief is entirely reasonable and warranted, given the ample misleading evidence of nonidentity that Superman/Clark has carefully strewn around Metropolis (and, I suppose, given the way Mr. Jerry Siegel depicted the faces and physiques of Superman and Clark respectively). Plantinga's arithmetical example may be tougher, in that while Lois has no way whatever of computing the necessary falsehood of her belief, and so cannot be blamed in any way whatever for holding it, the arithmetical belief may be provably contradictory and might in time be discovered to be false by Plantinga himself were he to compute long and carefully enough. But I am inclined to think the point about coherencelike inferential connections to other beliefs holds here as well. Unfortunately, to pursue the example further would require a vigorous foray into both the ontology and the psychology of believing necessary truths and necessary falsehoods.

In each of Plantinga's two other proposed counterexamples to necessity, a subject who has been persuaded that things of a certain type do not exist is confronted with a clear perception or memory of a real thing of that very type. An impressionable undergraduate has been convinced by philosophical argument that no one is ever appeared to redly, but is suddenly himself appeared to redly and, reflecting, accepts that he is; an arboreal expert who maintains (presumably on theoretical grounds) that the state of Washington contains no oak trees suddenly remembers seeing one in Bellingham. These new episodic beliefs sharply contradict, hence drastically fail to cohere with, their subjects' respective noetic structures as they had been; yet, Plantinga contends, they are warranted.

One might naturally respond that upon acquiring the new episodic beliefs, the subjects of course scrap their previous theoretical beliefs, because those beliefs have just been refuted, and so there is no incoherence. But that will not do, for surely there is a time lag between the perceptual/memory confrontation and the rejection or readjustment of the opposing theoretical beliefs. During that time interval, however short, the theoretical beliefs remain, and clash with the new beliefs.

I agree that the new beliefs are very quickly warranted and that they demand revision of the contrary theoretical beliefs rather than the other way around. Indeed, the two examples seem to be plain cases of a theoretical generalization's being refuted by a fact. But their force as putative counterexamples depends entirely on what we should say about the tiny transitional time interval. They succeed only if, during that interval, the theoretical beliefs are themselves still so internally coherent as to resist apparent disconfirmation (as when an undergraduate chemistry student's Thursday afternoon lab result flouts a well-established chemical equation), *and* the new perceptual/memory belief is not "wild," but tenable and perhaps coherent in my third and fourth ways as well. In light of the time lag's brevity and the unknown psychological relations and microevents that occur within it, one cannot be confident that both those conditions are fulfilled. Indeed, it is hard to see how they could be.

The examples are severely underdescribed. In particular, we are not told much about the grounds for the standing theoretical beliefs. If those beliefs are well enough supported, it may be that the new perceptual/memory beliefs are *not* warranted and should be rejected as erroneous (as Plantinga grants; cf. his cow example on p. 83). But I assume Plantinga means his cases to be ones in which the theoretical beliefs are not so impregnably supported and the perception/memory is a good clear one of the sort that does just plain disconfirm a fallible theoretical generalization. If that is so, then as soon as the subject acquires the well-justified perceptual/memory belief, the previous contrary theoretical belief *is no longer justified*, precisely because it has been disconfirmed. The new perceptual/memory belief is warranted by its tenability and third- or fourth-grade coherence, and it does not lose warrant through its failure to cohere with the theoretical belief, because the latter, having just been refuted by the former, is no longer justifed despite its inertial micropersistence.

This sort of response to Plantinga's examples had better not depend on the assumption that the theoretical generalizations are weakly enough supported to be simply refuted by an apparently conflicting perception/memory. For a smooth continuum connects such cases of clear refutation with cases like that of the undergraduate chemist, in which it is uncontroversial that the ostensible data are to be rejected rather than the well-entrenched theory they seem to "refute." Fortunately, my response does not depend on that assumption, though I made it for the sake of exposition. In any version of one of Plantinga's examples, the standing theoretical generalization will have some degree of antecedent justification, against which the new perceptual/memory belief will have to contend. It may be comparatively little, as I have assumed, or it may be much. But since the perceptual/memory belief is logically incompatible with the theoretical belief, the former will be warranted only to the degree that the latter is not, in strict inverse proportion. And so it will be positively warranted (as Plantinga intends) only so far as the theoretical belief is made dubious; my response stands.

(These points are clearer in the tree case than in the example of the impressionable undergraduate philosopher, because the latter contains two complications. One is that the new experiential belief in that example, if I understand Plantinga correctly, actually an introspective belief rather than an external-world perceptual one. To some philosophers that will make it all the more obvious that the belief is warranted, and I tend to agree, but the status of introspective beliefs is a special topic that would require a significant digression.[25] The second complication is that the impressionable undergraduate's evidence for his belief that no one is ever appeared to redly is purely philosophical, and so the undergraduate faces David Hume's problem of thinking with the learned while speaking with the vulgar. Like G. E. Moore, I myself hold that one ought not to believe, and rarely does actually believe, any proposition that contradicts an item of common sense and is defended on purely philosophical grounds,[26] but this is not the place to go into metaphilosophy either.)

Plantinga adds a specific objection to the necessity of BonJour's (*op. cit.*) impure-coherentist explicans (p. 112), but I think the objection turns on a special feature of BonJour's account that my theory does not share, viz., its apparent neglect of the fact that warrant comes in degrees, so I shall not address it here.

VIII

Plantinga makes several objections to pure coherence theories, and to BonJour's impure theory, in the form of counterexamples to sufficiency. In each case, naturally, a subject's beliefs are highly coherent but, according to Plantinga, not warranted.

(1) Oliver Sacks's[27] Lost Mariner, afflicted with Korsakov's syndrome, completely forgot the past thirty years of his life and (in 1975 when he was 49 years old) believed that it was 1945 and he was 19 (Plantinga, p. 81).

(2) One *S* suffers from a bizarre cognitive malfunction that makes him "believe . . . , whenever he is appeared to redly, that no one else is ever appeared to redly," and these occasional beliefs "are coherent . . . in any reasonable sense a coherentist might propose" (*ibid.*).

(3) Timothy admires Picasso to a pathological degree, reads in the *National Enquirer* that Picasso was an alien from outer space, forms the belief that he too is an alien, and makes the rest of his beliefs cohere with these views.

(4) While seated on a high ledge in the Grand Tetons and justifiably believing the things that visually appear to him to be so (that Cascade Canyon is down to his left, that there is a hawk gliding below him, etc.), Ric "is struck by a wayward burst of high-energy cosmic radiation . . . [with the result that] his beliefs become fixed, no longer responsive to changes in experience" (p. 82). After Ric's friends have got him down the mountain and back to town, his beliefs remain just as they were on the ledge, even during a performance of *La Traviata*. (Additional description of the example on pp. 179–80 of *Warrant and Proper Function* makes it clearer that Plantinga sees the pathological split as dividing Ric's *beliefs*—all of them—entirely from his experiences. He *has* experiences, presumably veridical experiences of hearing and seeing things like the opera performance, but they simply do not affect his beliefs in any way.)

(5) Suppose Plantinga is a madman of the sort described by René Descartes in his First Meditation.

> I think I am a squash, perhaps a pumpkin. This psychotic delusion is the pivot of my whole system of beliefs and the rest of my beliefs settle into a coherent pattern of beliefs around it. (Thus I believe that I was grown in a famous Frisian garden, that I alone among the vegetables have been granted rationality and self-consciousness, that the explanation for my having been thus exalted is to be found in God's middle knowledge about

what various possible gourds would freely do in various situations, and so on.) (pp. 110–11)

Example (5) is followed by a pair of similar evil-demon-type cases.

The issues raised by these examples are various. I shall postpone discussion of (3) and (5), because those arguments come closest to a certain standard objection to coherentism generally, a version of which has been made against my explanationist theory in particular. Let us turn to the others, in order.

Example (1) is vexed by the facts that (a) Jimmie G., Sacks's Lost Mariner, lacked recent (except for short-term) memory, and (b) that he did not live entirely in the past. He interacted conversationally and pleasantly with those around him, so long as the focus was on what had happened within the past few seconds. But he was constantly presented with anomalies, arising both from the mismatch between the then present (1975) and from his belief that it was still 1949, and from his—as the joke goes—always meeting new people, who inexplicably knew all about him. Sacks writes:

> Looking at the grey-haired man before me, I had an impulse for which I have never forgiven myself—it was, or would have been, the height of cruelty had there been any possibility of Jimmie's remembering it.
>
> "Here," I said, and thrust a mirror toward him. "Look in the mirror and tell me what you see. Is that a nineteen-year-old looking out from the mirror?"
>
> He suddenly turned ashen and gripped the sides of the chair. "Jesus Christ," he whispered. "Christ, what's going on? What's happened to me? Is this a nightmare? Am I crazy? Is this a joke?"—and he became frantic, panicked. (p. 24)

> I found another photo in a magazine and pushed it over to him.
>
> "That's an aircraft carrier," he said. "Real ultramodern design. I never saw one quite like that."
>
> "What's it called?" I asked.
>
> He glanced down, looked baffled, and said, "The *Nimitz*!"
>
> "Something the matter?"
>
> "The hell there is!" he replied hotly. "I know 'em all by name, and I *don't know* a *Nimitz*. . . . Of course there's an Admiral Nimitz, but I never heard they named a carrier after him."
>
> Angrily he threw the magazine down. (p. 27)

> "I see these beds, and these patients everywhere. Looks like a sort of hospital to me. But hell, what would I be doing in a hospital—and with

all these old people, years older than me. I feel good, I'm strong as a bull. Maybe I *work* here. . . . Do I work? What's my job? . . . No, you're shaking your head. I see in your eyes I don't work here. If I don't work here, I've been *put* here. Am I a patient, am I sick and don't know it, Doc? It's crazy, it's scary. . . . Is it some sort of joke?" (pp. 24–25)

This is not a highly coherent belief system.

Plantinga might fictionalize the example by isolating Jimmie G. in such a way that he gets no information that conflicts with his 1949 self-image; perhaps his helpers would indulge his delusion (as the family in *Arsenic and Old Lace* seemed to cater to Teddy in order to get him to bury the "yellow fever" victims in the cellar). That would be to assimilate example (1) to (3) and (5), to be addressed below.

Plantinga puts his case (2) cryptically, and I do not altogether understand it. Whenever S is appeared to redly, he believes that no one else is ever appeared to redly; fine, but Plantinga then just instructs us to "[a]dd that S's beliefs, on those occasions, are coherent . . . in any reasonable sense a coherentist might propose" (p. 81). Now, on its face, the example suggests that S's belief diminishes explanatory coherence fairly dramatically, because if S is appeared to redly and is aware that he is, then it would be extremely odd to think that no one else ever is. What could possibly explain S's being the only human being who can be appeared to redly? And why is redness thus restricted when the other colors are not? So S would have a belief that is both striking and, in each of several respects, unexplained to the point of anomalousness. So understood, this is not a case of high coherence without warrant.

On the other hand, Plantinga could tell a story as to how S does revise his other beliefs in order to explain the striking belief. If the story does resolve the anomalies and is also sufficiently coherent otherwise, then the belief may be warranted, but only because it now does cohere.

Case (4) is puzzling in a different way. We are asked to imagine a radical split between Ric's beliefs and his perceptual experience. This is hard to do. Some philosophers argue for a conceptual connection between perceiving and the formation of perceptual beliefs; e.g., D. M. Armstrong maintains (as a piece of conceptual analysis) that perception is nothing but a certain means of acquiring a belief.[28] *Chez* such a philosopher, Plantinga's example is simply incoherent. I am not among those, but I still find the case hard to imagine in detail.

First, I assume that Ric's veridical experiences are conscious; for if they were subconscious (supposing there is such a thing as a "subconscious experience"), their occurrence would not reflect badly on his continuing to hold the beliefs that are based on his most recent conscious experiences. But if the veridical experiences are conscious, what can this mean but that he experiences the opera, etc., *as such*, and how could that not affect his beliefs? Perhaps there is no conceptual incoherence there, but if the alleged conscious experiences are by hypothesis prevented from affecting Ric's beliefs in the slightest, then I strongly suspect they will be so far from playing anything like the normal functional role of a conscious experience as to fail to qualify metaphysically as such, and so case (4) would be metaphysically if not conceptually impossible. (I assume here that, like natural substances and natural kinds of things, mental states and events have metaphysical natures that are *a posteriori* and may someday be discovered by psychological science; Plantinga may not grant that assumption.)

IX

I have been arguing that my coherentist theory evades Plantinga's objections. But it may well be that he would not classify my theory as coherentist in the first place, and so would regard my defensive moves collectively as an *ignoratio elenchi*. I am not sure whether my theory does qualify as (impure) coherentist according to his official definition as quoted in Part I, according to which coherentism holds that "a belief *B* is properly basic for a person *S* if and only if *B* appropriately coheres with the rest of *S*'s noetic structure (or with some part of it, or with an appropriately purified version of it, or some part of *that*). . . ." I say my spontaneous beliefs are properly basic in Plantinga's sense, but only because of conservatism by way of the Principle of Credulity. I think of conservatism as a coherentist notion, but since conservatism gives a belief some slight warrant regardless of the belief's relation to any other belief, Plantinga may well disagree. Yet I think my explanationist view is close enough to a coherence theory properly so called, and so much the worse for Plantinga's taxonomy if he does not count me as such, for the following reasons.

(1) So far as "coherentism" is partially understood as opposed to "foundationalism," my "foundational" beliefs are the most highly defeasible the world has ever seen—indeed the most highly defeasible it is logically possible to be. All that justifies a spontaneous belief in the very beginning is conservatism, and that only slightly; the belief

can be knocked right out by any competitor's having any measurable theoretical advantage. My epistemic house is built, not even on sand, but on gossamer.

(2) The pragmatic virtue in virtue of which spontaneous beliefs first count as minimally justified is of a piece with the other standard pragmatic virtues—simplicity and power and fruitfulness and the rest—in that (so I argued in my book) it has exactly the same ultimate rationale. And those other virtues are invariably counted as coherentist.

(3) The spontaneous beliefs have nothing distinctive about them, or even in common, other than happening to be held. They may be on any topic whatever. There is no particular source or kind of source that they need have (it is especially important to see that). And they are justified by nothing whatever that lies outside the pragmatic virtues.

For these reasons, I count myself firmly as a coherentist, though (a) I doubt that such fine taxonomic questions matter much in this area, and (b) I would fault Plantinga for pointedly ignoring us explanatory coherentists even if explanatory coherentism is not a species of coherentism.

X

As I said, Plantinga's examples (3) and (5) are more familiar than the others. For they are cases of someone's starting with one or more weird ideas that have no foundation in the real world, and then constructing a coherent system of beliefs that surround and support those ideas. This is a version of the old objection (mentioned in section VI) that any system of beliefs might be made as coherent as anyone could wish, but still be entirely unjustified. Since the plausibility of that objection's premise depends heavily on what notion of "coherence" is in the field, I shall not try to respond to it on behalf of coherentists everywhere, but shall consider it just as directed against my own theory.

In fact, Alvin Goldman has made the same general objection expressly against my view.[29] He asks, what if a certain person's "wild" spontaneous belief does happen to achieve coherence of my third and fourth kinds? Suppose that person's other experience is consonant with the wild belief, and the person's metabeliefs happen to fall nicely into place and yield a coherent story as to the source of the wild belief, without internal implausibilities and without loose ends. According to my theory, this process could end up justifying wild beliefs that are crazy—bizarre religious visions, beliefs in magic, or the like, including of course Timothy's conviction that he and Picasso are aliens.

I reply that, first, this scenario is very unlikely. In the real world, the environment and human minds being as they are, suitably weird spontaneous beliefs are not going to find holistic support of this kind. But let us continue to suppose that, however improbably, our weirdo's spontaneous belief actually does get resolved without mess and does achieve at least the same degree of explanatory coherence exhibited by your belief system or mine. Then, I say, the weirdo *is* justified in accepting the wild belief and the system that goes with it.

There are two interestingly different subcases. First: Suppose the wild belief is grafted onto otherwise normal perception. That would be a very tricky thing for any environment to engineer, but if the internal display featured some extra form of perception, say, backed by a coherent explanatory account of its mechanism that (*per impossibile*) fit well with all the subject's normal beliefs about the physical world, the subject would be weird *not* to accept it.

Second subcase: The weirdo's experience is not at all normal, but magical throughout, all the day long. If it were chaotic and confusing, of course, the subject would not be justified in believing much of anything; but we are supposing that it is as coherent and as explanatorily watertight as is our own realistic experience, though magical and radically different from ours. If it *really is* all that coherent and convincing, then it seems to me idle, churlish, and false to deny that the subject is reasonable and justified in accepting her or his magical world as it presents itself. You or I would have accepted it, after all, knowing no better. If the evil demon could give an otherwise normal subject a completely justified but false belief in a world like ours, then the same demon or a close cousin could give a subject an equally coherent and regular but magical world with the same credentials.

Explanatory coherentism has more troubles of its own. But I think it is undamaged by Plantinga's arguments.[30]

Notes

1. Except that an unrelated informal remark of W. V. Quine's is paraphrased on p. 68.

2. Laurence BonJour, *The Structure of Empirical Knowledge* (Harvard University Press, 1985).

3. Especially the works of Gilbert Harman, notably "Inference to the Best Explanation," *Philosophical Review* 74 (1965), pp. 88–95; *Thought* (Princeton University Press, 1973); and *Change in View: Principles of Reasoning* (Cambridge: Bradford/MIT Press, 1986).

Richard Feldman seems to agree that explanationists are off the playing field: "[*Warrant: The Current Debate*] is a thorough discussion and criticism of all the prominent views in recent epistemology" ("Proper Functionalism," *Noûs* 27 (1993), p. 34).

4. A prior reason might stem from Plantinga's unusual explication of "warrant" partially in terms of "what distinguishes knowledge from true belief" (p. 4); someone might think that explanatory coherence could not make for *knowledge*, even if it can justify a belief to some degree.

But equally, someone might think the notion of *knowledge* entirely expendable, and that epistemology need concern itself only with degree of justification (cf. Keith Lehrer, "Why Not Skepticism?" in G. Pappas and M. Swain (eds.), *Essays on Knowledge and Justification* (Cornell University Press, 1978)); such an epistemologist would need a concept of warrant but could not accept Plantinga's definition. At a slight risk of *ignoratio*, I shall here neglect the possibility that a concern for knowledge in particular is what makes Plantinga ignore explanationism.

5. For fear of exegetical quagmire, I shall not try to say which actual explanationists take exactly this line, though I believe Gilbert Harman is the strongest candidate.

6. Keith Lehrer, *Knowledge* (Oxford University Press, 1974, Ch. 7). Lehrer discusses the problem primarily as formulated by Wilfrid Sellars in "Some Reflections on Language Games," in *Science, Perception and Reality* (Routledge and Kegan Paul, 1963); see also Sellars, "Givenness and Explanatory Coherence," *Journal of Philosophy* 70 (1973), and "More on Givenness and Explanatory Coherence," in G. Pappas (ed.), *Justification and Knowledge* (D. Reidel, 1979). But the problem is a special case of that raised by A. C. Ewing and C. I. Lewis for coherence theories generally (Ewing, *Idealism: A Critical Survey* (Methuen, 1934); Lewis, *An Analysis of Knowledge and Valuation* (Open Court, 1946)). Others have wrestled with it too, notably Nicholas Rescher (*The Coherence Theory of Truth* (Oxford University Press, 1973, Ch. 3); *Plausible Reasoning* (Van Gorcum, 1976); *Methodological Pragmatism* (Basil Blackwell, 1977); and *Induction* (University of Pittsburgh Press, 1980)). See also James Cornman, *Skepticism, Justification, and Explanation* (D. Reidel, 1980), and Alan Goldman, *Empirical Knowledge* (University of California Press, 1988, Ch. 7).

7. There are a number of reasons for granting this. Two are that there are scads of apparent examples, and that since explanations cannot be circular and regress must be blocked, there must be explained unexplainers (the classic topology generated by an antisymmetric philosophical relation: cycle, regress, or stoppers).

8. There is also the possibility of contending that the data propositions are explained because they explain themselves. But I think Keith Lehrer (*op. cit.*) discredits that view fairly thoroughly.

9. William G. Lycan, *Judgement and Justification* (Cambridge University Press, 1988).

10. I coined this unsurprising term in "Conservatism and the Data Base," in N. Rescher (ed.), *Reason and Rationality in Natural Science* (University Press of America, 1985). I note that Laurence BonJour has used it, independently, in much the same sense (*op. cit.*, pp. 117ff.).

In *Warrant and Proper Function* (pp. 180–82), Plantinga raises the important question of whether the coherence relation is defined just on the class of *beliefs* or whether other states, such as perceptual experiences, can stand in coherence relations to beliefs as well. BonJour (*op. cit.*) seems to accept the former view, but for rebuttals, see John Pollock, *Contemporary Theories of Knowledge* (Rowman and Littlefield, 1986), and J. L. Kvanvig and W. D. Riggs, "Can a Coherence Theory Appeal to Appearance States?" *Philosophical Studies* 67 (1992), pp. 197–217. (Pollock seems to think that coherence theories are committed to the view being rejected, but Kvanvig and Riggs point out that this is not so.) Riggs has pointed out to me in conversation that my own theory in *Judgement and Justification* was equivocal (not to say contradictory) on this point, but I now side with him and Kvanvig.

11. *Theory of Knowledge* (Westview Press, 1990, pp. 65–66).

12. W. V. Quine and J. S. Ullian, *The Web of Belief*, 2nd ed. (Random House, 1978, Ch. V). That the Credulity Principle does follow from the conservatist claim takes a bit of showing, since our spontaneous beliefs are not usually theoretical hypotheses being measured against competing hypotheses for comparative explanatory advantage. But consider our present belief set B and two theories, T and T'. T is either an axiomatization of B or logically stronger than B, while T' is incompatible with B though having a very large intersection with B. Suppose that T' is otherwise exactly equal to T in explanatory virtue. Then on grounds of conservatism, we should prefer T to T', and that is tantamount to saying that B is justified to some degree merely because it is already held by us, which goes in turn for any spontaneous belief entailed by B.

13. See also L. Sklar, "Methodological Conservatism," *Philosophical Review* 84 (1975), pp. 374–400, which directly inspired my own work.

14. Perhaps most notably Bas van Fraassen in *The Scientific Image* (Oxford University Press, 1980).

15. See particularly Ch. 7 of *Judgement and Justification, loc. cit.* I argue at some length for a heavily idealized utiliarianism as against a deontological and/or priggishly truth-obsessed conception of justification.

16. The single most damaging assault I know against conservatism is David Christensen's "Conservatism in Epistemology," *Noûs* 27 (1994). But I am not yet convinced that Christensen's arguments would not work against the other virtues.

17. I have been reliably told that the book is both more pleasant and more invigorating to read if one is reading a copy that one has bought and paid for (particularly a hardback copy).

18. I do not mean to endorse, and do not endorse, the idea that in order to have any serious degree of explanatory coherence at all, a belief system must itself be logically consistent. See the next section.

19. In my book I neglected to distinguish these third and fourth grades of coherence, lumping them together as "coherence of the third kind" (pp. 167–69).

20. It seems that in *Judgement and Justification* I did not adequately forestall that misunderstanding, which has been committed by more than one commentator. For me to require that the metabeliefs be true would be to make me into a reliabilist of some sort, and I have worked hard not to be a reliabilist.

A quick way of seeing why an explanationist should not insist on the metabeliefs being true is to note that that requirement would rule out brains-in-vats and evil-demon victims as *justified* believers; I take that to be damning, since I take the position that a smoothly and globally deceived victim is not only conceptually possible, but is exactly as well justified as is a comparable, counterpart subject whose experience is similar but veridical. Somewhat surprisingly, arch-reliabilist Alvin Goldman agrees, but in *Epistemology and Cognition* (Harvard University Press, 1986) he offers a different, reliabilist way of accommodating the evil demon intuition, involving the notion of a "normal possible world." I have some objections to that strategy, but in any case I could not employ it myself, since to require a four-year-old to have metabeliefs about "normal possible worlds" would seem to violate the child-labor laws of at least forty-six states.

21. A similar objection was made by Richard Foley in "Justified Inconsistent Beliefs," *American Philosophical Quarterly* 16 (1979), pp. 247–57.

22. As is well argued by Richard Foley, *op. cit.*; see also Part 4 of Foley's *Working Without a Net* (Oxford University Press, 1993). But (cf. the previous note) he thinks these points count against coherence theories: "[A] coherentist, who presents coherence as a necessary condition of justification, cannot accept [the claim that mutually inconsistent beliefs can each be justified] without giving up the heart of the coherence theory" (p. 257). If I must give up the heart, still I shall keep the lungs, stomach, and liver.

23. See, e.g., G. Priest *et al.* (eds.), *Paraconsistent Logic* (Philosophia Verlag, 19).

24. See Chs. 1 and 4 of *Judgement and Justification*.

25. For the basics, see my "Consciousness as Internal Monitoring," in N. Block, G. Güzeldere, and O. Flanagan (eds.), *The Nature of Consciousness* (Bradford/MIT Press, forthcoming 1996). N.B.: Although a foundationalist might think introspective beliefs are a focal topic in any discussion of proper basicness, I do not, because people's actual spontaneous beliefs are for the most part not introspective. Indeed, I think it is fairly seldom that people have introspective beliefs.

26. See Ch. 6 of *Judgement and Justification*.

27. Oliver Sacks, *The Man Who Mistook His Wife for a Hat* (Gerald Duckworth, 1985, Ch. 2). Quotes are from the 1986 Picador edition.

28. D. M. Armstrong, *A Materialist Theory of the Mind* (Routledge and Kegan Paul, 1968, Ch. 10).

29. "Lycan on Justification," the lead paper in a symposium on *Judgement and Justification*, held at the American Philosophical Association (Pacific Division) meetings in March 1990. D. M. Armstrong has pushed the same point in discussion, suggesting that I will be "outflanked on the left." Lynne Rudder Baker hinted at the objection in her review of the book (*Philosophical Review* 100 (1991), pp. 481–84).

30. I thank Geoff Sayre McCord for very useful discussion of these issues during the writing of this paper.

2

Proper Function versus
Systematic Coherence

Keith Lehrer

Alvin Plantinga's two volumes on epistemology[1] are an extraordinary contribution to scholarship and philosophy in the theory of knowledge and philosophy of religion. I count myself among his greatest admirers. Both volumes contain a great deal of sound and profound argumentation. He had not developed his view in detail when I wrote *Theory of Knowledge*,[2] and I did not discuss his views there. With the more complete articulation of his views before us, I appreciate the importance of them and am happy to have the opportunity to rectify my earlier omission. I wish to compare his views to my own, not just because of my attachment to the latter but, as his method reveals, because the best way to understand a view is to oppose another to it. This will necessitate some exposition of my own views as well as his to articulate the difference between the two theories and thereby achieve the illumination that the philosophical dialectic provides. I will focus on the disagreement between us, but I do agree with and appreciate much, indeed, most, of his argumentation and wish to say so before focusing on the matters where we differ.

Both of us are admirers of the writings of Thomas Reid[3] and appeal to his writings and ideas in defense of our own. Plantinga is, in some ways, closer to Reid in the central role that he gives to the functioning of our faculties, but I attach greater importance than Plantinga does to a central principle of Reid's, the seventh of Reid's first principles concerning contingent truths, which affirms that "our natural faculties by which we distinguish truth from error are not fallacious"[4] and are worthy of our trust. Reid says that our assent to all the other principles is grounded upon this one.[5] He also says in his the discussion of first principles that they are joined together like links in a chain and that one who would not lift up the whole should not try to lift the parts.[6] This seventh principle is a kind of metaprinciple because it vouches for the convictions resulting from our faculties and thus offers internal evidence for them, as it also vouches for itself and offers internal evidence for itself. These are his words:

> How then come we to be assured of this fundamental truth on which all others rest? Perhaps evidence, as in many other respects resembles light, so in this also-that, as light, which is the discoverer of all visible objects, discovers itself at the same time, so evidence, which is the voucher for all truth, vouches for itself at the same time.[7]

According to Reid, our faculties do not simply produce belief as the result of proper functioning, they produce internal evidence for those beliefs. The metaprinciple just cited vouches for the others as it vouches for itself. Reid is no simple externalist. He thought there was internal evidence for the truth of the beliefs resulting from the proper functioning of our faculties. Plantinga need not depart from Reid on this point, and perhaps he does not, but that is a question I wish to pose.

I shall argue in favor of the following theses. Plantinga has not refuted the coherence theory, according to which internal coherence with a system combined with truth within that system is what converts true belief into knowledge. I shall argue that his own theory contains the primary defect of externalism, cognitive opacity concerning the information believed, and thus that it requires supplementation. Finally, I shall argue for the falsity of his claim that theology supplies a better defense than evolutionary theory of the connection between proper functioning and the truth of what is believed.

Plantinga on Warrant

I shall proceed in the reverse order to place emphasis on Plantinga's own views before turning to my own for comparison. Here is his analysis of warrant.

> A belief has warrant for you if and only if (1) the cognitive faculties involved in the production of B are functioning properly (and this is to

include the relevant defeater systems as well as those systems, if any, that provide *propositional* inputs to the system in question); (2) your cognitive environment is sufficiently similar to the one for which your cognitive faculties are designed; (3) the triple of design plan governing the production of the belief in question involves, as purpose or function, the production of true beliefs (and the same goes for elements of the design plan governing the production of input beliefs to the system in question); and (4) the design plan is a good one: that is, there is a high statistical or objective probability that a belief produced in accordance with the relevant segment of the design plan in that sort of environment is true.[8]

Having given this analysis, he proceeds to ask the question of whether naturalism based on the theory of evolution can supply us with any reason for thinking that our faculties function in such a way as to provide us with true beliefs.[9] I understand and agree with his argument and the opinion of Charles Darwin himself to the contrary conclusion. The assumption that the way we function in forming beliefs is the result of the evolutionary process fails to support the conclusion that those beliefs are true. He appears, however, to go beyond this negative conclusion, that evolutionary theory does not yield the conclusion that beliefs resulting from them are true, to the much stronger conclusion that our beliefs are likely to be false if evolutionary theory is correct. Plantinga proceeds by agreeing that evolution does not yield the conclusion that our beliefs are true, assuming our faculties have arisen from an evolutionary process, to the conclusion that they are not likely to be true. But this does not follow. It does not follow from evolutionary theory that we have no features, including our belief forming faculties, that are not essential for our survival. The truth of our beliefs may not be essential for our survival, and in my opinion, it is not essential. If all our beliefs were close to the truth, as close, for example, as the readings on my inexpensive watch are to the correct time, we would have what we need for our survival as a species without our beliefs being true. However, it does not follow from this that truth is of no use, that proper functioning that yields truth is of no use, for the simple reason that, though our beliefs need not be true for us to survive, their truth may, nonetheless, be useful. It does not follow from the fact that truth is not necessary for survival that it is not useful. The evolutionary argument for the truth of our beliefs is not valid, but this fact is no argument against any naturalist except one who holds that we have no features except those that are essential to our survival. And any naturalist who holds that view is worthy of our neglect.

Nevertheless, Plantinga is correct, or so it seems to me, in denying the validity of the inference from the premise that we have resulted from an evolutionary process to the conclusion that the proper functioning of our faculties yields beliefs that are true. So, there is the possibility that supernaturalism might be more useful than naturalism in reaching the conclusion that the proper functioning of our faculties yields beliefs that are true. If we are the result directly or indirectly of God, endowed with knowledge, goodness, and power, that might seem a premise from which we could conclude that the proper functioning of our faculties would yield beliefs that are true because they are designed to yield true beliefs. I shall argue that this conclusion does not follow.

First let me note that the justification or warrant of our beliefs cannot depend on this premise concerning God because we had the beliefs and were justified in them long before we believed in the existence of God. However, it may be that, though our justification or warrant for the things we believe does not depend on an argument concerning God, the existence of God does supply a better philosophical explanation for why the proper functioning of our faculties yields true beliefs or has a trustworthy if fallible tendency to do so. That strikes me as an interesting issue.

The Problem of Evil

However, the argument, though it has the support of Plantinga,[10] seems to me invalid. The problem with the argument is a simple one. It is the problem of evil. Plantinga has argued, brilliantly enough, that the solution to the problem of evil depends on recognizing that it does not follow and, indeed, that there is no good argument from the existence of God to the absence of evil. To quote him:

> Less trivially, consider
>   (1) There is an omnipotent, omniscient and perfectly good God
>   (2) There are 10^{13} turps of evil
> and
>   (3) Possibly, for any world W which is as good as the actual world, but contains less that 10^{13} turps of evil, it is not within the power of God to actualize W, despite his omnipotence and omniscience.
> I might argue that the probability of (1) on (2) is not as low as you might think by pointing out that (2) is equivalent to (2)&(3) (because (3) is necessarily true).[11]

The Problem of Deception

Now notice that if incredible turps of evil do not yield the conclusion that God does not exist, and, hence, the existence of God does not yield the conclusion there are not incredible turps of evil in the world, nor even render this highly probable, we can argue in the same way concerning deception. Suppose the unit of deception is a decep. Then we can, using exactly the same argument as Plantinga has used concerning evil, argue that incredible deceps of error do not yield the conclusion that God does not exist, or even render this highly probable, and, hence, the existence of God does not yield the conclusion that there are not incredible deceps of error in the world, or even render this highly probable. Moreover, the very explanation that Plantinga uses to account for the possibility of evil, namely, that it is the product of free will, may be used explain the fact that we deceive ourselves and others. It is by the exercise of our free will.

Much human error is the result of our leaping beyond the reasonable bounds of valid argumentation and deceiving others by an exercise of free will. That is not the end of the possibility of error produced by free agents within Plantinga's theism, however. Human free agents exercise their free will to deceive each other as our awareness of human deception, our own included, will persuade us. But the matter is still worse. To explain evil beyond the prodigious evil resulting from human freedom, Plantinga notes that theism, at least of the sort he favors, holds to the existence of Satan and his cohorts who may, for all we know, produce all the evil we do not produce by an exercise of their freedom. But just as there is evil that cannot be explained by an exercise of human free will, so there is error that cannot be explained by an exercise of human free will. These deceps of error might be explained according to the theist by work of Satan and his cohorts who exercise their freedom to deceive us. In short, then, if Plantinga is right that we cannot conclude, deductively or probablistically, from the existence God that it is false that there are 10^{13} turps of evil, for the same reason he cannot conclude, deductively or probablistically, that it is false that there are 10^{13} deceps of deception.

Compare, finally,

S.   Satan and his cohorts produce incredible deceps of error

with

E.   Evolutionary processes produce incredible deceps of error.

I find little to choose between them. A naturalist wishing to assign a high probability to the conclusion that the proper functioning of our faculties yields truth because they are the result of evolution must assign a low probability to E, while a supernaturalist wishing to assign a high probability to the conclusion that the proper functioning of our faculties yields truth because they are designed by God must assign a low probability to S.

An argument against S or E might be based on our commonsense assumption that the proper functioning of our faculties yields truth, which, I think, is based on the Reidian metaprinciple that our faculties are trustworthy and not fallacious. The argument depends on coherence as I shall argue below. The theist may accept that God is responsible for the proper functioning of our faculties to yield truth, admitting that he does not know why Satan and his cohorts do not undermine that functioning, and the naturalist may accept that evolution is responsible for such proper functioning, admitting that he does not know why evolutionary processes do not undermine such proper functioning. Both theists and atheists have thought that such proper functioning yielding truth was useful to our survival and adaptation and rejected S and E accordingly. I suspect that too much truth would lead to our demise, being the pessimist that I am, and I have argued for that conclusion. This kind of moral pessimism might be shared by a theist and an atheist, however, and each will think we are lucky not to have greater capacities to discover the mysteries of the universe than we do.

Neither the hypothesis of evolution nor of the existence of God enables us to deduce that proper functioning will yield truth, or, therefore, to provide a deductive explanation of why it does. Induction and inductive explanation will depend on the assignment of initial probabilities to hypotheses about how Satan and cohorts would behave in the one case and to initial probabilities about how evolutionary processes would behave in the other. Both deductive arguments are invalid and both inductive arguments rest on speculative probabilities. To argue on the basis of either kind of speculation is a mistake. We are much better warranted in believing that the proper functioning of our faculties yields truth than we are in believing anything about these speculative matters.

Proper Functioning and Externalism

Is proper functioning enough to yield warrant and, combined with true belief, knowledge? It is a bit hard for me to tell because I am not sure

I understand what Plantinga regards as proper functioning and, as a result, I find it difficult to know what would count against the account. Having introduced the idea into the literature with Thomas Paxson[12] that undefeated justification plus true belief is knowledge, and having subsequently argued that knowledge is undefeated justification, I find that the presence of reference to a defeater system in the analysis leaves me suspicious that the notion of defeat can be used to meet any counterexample. Moreover, any counterexample in which there is proper functioning but no warrant because of some feature F not included in Plantinga's account faces the prospect of being treated by Plantinga as an interesting illustration that properly functioning systems must have feature F, thus calling for a minor amendment. It is difficult, for that reason, to show that the account or some minor amendment of it is not sufficient for warrant, but I shall now try in order to press Plantinga for further clarification. The way to illuminate the consequences of a definition is to consider possible counterexamples, and so I shall proceed to the task.

Mr. Truetemp

The counterexamples I shall offer here are ones I offered against externalism.[13] They were not offered merely as refutations but as examples illustrating the features that a correct account of knowledge must possess. The most critical feature of an account of justification, or warrant, is that justification or warrant arises from epistemic evaluation of what one believes or considers rather than from the way in which the belief or consideration arose. So, first consider a counterexample against the sufficiency of Plantinga's account. Consider an example which, though it stretches the imagination a bit, does not, I think, tear it lose from philosophical relevance. Imagine progress in neural and cognitive science that makes it possible to install devices in the brain of a normal person that produce belief limited to a specific subject, for example, beliefs about one's temperature, beliefs that one might express by saying things like "My temperature is 98 degrees."

Now suppose that a doctor is dealing with a group of patients whose temperature variation is a critically important indication of the state of a brain malady and the need for medication to treat it. The brain malady produces an apathetic state that leads the patients to neglect to monitor their own temperature with the result that they do not get the medication in time to prevent dysfunction. It occurs to the doctor that if she could design a device that could be installed in the brain which would produce correct beliefs at regular intervals, say once an hour, about the temperature of the patient, the patient would have a correct belief about his temperature in time to take the medication and avoid the dysfunctional set of symptoms. The doctor works on developing such a device, which she calls "doxatemp," with a neurologist and a cognitive scientist. They develop a prototype which their experimental efforts indicate will produce correct beliefs about the temperature of the brain when implanted in the brain of the subject.

They then acquire a patient who has the malady and requires brain surgery to remove a small tumor, which is characteristic of the malady, and they implant the device in the patient who, for the obvious reason, they refer to as "Mr. Truetemp," hoping the device they have designed to produce correct temperature beliefs in him every hour will work. There is no doubt that the device will measure the temperature of Mr. Truetemp's brain accurately, but the question is whether it will make Mr. Truetemp believe that is his temperature. The doctors wait impatiently as Mr. Truetemp regains consciousness. After a short time, Mr. Truetemp awakes from the sedative, remarks that he has very little pain, and then suddenly says, "You know I am suddenly convinced that my temperature is 98 degrees, but I do not have the slightest idea why I believe that." The doxatemp has worked just as it was designed to do and is functioning properly to produce true beliefs on the hour about the brain temperature of Mr. Truetemp.

No problem for the proud doctors, but a problem for Plantinga, because Mr. Truetemp, completely puzzled as to why he is suddenly convinced his temperature is 98 degrees adds, "I am convinced that my temperature is 98 degrees, but I don't know whether that is my temperature, I am just completely convinced that it is." We can imagine, if we wish, that neither he nor the physicians ever check to see if the device is working properly, though, in fact it is. I claim this. Mr. Truetemp has true beliefs about his temperature produced by a device that is properly functioning to produce true beliefs as it was designed to do in the environment it was designed for. It appears to me to fulfill Plantinga's conditions for warrant in addition to true belief, but Mr. Truetemp does not know that his temperature is 98 degrees when he believes it is, nor does anybody else—the accuracy of the beliefs produced by the device being unchecked—because he has no idea whether his conviction is correct and he is totally mystified by the existence of it.[14]

The problem, I shall argue, is that Mr. Truetemp is not in a position to evaluate his belief favorably or respond to any objection to it, and that an adequate account of warrant and justification which convert true belief into knowledge requires that one be in a position to evaluate the belief in terms of a background system with which it coheres and which enables one to respond to objections to the belief. In short, proper functioning is not sufficient. You need to add coherence with a background system. This example illustrates a problem common to all externalist accounts, namely, the problem of the *opacity* of the external connection to the subject of belief.

Transcending Origins of Belief: Ms. Prejudice

The proper functioning condition is also not necessary. The reason is that a belief might arise from improper functioning—racial prejudice, for example—but become warranted later by the acquisition of evidence. Imagine, for example, the case of Ms. Prejudice, who out of prejudice against a race believes that the members of the race who have a certain disease get the disease because of their genetic makeup. Of course, she, being very racist, believes this is a sign of their racial inferiority, and she is totally convinced because of her racism that the disease is the result of the genetic constitution of the race. Now imagine that Ms. Prejudice becomes a medical student and learns, to her pleasure, of the medical evidence that supports her prejudiced conviction. She becomes, however, a medical expert of the highest quality, fully capable of separating her prejudices from her scientific studies. As luck would have it, she becomes part of a research team assigned the task of checking on the genetic basis of the disease. Her coinvestigators know of her prejudice, but they also know of her scientific discipline, and decide that she will make an excellent devil's advocate for the thesis that the disease is not genetically caused. She wants to make sure it really is, and she will force them to investigate with the greatest care every reason for doubting that the disease is genetically caused. She wants to make absolutely sure that she cannot be charged with concluding on the basis of the scientific evidence that the disease is genetically caused because of prejudice. Of course, her belief that the disease is genetically caused is the result of her still very intense prejudice, but her scientific evaluation of the evidence in favor of this belief must be rigorously tested.

Every objection to the claim is considered and refuted by the team, all of whom, except for Ms. Prejudice, who plays devil's advocate, are completely without prejudice. They all conclude that the scientific evidence shows conclusively that the disease is genetically caused, as Ms. Prejudice has believed all along. After the investigation, her belief has warrant, all the warrant the matter admits of, and she knows that the disease is genetically caused. She has the same evidence, and thus the same warrant, for believing this as the other members of her team, and if they know that the disease is genetically caused, so does she. But her belief is the product of an improperly functioning system of racial prejudice.

Externalists are inclined to reply to this sort of example that at the time at which Ms. Prejudice has warrant and she knows that the disease is genetically caused, which is only after she gets the scientific evidence, her belief is now causally or counterfactually sustained by processes connected with the evidence she has for her belief. I think the evidence of psychology opposes this cheery perspective. Should her prejudice suddenly vanish, perhaps her belief would as well. Perhaps her belief is so powerfully supported by her prejudice that the collapse of the latter would fill her with doubt and uncertainty about all matters pertaining to former objects of her prejudice. Perhaps, even if she were to cease to believe what she did out of prejudice but continued to believe it, some other prejudice would be the cause instead, and still not the evidence. The critical point is that it does not matter whether the evidence has any causal or counterfactually causal effect on the belief. All that matters for her to have warrant is that she understands, as well she does with her robust scientific understanding of evidence, that this evidence shows that the content of her belief, the claim or proposition that the disease is genetically caused, is true. It is that understanding and not the causal or counterfactually causal influence on the belief that gives her warrant and knowledge.[15]

There are typical externalist responses to these examples that seem to me to amount to biting the bullet which has a nasty effect on the teeth. To the example of Mr. Truetemp, it is common to reply that Truetemp does know that his temperature is 98 degrees but does not know that he knows. I regard this as implausible. Truetemp has no idea why he suddenly believes that his temperature is 98 degrees and does not know that what he believes is true, though he does know that he believes it. But if he does not know that what he believes is true, though he does know that he believes it, then he does not know that his temperature is 98 degrees. Consider the difference if the doctor knows that the device is effective and tells Truetemp about the implantation of the device and what it does. Then Truetemp knows that his beliefs are true.

The standard externalist reply to the case of Ms. Prejudice is that she does not know because her appeal to the evidence is just rationalization for her prejudiced belief. This seems incorrect to me. She really understands the relevance of the evidence to what she believes, and it is that understanding that gives her knowledge. I would distinguish between the attitude of belief and the attitude of positive evaluation based on the evidence, which I have called acceptance. I do not deny that this positive evaluation, the higher-order attitude, might be caused by the evidence, but the belief may rest below this level of reflection mired in prejudice.

It is important to notice that there are other ways Plantinga might reply to these examples if he admits that Truetemp is ignorant and that Prejudice knows. He could say, as I would be inclined to say, that Truetemp's ignorance concerning why he believes what he does is a defeater. That would constitute a modification of his account to accommodate defeaters of this sort, but it is possible to say that proper functioning requires positive evaluation of the belief and not just the belief itself. I hope that he might make that reply, for it is one that would bring him close to my own position. He could say that Prejudice's knowledge is the result of proper functioning in production of higher-level positive evaluation or acceptance rather than in the production of belief at the first level and modify his account to allow that warrant might arise from the proper functioning in production of evaluation or acceptance of something believed from prejudice. I think he should admit this, for there is no reason to tie an account of warrant to how a belief is produced as opposed to how it is evaluated. Again, such a modification would bring Plantinga closer to the sort of account I defend.

The Example of Divine Illumination

There is a final example which I take seriously. It seems to me that on Plantinga's account it is beyond the power of anyone, even God, to bypass our usual cognitive faculties and give us knowledge. Suppose that God wants Abraham to know something, that Isaac will have children. Now he might have some angel appear before Abraham and tell him, thus making use of Abraham's cognitive faculties in their proper functioning way. Or Abraham might have a special faculty for discerning spiritual matters, some *sensus diviniatis*[16] that God might use to produce that belief in Abraham. But is there nothing God can do to miraculously give Abraham such knowledge in some other way, bypassing the usual sort of functioning of Abraham's faculties?

Put the question another way. Suppose that knowledge arising in the natural way is the product of the proper functioning of our cognitive faculties. Is it beyond the power of God to produce knowledge in some other way without producing it through the proper functioning of our faculties? It seems to me a serious objection to Plantinga's view to disallow that warranted belief can arise from divine illumination that miraculously bypasses production by our cognitive faculties. Why, in short, should God be limited in this way? The point is that Plantinga, like the externalists he resembles, restricts knowledge to belief with a certain kind of history, and that seems to me to be a critical mistake. The history of a belief may explain how you know what you believe, but it is possible that you might have known the same thing in another way, by divine intervention, for example. Of course, if the content of the belief is historical or causal, such as my belief that I am now seeing a computer, that a computer is causing my present experience, you have to have causal knowledge to know that the belief is true, but not all beliefs have a causal content connected with their production in this way.

To raise objections against a theory is, however, not sufficient in philosophy. One must also show that one can construct a theory that avoids the objections and, moreover, that clarifies the underlying problem. The basic underlying problem is that Plantinga, like externalists generally, has supposed that how a belief is produced is what determines whether it has warrant. That is a mistake. What does determine whether a belief has warrant? In part, it is the very thing that Plantinga has rejected, the coherence of the belief with a system of beliefs. I do not say that coherence suffices for warrant. It does not. But it is necessary, at least as I conceive of coherence, and it is the role of coherence that Plantinga has neglected. He could, if he wished, and I hope he might yet do so, include coherence in his account of proper functioning, for that is essential for the solution of the problems of Truetemp, Prejudice, and others of the sort.

Coherence Defended

Plantinga has reiterated the claim that coherence will not work. His basic arguments against the coherence theory are variations of isolation arguments. These are arguments indicating that a doxastic system can be isolated from sensory experience and from external reality and can remain unresponsive to it.[17] This will happen when our cognitive faculties are frozen or assaulted and do not function properly. Coherence is, consequently, not sufficient for the conversion of true belief into knowledge, though I have never thought or suggested that it was. However, that leaves open the possibility that coherence with a doxastic system is necessary, which it is, and that when coherence is combined with requisite freedom from error in the doxastic system, it is sufficient, which it also is.

It would not be appropriate for me to repeat the theory of personal justification, which is coherence with an acceptance system, which when undefeated by corrections of errors in the acceptance system yields undefeated justification, though I include my definitions in an appendix. I claim in *Theory of Knowledge* that undefeated personal justification, which is a blend of coherence with an acceptance system undefeated by errors in it, is knowledge. Let us first consider how the addition of a requirement of coherence with an acceptance system meets the objections concerning Truetemp and Prejudice. I have developed a theory of coherence with a background system in terms of beating and neutralizing competitors, but here I shall appeal only to the basic idea. Justification results, not from the coherence *of* a system as some coherence theorists maintain, but from coherence *with* a background system, an acceptance system.

Moreover, I distinguish the natural state of belief from the positive evaluation of it in terms of the goal of accepting what is believed if and only if it is true. This positive evaluation, which may not involve conscious deliberation, is acceptance. The acceptance system is a set of acceptances, of states of acceptance, and not merely the things accepted. The reason is that our acceptance of something, and not merely the content of the proposition accepted, is relevant to justification, as we shall see. Suppose I accept p. What is required for my acceptance of p to cohere with my acceptance system? Obviously, I must accept p itself; that must be part of my acceptance system, but that is not enough. The reason is that my acceptance of p might be defenseless against objections to it. My acceptance of p coheres with my acceptance system just in case my acceptance system contains replies to objections to it—more technically, in case all the competitors are beaten or neutralized.

Truetemp and Coherence

With this idea of personal justification and coherence before us, we can understand why Truetemp's belief that his temperature is 98 degrees does not cohere with his acceptance system and why he is not personally justified in accepting this. One fundamental objection to anything one believes is the denial of it. Another and equally important objection to any belief, which does not raise any objection to the truth of what is believed, is that the person cannot tell whether or not the thing she believes is true and, hence she is untrustworthy in believing it. The latter objection is one that Truetemp cannot meet in terms of his acceptance system because he does not think he can tell whether what he believes about his temperature is true, nor does he accept that he is trustworthy in believing such things. For he has no idea why he does believe it, and thus does not accept what he finds that he believes about his temperature. Thus he is not personally justified in accepting that his temperature is 98 degrees, because his believing it is not positively evaluated in terms of his acceptance system and does not cohere with it. His belief may be consistent with the things he accepts, but that does not suffice for coherence with the background system. His belief coheres with his acceptance system only if it contains replies to objections against his belief, which it does not.

Prejudice and Coherence

Consider Prejudice who has an acceptance system full of information about the disease and the causes of it. She is an expert, and her acceptance system contains the answers to objections against her acceptance system. The crucial objection is that she believes what she does out of prejudice and is not influenced by science in her belief— only by prejudice. She has an answer, which I find sufficient, which is that her acceptance of what she believes is explained by the scientific evidence she accepts. She has a sound and correct scientific justification of what she accepts on the basis of her acceptance system, and this justification is undefeated by error.

Her critic might persevere and claim that because she believes what she does out of prejudice, she is untrustworthy in accepting it, and hence not justified. Her reply is that how she came to believe it may not be trustworthy but her acceptance and positive valuation of the proposition she believes based on her evidence are trustworthy, and thus her acceptance is justified on the basis of her acceptance system.

It is how we evaluate evidence for what we accept that makes us trustworthy in accepting it and not the origin of our original belief. Belief is often, more often than we choose to admit, beyond our control and beyond our understanding. It is the evaluation of what we believe in terms of our evidence for it that determines whether we are justified in accepting the things we believe rather than the obscure doxastic origins of it all. Ms. Prejudice transcends beyond mere rationalization to sound scientific evaluation, and such evaluation gives her justification and knowledge.

The Isolation Argument and the Gettier Problem

Let us close in on the objection to the coherence theory that Plantinga has reiterated, the isolation objection. The solution to this problem for the coherence theorist depends on recognition of the fundamental insight of the Gettier problem: that of falliblism, the doctrine that justified belief may be false.[18] In the formulation of his problem Edmund Gettier made an enormous impact, beyond that of Bertrand Russell[19] who formulated a problem with the same formal structure, because, unlike Russell and those who preceded him, Gettier understood the implications of the problem resulting from the fundamental insight of falliblism.

The point is that proper functioning systems, reliable processes, and all the wondrous externalist things invented after Gettier are fallible in the sense that, however often they lead to truth, they sometimes lead to error. This they share with beliefs justified without inference and beliefs justified by inference and, yes, those justified by coherence. That is what makes the Gettier problem interesting. I think that Plantinga's treatment of this problem is the least satisfactory part of his book, for he attempts to explain it in terms of some failure of proper functioning, much in the tradition of externalists who always try to deal with the problem by appeal to the way the true beliefs are produced.[20] But that is not the problem.

Specify your process or functioning or inference or coherence or other favorite, and you will be left with the conclusion that resulting beliefs can meet your condition and be false nonetheless, unless, of course, you arbitrarily refuse to give your favored epistemic award to anything false. The reason is that our faculties are fallible. The consequence is that whatever condition you append to true belief to obtain knowledge will, unless you fill in some special condition to ensure against defeat by error, reproduce the Gettier problem. Our best epistemic efforts may go astray. That is the human condition.

The result of this is very favorable to the coherence theory. Though coherence does not suffice to convert true belief into knowledge, this fact does not distinguish coherence from other conditions, like Plantinga's, for example, because you have to add some condition to ensure that the warranted belief is not defeated by some error. However, once you add that condition to coherence—that is, that the personal justification resulting from coherence with the acceptance system is not defeated by any error in the acceptance system—you have a combination of coherence and truth that converts true belief into knowledge. Hence, as I have argued, undefeated justified acceptance is knowledge. Of course, one needs a technically satisfactory account of this idea of not being defeated by error, which is difficult. It is, however, a matter of technical fine-tuning, which I have attempted in some detail, but it is not a problem unique to the coherence theorist.

How does undefeated justification based on coherence avoid the isolation problem? Simply enough. My justification for accepting what I do, especially in matters of perception concerning what I perceive, must answer the objection that I am isolated, doxastically frozen, and other isolationist favorites. To meet them my acceptance system must answer these objections, most simply, perhaps, by replying that I am not cut off from the world, and hence not isolated in the ways imagined. Now my accepting what I do to answer these objections must not be defeated by error in what I accept, and therefore what I accept to answer these objections must be true. Hence undefeated justification, undefeated coherence with my acceptance system, excludes the possibility of isolation. I must accept that I am not isolated, though I need not have reflected upon this, or my acceptance fails to cohere with my acceptance system, and I must be right in accepting this or my justification based on coherence will be defeated. That is how undefeated justification yields knowledge.

Coherence and Divine Intervention

Finally, to see how this theory solves the problem of divine intervention, note that the objection to what I learn from God by direct intervention may be accompanied by my acceptance that my belief has come from a trustworthy source and I can tell that I am so informed and not deceived. Now this meets the objection that what I believe is not the product of proper functioning. For my answer is, "Yes, that is true, it is the product of a better source, grace." Now the atheist will not be convinced by this any more than the skeptic will be convinced by my reply to the claim that my beliefs are provided by a powerful demon bent on deceiving me when I say I can tell that I perceive the world before me and am not deceived. In both cases my answers to the objections, if admitted, will, with a qualification I shall add, be sufficient. If my source of information is trustworthy and I can tell that it is, the objections are answered and undefeated justification results. There are better things in life and epistemology than proper functioning, and undefeated justification is one of them.

Conclusion

Let me answer one final objection of Plantinga and of detractors to the view just considered. There is a fundamental objection to anything that I accept, namely, that I am not trustworthy in what I accept. To answer this I must accept that I am trustworthy in what I accept, and this principle, which I accept, might be formulated as follows:

T.   I am trustworthy in what I accept and I accept this too.

This principle, which reminds one of Reid's metaprinciple, contains a loop. Plantinga speaks of vicious loops of argumentation. The principle does, of course, refer to itself and loops back onto itself. This has the consequence that the principle which plays a general role in justification of whatever we accept is self-referential. However, principle T is not a premise in a proof, it is part of an acceptance system, and though a central part, it is justified by other things that we accept. This metaprinciple, like Reid's, vouches for itself as it vouches for other things, but it is also supported by the other things that it supports as they support it. Is principle T a foundation? That is a poor metaphor because of the mutual support between the principle and other things one accepts. A better metaphor is that of a keystone in an arched roof. You place it in the top and it holds the sides of the arch in place as they hold it in place. You could not use principle T to prove that the skeptic is in error when he affirms that you are not trustworthy. But that does not mean that principle T plays no role in justification. On the contrary, it is a keystone of justification and, hence, of undefeated justification. The role of principle T is not to prove the skeptic wrong but to explain how coherence yields justification and knowledge, including the knowledge that the skeptic is wrong.

Is principle T a principle of reliability and of proper functioning? No, it is not. It is not a naturalistic principle, any more than it is principle of epistemic obligation or permission. It is a principle of worth. To say that I am trustworthy in what I accept is to say that acceptance of the things I accept is more worthy of my trust than nonacceptance. I end with the claim that epistemic worth is not simply a matter of a high objective probability or statistical frequency of attaining truth.

Mr. Cartupe and the Demon

Consider the example of Mr. Cartupe, duped by reading Descartes into thinking the famous deceptive demon exists because he believed that Descartes intended to claim that the demon exists rather than just using him as an instrument of hyperbolic doubt. Cartupe is, moreover, quite strict in the way in which he incorporates this new conception into his doxastic ways and teaches himself to preface his beliefs with, "As the demon has deceived me into believing. . . ." Now, and this will strain your imagination, but not beyond what Descartes asked of us, suppose that the demon really exists and deceives us. Then Cartupe will be right with a high objective probability and the rest of us wrong with a high objective probability.

I do not think that he is trustworthy in what he accepts, however, even given the high probability of the truth of what he accepts. The reason is that his whole system of acceptance is based on his foolish error of thinking that Descartes was claiming that the demon existed and believing what he thus mistook for Descartes's intention. What he believes is not worth believing, even for someone interested in believing what is true, because it is based on foolishness. There is more to trustworthiness than being right, even with a very great frequency.

I end with a question. Suppose that some powerful being, perhaps the demon himself, wished that Cartupe should have the truth when no one else did and hence that his system is functioning properly and by design to produce true beliefs. Is that knowledge? A coherence theorist who accepts principle T would not think so, and I do not. I suspect Plantinga would not either. Let us leave it to the reader to decide why. Knowledge is often explained by proper functioning. There Plantinga is right. But proper functioning is not necessary or sufficient for knowledge. Knowledge is a matter of coherence incorporating trustworthiness. Knowledge is a matter of trustworthiness and not natural or supernatural success. I think that probably Plantinga and I are closer together than I represent us as being, for our proper functioning, if the result of God's benevolent design, should enable us to evaluate what we accept to protect ourselves from deception. I am not sure that I am trustworthy in thinking this, however, and, consequently, I shall wait for Plantinga's reply before accepting a conclusion.

Appendix: Definitions

D1.   A system X is an acceptance system of S if and only if X contains just statements of the form—S accepts that p—attributing to S just those things that S accepts with the objective of accepting that p if and only if p.

D2.   S is justified in accepting p at t on the basis of system X of S at t if and only if p coheres with X of S at t.

D3.   S is justified in accepting p at t on the basis of system X of S at t if and only if all competitors of p are beaten or neutralized for S on X at t.

D4.   c competes with p for S on X at t if and only if it is more reasonable for S to accept that p on the assumption that c is false than on the assumption that c is true, on the basis of X at t.

D5.   p beats c for S on X at t if and only if c competes with p for S on X at t, and it is more reasonable for S to accept p than to accept c on X at t.

D6.   n neutralizes c as a competitor of p for S on X at t if and only if c competes with p for S on X at t, the conjunction of c and n does not compete with p for S on X at t, and it is as reasonable for S to accept the conjunction of c and n as to accept c alone on X at t.

D7.   S is personally justified in accepting that p at t if and only if S is justified in accepting that p on the basis of the acceptance system of S at t.

D8.   S is justified in accepting that p at t in a way that is undefeated if and only if S is justified in accepting p at t on the basis of every system that is a member of the ultrasystem of S at t.

D9.   M defeats the personal justification of S for accepting p at t if and only if S is personally justified in accepting p at t, but S is not justified in accepting p at t on system M at t where M is a member of the ultrasystem of S at t.

D10.   A system M is a member of the ultrasystem of S at t if and only if M either is the acceptance system of S at t or results from eliminating one or more states described by statements of the form—S accepts that q—when q is false, replacing one or more statements of the form—S accepts that q—with a statement of the form—S accepts that not-q—when q is false, or any combination of such eliminations and replacements in the acceptance system of S at t with the constraint that if q logically entails r which is false and also accepted, then—S accepts that r—must be also be eliminated or replaced just as—S accepts that q—was.

These definitions yield the following definition of knowledge:

DK. S knows that p at t if and only if (i) S accepts that p, (ii) it is true that p, (iii) S is personally justified in accepting that p at t, and (iv) S is justified in accepting that p at t in a way that is undefeated.

We may obtain the following reduction of the analysis:

DK*. S knows that p at t if and only if S is justified in accepting that p at t in a way that is undefeated.

Notes

Research for this paper was supported by the National Endowment for the Humanities Grant #RO-22582–93. I am indebted to many of my colleagues and students for their comments on this paper, most especially Laura Ekstrom, Joseph Tolliver, Mark Patterson, Joel Pust, and Linda Radzick.

1. A. Plantinga, *Warrant: The Current Debate* and *Warrant and Proper Function*, New York and Oxford: Oxford University Press, 1993.

2. K. Lehrer, *Theory of Knowledge*, Boulder and London: Westview Press and Routledge, 1990.

3. T. Reid, *The Works of Thomas Reid, D.D.*, 8th ed., edited by W. Hamilton, Edinburgh: James Thin, 1895, is the most readily available out of print complete edition, though earlier editions are more accurate. For selections of Reid, see T. Reid, *Inquiry and Essays*, edited by R. Beanblossom and K. Lehrer, Indianapolis: Hackett, 1983.

4. T. Reid, *Works*, p. 447, *Inquiry and Essays*, p. 275.

5. T. Reid, *Works*, p. 447.

6. T. Reid, *Works*, p. 439.

7. T. Reid, *Works*, pp. 447–48.

8. A. Plantinga, *Warrant and Proper Function*, p. 194.

9. A. Plantinga, *Warrant and Proper Function*, chapter 12, passim.

10. A. Plantinga, *Warrant and Proper Function*, pp. 236–37.

11. A. Plantinga, *Warrant and Proper Function*, p. 175.

12. K. Lehrer and T. Paxson, Jr., "Knowledge: Undefeated Justified True Belief," *Journal of Philosophy*, 66 (1969).

13. K. Lehrer, *Theory of Knowledge*, chapter 8.

14. Cf. K. Lehrer, *Theory of Knowledge*, pp. 163–64.

15. Cf. K. Lehrer, *Theory of Knowledge*, pp. 168–72.

16. Cf. A. Plantinga, *Warrant and Proper Function*, pp. 42–43.

17. A. Plantinga, *Warrant and Proper Function*, pp. 178–82.

18. E. Gettier, Jr., "Is Justified True Belief Knowledge?" *Analysis*, 23 (1963), pp. 121–23.

19. B. Russell, *Problems of Philosophy*, London: Oxford University Press, 1959, p. 132.

20. A. Plantinga, *Warrant and Proper Function*, pp. 31–35.

Plantinga on Knowledge and Proper Function

Laurence BonJour

In his two books *Warrant: the Current Debate* and *Warrant and Proper Function*,[1] Alvin Plantinga attempts nothing less than a major reorientation of contemporary epistemological thought. The first of these two volumes contains elaborate objections to the main kinds of epistemological positions that have been advanced in recent times, objections that Plantinga claims to be more or less decisive; and the second offers a positive view that, although bearing some family resemblance to recent versions of reliabilism, is strikingly novel in both its details and its implications. I have learned and will continue to learn a great deal from these tightly argued, extremely knowledgeable, and also highly entertaining volumes. But despite my great admiration for Plantinga's accomplishment, his criticisms of other views seem to me both less clear and less decisive than he thinks, and his positive proposals strike me in the end as deeply unsatisfying.

In the first section of the paper, I will consider Plantinga's main line of objection to opposing views, especially to those of an internalist sort; while there is a serious problem with the way in which the objection is couched, I will try to show that this does not prevent it from posing, at the very least, a major challenge to the positions at which it is aimed. The second and third sections will then explore some of the bases for my dissatisfaction with Plantinga's positive position.[2]

I

The place to begin, I think, is with the concept that figures prominently in the titles of both books: Plantinga's rather idiosyncratic idea of *warrant*. Warrant, we are told, is "a normative, possibly complex quality that comes in degrees, enough of which is what distinguishes knowledge from mere true belief" [*WCD* 4]. Plantinga rejects the more standard term "justification" as a label for this quality, on the ground that it is biased in favor of internalist, deontological conceptions of what is required for knowledge, the very conceptions that he in fact most strongly wants to reject. Noting that "warrant" also has its deontological connotations, he suggests in passing that Roderick Chisholm's term "positive epistemic status" or Ernest Sosa's term "epistemic aptness" might have been better for what he has in mind.

"Warrant," then, as employed by Plantinga, appears to be something of a technical term: it stands for whatever it is that has to be added to true belief to yield knowledge, but the term itself is not supposed to convey in any very straightforward way just what that something might be. (For the rest of this paper, I will use scarequotes as a reminder that the term "warrant" is being used in this somewhat artificial and, I believe, potentially misleading way.) Nor, beyond the very general reference to normativity, are we initially given any other intuitive account or explanation that we might appeal to in determining whether "warrant" is present in a particular case. Thus if we are to evaluate the claim that "warrant" is or is not present in such a case, a kind of claim that Plantinga makes over and over again and that forms the main basis for his criticisms of other positions, the only way to proceed is apparently this: suppose or imagine that the belief in question is true, and then determine intuitively whether on this supposition it would count as knowledge. And this seems indeed in the main to be Plantinga's procedure, though more often than not he is less than fully explicit about it.[3]

If this is the way we are to think about claims concerning "warrant," then a great deal of weight will obviously rest on our intuitions about the presence or absence of knowledge in a described case. And here, I would suggest, there are at least two reasons for concern, one of which will be considered now and the other later, in section III. The first reason has to do with the structure of the concept of knowledge. As Plantinga himself notes, specifying the idea of "warrant" in the way that he does leaves open the possibility that "warrant" may not be "a simple property or quantity"; "perhaps," he suggests, "it is more like a vector resultant of other properties or qualities" [*WCD* vi]. But while this remark recognizes that what has to be added to true belief to yield knowledge need not be one simple property, it still seems to assume without any apparent justification that if multiple properties are involved, these will at least be such as to combine together in some way to yield a single "resultant" property. Why might not knowledge require instead two (or even more) distinct and incommensurable properties over and above truth and belief? And if this were so, "warrant," as understood by Plantinga, would in fact be merely a conjunction of independent properties; and establishing that "warrant" was absent in a particular case would in itself say nothing as to which of the component properties was missing.

Indeed, as it happens, the general account of knowledge that has been more or less standardly accepted in recent epistemology, and that is adopted or assumed by most of the specific positions that Plantinga is criticizing, takes precisely this form. On this account, knowledge requires the satisfaction of two distinct conditions in addition to belief and truth. The *third* condition, for which the term "justification" is most standardly employed, has to do with the presence of something like a reason or ground for the truth or likely truth of the belief. It is this condition that is the locus of the dispute between internalists and externalists, internalists insisting and externalists denying that this reason or ground must be accessible to the believer himself.

The *fourth* condition, on the other hand, is intended to exclude counterexamples of the general sort made famous by Edmund Gettier: counterexamples, very roughly, in which, although the other three conditions are satisfied, the truth condition is satisfied in a way whose accidental or quirky character seems incompatible with knowledge. Thus, for example, in a variant of one of Gettier's original examples, I might have overwhelming (but ultimately misleading) evidence that a particular one of my departmental colleagues owns a BMW and come to believe on this basis the more general claim that one or another of my colleagues owns a BMW; if the specified colleague does not own a BMW, but some other colleague (about whom I have no evidence relevant to the possession of a BMW) does, then the general belief is both true and apparently justified, but intuitively not a case of knowledge.[4] It will be useful, in the context of the present paper, to have a specific version of a fourth, anti-Gettier condition in mind, and I will adopt for that purpose a condition (adapted a bit from a condition originally proposed by Peter Unger[5]) which though technically less sophisticated, has the virtue of being relatively transparent from an intuitive standpoint: the condition that it not be an *accident* in relation to whatever satisfies the third condition that the belief is true.

The idea that a correct account of knowledge should take this form, with two separate conditions in addition to the requirements of belief and truth, may of course be mistaken in some way; but Plantinga, in criticizing views that are so formulated, obviously cannot simply assume that this is so. I believe that his inattention to this point seriously compromises his arguments against many of the views he discusses.

One of Plantinga's standard modes of objection to other epistemological views, especially to those of the internalist, deontological variety with which I will here be mainly concerned, is to offer a counterexample in which the account of the third condition offered by the view in question is satisfied, but in which "warrant" in Plantinga's sense is intuitively not present, i.e., (presumably) which is intuitively not a case of knowledge even if the belief in question is in fact true. Thus, e.g., in opposition to the view he calls "post-classical Chisholmian internalism,"[6] we are offered the following case:

> Suppose . . . I am being arbitrarily manipulated by an Alpha Centaurian or Cartesian demon or some other pathology-inducing condition, and consider the phenomenology, the purely psychological properties, that go in fact with perceiving a large oak tree at 40 yards: suppose the Alpha Centaurians give me those properties at random intervals, with no correlation at all with my being in the presence of oak trees. Naturally enough, on those occasions I believe that I perceive an oak. These beliefs, however, will surely have little by way of warrant for me, despite the fact that they are accompanied by evidence bases that in other, more happy circumstances accompany that belief's having a high degree of warrant for me. [*WCD* 61]

Presumably the point is that even if in a particular case, there actually is an oak tree present at the specified distance so that the belief is true, this is still intuitively not a case of knowledge. Analogous counterexamples, appealing variously to brain lesions, random bursts of radiation, Cartesian demons, Alpha Centaurians, and the like, are also offered in opposition to the earlier and more familiar version of Chisholm's foundationalism, to a generic version of coherentism, to my own version of coherentism, and to the "evidentialism" of Richard Feldman and Earl Conee. Plantinga's suggestion seems to be that such a counterexample can be found for any internalist view.[7]

Such examples are supposed to show that the third conditions proposed by the views in question are insufficient for "warrant" and thus mistaken. But the possibility must be considered that what has gone wrong in such cases is not that the proposed third condition is mistaken, but rather that the *fourth* condition (which may be assumed rather than explicitly stated) is simply not satisfied, i.e., that the case in question is just a Gettier case, in which case there need be nothing wrong with the account of knowledge being criticized.[8] In the case just quoted, this possibility seems in fact to be realized: in relation to whatever justification the perceptual experience of an oak tree might provide for the belief that an oak tree is present, it is simply an accident that such a belief happens in a particular instance to be true, given that the experience was caused in a way that had nothing to do with whether or not such a tree was present. And the same seems to be the case for many or all of the parallel counterexamples that Plantinga gives—at least once they are sufficiently elaborated to clearly satisfy the various third conditions in question.[9]

Plantinga has replied to the foregoing line of criticism, both by anticipation in *WCD* [111] and in a subsequent article.[10] In these places, he makes two main points: First, counterexamples like the one quoted above differ from the usual run of Gettier examples in that they involve cognitive failures of a much more thoroughgoing and elaborate sort. And, second, such examples show in any case that satisfying the various proposed third conditions is not, contrary to the alleged claims of the proponents of these views, even "*nearly* sufficient" for "warrant," i.e., not even, when combined with true belief, a close approximation to knowledge. The significance of the first point is, however, rather obscure: while the examples are perhaps somewhat atypical, they seem to still conform to the familiar proposals for anti-Gettier conditions, such as the one provisionally adopted here. And the second response seems to betray, as Plantinga himself half acknowledges,[11] a confusion about the structure of the proposed concept of knowledge: the proposed fourth conditions are after all supposed to be necessary conditions, and a case that fails to satisfy them accordingly won't be a case of knowledge at all. If the proponents of such conceptions have sometimes sounded as though the fourth conditions were relatively insignificant additions or said (as I myself did[12]) that the justified true belief account of knowledge is still "approximately correct," this was a way of pointing out the relative rarity of the kinds of cases that the fourth condition is intended to exclude, not of claiming that a case might somehow be very close to knowledge even when that condition is not satisfied.

It is worth noting at this point that Plantinga's own account of "warrant" (discussed below) will presumably also itself be subject to Gettier cases and thus will itself require a fourth condition—so that "warrant" on the account he eventually gives will not in fact include everything necessary to convert true belief into knowledge. At least this will be so as long as it is possible for a belief to satisfy Plantinga's account of warrant and still be false, for then it will also be possible for it to be true in the accidental way that yields a Gettier case. I say "presumably" because it is difficult to be sure about Plantinga's views on this point. He discusses what he calls "quasi-Gettier cases" [*WPF* 40], or sometimes "semi-Gettier cases" [*WPF* 83] ("quasi" or "semi" because they pertain to "warrant" rather than justification), and goes to substantial pains to refine his account of "warrant" to exclude them [*WPF* 38–40, 82–86]. But he also seems to allow for beliefs that are mistaken even though "warranted" (perhaps most clearly in the discussion of fallible a priori "warrant" [*WPF* 109–13]), and it seems in any case quite hard to believe that he would want to claim that his account of warrant, however refined, is enough to completely guarantee truth.

For these reasons, counterexamples like the one quoted above do not, I believe, show what Plantinga claims that they do. From the standpoint of the general account of knowledge that these views reflect, the problem is that Plantinga's concept of "warrant" in effect lumps together two very different and basically incommensurable sorts of conditions. Thus he is led to construe a failure of an example to satisfy one of these conditions as showing that the view he is criticizing has made a mistake in the other condition. (Plantinga, of course, has other arguments against the various views he considers. In addition to criticisms pertaining specifically to each of the various views, which there is no space to go into here, there are also counterexamples designed to show that the various third conditions that he criticizes are not necessary for "warrant," i.e., that there can be cases of knowledge where a particular such condition is not satisfied. Such examples seem to me to vary a good deal in plausibility, but many of them are quite forceful.)

There is, however, an interesting potential rejoinder available to Plantinga on this point, one that highlights what I regard as the single most important issue raised by his epistemological work. The discussion so far might seem to suggest that some internalist view may be, despite counterexamples of the sort just considered, perfectly adequate as an account of the third condition for knowledge, i.e., roughly, as an account of what it is for a person to be epistemically justified, to have an appropriate reason for thinking that his belief is true. Such an account would still need to be supplemented by some version of the fourth condition in order to rule out relatively rare cases where the truth of the belief is a mere accident or fluke. But this is nonetheless quite compatible with its essential correctness as an account of the third condition.[13]

It seems to me, however, that Plantinga would want to question, on the basis of this very sort of counterexample, whether a purely internalist condition can really play such a role. What reflection on such counterexamples really shows, he might want to argue, is that it is *always* something like an accident when a belief that is merely specified as satisfying some particular internalist condition turns out to be true. And this in turn might seem to make the internalist third condition merely idle, with the fourth condition, which is after all fundamentally externalist in character, doing all the real work.

We may develop this point by returning to the example quoted above, the case of the person whose oak tree experiences are caused at random by Alpha Centaurians (or analogously by a Cartesian demon or a brain lesion or a random burst of radiation that somehow affects his senses) and who believes on that basis that an oak tree is present. Such beliefs, as we have seen, clearly fail the anti-Gettier condition. But do they nonetheless still at least satisfy the third condition for knowledge? I.e., in first approximation, does the occurrence of the experience constitute a good internalist reason for thinking that such a belief is true? Here it will be helpful to focus the question a bit by distinguishing, in a way that parallels Plantinga's own distinction between objective and subjective epistemic duty [*WCD* 16–17, 19–21], between an *objectively* good reason and a *subjectively* good reason: to have an objectively good reason is to have some basis or ground which establishes that the belief in question is objectively likely to be true; whereas merely to have a subjectively good reason is to have a basis or ground that seems from one's subjective point of view to constitute an objectively good reason but perhaps does not genuinely do so. In these terms, it seems apparent that an adequate third condition for knowledge must be one whose satisfaction yields an objectively good reason, not merely a subjectively good one, which is just to insist that justification or warrant must be objectively, and not merely subjectively, truth-conducive. The question then is whether the oak tree experiences in the sort of case in question are objectively good reasons or merely subjectively good reasons for thinking that an oak tree is present.

The answer to this question seems to hinge in large part on just how unusual this kind of case is in relation to the total class of actual and possible oak tree experiences. If oak tree experiences caused by Alpha Centaurians or Cartesian demons or analogous aberrant causes, as we may refer to them, are relatively rare in relation to experiences caused in the normal way (as we regard it) by genuine oak trees,[14] then as far as I can see (and contrary to Plantinga's claim), even an aberrantly caused experience may still be an objectively good reason for thinking that the belief that an oak tree is present is true, since experiences with that content are in general strongly correlated with the occurrence of oak trees. But if aberrantly caused oak tree experiences are more common or even as common as normally caused ones, or, perhaps still worse, if there is simply no objective fact of the matter as to the relative proportions, then an oak tree experience would apparently fail to be an objectively good reason for believing that an oak tree is present, however subjectively compelling it might seem. Moreover, since it is an internalist version of the third condition that is in question, it will not be enough for the experiences in question to be as a matter of external fact strongly correlated with oak trees; so long as the believer in question has no access to this fact, the experiences will still fail to constitute an objectively good reason for him.

One possible response to this problem would be to attempt to argue on a priori grounds that aberrantly caused oak tree experiences are sufficiently rare to make it objectively likely that such an experience will be accompanied by an oak tree. (An empirical argument would seem to be obviously question-begging in relation to the larger problem of whether all of our perceptual experiences might be caused in some aberrant way.) I myself have elsewhere attempted an argument of at least approximately this sort.[15] But it must be conceded that the prospects for success are extremely cloudy at best, and that very many recent philosophers would regard the project as completely hopeless.[16] Plantinga's own view appears to be that we have in general no possible way to know the a priori probabilities that would be needed to give such an argument [*WCD* 109] and perhaps, at least in relation to some issues, that aberrantly caused beliefs are at least as common as normally caused ones [*WPF* 125, discussing the problem of induction].

If no such argument can be given, then the satisfaction of an internalist standard that appeals merely to the occurrence of such experiences will fail to constitute an objectively good reason or justification for believing that there is an oak tree present. As long as it is not also specified as an external condition that the experiences are not aberrantly caused, i.e., that cognitive faculties of the person in question are functioning normally or properly in a sense that excludes the influence of demons and the like, the satisfaction of such an internalist condition will apparently have no tendency at all to show that the belief that results is objectively likely to be true. And this conclusion will of course generalize to all kinds of perceptual experiences—and, Plantinga would argue, to memory beliefs, a priori beliefs, and all other kinds of beliefs to which internalist justification might seem to pertain. Since an analogous argument can apparently be made in relation to any sort of internalist account, the indicated result is that no purely internalist condition can capture the idea of an objectively good reason and thus that such accounts fail even as accounts of the third condition of knowledge. And, as already noted, it is obviously not an adequate response to this problem to point out that aberrant causes of experience or belief are ruled out by the fourth, anti-Gettier condition, since this would be to admit that the internalist third condition by itself is inadequate as an account of justification.

It is something like the foregoing line of argument, that seems to me to be latent in Plantinga's criticisms of internalist views, partially obscured by his insistence on couching matters in terms of his unfortunate concept of "warrant." While the underlying concern is hardly new, his examples seem to me to bring out very forcefully just how serious a problem such an argument poses for the internalist. I am not yet convinced that the argument is correct, mainly because I am not yet ready to abandon the idea of an a priori metajustification of an internalist account of justification. But it seems to me to have a great deal of force, especially against the many who have already given up on such a metajustification. And if it is correct, then no purely internalist account of the third condition of knowledge will do, since some appeal to an external condition will be needed to guarantee the presence of an objective reason.

It is important to insist, however, that even if some such argument succeeds in the end in showing that the third condition of knowledge must itself have an externalist ingredient of some sort, it still does not show, or have any real tendency to show, that a *purely* externalist third condition, one according to which the possessor of a "warranted" belief need not have even a subjective reason for thinking it to be true, is acceptable. After considering in the next section whether

Plantinga's positive view is itself vulnerable to counterexamples, I will attempt in the final section to show both that it has this purely externalist character, and also that such a position is highly unsatisfactory from an intuitive standpoint.

II

I turn then to Plantinga's positive account of "warrant," beginning with his own summary of the view:

> a belief has warrant for me only if (1) it has been produced in me by cognitive faculties that are working properly (functioning as they ought to, subject to no cognitive dysfunction) in a cognitive environment that is appropriate for my kinds of cognitive faculties, (2) the segment of the design plan governing the production of that belief is aimed at the production of true beliefs, and (3) there is a high statistical probability that a belief produced under those conditions will be true. Under those conditions, furthermore, the degree of warrant is an increasing function of degree of belief. . . . [*WPF* 46–47]

This passage seems to say only that the enumerated conditions are necessary for "warrant," but it seems clear that his view is that they are also at least approximately sufficient [see, e.g., *WPF* 194], and I will so interpret him here.

While there is much that could be said in elaboration and explanation of these conditions, a few brief explanatory comments will have to suffice for now. In the first place, it is important to emphasize that condition (1) is supposed to exclude not only internal malfunction, but also external manipulation by Cartesian demons, Alpha Centaurians, and the like. Second, both condition (3) and implicitly condition (1) rely on the idea of a *design plan*, a set of specifications according to which human beings (and presumably other beings) are constructed. Such a design plan will delineate, among other things, the various specific faculties or "modules" that go to make up our overall cognitive apparatus, together with the aim or purpose of each. In clarifying and elaborating this idea, Plantinga relies heavily on artifacts as examples. And while he claims that the employment of the concept of proper function and the correlative concept of design does not immediately presuppose that human beings were literally designed by an intelligent being, rather than, say, by evolution, he does ultimately argue that only a theistic view can give an adequate account of these concepts. Third, condition (3) reflects the way in which Plantinga's view resembles the reliabilist views of Alvin Goldman and others. His claim, which I will not challenge here, is that embedding reliabilism within a proper function account avoids two otherwise severe problems: (i) the generality problem, and (ii) the problem of accidental reliability.[17]

As noted above, it seems most unlikely that Plantinga really wants to claim that satisfying these conditions yields the guarantee of truth that would be necessary to avoid the need for an anti-Gettier condition and thus qualify as a complete account of "warrant" in his specified sense. Therefore I will take him instead to be offering an account of only the third condition of knowledge, an account that is thus supposed to play the same role in the overall concept of knowledge as the various internalist and externalist conditions that he criticizes, but to do so more adequately. (I will, however, for lack of a better alternative, continue to use "warrant"—with the quotes—to refer to the property that satisfies this condition.)

There are many questions that could be raised about this account, most of which will not find their way into the present discussion. But the obvious place to start is to ask just what the argument for the correctness of Plantinga's view is supposed, according to him, to be. The answer to this question is in fact less than completely clear. Part of the argument is clearly the criticisms of opposing views and especially the way that the idea of proper functioning emerges as a kind of ongoing theme of those criticisms. But, as noted above, those criticisms show at most that some externalist requirement, perhaps something like a requirement of proper functioning, is needed as one ingredient in the third condition, not that it is the whole story. Even if it can be established that satisfying an internalist account is insufficient by itself for "warrant" (and also, as Plantinga also argues, that satisfying the various specific internalist accounts that he considers is not necessary), this hardly shows that no internalist ingredient at all is required for an adequate third condition.[18]

Why then, apart from the problems with other positions, are we supposed to think that Plantinga's specific account is correct? Presumably a good part of the reason is supposed to be the implicit claim that his account is free from the counterexamples that allegedly plague others. I will take a stab at constructing some counterexamples momentarily. But before doing so, it is worth noting that the specific character of Plantinga's account tends to make really compelling counterexamples difficult to come by, but in a way that on careful consideration lends no genuine support to his position. A counterexample designed to show, e.g., that Plantinga's conditions are insufficient for "warrant" would have to be a case in which his conditions are clearly satisfied, in particular in which the belief results from the proper functioning of a module of my design plan aimed at truth, but in which "warrant" is clearly absent, i.e., which is not a case of knowledge even if true (and even if an appropriate anti-Gettier condition is satisfied). And the problem is that while I have some rough idea of how I usually function, I have no information that seems to me at all reliable about what "proper functioning" in accordance with my "design plan" really amounts to, and still less about whether various aspects of my design plan are genuinely aimed at truth—or indeed whether, in Plantinga's sense, I have a design plan at all. These matters can, of course, be simply stipulated, but this inevitably makes such examples less intuitively convincing and assessable than is the case with the usual run of philosophical examples; and this will be the case whether or not Plantinga's view is correct.

But, with this disclaimer, here is an attempt in this direction. Suppose that a certain person, call him Boris, was indeed designed by God and that deep within his brain or psyche, God has implanted a very narrow and specialized module designed to guarantee that Boris will have a true belief about some monumentally important matter. To be specific, suppose that this module is so constructed that at some appropriate temporal interval before the mundane world comes to an end with the Second Coming, Boris will be caused to believe with maximal firmness and conviction that this is about to occur. We may suppose that the belief is accompanied by no distinctive phenomenology, beyond the strong impetus to belief itself.

Now the time has come, and Boris finds himself believing that the world will soon end, and believing it as firmly as he believes that $2 + 2 = 4$ or that he is a human being. In this case, Plantinga's account of "warrant" appears to be satisfied: the faculty or module is functioning properly; there is no problem about the environment; the module in question is aimed at producing a true belief; and, we may suppose, its reliability under the existing conditions is extremely high. Moreover, Boris's belief, we are supposing, is true, and there is no Gettier-type problem. In addition, Boris's degree of warrant for this belief will apparently be maximal, thereby effectively eliminating any worry about conflicting evidence.

Does Boris then have maximally "warranted" *knowledge* that the world will soon end? While it is far from obvious to me that he does, it must be confessed that the issue is far from easy to resolve, with attempts to argue for one answer or the other running a serious danger of begging the question. Thus, for example, it seems highly doubtful that it would be *rational* for Boris to *act* on this belief, e.g., by selling his house to buy full-page ads proclaiming the forthcoming event or canceling his life insurance policies (as of the date of the expected occurrence). He has lots of reasons for being suspicious of beliefs of this kind and none that is apparent for trusting them; moreover, the catastrophic consequences if he is wrong seem to provide strong reasons for caution and restraint. But while there is surely something puzzling about it being less rational to act on a maximally "warranted" case of knowledge than on less "warranted" beliefs, Plantinga may simply want to deny that there is any connection of this sort between knowledge and rational action.

Thus although I believe, with an important qualification to be noted below, that the example just given *is* a counterexample to Plantinga's view, the more important point is the rather serious intractability of this whole question. And this points, I think, to a second main reason (in addition to the one developed in section I) why Plantinga's primary reliance on intuitions about knowledge is quite problematic at best: it is far from clear that our intuitions about whether examples of this sort are cases of knowledge are clear and unequivocal enough to be very strongly relied on.

There is one particular aspect of this general worry that seems to me particularly important in thinking about Plantinga's view: the possibility that there is more than one kind or species of knowledge, with different species having importantly differing requirements, so that a bald appeal to undifferentiated intuitions about whether a particular case is or is not knowledge would risk serious confusion. While other philosophers have at least suggested the sort of distinction among kinds of knowledge (or senses of "knowledge") that I have in mind, the following two formulations are perhaps the most explicit.

In a discussion of Locke's views on innate ideas, J. L. Mackie puts the following objection to innate knowledge into the mouth of a "judgment empiricist":

> If a belief, however confident and however true, simply arose in a person as something like an instinct, whether as a result of evolutionary processes or by what Locke's contemporaries called being implanted or imprinted or inscribed in the soul by God, that person could not properly be said to know whatever he thus truly, instinctively, believed. He

would not have good reasons for believing as he did; he would not be
authoritative about it; he would not be epistemically justified; he would
have no 'right to be sure'.[19]

Obviously this objection could just as well be directed against
Plantinga's account, as it relates to the case of Boris. Mackie's view,
however, is that the objection is not conclusive. There is, he suggests,
a whole spectrum of possible senses of "know": at one end is a
"minimal" sense, in which knowledge is merely nonaccidentally true
belief; at the other end, we have what Mackie calls "authoritative,
autonomous, knowledge," "the knowledge of the man who himself
has epistemic justification, the right to be sure."[20] And thus, while the
innate belief falls far short of "authoritative knowledge," it may still
be an instance of "minimal knowledge."

A similar distinction is drawn by Ernest Sosa, who distinguishes
what he calls "animal knowledge" from what he calls "reflective
knowledge": whereas animal knowledge arises as a direct response to
stimuli of various kinds "with little or no benefit of reflection or
understanding," reflective knowledge involves a wider understanding
of how the belief comes about and how it is related to the fact that is
its object.[21] Animal knowledge is essentially the variety of knowledge
for which something in the vicinity of a pure reliabilist account might,
depending on other problems, be adequate; reflective knowledge, in
contrast, essentially involves an internalist dimension of critical reflection.

I do not want to endorse every aspect of Mackie's and Sosa's views
on this point, nor do I think that the distinctions they have given are
exactly the same. (In particular, it seems likely that Sosa's animal
knowledge requires somewhat more than is required by Mackie's
minimal knowledge.) But it seems to me highly plausible that there is
a viable distinction to be drawn roughly along these lines, and that a
good deal of epistemological mischief, in particular much of the
seemingly intractable character of the internalism-externalism debate,
has stemmed from ignoring it.

In these terms, my suggestion is that while Boris has something like
animal knowledge or at least minimal knowledge that the world is
about to end, he clearly does not have reflective or authoritative
knowledge. And, more generally, I believe that Plantinga's account of
"warrant" and the conception of knowledge that results from it captures at best some close approximation to animal knowledge, not the
reflective knowledge that is distinctively human. I will develop this

suggestion a bit further in the final section of the present paper, via a consideration of some aspects of Plantinga's discussion of particular varieties of knowledge.

Before doing that, however, I want to look briefly at the possibility of a different sort of counterexample. The previous example was designed to show that a belief's satisfying Plantinga's account is not *sufficient*, when combined with truth and the absence of Gettier problems, to make it a case of knowledge, at least not knowledge of the distinctively human, reflective variety. But is it *necessary* either? Can't we imagine a being, call him Frank, whose cognitive faculties are entirely produced at random, perhaps via a very complicated and unlikely set of mutations, but who ends up with faculties that are close to or even identical to those of a normal human being? Frank might receive what would appear to be a normal education, might obtain a job in some cognitively demanding field like one of the sciences, and might eventually make, or at least appear to make, important contributions to human knowledge. All of this appears to be quite possible in the broadly logical or metaphysical sense to which Plantinga himself so frequently appeals. Since Frank's faculties were randomly produced, however, he apparently has no cognitive design plan, and hence his faculties could not be correctly said to be functioning properly or to be aimed at truth. And this would mean in turn that none of the beliefs that resulted from those faculties would be "warranted" or would constitute knowledge.

But isn't this a quite implausible result? Frank might be indiscernible in every way from the rest of us as regards his cognitive functioning, might be an apparently excellent source of information or even an apparently great teacher, and would surely believe (or seem to believe) that he had "warranted" beliefs and knowledge. He might appear to satisfy every cognitive virtue to the highest possible degree. Moreover, if Plantinga is right that making good sense of the notion of proper function ultimately requires theism [*WPF*, ch. 11] and if God does not in fact exist, we are all in essentially the same situation as Frank. While I emphatically do not want to rule out the very possibility that a thoroughgoing skepticism might turn out to be correct, surely this way of arriving at it is too easy.

How would Plantinga respond to this sort of objection? In *WPF*, he considers a somewhat parallel example that he attributes to William Hasker, in which one Geoffrey, through a random genetic mutation, acquires a new and unusual apparent cognitive ability: the ability to locate himself and make his way around by sensing magnetic fields

[*WPF* 29–30]. The issue in this case is whether Geoffrey's beliefs about his location are "warranted" and at least sometimes constitute knowledge, despite the fact that the apparent cognitive ability in question is presumably not specified in his design plan. Plantinga's initial and rather surprising response to Hasker's example is to suggest that Geoffrey may simply have acquired a *new* design plan:

> If evolutionary theory is fundamentally correct, organisms acquire their design plans by way of random genetic mutation (or some other source of variation) and natural selection. Well, can't Geoffrey have acquired his new design plan by way of a sizable (and improbable) random genetic mutation? Then his cognitive faculties would be working properly according to the new design plan . . . and there would be no reason to deny his belief's warrant. [*WPF* 30]

This response is somewhat disingenuous, since Plantinga himself ultimately denies that a naturalistic account of proper function and of the possession of a design plan is possible. But it would be unacceptable in any case, for if there is any plausibility at all to the idea that evolution can be literally said to design organisms, the natural selection step is clearly essential, since it is this step that provides something like an analogue of the designer's choice of one configuration over another. And in neither Geoffrey's case nor Frank's has natural selection yet had a chance to operate.

In considering a somewhat similar example proposed by Sosa (following Donald Davidson), Plantinga again suggests that a being whose capacities resulted from chance might still nonetheless possess a design plan. Since Sosa's example rules out any appeal to evolution, the suggestion this time is that it would still make sense to say that the being's faculties function well or ill and that the "notions of design plan and proper function are correlative: a thing is working properly, in doing **A** in circumstances **C**, if and only if its design plan calls for it to do **A** in **C**."[22] I am inclined to think that this last claim is essentially correct. But what it shows, I think, is that ascriptions of proper functioning, in the relevant respects, to beings like Frank or the being in Sosa's example should not be taken in the fully literal way that would require a design plan, for the absence of such a design plan in such cases is surely far clearer than is the literal presence of proper functioning. And if it still seems intuitively correct that such beings might have "warranted" belief and knowledge, as I believe that it does, then satisfying Plantinga's conditions is shown to be unnecessary for "warrant."

III

In this final section, I want to look further at Plantinga's accounts of "warrant" and knowledge, and in particular at some of his accounts of specific kinds of apparent knowledge, as they are presented in the middle chapters of *WPF*. My ultimate aim is to buttress the suggestion that what Plantinga has given us is, at best, an account of something like animal knowledge in Sosa's sense. But I will approach this issue by focussing on two more specific questions with regard to a given category of alleged knowledge: do we, on Plantinga's view, have any good (non-question-begging) reasons of any sort for thinking either (1) that most or even any of our beliefs in the area in question are true, or (2) that Plantinga's conditions for warrant are satisfied for most or even any of those beliefs? In other words, if the truth or "warrant" of our beliefs in the specified area were questioned, either by some external skeptic or by our own critical reflection, is there anything that we could say to respond to the resulting challenge?

As will emerge more fully below, but is perhaps obvious enough even at this point, the answer to both of these questions appears to be "no." On Plantinga's view, as with any externalist view, being "warranted" does not bring with it any access to a reason for thinking that the belief is true (though it does sometimes involve "evidence"—see below for a consideration of what this amounts to). Moreover, perhaps even more seriously, the crucial factor in "warrant," viz., the cognitive design plan, is not something that we even have any very specific beliefs about, making it difficult to see how we could possibly have any good reason for thinking that the specific conditions required for warrant are satisfied.

But if this is right, then a further question arises: why isn't Plantinga's view itself a deep and troubling version of skepticism? On his view, while we may have "warrant" and even knowledge *if* the right conditions are satisfied, we apparently have no way to tell from the inside whether those conditions are ever satisfied, nor any reason at all to think that they are (though we might still, of course, be "warranted" in believing and even know that they are satisfied, if the belief that they are satisfied should itself happen to satisfy Plantinga's conditions). If a particular belief is called into question, either theoretically or as a possible basis for action, we are apparently helpless to resolve the resulting issue in any way that we can understand to be adequate, as helpless as the dumbest, least reflective animal. One important upshot of this problem is that Plantinga's accounts of various species of alleged knowledge all have an implicitly conditional character: *if* such-and-such more specific conditions are satisfied, then our beliefs are "warranted."

While such an appeal is not fully explicit, it seems reasonably clear that Plantinga, like his acknowledged intellectual forebear Thomas Reid, would respond to concerns of these sorts by invoking our commonsense convictions that we do have knowledge of the various kinds in question and hence that whatever conditions are required for knowledge must be satisfied (cf., e.g., *WPF* 90). But whatever the force of such an appeal in general (I am inclined to think that it is usually substantially overrated), it is especially problematic in the context of a view like Plantinga's. For if knowledge indeed requires "warrant" in Plantinga's sense, then it requires the satisfaction of conditions to which common sense has no apparent access of any sort, making it in turn most unclear why commonsense convictions in this regard should be given any serious weight.

All of these matters may be illustrated and elaborated by looking at some of the accounts that Plantinga offers of particular species of knowledge, beginning with his account of perceptual knowledge of the physical world. While such knowledge is clearly dependent in some way on perceptual experience, Plantinga, following Reid, denies that there is or needs to be any good argument, "inductive, deductive, or abductive," from the claim that my experience is of a specific sort to the truth of a claim about the physical world. Even more strikingly, Plantinga seems to deny that there is any sort of logic or rationale to the relation between experience and corresponding belief [cf. *WPF* 92–93, 98–99]: what makes it the case that a certain belief comes to be warranted when I am "appeared to" in a certain way is simply the fact that "this sort of belief formation under that sort of circumstance is dictated by our design plan." But there is apparently no further rationale, at least none accessible to us, as to *why* the design plan dictates this correlation between experience and belief rather than some other one. Thus, for example, while a normally functioning human being when appeared to in a certain distinctive way forms the belief that there are tiger lilies blooming in the backyard rather than that there are tigers in the backyard, there is no intelligible connection between the character of the experience and the content of the belief that explains why the one belief is more appropriate than the other. To be sure, we may appeal to the (assumed) fact that the design plan is aimed at truth. But here as elsewhere (see below), we seemingly have on his view no insight of any sort as to why having this design feature is a good way to achieve true beliefs.

Thus all that we can apparently say is that:

> a perceptual judgment . . . constitutes knowledge if and only if (roughly speaking) that belief is true, sufficiently strong, and produced by cognitive faculties that are successfully aimed at truth and functioning properly in an epistemic environment that is right for a creature of my perceptual powers. Most of us take it utterly for granted, with respect to many occasions and many perceptual judgments, that these conditions are in fact met. *If* we are right, then on those occasions the perceptual judgment in question constitutes knowledge. . . . [*WPF* 89; my italics]

That we do for the most part take both the truth of our perceptual beliefs and the satisfaction of whatever conditions are required for knowledge for granted seems undeniable. But as already noted above, the specific character of Plantinga's conditions makes it extremely hard to see how this confidence could be well taken. And for this reason, the conditional character of Plantinga's conclusion should, I would suggest, be taken much more seriously than he seems to take it: that these conditions are indeed satisfied is an assumption for which we have no clear rationale about a matter to which we have no apparent access.

There is one further wrinkle to be considered in this area. In both the discussion of perception [*WPF*, ch. 5] and a subsequent discussion of the "evidentialist" view advanced by Richard Feldman and Earl Conee [*WPF*, pp. 185–93], Plantinga suggests that perceptual experience constitutes *evidence* for the perceptual judgments that it prompts, and it is worth pausing briefly to see what he means by this. As Plantinga seems to be using the term, something A constitutes evidence for a belief B if the following conditions are satisfied: (1) B is accepted in response to A; (2) there is ("if things are going properly") a relation of objective probability between the occurrence of A and the truth of B; and perhaps also (3) there is a "differential response to differential input," i.e., variations in A-like conditions yield corresponding variations in belief [*WPF* 186, 190].[23] As the examples cited and the discussion of them elsewhere makes clear, the relation of objective probability really obtains, on Plantinga's view, not between the occurrence of A by itself and the truth of B, but rather between the occurrence of A *together with the other conditions required for warrant* and the truth of B.

Now while Plantinga can of course use the term "evidence" in any way that he chooses, there are at least two ways in which this conception of evidence is potentially misleading. First, contrary to what Plantinga seems to suggest, it is clear that Feldman and Conee intend a much stronger conception of evidence, roughly one that would require (a) that the relation of probability obtain between the evidence alone and the truth of the belief, and (b) that the person in question have "collateral evidence" supporting the existence of this relation of probability.[24] Second, and more importantly, it does not follow from the fact that a person has evidence in Plantinga's relatively weak sense that he has anything that he can *recognize* as a reason for thinking that the corresponding belief is true or likely to be true, nothing that could provide even the hint of an answer to a skeptical or critical challenge to the truth or "warrant" of B. Such a person need not and in general will not have any access to either the truth of the additional required circumstances or the relation of objective probability, and thus has no way to tell from his own perspective that the evidence in question really is evidence.[25]

Consider next the venerable issue of other minds. Plantinga considers and rejects the three more or less standard responses to this problem in the literature, viz. the argument from analogy, the appeal to some sort of theoretical or explanatory inference, and the Wittgensteinian notion of "criteria." He then invokes his own account:

> But if the connection between *B* [behavior and other circumstances] and *S* [a mental state] isn't inductive or deductive, what is it? . . . The answer . . . is just that a human being whose appropriate cognitive faculties are functioning properly and who is aware of *B* will find herself making the *S* ascription . . . . *if* the part of the design plan governing these processes is successfully aimed at truth, then ascriptions of mental states to others will often have high warrant for us. . . . [*WPF* 75; my italics on "if"]

This seems to me to be a particularly revealing formulation. While B still presumably constitutes "evidence" in the sense just discussed, it gives the person who arrives at the belief nothing like an intelligible indication of any sort that the ascription is true. Instead, upon becoming aware of B, she just "finds herself" making the ascription. This is presumably more or less what animals do, but it is both alarming and hard to believe that nothing more can be said in the case of supposedly more enlightened and reflective human knowledge.

At the end of his discussion of other minds, Plantinga considers explicitly a skeptic who appeals to the various ways in which the apparent awareness of behavior and circumstances might fail to be associated with the actual existence of mental states in other minds: cases where the experiences in question are caused by a Cartesian demons and the like.[26] His response is that while such situations are indeed possible "in the broadly logical sense," this means only that beliefs about other minds don't possess Cartesian certainty, i.e., immunity from all doubt. But this response grossly understates the problem. If behavioral "evidence" offers no reflectively intelligible indication of any sort that the corresponding beliefs are true, if the only claim about either "warrant" or truth that I am in a position to defend is conditional in the way already noticed, if all I can say is that I just seem to make *this* sort of mentalistic ascription when I am aware of *that* sort of behavior, then what is lacking is not merely certainty but any sort of intelligible reason to think that a belief about another mind is true. And this in turn seems to provide the basis for a much less easily dismissed version of skepticism.

Consider, finally, Plantinga's discussion of induction, specifically the "old riddle of induction." Here his response to the sort of skeptical challenge raised by Hume takes the form of questioning whether there is really any problem at all:

> But what, precisely, is the complaint? Is it that I am *irrational* in reasoning in this way? That seems unlikely. Here once more we meet the protean, many-sided character of 'rationality'. . . . [*WPF* 126]

Plantinga proceeds to distinguish three different senses of "rationality" in which inductive reasoning fails to be irrational.

> Is the claim instead that we are *deontologically* unjustified in reasoning in this way? That seems obviously wrong: there are no intellectual duties—at any rate none any of us know of—to refrain from forming beliefs in this way. . . . [*WPF* 126]

And so on.

But this great display of puzzlement is very hard to take seriously. Inductive reasoning, as the very term suggests, purports to be a mode of *inference* or *argument*, in which one moves from a premise concerning observation, something roughly of the form "all observed cases of *A* have been cases of *B*," to a conclusion that goes beyond observation, most typically something of the form "all cases of *A* are cases of *B*." The problem here isn't that such an argument isn't deductively valid or that the conclusion isn't guaranteed to be true, concerns that Plantinga also suggests and rejects. Rather Hume's claim, which Plantinga himself clearly endorses [*WPF* 125], is that the conclusion of such a supposed argument simply *does not follow*, even with probability, from its premise, i.e., that the premise does not provide any intellectually discernible reason to think that the conclusion is any more likely to be true than it would be without such a premise. And this surely seems to be a problem, since it would mean that the supposed argument was simply no good, entirely lacking in cogency, no matter how well accepting beliefs in this way may in fact fit our design plan—which in turn, I would suggest, gives a perfectly clear meaning to saying that "reasoning" in this way is irrational.

Plantinga can still, of course, make the same response that he makes to the objection that the argument is not deductively valid (which objection he mistakenly ascribes to Hume):

> On the present account of warrant, at any rate, the absence of such an argument is no bar to an inductively formed belief's having warrant. What counts instead is whether we do *in fact* reason in this way when our faculties are functioning properly, whether we do in fact reason from correlations we have observed to correlations we have not. The answer, of course, is obvious; it is the person (if there is one) who *can't* (or won't) reason thus who displays pathology. [*WPF* 127]

But this response seems unsatisfactory in two different respects. First, as already noted, it is hard to see how the answer at the end can really be obvious to us, however initially obvious it might seem. Second, while the conditions of Plantinga's account may in fact be satisfied in a particular case, this does not seem to yield anything that deserves to be called "reasoning" in any but the most Pickwickian sense. It would be more accurate to say, echoing the earlier discussion of other minds, that a person who believes the "premise" of such an argument simply "finds himself" believing the "conclusion."[27]

Similar questions and problems could, I believe, be raised about each of the other areas of putative knowledge that Plantinga discusses, but the foregoing will have to suffice for present purposes. What these problems seem to me to indicate, as already suggested, is that while Plantinga's epistemological view may be an adequate account of the knowledge of animals and very young children, it is extremely unsatisfying as an account of the more distinctively human brand of knowledge that we all believe ourselves to possess. We often seem at least to have intellectually discernible reasons for thinking that our beliefs are true and that the conditions for knowledge are satisfied, but Plantinga's view apparently gives us nothing but beliefs that we ineluctably find ourselves having under various circumstances and that we believe for no discernible reason to be "warranted" and to constitute knowledge.

All that having been said, it must be confessed at once that no one has yet succeeded clearly in elaborating an epistemological position that shows how we can really have the kind of knowledge that we think we do. In addition, Plantinga's challenge to internalist views, discussed at the end of section I above, provides one serious reason for doubting whether such an intuitively satisfying epistemological position is really possible, since it suggests that any defensible conception of a reason for thinking that a belief is true may have to have an externalist dimension. But even if Plantinga should turn out to be right on this point, it would not show that the internalist dimension can be dispensed with entirely, and we have just seen the catastrophic consequences of doing so. Whether some intuitively satisfying amalgam of internalism and externalism is possible remains to be seen, but it is surely in this direction that one who accepts Plantinga's anti-internalist point should look.

There is one final remark that seems worth making. It is somewhat odd that Plantinga does not seem to be worried about or even indeed to notice the radically skeptical implications of his position. The natural explanation is that one who is utterly convinced of the existence of a good God, a God who is, in Descartes's phrase, "not a deceiver," would have on that basis what might seem to be an independent reason for thinking that our instinctive cognitive behavior reflects proper functioning according to a good design plan. And indeed, despite one explicit disavowal [*WPF* 236–37], there are many passages in these two books, especially the second, where such a neo-Cartesian view seems to be lurking just beneath the surface. But if this is what Plantinga has, however implicitly, in mind, it must be insisted that such reassurance is legitimately available only to someone who has good, intellectually cogent reasons for thinking that such a being exists, not to someone who, on whatever other basis, merely "finds himself" believing in one.[28]

Notes

1. New York: Oxford University Press, 1993. References to the pages of these two volumes will use the abbreviations *WCD* and *WPF*.

2. It may be worth saying at the outset that I will not concern myself here with the more specific task of resuscitating either coherentism in general or my own coherentist position in particular in the face of Plantinga's assault. That project, if it can be accomplished at all, would require a substantially larger canvas than I have available here.

3. There is some room for doubt here: Plantinga sometimes seems to make claims about the presence or absence of warrant as though they were matters of direct insight and without explicitly formulating the case in question in such a way as to make possible an appeal to intuitions about knowledge.

4. See Edmund Gettier, "Is Justified True Belief Knowledge?" *Analysis*, volume 23 (1963), pp. 121–23. The example in the text is actually a further variation on a variation of Gettier's original example originally proposed by Keith Lehrer.

5. See Peter Unger, "An Analysis of Factual Knowledge," *Journal of Philosophy*, volume 65 (1968), pp. 157–70.

6. This is Plantinga's label for the modified Chisholmian view he finds in Chisholm's "The Place of Epistemic Justification," *Philosophical Topics*, volume 14 (1986), pp. 85–92; and in Chisholm's "Self- Profile," in Radu Bogdan (ed.), *Roderick M. Chisholm* (Dordrecht: D. Reidel, 1986).

7. Plantinga's objections to the externalist and quasi-externalist views that are more akin to his own are rather different in character and will not be specifically considered here.

8. As Plantinga notes [*WCD* 111], I made this suggestion briefly about a roughly analogous sort of case in *The Structure of Empirical Knowledge* (Cambridge, Mass.: Harvard University Press, 1985), p. 150; it is also made and further elaborated by Richard Feldman in his paper "Proper Functionalism," *Nous*, vol. 27 (1993), pp. 35–39.

9. See Feldman, op. cit., pp. 38–39, for a discussion of the need for elaborating the examples.

10. "Why We Need Proper Function," *Nous*, vol. 27 (1993), pp. 69–71, replying to Feldman, op. cit.

11. Ibid., p. 70.

12. In *The Structure of Empirical Knowledge*, cited above, p. 3.

13. This seems to be Feldman's suggestion. See Feldman, op. cit., pp. 36–37.

14. This would seemingly be compatible with the existence of, e.g., demon worlds where all such experiences are caused by Cartesian demons, so long as such worlds are themselves objectively rare.

15. In *The Structure of Empirical Knowledge*, cited above, chapter 8.

16. Plantinga would also no doubt object that a priori beliefs are just as subject to this general problem, making such an argument question-begging. I am not convinced that this is so, in part because I think that his account of a priori knowledge as being based merely on a distinctive sort of phenomenology (see *WPF*, ch. 6) is highly misleading as best. But there is no space to go into this issue here.

17. But see Feldman, op. cit., for criticisms on these points.

18. To be sure, Plantinga's account of various aspects of our cognitive functioning often mentions states or processes that are internally accessible; but, as we will see further below, there is no requirement of anything like an internally accessible reason for thinking that one's beliefs are true. Moreover, the account seems to allow a cognitive process to yield "warranted" belief even when the belief itself—including the firmness with which it is held—is the only internally accessible element.

19. J. L. Mackie, *Problems from Locke* (London: Oxford University Press, 1976), p. 217.

20. Ibid., pp. 218–20.

21. Ernest Sosa, *Knowledge in Perspective* (Cambridge: Cambridge University Press, 1991), p. 240.

22. "Why We Need Proper Function," loc. cit., p. 78.

23. Presumably, though Plantinga does not say so explicitly, A also has to be something of which the person can be subjectively aware.

24. See Richard Feldman and Earl Conee, "Evidentialism," *Philosophical Studies*, vol. 48 (1985), pp. 15–34, especially the discussion of my clairvoyance example at pp. 29–30.

25. Plantinga's notion of evidence is closer to the idea of an "adequate ground" advanced by William Alston in "An Internalist Externalism," reprinted in Alston, *Epistemic Justification* (Ithaca, N.Y.: Cornell University Press, 1989), pp. 227–45. But even Alston seems to require that the requisite relation of objective probability obtain between the ground by itself and the truth of the belief (see p. 232).

26. It is interesting, however, that the situations that are actually mentioned are cases where it is my beliefs about the physical world that are false, i.e., cases in which the other bodies whose behavior I seem to be aware of aren't really there at all. Plantinga does not consider explicitly the sort of skepticism that would pertain specifically to other minds but not to bodily behavior, e.g., the possibility that everyone else is a mechanical robot of some kind.

27. As far as I can see, Plantinga would say essentially the same thing about deductive arguments. Thus if we insist that any genuinely cogent argument requires that it be intellectually discernible or intelligible that if the premises are true, the conclusion either must be true or is probably true, it seems to follow that for Plantinga there are no genuinely cogent arguments. Instead there are simply cases where a person who believes one set of things "finds himself" believing a further thing. And this, of course, will apply to Plantinga's own arguments as well. But while I ultimately have doubts about many of those arguments, it will be clear to any reader of these books that this result does not do them justice.

28. I am grateful to the participants in my epistemology seminar in the fall of 1994, in which many of these issues were discussed, and especially to Bill Talbott. Ann Baker made many valuable comments on earlier drafts.

4

Plantinga on Epistemic Internalism

Ernest Sosa

What does it take for a belief to be epistemically justified? What sort of status does a belief have in being epistemically justified? Important in contemporary epistemology, these are main questions posed by Alvin Plantinga in his penetrating three-chapter discussion of epistemic internalism and Roderick Chisholm's epistemology. What follows will first present the core results of that discussion, and will then examine it critically.

What Is Internalism?

1. From p. 19 of *Warrant: The Current Debate*:

> According to Locke and Descartes, epistemic justification is *deontological* justification. And here they are clearly thinking of *subjective* duty or obligation; they are thinking of guilt and innocence, blame and blamelessness. If I do not have certainty but believe anyway, says Descartes, "I do not escape the blame of misusing my freedom." Locke, clearly enough, is also thinking of subjective duty ("This at least is certain, that he must be accountable for whatever mistakes he runs into"). But then the First Internalist Motif follows immediately:
>
> M1.   *Epistemic justification (that is, subjective epistemic justification, being such that I am not blameworthy) is entirely up to me and within my power.*
>
> All that is required is that I do my subjective duty, act in such a way that I am blameless. All I have to do is my duty; and, given that ought implies

73

can, I am guaranteed to be able to do that. So justification is entirely within my power; whether or not my beliefs are justified is up to me, within my control.

2. From p. 20:

[There is a] . . . Second Internalist Motif:

M2.   *For a large, important, and basic class of objective epistemic duties, objective and subjective duty coincide; what you objectively ought to do matches that which is such that if you don't do it, you are guilty and blameworthy.*

And the link is provided by our nature: in a large and important class of cases, a properly functioning human being can simply see whether a given belief is or is not (objectively) justified for him.

3. From pp. 20–22:

The Second Internalist Motif has three corollaries.

First: if it is your subjective duty to regulate your belief in this way, then you must be able to see or tell that regulating belief this way is indeed your duty. . . .

C1.   *In a large and important set of cases, a properly functioning human being can simply see (cannot make a nonculpable mistake about) what objective epistemic duty requires.*

To grasp the second corollary, we must note first that (according to both Descartes and Locke) I do not determine *directly*, so to speak, what it is that I am obliged to believe and withhold. . . . I have a way of determining when a belief is justified for me; to use a medieval expression, I have a *ratio cognoscendi* for whether a belief is justified for me. . . . So the second corollary:

C2.   *In a large and important class of cases a properly functioning human being can simply see (cannot make a nonculpable mistake about) whether a proposition has the property by means of which she tells whether a proposition is justified for her.*

[For Descartes and Locke] . . . the ground of justification (the justification-making property) is identical with the property by which we determine whether a belief has justification: *ratio cognoscendi* coincides with *ratio essendi*. (This is not, of course, inevitable; in the case of measles, velocity, blood pressure, weight, and serum cholesterol our *ratio cognoscendi* does not coincide with the *ratio essendi*.) . . . So the third collorary:

C3.	*In a large, important and basic class of epistemic cases a properly functioning human being can simply see (cannot make a nonculpable mistake about) whether a proposition has the property that confers justification upon it for her.*

4. From pp. 22–23:

There is still another and somewhat less well defined internalist motif here. According to Locke and Descartes, I have a sort of guaranteed access to whether a belief is justified for me and also to what makes it justified for me: I cannot (if I suffer from no cognitive deficiency) nonculpably but mistakenly believe that a belief is justified or has the justification-making property. This is the source of another internalist motif; for it is only certain of my states and properties to which it is at all plausible to think that I have that sort of access. . . . These states are the ones such that it is plausible to hold of them that I cannot make a nonculpable mistake as to whether I exhibit them. But they are also, in some recognizable, if hard to define sense, internal to me—internal to me as a knower or a cognizing being. Thinking of justification in the deontological way characteristic of classical internalism induces *epistemic* internalism: and that in turn induces internalism of this different but related sort [which he calls "personal"].

5. From pp. 32–34:

Chisholm endorses a fundamental intuition of the classical internalist tradition: there are epistemic duties; and justification, being justified in one's beliefs, is the state of forming and holding beliefs in accord with those duties. Here Chisholm endorses, at least by implication, the First Internalist Motif. . . . The basic idea . . . is that our epistemic duty or requirement is to try to achieve and maintain a certain condition—call it 'epistemic excellence'—which may be hard to specify in detail, but consists fundamentally in standing in an appropriate relation to truth. . . .

So my obligation is to try to achieve epistemic excellence, and the way to do so is to act on what I believe is the way to achieve that state. But then the Second Internalist Motif and its corollaries . . . are also satisfied. The ground of warrant, that which confers warrant upon a proposition for me, is the aptness for fulfilling epistemic duty of my accepting that proposition. But in the typical case the degree of that aptness will depend upon the degree to which the proposition in question seems to me to be true; and that is something to which I have a sort of guaranteed access. Thus C2 . . . is satisfied. But so is C3. . . . For what is my *ratio cognoscendi* here; how do I tell whether a given proposition is such that accepting it will contribute substantially to the fulfillment of duty to try to achieve epistemic excellence? Well, one way would be by determining how much or how strongly it seems to me to be true. The more strongly the proposition in question seems to me to be true, the more apt accepting it is for fulfillment of my epistemic duty. *Ratio essendi* and *ratio cognoscendi*, therefore, coincide. And of course the third motif is also exemplified: for *trying to do something or other* is surely in an important and recognizable (if hard to define) sense internal.

Critique of Plantinga on Internalism

1. Plantinga argues that deontology, (epistemic) justification, and internalism are closely connected, and that we can understand Chisholm's internalism if we are clear on the connections.

   a. By "internalism" he means mostly "epistemic internalism," i.e., the view that we have special epistemic access to the epistemic status of our beliefs (or at least to the status of being justified). And the special access he (and Chisholm) seem to have in mind is access by means of unaided armchair reflection.
   b. According to the deontological view of epistemic justification, such justification consists in an appropriate relation to one's epistemic obligations or duties. Thus the following principle (principle D) emerges from Plantinga's two "internalist motifs":

   One is epistemically justified (and one is not blameworthy) in ø'ing if and only if in ø'ing one does one's epistemic duty—or, at least, that is so for a large, important, and basic class of epistemic duties.

2. According to Plantinga, for a correspondingly large, etc., class of cases where one adopts a belief, one is justified in believing as one does iff one does one's duty. Thus, in such cases one is culpable, blameworthy, iff one fails to do one's duty. And this implies, on plausible assumptions, that for such a class of cases (as emerges from his three "corollaries"):

   a. One cannot make a nonculpable mistake about what one's duty requires with regard to the relevant belief options.
   b. One cannot make a nonculpable mistake about whether a belief option has the property by means of which one can tell whether it is a justified option (the *ratio cognoscendi*).
   c. One cannot make a nonculpable mistake about whether a belief

option has the property that makes it a justified option (the *ratio essendi*).

3. Moreover, according to Plantinga, if the foregoing is right, it "induces" not only epistemic internalism, but also what he calls "personal" internalism: namely, the view that the justification-making properties will be constituted by states that are "in some recognizable, if hard to define sense, internal to" the believer.

4. According to Plantinga, then, if Chisholm means such *deontological* justification when he speaks of "epistemic justification" and of other such epistemic statuses, then we can understand thereby his commitment to internalism, to the idea that we must have special access, by pure reflection, to the justification of our beliefs. And Plantinga adduces strong textual evidence that Chisholm does view epistemic justification as something very much like our deontological justification.

5. We can distinguish among three grades of justification as follows. First two preliminary concepts:

   a. In ϕ'ing, S *abides by* an objective duty iff given S's circumstances and past, S ought to ϕ and S does ϕ.
   b. In ϕ'ing, S *violates* an objective duty iff in ϕ'ing S *culpably* fails to abide by an objective duty.

And now the three grades:

   c. S is *justified$_1$* (justified to the first degree) in ϕ'ing iff in ϕ'ing S does not violate an objective duty.
   d. S is *justified$_2$* (justified to the second degree) in ϕ'ing iff in ϕ'ing S is justified$_1$, and S then has a choice on whether to ϕ; that is, whether to ϕ or not is then within S's control.
   e. S is *justified$_3$* (justified to the third degree) in ϕ'ing iff in ϕ'ing S abides by an objective duty through a knowledgeable choice or at least through a choice based on a correct belief as to what one ought then to do (which implies that S then *has* a choice on whether or not to ϕ, and implies also that in ϕ'ing S is justified$_2$).

6. People might now in various ways *nonculpably* fail to abide by their epistemic duty. This might happen, for example, because (a) they cannot help believing that p, (b) nor could they earlier have helped

getting into a situation where they would now be unable to help believing that p, while yet (c) in believing that p they are not abiding by any duty; nor, given their lack of choice, are they *culpably* failing to abide by any duty. Consequently they are not *violating* any duty, and hence they are justified to the first degree in believing that p. Circumstances might make inevitable someone's believing something epistemically crazy, in which case they would be justified to the first degree in their (crazy) belief.

However, people cannot be justified to the second degree in that way. In order to be justified to this higher degree in ø'ing, ø'ing must be within your control. How might someone be justified to the second degree in believing something? Consider first a second way in which someone might be justified to the first degree in believing something epistemically very questionable: namely, through nonculpably failing to realize what their epistemic duty requires in the circumstances. In that case it might be up to them whether they believe that p or not; it might be a matter within their control and subject to choice. Yet they might nonculpably do the wrong thing simply through nonculpable failure to identify the right choice in the circumstances. And this is a way in which people might be justified not only to the first degree, but to the second degree as well. People might thus be justified to both the first and the second degree in believing something even though they neither know nor even believe correctly that they are so justified.

Recall the deontologism identified by Plantinga in principle D:

> One is epistemically justified (and one is not blameworthy) in ø'ing if and only if in ø'ing one does one's epistemic duty—or, at least, that is so for a large, important, and basic class of epistemic duties.

It is only if we interpret "epistemic justification" here as justification to the *third* degree that D is most plausible and that the corollaries 2a–2c can be derived most plausibly. Alternatively we can restrict the class of beliefs and/or believers involved so as to rule out the possibility of failure of control over what one believes and the possibility of failure of knowledge or correct belief as to what one ought to believe and as to what one would be justified in believing. For that restricted class of cases, as soon as one has justification to the lowest degree, one has it also for each of the higher degrees.

7. That is all just fine, and interesting. But where's the *internalism*? Even if we grant 2a, for example, how do we arrive at the result that

when one knows what one's duty requires, and when one believes correctly (without mistake) what one's duty requires, one knows this *by reflection*, or in any such "internalist" way?

One might appeal here to the intuition that the evil demon's victim would be as well justified as we are, and indeed to the intuition that the solipsist heroine might be equally justified without the (dubious) benefit of any demon's intervention, there being no demon, and indeed there being nothing external to our heroine. Our heroine must be justified in virtue of properties *internal* to her, or so it might be argued. And since for any actual flesh and blood thinker there is such a corresponding demon's victim or solipsist heroine, who is identical to him or her in all internal respects, therefore the justification of actual people must also derive from properties *internal* to them.

So, if 2a–2c still apply to our victim or solipsist, as they may well be meant to apply, then she must know about her own justification, and about its sources, on the basis of knowledge of internal properties of hers. That's fine, but still: how do we get that this knowledge must be *by reflection*? Well, what does "by reflection" (or "by armchair thought") mean? It usually means approximately the following: "by some combination of introspection and memory, along with intuitive and inferential reason." But how do we know that the solipsist heroine would know about her own justification and its sources by means of *such* faculties only? On reflection, this does not seem a serious problem for our internalist, however, since he might just define reflection as "cognitive processes involving only a priori thought about necessary truths, along with introspective knowledge of one's own internal properties, aided by memory and reason."

More problematic for Plantinga is the fact that this line of reasoning from a deontological conception of epistemic justification to an epistemic internalism, makes essential use of an *assumption* of personal internalism. This line of reasoning *assumes* that the solipsist heroine would be equally justified as her flesh and blood counterpart, and that the justification of the heroine would (of course) derive at most from her internal properties (there being nothing external). It is only on the basis of that assumption that we are able to invoke the 2a–2c corollaries of the deontological conception and derive from them a doctrine of epistemic internalism: the doctrine that one could always know *by reflection* how things stand with regard to one's own epistemic justification. On this line of reasoning, therefore, it would not be true that one could just start with a deontological conception of epistemic justification, and derive *both* epistemic internalism *and* personal internalism from that. On the contrary, it is only by first assuming personal internalism that one can then derive epistemic internalism from the view of epistemic justification as deontological.[1]

8. Moreover, the conception of epistemic justification as deontological has certain further limitations that emerge more clearly in light of the fact that it amounts in effect to a notion of justification *in the third degree*. Plantinga sets up things somewhat differently, but this is the upshot anyhow. Plantinga delimits the scope of his claim that epistemic justification is subject to the three corollaries, 2a–2c. He delimits the scope of that claim to a "wide and important class of cases"—in effect cases in which the subject is functioning properly, which means (a) that he is knowledgeable enough about the particulars of his situation and about the abstract requirements of epistemic duty, and (b) that he is smart and alert enough that he can put that knowledge to use appropriately in determining what epistemic duties are in fact binding on him at the time, as to whether he is to accept the belief in question or not.

However, few would deny that if we delimit thus the class of relevant cases, then *in any such case* the subject will be justified only if he knows that he is justified. What is more, consider the large and important class of cases where epistemologists generally would agree that one would be equally justified in solipsistic isolation. Epistemologists would agree generally that one's knowledge or awareness that one is justified in any such case will be internalistic, by reflection. Most epistemologists, of whatever persuasion, externalist or not, will surely grant that for a large and important class of cases, what Plantinga claims on behalf of the internalist is likely to be true. Take any case where one knows something or one is epistemically justified in believing something purely on the basis of reflection. Many epistemologists, externalist or not, will agree that in any such case one can know internalistically, by reflection, that one's belief has its positive epistemic status. Real disagreement will begin to arise over cases where one's knowledge is perceptual or depends essentially on perceptual knowledge. Of course, even here one might argue that one must be able to know or believe correctly, simply on the basis of reflection, that one's belief is justified, but now the argument will have to rely on an independent claim that *personal internalism* is true; or so it was argued above.

9. Anyhow, there are further important limitations of the conception of epistemic justification as deontological. The problem is not so much

that there isn't such a notion, nor is it that the scope of such epistemic justification is too narrow, given our very limited control over what we believe. These are problems, I believe, but they are not the main problems I wish to highlight. My main problem is rather that of whether this notion of "epistemic justification" captures an epistemic status of primary interest to epistemology, *even to "internalists" generally*. Don't we fall short in our effort to throw light on internalist epistemic justification if we stop with the explicated deontological justification in the third degree? After all, there are other desirable statuses for our beliefs to attain. Thus it is good that one's beliefs not derive from a deliberate effort on one's part to believe what is false, from a sort of "epistemic masochism." And it is a good thing that one's beliefs not derive from uncaring negligence. These are moreover sorts of things that one could know about the derivation of one's beliefs on the basis of armchair reflection. So one could secure internalism, and define a sort of "epistemic justification" even without invoking the full deontological machinery. But surely we would then fall short in our attempt to throw light on matters epistemic. Avoiding epistemic masochism and uncaring negligence are only two of the things involved in epistemic excellence. And a similar question could now be pressed against the deontologist: In opting for a deontological conception of epistemic justification, are we capturing all relevant aspects of "internal" epistemic excellence that we wish to illuminate? Or are we falling short in ways analogous to the ways in which we fall short if we stop with mere masochism-avoidance or negligence-avoidance conceptions of justification?

10. Let us focus on epistemic justification of the third degree—the sort of epistemic justification used by Plantinga to defend deontologism as a route to epistemic internalism. If we focus on the content of epistemic justification to that degree, I believe we can see that it will inevitably miss respects of epistemic excellence, of internal epistemic excellence.

a. Consider our correct beliefs about what duty requires in various circumstances, and our correct beliefs about the particulars of our own situation in terms of which we would need to determine our epistemic duties in that concrete situation. Presumably, these beliefs are also assessable as epistemically justified or not. What is more, one could hardly attain deontological *epistemic* justification if the duty-specifying beliefs that govern one's epistemic choice are wholly *unjustified*. So, there must be an assumption that these beliefs are epistemically justified in some sense. But, on pain of vicious circularity, the sense involved cannot be that of deontological epistemic justification.

b. Second, what are we to say of beliefs that do *not* result from a knowledgeable choice on the part of the believer? Take, moreover, beliefs that the believer is in no way responsible for and could not have avoided, *or* could not have known to be wrong beliefs to hold in the circumstances, so that the believer bears no responsibility for his lack of pertinent control *or* lack of pertinent knowledge or correct belief as to his choice of cognitive attitude in that actual situation. This could presumably happen even with wholly internal beliefs that are introspective or reflective and independent of perception. If we restrict ourselves to justification in the third degree as our only conception of epistemic justification, then all such beliefs turn out to be indistinguishable in respect of epistemic justification—they are all equally unjustified. But can there be no difference in relevant epistemic status between the following two classes of beliefs? Consider, *on one hand*:

C1 the belief that $1 + 1 = 2$, or the belief of someone with an excruciating headache that she suffers a headache, beliefs which presumably one cannot help having—and the great class of such obvious, nonoptional beliefs;

and, *on the other hand*:

C2 the convictions of the victim of a cult who has been brainwashed; or the beliefs of a naïf with a crude conception of what justification requires in a certain ambit, who acquires his beliefs in ways that he is convinced are methodologically sound, simply because he was raised in a culture where such ways are instilled, so that now, through no fault of his own, our naïf does not properly know what to believe and what not to believe in that ambit.

These two classes of belief can hardly count equally as beliefs internally unjustified in any sense of much importance for epistemology. Clearly, we must go beyond the concept of deontological justification in the third degree, if we wish to explicate the fact that the beliefs in C1 are internally justified while those in C2 are not. The claim is *not* that there is *no* sense in which both sets of beliefs are on a par in respect of internal justification: indeed, *both* do fail to be "deontologically justified in the third degree," and that does seem an understandable sense of internal justification. The claim is *rather* that there is likely some further important sense of internal justification that remains uncaptured by the notion of deontological justification in the third degree. With this notion we fall short, in a way in which we would fall short in our effort to explicate internal justification if we were to stop with just the notion of belief nonnegligently acquired and sustained. The broader notion of internal justification would perhaps need to take account both of the avoidance of negligence and of the securing of deontological justification in the third degree—these would both be relevant, in different ways, to internal epistemic justification. But, as we have seen, the broader notion would need to go beyond these as well. The contours of that broader notion have yet to be traced. Nevertheless, to the extent that we find it plausible that in some sense the beliefs in C1 are internally justified while those in C2 are not, we should be willing to hold open the possibility, worth exploring, that there is such a broader notion, even if its contours remain obscure.[2]

Notes

This paper benefitted from discussion in my seminar at Brown, and especially from the comments of Matthew McGrath.

1. Actually, it is not ruled out that personal internalism receive some independent support; the important point is that, so far as we have been able to determine, it seems needed as a prior premiss for any argument we have been able to devise that moves from deontologism of justification to epistemic internalism.

2. My main conclusion should be viewed *not* as an objection, but as a supplement to Plantinga's discussion, from which, as always, I have learned a great deal.

Part II

Defeasibility, Knowledge, and the Gettier Problem

5

Knowledge Is Accurate and Comprehensive Enough True Belief

Richard Foley

In 1963 Edmund Gettier asked a simple question that spawned an enormous literature, what has to be added to true belief in order to produce knowledge? At the time, the standard answer was, justification; knowledge is justified true belief. Gettier described two cases that convinced most philosophers that this answer cannot be correct.[1]

One of the cases is as follows: Smith justifiably believes proposition F, "Jones owns a Ford." Despite Smith's overwhelming evidence, F is false. Smith recognizes that F implies P, "Jones owns a Ford or Brown is in Barcelona." Smith has no evidence of the whereabouts of Brown; he believes P only because it is implied by F. As it happens, P is true; Brown is in Barcelona. So, Smith has a justified true belief in P, but he does not know P.

Gettier's examples inspired others, and soon there was a huge variety of Gettier-style counterexamples in the literature. Epistemologists reacted to the counterexamples in one of two ways. The first camp searched for a way to qualify the kind of justification that when added to true belief produced knowledge. Thus, some philosophers argued that knowledge is true belief that is nondefectively justified, where a justification is nondefective if it doesn't justify any falsehood. Others argued that the justification must be nondefeasible, in the sense that no truth, if known, would defeat it. There have been other proposals as well.[2]

A second camp, led by Alvin Goldman, looked for an external relation that could be tacked on to justified true belief to produce knowledge. In a 1967 article, he contended that knowledge involves there being "an appropriate causal connection" between the fact P and the person's believing P.[3] The proposal nicely handled the original cases described by Gettier, but it ran into other problems. Knowledge of mathematics and general facts proved especially thorny.

Nevertheless, Goldman's recommendation captivated many epistemologists, in part because it shifted the focus away from issues of justification. Indeed, some epistemologists were questioning whether justification, at least if understood in the usual foundationalist or coherentist ways, is even necessary for knowledge. Being justified in believing a proposition P is typically thought of as an internal condition; it is a matter of the believer having, or being able to construct, an argument for P. But to insist that this is a prerequisite of knowledge, they argued, is to overintellectualize the notion. Some kinds of knowledge, especially highly theoretical knowledge, might involve argument, but other kinds typically do not, for example simple perceptual knowledge.

Thus, these epistemologists abandoned the strategy of trying to find something that can be added to justified true belief to produce knowledge and instead began to look for something less explicitly intellectual that could turn true belief into knowledge. According to this approach, in order to know P it is not necessary for an individual to have an appropriate internal argument for P. Rather, it is necessary for the individual to stand in the appropriate external relation with P. The philosophical task is to identify the precise relation. Since a simple causal relation between the fact P and the belief P won't do, some other relation needs to be found.

There has been no shortage of candidates. David Armstrong has declared that one knows P only if there is a lawlike connection between one's belief P and the state of affairs that makes it true.[4] Fred Dretske has said that one knows P only if there are reasons R such that one believes P because of R and R would not be the case unless P were.[5] In a similar spirit, Robert Nozick has suggested that one knows P only if one's belief tracks the truth, where this is a matter of it being the case that in close counterfactual situations in which P is false one would not believe P and in close counterfactual situations in which P is true one would believe P.[6] For Ernest Sosa knowledge is a matter of apt true belief, where an apt belief is a product of intellectual virtues and where an intellectual virtue is a truth-conductive disposition rooted in one's abilities and faculties.[7]

There have been other proposals as well, but it was Goldman again who formulated the view that had the widest appeal. In his 1986 book, *Epistemology and Cognition*, he defended a reliability theory of knowledge. To know P it is not necessary for the fact P to cause the belief P, although this will often be the case. Rather, it is necessary for the processes, faculties, and methods that produced or sustain the belief to be highly reliable.[8]

Since 1986 there have been refinements to the reliability theory, some suggested by Goldman himself.[9] In addition, the theory has motivated a major successor theory. Alvin Plantinga has argued that the key to understanding knowledge is not reliability but rather proper functioning. Knowledge is a matter of having true beliefs that are produced by cognitive faculties functioning properly in the environment for which they were designed to function, where design can be explicated either naturalistically (the processes of natural selection) or supernaturally (God's design). Since cognitive equipment that is functioning properly will normally be reliable, the differences between Plantinga's and Goldman's accounts are subtle, but Plantinga argues that his account has significant advantages, the principal one being that it can do justice to cases in which a true belief is the product of cognitive malfunctions that are "accidentally reliable."[10]

There are other important differences of opinion among Goldman, Armstrong, Dretske, Nozick, Sosa, and Plantinga, but they all share the view that in order for one to have knowledge, there has to be an appropriate fit between one's beliefs, faculties, and methods on the one hand and one's environment on the other, where "appropriate fit" is to be understood causally (the early Goldman) or counterfactually (Dretske and Nozick) or in terms of the reliability of one's faculties in one's environment (the later Goldman and Sosa) or in terms of one's faculties functioning properly in the environment for which they were designed (Plantinga).

Together, these views constitute a movement in epistemology and an undeniably rich one at that. My belief, however, is that the entire movement is mistaken, and mistaken not just in detail but irreparably mistaken.

Why the Tradition Is Mistaken

Imagine that your beliefs are as accurate and as comprehensive as is humanly possible. You have true beliefs about the basic laws of the universe, and in terms of these basic laws, you can explain everything that has happened, is happening, and will happen. You can explain the origin of the universe, how life came into existence on earth, the mechanisms by which cells age, and so on. You can even explain how you came to have all of this information. You have a perfectly veridical and explanatorily perfect belief system, or as close to this as is humanly possible.

Then you have more knowledge than I, and you have more knowledge than anyone else as well. But notice, your having a perfectly veridical and explanatorily perfect belief system is consistent with your beliefs having been produced in strange, nonstandard ways. For example, it is possible that you have been struck by a lightning bolt, and this in some curious way has caused you to believe what you do.

But if so, your having a perfectly veridical and explanatorily perfect belief system is consistent with most of your beliefs not being caused by the states of affairs that make them true. They are instead the products of the lightning bolt, which against all odds has had the effect of generating a perfectly veridical belief system. Thus, your having this perfect belief system is consistent with the conditions of Goldman's early account of knowledge not being satisfied.

Similarly, it is consistent with the conditions of Goldman's later account of knowledge not being satisfied, since the lightning bolt need not be a reliable way of acquiring beliefs. By hypothesis it has produced nothing but true beliefs in this instance, but we can stipulate that in other close counterfactual situations it would not have had this effect. Thus, it is not a reliable way of acquiring beliefs.

Likewise, your having this perfectly veridical and explanatorily perfect belief system is consistent with your beliefs not being the products of intellectual virtues and not being products of your cognitive faculties functioning properly. Hence, it is also consistent with the conditions of Sosa's and Plantinga's accounts not being satisfied.

So, even though you have a perfectly veridical and explanatorily perfect belief system, if your beliefs are the products of a lightning bolt or of some other similarly strange process, the accounts of Goldman, Sosa, Plantinga, and other like-minded theorists force us to deny that you have knowledge. Indeed, on the assumption that my cognitive faculties sometimes operate reliably and properly, these accounts imply that I know more than you about the origin of the universe, how life came into existence on earth, and the mechanisms by which cells age. But this is absurd. You know far more about these things than I do, and any account that suggests otherwise is inadequate.

An Objection from the Theory of Mental Content

Some accounts of mental content imply that having a rich set of beliefs about the world is possible only if one has a correspondingly rich and systematic set of causal or nomological relations with the objects that make up the world. But if so, a stray lightning bolt could not possibly produce an extensive set of beliefs, much less extensive knowledge.[11]

An objection of this sort is only as strong as the account of content on which it is based, and it is an understatement that no account of content is noncontroversial. So at best, the objection has only doubtful force. In addition, it is subject to a dilemma. Either the theory of content on which the objection is based is implausible, or the objection merely pushes the problem for reliabilist and reliabilist-inspired accounts back a level, where it can be raised again.

Consider any account of content. Given the account, either the prerequisites of having a rich set of beliefs imply that the conditions of knowledge are also generally met, or they do not. If the former, the account is implausible. It does not leave enough room for error. An account of content is plausible only if it allows for the possibility of widespread error. There may be limits on how extensive one's errors can be while still having beliefs, but the limits are at best distant ones.[12]

On the other hand, suppose that a theory of content leaves adequate room for error, as most do. Then it will be possible for you to have a perfectly veridical and explanatorily perfect belief system, or at least something approaching this, and for the system to be maximally delicate, in the sense that if anything had been different you would have had seriously mistaken beliefs instead of perfectly true ones. For example, suppose it is the world in its totality, rather than a stray lightning bolt, that causes you to have a perfectly veridical and explanatorily perfect belief system, and suppose that the way in which it does so is maximally delicate; if anything had been slightly different about the world or you, you would have instead come to have a deeply flawed belief system. Then the original problem for reliabilist and reliabilist-inspired accounts reappears. In this scenario, your beliefs need not be virtuous in Sosa's sense. Nor need they be reliably produced in Goldman's sense. And they need not be the products of cognitive faculties functioning properly in Plantinga's sense either. And yet, you have knowledge, indeed lots of it.

Knowledge and Lack of Stability

If knowledge were a matter of there being an appropriate causal or counterfactual fit between one's environment and one's intellectual faculties, habits, and methods, then knowledge of necessity would have a large degree of stability. However, it is a mistake to think that knowledge is necessarily stable. It is not impossible to have fleeting moments of insight. I may suddenly see how to complete a proof but then almost immediately lose it, but this doesn't mean that I did not have knowledge during that brief moment.

There are more exotic examples as well. Think of mystics who claim that the most important kinds of knowledge cannot be cultivated, because they are so fragile. When every circumstance is exactly right, powerful insight is possible, but when the smallest detail is altered, the insight is lost. On this view, mystical knowledge cannot help but be unstable and of short duration.

This is not to say that the claims of professed mystics should be accepted. The point is a much more modest one. Namely, their claims to knowledge are not to be rejected as inherently incoherent on the ground that knowledge is by definition stable.

Is Knowledge Indefeasibly (or Nondefectively) Justified True Belief?

If you have perfectly veridical and explanatorily perfect beliefs, your beliefs are also internally coherent. Thus, given a coherence theory of justification, they are justified. Moreover, since your belief system is a perfectly accurate and comprehensive, the justifications for your various beliefs are nondefective; they don't justify any falsehoods. Likewise, they are indefeasible; there are no truths, if known, that would defeat them.

Nevertheless, it is a mistake to conclude that knowledge is best understood as nondefectively justified, or indefeasibly justified, true belief. Having a perfectly veridical system is sufficient for knowledge. It may also be sufficient, depending on one's account of justification, to ensure that one's beliefs are justified. Even so, justification doesn't have to be invoked to explain why a perfectly veridical believer has knowledge. Justification is a by-product. It is not doing the work in generating knowledge. True beliefs are doing that.

The same is true of less idealized cases, in which we have knowledge but lack a perfectly veridical belief system. In these more ordinary cases, justification is again not the crucial consideration, even if it is frequently a by-product. The key consideration is whether our beliefs are accurate enough and comprehensive enough to count as knowledge.

Knowledge is Accurate and Comprehensive Enough Belief

Knowledge is a matter of having accurate and comprehensive enough beliefs. One knows P if and only if one has accurate enough beliefs about P and also comprehensive enough beliefs about P.[13]

If one has a perfectly veridical and explanatorily perfect belief system, these conditions of knowledge are automatically satisfied, but they also can be satisfied when one's beliefs are far less than perfect. It is enough to have enough true beliefs. What counts as enough is context dependent. It varies with our interests and needs as well as the perspective of those attributing knowledge.

All Gettier-style counterexamples can be handled by this approach, since they all depend on there being some important truth of which the believer is unaware. We from the outside are aware of the believer's lack of awareness, which is why the example has force. We see that the believer has a less than complete picture of the actual situation, and this convinces us that the believer lacks knowledge. To explain the lack of knowledge, we need not invoke conditions of reliability or proper functioning. Nor need we invoke the defeasibility of the believer's justification. The simplest and best explanation is the lack of true beliefs. There is no knowledge because the believer lacks an accurate enough or comprehensive enough "picture" of P and "its surroundings." The believer either has an inaccurate belief about some feature of the situation that we regard as crucial or lacks a true belief about this feature.

For example, consider Goldman's barn case.[14] You are driving in the country and stop in front of a barn. Unbeknownst to you, the surrounding countryside is filled with barn facsimiles. The facsimiles are so detailed that if you had stopped in front of any of them, you would have been fooled into thinking you were looking at a real barn. But by luck, you have stopped in front of one of the few real barns left in the area. You have a true belief that you are looking at a barn but you lack knowledge. Why? Because you are unaware of the barn facsimiles and because the story has been told in a way that convinces us that this is an important lacuna in your belief system. The story emphasizes that there are a large number of barn facsimiles that would have fooled you and moreover the facsimiles are in the immediate area. In addition, there is nothing in the story to suggest that there is something especially meaningful about your having a true belief about the barnlike thing in front of you as opposed to the other barnlike things in the vicinity.

Suppose we retell the story to make it clear that having true beliefs about things in the nearby vicinity is insignificant in comparison with having true beliefs about the thing in front of you. For example, suppose we stipulate that you will spend the rest of your life within sight of the barn that is now in front of you and hence will never have the opportunity to be fooled by the barn facsimiles in the vicinity. Or suppose we stipulate that this barn was involved in some memorable incident in your childhood and that this memory motivated you to locate the barn again as an adult. Then we may begin waver as to whether you lack knowledge that the thing in front of you is a barn, and our reservations correspond to our having doubts about the importance of your not being aware of the barn facsimiles in the area.

Other Gettier-style cases can be dealt with in a similar way. In each case, the example is described so as to focus our attention on some aspect of the situation about which the person lacks true beliefs. Moreover, the example is described in such a way as to convince us that the aspect is important; it is important to the believer or to us or merely important in understanding what is "really" going on in the situation. As a result, we are led to conclude that the believer's grasp of the situation is incomplete or faulty in some important way. Hence, the person lacks knowledge. The person's beliefs are either not accurate enough or not comprehensive enough to count as knowledge.

Notes

A much abbreviated defense of the views in this paper can be found in Richard Foley, "The Epistemology of Sosa," in E. Villanueva (ed.), *Truth and Rationality*, (Atascadero, Calif.: Ridgeview, 1994), section 5.

1. Edmund Gettier, "Is Justified True Belief Knowledge?" *Analysis* (1963), 121–23.

2. For a survey of the literature, see Robert Shope, *The Analysis of Knowledge* (Princeton: Princeton University Press, 1983).

3. Alvin Goldman, "A Causal Theory of Knowing," *Journal of Philosophy*, 64, 357–72.

4. D. M. Armstrong, *Belief, Truth, and Knowledge* (Cambridge: Cambridge University Press, 1973).

5. Fred Dretske, *Knowledge and the Flow of Information* (Cambridge: MIT Press, 1981).

6. Robert Nozick, *Philosophical Explanations* (Cambridge: Harvard University Press, 1981).

7. Ernest Sosa, *Knowledge in Perspective* (Cambridge: Cambridge University Press, 1991).

8. Alvin Goldman, *Epistemology and Cognition* (Cambridge: Harvard University Press, 1986).

9. For example, see Alvin Goldman, "Strong and Weak Justification," *Philosophical Perspectives*, 2 (1988), 51–70.

10. Alvin Plantinga, *Warrant: The Current Debate* (New York: Oxford University Press, 1993); see especially his examples of accidental reliability on p. 192 and p. 210.

11. For example, see Donald Davidson, "A Coherence Theory of Truth and Knowledge," in E. LePore (ed.), *The Philosophy of Donald Davidson, Perspectives on Truth and Interpretation* (London: Basil Blackwell, 1986), 307–19.

12. For a defense of this claim, see Richard Foley, *Working Without a Net* (New York: Oxford University Press, 1993), especially pp. 67–75; also see Peter Klein, "Radical Interpretation and Global Skepticism," and Colin McGinn, "Radical Interpretation," both in E. LePore (ed.), *Truth and Interpretation* (Oxford: Basil Blackwell, 1986).

13. Contrast with Crispin Sartwell who argues that knowledge that P is simply a matter of having a true belief that P. See Sartwell, "Knowledge Is Merely True Belief," *American Philosophical Quarterly* (1991), 157–65.

14. Alvin Goldman, "Discrimination and Perceptual Knowledge," *Journal of Philosophy* 73 (1976), 771–91.

6

Warrant, Proper Function, Reliabilism, and Defeasibility

Peter Klein

Introduction

"Warrant" is defined by Alvin Plantinga to be *whatever* it is that distinguishes mere true belief from knowledge.[1] In other words, knowledge is defined as true, warranted belief. The crucial question, then, for epistemologists becomes "what is warrant?"

It is important to note that "warranted belief" is not a sophisticated equivalent of "justified belief." If it were, the definition of knowledge as true belief that is warranted would be subject to the Gettier counterexamples. For Edmund Gettier showed that true, justified belief is not sufficient for knowledge when justification is given a purely internalist explication.[2] For example, if we say that a belief, p, is justified for a person, S, just in case S has adequate evidence for p, then since a false, justified belief can entail a true belief and, at least on some occasions, provide an adequate justification of a true belief, q, for S, then q would be a true, justified belief—but it is not knowledge.

Because "warrant" is not the philosopher's counterpart of "justified," when we agree that warrant is whatever has to be added to true belief to convert it into knowledge, we have not agreed to very much. For "warrant" is merely a placeholder until we arrive at an account of what converts true belief into knowledge.

Nevertheless, I think we can appeal to a deeply held intuition that underlies virtually all attempts to characterize warrant at least since the modern period. That intuition is that a warranted belief is one that is not held on the basis of mere luck or chance.[3] A belief is warranted when it is not an accident, *from the cognitive point of view* (as Plantinga puts it in WCD, 195, quoted later in this paper) that it is both true and believed. Passages cited by Plantinga from René Descartes and John Locke indicate that, as he calls them, the "two fountainheads of Western theory of knowledge" shared that view.[4] (I have italicized the relevant portions of the passages.) Descartes says:

> If I abstain from giving my judgment on any thing when I do not perceive it with sufficient clearness and distinctness, it is plain that I act rightly. . . . But if I determine to deny or affirm, I no longer make use of my free will, and if I affirm what is not true, it is evident that I deceive myself; *even though I judge according to the truth, this comes about only by chance*, and I do not escape the blame of misusing my freedom. . . . (WCD, 12)[5]

And Locke says:

> He that believes, without having reason for believing, may be in love with his own fancies; but neither seeks the truth as he ought. . . . He that does not this to the best of his power, *however he sometimes lights on the truth, is in the right by chance; and I know not whether the luckiness of the accident will excuse the irregularity of his proceeding.* (WCD, 13)[6]

Although both Descartes and Locke hold that by using our faculties as we ought to, we can arrive at knowledge, the important point I wish to draw attention to here is that both of them base that claim on an appeal to the intuition that true belief had by chance is not knowledge. As we will see, Plantinga employs that very intuition at key points in his account of warrant. Further, as Plantinga correctly points out, Gettier showed that even true belief arising out of our epistemic duties can also be an accident, from the cognitive point of view. Hence, warrant cannot be construed as true beliefs that we ought to hold on the basis of the evidence which is available to us through introspection alone.

So let us start with the basic assumption that knowledge is true belief that is not accidentally true from the cognitive point of view. Hence, if warrant is what has to be added to true belief to convert it into knowledge, warrant is that property of a true belief in virtue of which it is not accidentally true. So the question "what is warrant?" is more fully elaborated as this question: What converts an accidentally true belief, from the cognitive point of view, into one that is not accidentally true, from the cognitive point of view? Simple question; difficult answer. For there are more ways to answer that question than there are epistemologists![7]

This is not the place to review all of those attempts to provide an account of nonaccidentally true beliefs. But this is the place to consider Plantinga's answer to that question in the context of some other general approaches to answering it. Plantinga's basic claim in WCD and WPF is that a belief is warranted just in case it is produced by a cognitive faculty functioning properly. It isn't an accident because S's cognitive faculties are doing what they were designed to do. Of course, such talk inevitably invokes thoughts of a designer, a design plan, and the environment in which the artifact was designed to operate. And that is not a coincidence, since Plantinga thinks of human capacities as the result of a design plan and that such a plan cannot be given a purely naturalistic, nontheistic, characterization.[8]

One of the basic claims in this paper is that this cannot be a correct account of warrant. It is tempting to explore the very deepest issue here—namely, are human capacities "designed" in any sense whatsoever? But, tempting though that is, I won't succumb. Rather, my strategy will be to explore whether warranted belief can be correctly characterized as just those beliefs that result from the employment of our cognitive faculties functioning properly. I hope to show that proper function is neither a sufficient nor a necessary condition for warrant. There are beliefs that are the result of properly functioning cognitive faculties which are accidentally true, from the cognitive point of view; and there are beliefs that are not produced by properly functioning cognitive faculties (at least given what Plantinga means by "properly functioning cognitive faculties") that are true, and not accidentally so, from the cognitive point of view. In addition, I hope to show that there is a better account of warrant available, namely the defeasibility theory of warrant. I will do that by contrasting three externalist accounts of warrant: strict reliabilist accounts, Plantinga's proper function account, and the defeasibility account.[9]

The paper has three parts. Part I introduces a straightforward case in which to test the three views. In Part I, I will contrast the ways in which a strict reliabilist and a proper functionist ought to treat the test case. Examining the test case will help to set the stage for the more detailed discussion of the proper function account of warrant that occurs in Part II. Specifically, in Part II, I will give my reasons for thinking that such an account cannot provide sufficient or necessary conditions for warrant. In Part III, I want to characterize the defeasibility theory in general and explain how a properly crafted defeasibility theory (one which can adequately distinguish between genuine and misleading defeaters) can explain the justifiably conflicting intuitions about the test case described in Part I. In addition, I want to show how such a properly crafted defeasibility theory can handle an objection first developed by Robert Shope and reiterated by Plantinga. The last point is important since this objection is the only one that I am aware of that has not been answered effectively in the literature on the defeasibility theory.

Part I: The Test Case

Here is the test case:

> Mr. Damage has had perfectly functioning cognitive equipment up until the unfortunate day that he suffers some serious brain damage. He no longer gets many things right and most of his knowledge is wiped out. His brain damage causes all sorts of abnormal perceptions and causes him to make rather peculiar inferences. But along with causing Mr. Damage to believe all sorts of false propositions, his brain damage causes him to believe that he has brain damage. Thus, his particular form of brain damage and the laws of nature are such that his brain damage causes him to believe at least one true proposition along with many false ones.

This case is not original with me and it is discussed by Plantinga.[10] Let me suggest what the strict reliabilists ought to say about this case. They hold that a belief, if true and reliably produced, is knowledge. Of course, there are varying accounts of reliably produced beliefs which become increasingly sophisticated to meet increasingly complex counterexamples. In addition, a central problem for reliabilist accounts is the so-called "generality problem." Briefly, for *every* process that results in a true belief, there will be some *very specific* description of the process (one that picks out just this process and very few others) such that processes of *that* sort will always result in true beliefs. But such a description will not give much, if any, insight into what makes a process truth conducive.

For the purposes of this paper, we can set aside this worry and stipulate that there will be some insightful description (perhaps employing some categorically basic terms in mature sciences) of the process resulting in Mr. Damage's belief that he has brain damage which is such that it is generalizable to other people with similar damage. My suggestion to reliabilists is that they bite the bullet and assert that although beliefs resulting from brain damage are not typically reliable indicators of the truth, in this case, because the belief that Mr. Damage acquires is the causal product of his brain damage, it is not accidental, from the cognitive point of view, that he believes that he has brain damage.[11] After all, the "laws of nature" are such that Mr. Damage's belief and the beliefs of other people suffering similar damage are such that they are true and reliably caused. The reliabilist ought to say that Mr. Damage knows he has brain damage.[12] Of course, he doesn't know it in the typical way that others know such things. But so what? Consider the case of a gypsy fortune teller.[13] In that case, the fortune-teller acquires knowledge that is normally acquired in other ways. For example, the fortune-teller knows which horse will win a race but doesn't arrive at that true belief by examining the winner's previous record and the previous records of its competitors. Similarly, in the Brain Damage Case, Mr. Damage acquires the belief in a nonstandard way but a sufficiently reliable way. So the strict reliabilist ought to say that Mr. Damage has knowledge that he has brain damage.

Consider one more case: telepathy. Whether or not such a thing happens, we would not want our account of knowledge to rule out that possibility a priori; and in such cases it appears that the telepathist would gain knowledge in a manner that somewhat parallels the way in which Mr. Damage acquires knowledge. The telepathist, or at least one who has not investigated the reliability of his telepathic powers, would have no "reason" or "evidence" for his beliefs. The beliefs just seem to come to him from out of the blue. Nevertheless, if there are telepathists, they would have knowledge according to the reliabilists. They might not have iterated knowledge. That is, they might not know that they know—indeed, they might not even believe that they possessed knowledge. But that would not prevent them from having knowledge.

No doubt, there will be those who take the Test Case to be a clear counterexample to reliabilism. Indeed, that is just Plantinga's reaction. Here is what he says:

> But surely [Mr. Damage] does *not* know that he is suffering from a brain lesion. He has no evidence of any kind—sensory, memory, introspective, whatever—that he has such a lesion; *his holding this belief is, from a cognitive point of view, no more than a lucky (or unlucky) accident.* (WCD, 195, italics mine)

Note that Plantinga appeals to the very grounds I claimed provided the basis for many of our intuitions about what constitutes knowledge— namely that knowledge is not accidentally true belief. But—and this is a crucial point—the reliabilist will not agree that "from the cognitive point of view" a belief lacking evidence is, ipso facto, accidentally true. Far from it. The reliabilist will look at the process resulting in the true belief in order to determine whether it would result in true beliefs sufficiently often. It would be accidentally true "from the cognitive point of view" only if the belief is true but the process which produced it typically does not result in enough true beliefs. Thus, the test case reveals that there will be a conflict of intuitions about what constitutes accidentally true beliefs. What are we to make of this?

It appears from the passage cited above that Plantinga thinks the problem here is that there is a lack of evidence for the belief. He does, after all, say that. But I think his considered view is presented a few paragraphs later. Roughly, the reason that it is an accident from the cognitive point of view is not that there is a lack of evidence; rather it is an accident because the belief arose as a result of a "cognitive abnormality." Here is what he says (I have changed the quotation somewhat to make it compatible with the abbreviations and terminology I use throughout this paper; see WCD, 197, for the exact wording):

> Clearly, there are as many counterexamples of this sort as you please. One recipe for constructing them is just to consider some event, *e*, that causes S to believe that *e* occurs where *e* causes S to form the belief in question by virtue of some cognitive abnormality, *and in such a way that it is just an accident, from a cognitive point of view, that the belief is true.* . . . As I argue in *Warrant and Proper Function*, they can be related in this way but fail to be in the way required by the design plan of our noetic structure; but then my belief is not knowledge. . . . What these examples show is that something further must be added; we must add, somehow, that S's noetic faculties, or those involved in the production of the belief in question, are functioning properly, are in good working order. (WCD, 197, italics mine)

Thus Plantinga's considered view is that it is not the lack of evidence that is central to these cases. Forming a belief such as "I have brain damage" might typically require evidence. But the reason he thinks this is not a case of knowledge is that the belief is not produced by our cognitive equipment functioning properly. The belief is a cognitive accident. That, alone, makes the belief unworthy of being accepted. Put another way, some beliefs might be knowledge only if they are supported by evidence, but that is because those beliefs, when produced by properly functioning cognitive equipment, are formed only on the basis of evidence. If our cognitive equipment could function properly and not employ evidence, these beliefs would be knowledge.

So we have two conflicting reactions to the test case:

1. The reliabilist account which holds that Mr. Damage *has knowledge* because the true belief, from the cognitive point of view, *is not accidentally true.*
2. The proper functionist account which holds that Mr. Damage *does not have knowledge* because the true belief, from the cognitive point of view, *is accidentally true.*

The test case reveals a stark clash between the reliabilist's and proper functionist's intuitions regarding what constitutes an accident from the cognitive point of view. The defeasibility theory characterizes accidents from the cognitive point of view in still a third way. We will consider that account of warrant in some detail later, but let me look ahead *just* a bit. The general defeasibility theory holds that a belief is accidentally true if there is evidence which defeats it that is unknown to the believer. The believer arrived at a true belief, but in light of some of the relevant evidence that the believer does not possess, the believer is lucky to have arrived at a true belief. Had the believer come to know the other relevant counterevidence, the true belief would not be justified.

In Part III, I will illustrate the advantages of the defeasibility theory over both of the accounts we have discussed so far. Again, to look ahead a bit, a primary advantage of the defeasibility theory is that it, alone, can account for the conflict of intuitions in the test case. But first, I want to show that the proper functionist account provides neither sufficient nor even necessary conditions for knowledge. That is the task of Part II.

Part II: Problems with the Proper Functionist Account

Plantinga's account of warrant is given in the following passage:

> According to the central and paradigmatic core of our notion of warrant (so I say) a belief *B* has warrant for you if and only if (1) the cognitive faculties involved in the production of *B* are functioning properly (and

this is to include the relevant defeater systems as well as those systems, if any, that provide *propositional* inputs to the system in question); (2) your cognitive environment is sufficiently similar to the one for which your cognitive faculties are designed; (3) the triple of the design plan governing the production of the belief in question involves, as purpose or function, the production of true beliefs (and the same goes for the elements of the design plan governing the production of inputs to the system in question); and (4) the design plan is a good one: that is, there is a high statistical or objective probability that a belief produced in accordance with the relevant segment of the design plan in that sort of environment is true. . . . This account of warrant, therefore, depends essentially upon the notion of proper function. (WPF, 194)[14]

Now, there are some caveats, bells and whistles, and clarifications needed here and there. But the basic view is clear. A belief, p, is warranted for a subject, S, just in case S's cognitive equipment that aims at the truth is functioning properly in an environment sufficiently similar to the one in which S's cognitive equipment was designed to function. If such a belief is true, it is knowledge.[15] My claim is that this account does not correctly characterize either a sufficient or necessary condition of warrant. A belief produced in such a fashion, even if true, could be accidentally true from the cognitive point of view; and, given what Plantinga calls the paradigmatic use of notions like "proper function" or "design plan," a true belief need not be produced by our cognitive faculties functioning properly in order to be knowledge.

Let me begin by recalling how Plantinga treats Gettier problems. The main lesson Plantinga draws from them is that their

essence . . . shows internalist theories of warrant [are] wanting. What the Gettier problems show, crudely stated and without necessary qualification, is that even if everything is going as it ought to with respect to what is internal (in the internalist sense), warrant may still be absent. (WPF, 36)

The "internalist sense" mentioned in the citation is whatever is accessible by introspection alone to the believer. In other words, the main lesson to be learned from the Gettier problems, according to Plantinga, is that we can fail to have knowledge because something not accessible to the believer through introspection alone has gone wrong. In particular, our cognitive faculties might not be functioning properly because they are damaged; or the environment might contain deceptive elements and, hence, our cognitive mechanisms might be operating in environments for which they were not designed. Plantinga is, no doubt, right that many of the cases in the Gettier literature involve deception—sham Ford owners, tricksters with holographic projectors, and hucksters in phony barn country attempting to dupe unsuspecting tourists. Plantinga can handle those cases easily since our faculties were not designed to deal with such situations.

In addition, I fully agree with him that the Gettier cases show that a purely internalist account of warrant cannot succeed. Try as we might, we could have arrived at our beliefs (though true) through some sort of cognitive accident. Following all the rules of good reasoning, we could arrive at a false but justified belief and infer a true justified one from it. Yet the inferred proposition, though true, justified, and believed is not knowledge.

But I think our cognitive equipment can also be functioning absolutely perfectly, according to the conditions developed by Plantinga, and yet it is merely accidental, from the cognitive point of view, that we have arrived at a true belief. Consider the following case of Lucky Ms. Jones:

> Jones believes that she owns a well-functioning Ford. She forms this belief in perfectly normal circumstances using her cognitive equipment that is functioning just perfectly. But as sometimes normally happens (no deception here), unbeknownst to Jones, her Ford is hit and virtually demolished—let's say while it is parked outside her office. But also unbeknownst to Jones, she has just won a well-functioning Ford in the Well-Functioning Ford Lottery that her company runs once a year.

Unlike the test case, I gather that everyone's intuitions are clear here. Jones's belief that she owns a well functioning Ford was formed by her cognitive faculties that aim at the truth functioning properly in an appropriate environment. And the belief is true. But it isn't knowledge because it is an accident, from the cognitive point of view, that her belief is true.

Indeed, there is a very general lesson to be learned here. There is a potential Generalized Gettier Problem that can be formulated. *If* warrant can transfer from a false, warranted belief through the proper exercise of our faculties to a true belief, then that true belief will be warranted but not knowledge.[16]

There are four alternatives available to the proper function theory to resist this counterexample.[17] The first is to deny that a warranted belief can be false. The second is to claim that warrant can be transferred *only from a true belief* to another belief. The third is to deny that warrant can be transferred at all. The fourth is to claim that Ms. Jones's beliefs aren't warranted. Let us consider those alternatives in order.

There is no principled reason available to the proper function theory for holding that a warranted belief must be true. Indeed, Plantinga explicitly recognizes that a false belief can be warranted. He says:

> On an adequate account of warrant, what counts is not whether my experience *guarantees* the truth of the belief in question (and how *could* it do a thing like that?), but whether I hold it with sufficient confidence and whether it is produced in me by cognitive faculties successfully aimed at the truth and functioning properly in an appropriate environment. If so, it has warrant; and if it is also true it constitutes knowledge. (WPF, 55, emphasis in the original)

So, according to the proper function account, a belief can be warranted and false.

What about the second alternative, namely, that warrant cannot be transferred from a false belief? Such a stipulation will not vouchsafe the proper function theory from a modified version of this counterexample. As the long history of the Gettier literature shows, this restriction that warrant cannot be transferred from false beliefs to true ones is both too strong and too weak. Indeed, one of the first responses to the Gettier cases was to suggest this very "fix."[18] That fix didn't work and it was quickly seen how serious a problem the Gettier Problem was.[19]

The restriction is too strong because cases can be constructed so that a belief is known (hence warranted) even though based on a false proposition, when what makes the proposition false is not, so to speak, fatal. For example, suppose that my belief that I have an appointment at 3:00 p.m. on April 10th is based on my warranted but false belief that my secretary told me on April 6th that I had such an appointment. If my secretary told me that I had such an appointment, but she told me that on April 7th (not the 6th), my belief that I have an appointment at 3:00 p.m. can still be knowledge, even though the belief that supports it is false.

But, more importantly for our purposes here, the restriction is too weak because Ms. Jones's reasoning could be constructed so that only true beliefs are employed by the cognitive faculties and the resulting belief is still accidentally true.[20] For example, suppose that Jones is a *very* cautious reasoner and comes to believe that she owns some well-functioning Ford *without ever forming the false belief that the Ford which she has been driving up until the day of the accident is still well functioning.* Jones could reason as follows: "I had a well-functioning Ford when I arrived at the office this morning and the chances of anything happening to it while it is parked outside of my office are very slim. Of course, something could happen to it. I've heard of cars being hit while parked. But I did enter the Well-Functioning Ford Lottery. So, either I own a well-functioning Ford that I parked outside my office or I've won one. But in either case, I own a well-functioning Ford." Thus the restricted warrant transfer principle won't save the proper function theory from this modified counterexample.

So the question becomes: Can the proper function theory block the warrant transfer principle in general? That brings us to the third alternative.

Perhaps Plantinga could hold that warrant does not "transfer" under any circumstances. Justification might. Knowledge might. But warrant doesn't. That seems possible; and, further, since "warrant" is a philosopher's invention acting merely as a placeholder until whatever it is that converts a true belief into knowledge is specified, there will not be many, if any, intuitions to which one could appeal. I think it will be difficult, but not impossible, to explain how knowledge could be closed under the appropriate forms of inference if warrant is not also closed under those forms of inference.[21] But let us grant that warrant does not transfer.

Nevertheless, it remains clear that even if we grant that warrant cannot be *transferred* from one proposition to another, the case of Lucky Ms. Jones is still a counterexample to Plantinga's account. For Jones's belief that she owns a well-functioning Ford is the result of her cognitive equipment functioning properly and is, for that reason alone, warranted according to the proper function account. In other words, although the counterexample *could* be understood as employing a warrant transfer principle, it *need not* be understood that way.

Finally, what if Plantinga were to suggest that Jones is not warranted in believing that she owns a well-functioning Ford? That response leads directly to skepticism with regard to the past. To see that, change the case by making everything to be as she thinks it is. Her Ford is fine. It wasn't virtually demolished while parked outside her office. If her belief that she owns a well-functioning Ford isn't warranted in the case as originally described (when her car was virtually demolished), then her belief isn't warranted in the case in which everything is as she thinks it is. For her equipment is working in exactly the same way in both cases. Of course, the "environment" is different, but the only difference is that in the revised case all of her relevant beliefs are true and in the original case some of them are false. But we have already seen that the (mere) truth of a belief cannot convert it from an unwarranted to a warranted belief. So Plantinga would be forced to assert that Jones isn't warranted in believing that she owns a well-functioning Ford in the case in which everything is as she believes it to be. That might be a consequence some skeptics would embrace, but it would surely prompt most people to reject the proper function theory. So this alternative will not provide an acceptable way to avoid the counterexample.

In sum, I take it that the Lucky Ms. Jones Case shows that even when our cognitive equipment that aims at the truth is functioning properly in an environment which is sufficiently similar to the one in which the equipment was designed to function employing strategies that arrive at the truth sufficiently often, we might still arrive at belief that is accidentally true *from the cognitive point of view*. As long as Plantinga allows that a false belief can be warranted and that its warrant can be transferred to a true belief, the Generalized Gettier Problem provides a recipe for constructing as many counterexamples as you please. And if Plantinga were to require that warrant can transfer only when the warranted proposition is true, the cautious reasoner variation on the Lucky Ms. Jones case shows that proper function is not sufficient for warrant. And even if Plantinga were to deny that warrant transfers in any case, it is clear that the example need not assume that it does. And, finally, the suggestion that Jones's belief that she owns a well-functioning Ford isn't warranted would lead directly to an unacceptable form of skepticism. Thus I think this case shows that warrant as characterized by the proper function theory is not sufficient to fill the gap between mere true belief and knowledge.

Let me now turn to my claim that a properly functioning cognitive faculty is not even necessary for the production of knowledge. If the reliabilist intuitions in the test case were universally shared, we would already have found a case that shows that properly functioning cognitive equipment is not necessary for knowledge. But Plantinga has discussed such cases and stated his intuitions about them. He claims that the beliefs which arise from damaged faculties, even though reliable, are not knowledge. I think we must respect those intuitions. (I will return to this question in Part III and show how we can account for those intuitions without embracing the proper function theory.) So a more careful look at Plantinga's account of warrant as proper function is required.

As Plantinga correctly points out, the basic or fundamental meaning of "proper functioning" is employed when we are speaking of artifacts. He says, "Our paradigm cases of design and proper function . . . are artifacts, things designed by conscious agents" (WPF, 196). I agree. The root meaning of "proper function" arises with regard to artifacts and is applied only in some extended sense to objects that we believe were not created through the exercise of intelligent planning. My claim that our cognitive equipments' functioning properly is not a necessary condition of knowledge is aimed at the root notion of proper function.

Consider this case, a variation of the familiar Pinocchio story. Geppetto creates a puppet, Pinocchio, to entertain the audiences that come to the puppet shows. Since the proper function of an artifact is determined solely by the intentions of the creator of the artifact, Geppetto has the authority to assign a proper function to the puppet— *entertain the audience!* Pinocchio was not made to gain knowledge, have fun, or rebel against his creator. If he were to suddenly "come alive" and gain knowledge, or have fun, or rebel against Geppetto, he would not be fulfilling his proper function.

Indeed, were Pinocchio—the object rigidly designated by "Pinocchio" in our story—to do anything but entertain the audiences, he would not be fulfilling his design plan. But I take it that our intuitions are that Pinocchio could suddenly "come alive" and do all those things. Maybe not easily. Maybe something mysterious would have to happen. But if it were to happen, Pinocchio could gain knowledge— and that's enough for my purposes.

The case is built on a simple claim. The proper function of an artifact is determined by the artifact's creator. In some cases it is difficult, if not impossible, to ascertain from an examination of the artifact itself what its proper function is.[22] Even something as simple as a hammer would not reveal its proper function by an examination of its properties alone. We need to know, for example, that it was made by creatures who are large enough to hold it. Its function would be very different if it were created by intelligent ant-sized creatures.

The Pinocchio case shows, I think, that Pinocchio could, if he came alive, gain knowledge even if he were not designed to do so. But some will object. How is this relevant to the human case?

Well, consider what we can call the Garden of Eden Case. Suppose that we, humans, are artifacts. That is, suppose some theistic hypothesis is correct. Some god created us with the intention, say, that we remain in some sort of wonderful place, some sort of garden, say. Perhaps the creator calls it "Eden." Now, this creator has given us many proper functions: We are to name the plants and animals. We are to have a bit of fun. We are to worship the creator. In addition, when we are functioning properly we gain knowledge of all sorts of things, but we are not supposed to gain knowledge of some deep secrets—the secrets of the Tree of Life. These are things we are not supposed to know. That is not our proper function. And since we are artifacts, our proper functions are just those in our creator's design plan that are executed in us.

Ah! But we are rebellious. Like Pinocchio, we rebel against our creator and gain the knowledge we were not intended to gain. Is that an inconceivable story?

I think it's a false story. But I don't think it is inconceivable that we do things, including gaining knowledge, that we were not intended to do by our creator (if there were one). We can gain knowledge that we were not supposed to gain—we might even pay a price for gaining it, like being thrown out of Eden—but we gained it nevertheless.

To make my claim here clearer, let me hasten to add that I am not engaging in amateur hermeneutics. Maybe there are ways of telling the Garden of Eden story within the religious traditions that employ the Book of Genesis without attributing a design plan to a creator such that we are violating it by gaining some of our knowledge. Perhaps freedom of the will is part of our design plan and is required, for example, to worship the creator. Thus, maybe there is what Plantinga would refer to as a "trade off" between two features of our design plan (WPF, 32–40). Our gaining knowledge would not violate the design plan since we would be designed so as to make it possible that we can gain such knowledge even if our creator desires that we not do so because without that ability (free will) we could not properly worship our creator.

But whether that story is better hermeneutics or not doesn't matter. What matters is that the story I am telling is a possible story and that's enough to show that proper functioning is not a necessary condition of knowledge. My story shows that we can pull apart our having knowledge from the intentions of our maker—if there were one. Were our maker to intend that we remain ignorant and design us with that plan in mind, we could rebel and gain knowledge. In other words, I think the root notion of proper function is such that we *can* gain knowledge, even though doing so would not be to function properly.

Plantinga considers a case in some ways similar to the ones we have been discussing. Call it the Rock and Radio Case. He imagines a radio that, as luck would have it, functions better than it was intended to function because a small rock hits it and its fidelity is improved. Here is what he says about that case.

> Perhaps what we must say here is this: in the paradigm or central cases, a properly functioning device does what it was designed to do and does it the way it was designed to do it; there will be analogical extensions of the term to the sorts of cases where it does was it was designed to do but by some fortuitous circumstance doesn't do it in the way it was designed to do it; *but there are not analogical extensions of the sort of case where it functions in accord with its design plan, but doesn't at all perform the function the designer was aiming at.* (WPF, 28; italics mine)

I agree that there is no analogical extension of "proper function" such that an artifact is functioning properly but is not doing what its designer was aiming at. Indeed, the Pinocchio Case and The Garden of Eden Case depend on that. In those cases knowledge is gained contrary to what "the designer was aiming at."

Now, consider an important variation of the Rock and Radio Case—call it the Radio/Filling Case—in which there was no intention to create something that received radio broadcasts. Suppose a dentist puts some fillings in my teeth. The fillings are designed to restore the functions of my teeth and prevent further cavities. But after the fillings are implanted, I start hearing strange noises: muffled music, unclear voices. I begin to doubt my sanity. But the strange noises are traced to the new fillings that are receiving radio broadcasts. I am not insane. My fillings were certainly not designed to receive such signals. But they do anyway. Now I don't know if that's at all physically possible; but it doesn't matter. My response to such cases is not "They can't be receiving radio transmissions. They weren't designed to do that."

The point is that I can do things, either like hearing radio broadcasts the hearing of which is not part of my design plan or like gaining knowledge of things about which I was designed to remain ignorant. More specifically, even if we were designed by some conscious being, we can do things—including gaining new general cognitive capacities or particular bits of knowledge—that were not in any way part of our design plan. That can happen either by dint of effort or by some accident. We could happen to be struck by lightning which causes some significant rearrangements of our cells which in turn gives us new cognitive capacities. For example, suppose we are able to sense the density of objects after being struck by lightning. We can tell whether one object is more dense than another, although we were not designed to know such things. Surely we would have knowledge in such cases but gaining that knowledge would not have been part of our design plan.

Of course, the same result obtains if "proper function" were given some of the more common naturalistic analyses. For example, suppose that we adopt an account such that we are "functioning properly" (or some part of us is functioning properly) just in case we are doing something which has been evolutionarily beneficial.[23] Lightning could strike and we could gain new capacities and, hence, new knowledge that would not result from our functioning properly. Or suppose that we adopt an account of "functioning properly" such that we are functioning properly (or some part of us is functioning properly) just in case we are doing something that gives us some current advantage over our competitors. Lightning could strike and we could gain new capacities and, hence, new knowledge that might not be useful in our competitions. Perhaps we become so fascinated by what we are learning, we don't see our predators creeping up on us! Such individuals would probably not survive for a long time, but in the interval between their previous ignorance and their demise, they surely gained new knowledge.

This concludes my discussion of Plantinga's account of warrant. I hope to have shown that his account provides us with neither a sufficient nor a necessary condition of warrant.

Part III: The Defeasibility Theory

This is not the place for a full-blown presentation and defense of a correctly formulated defeasibility theory.[24] But I will (a) state the theory in its most general form, (b) distinguish what I call its correct form from another close, but I think, incorrect form—the form that apparently Plantinga thinks is the most plausible version, (c) show how it can account for the valid intuitions that underlie the test case presented in Part I, and (d) point out how it handles the objection to it that is presented by Plantinga that was first developed by Robert Shope.[25]

The General Form of the Defeasibility Theory

Underlying the defeasibility theory is the same intuition that motivates reliabilism and Plantinga's proper functionist account of warrant: Pure internalistic accounts of warrant cannot avoid the Gettier Problem and, whatever warrant is, it must be that feature of knowledge in virtue of which the true belief is not accidentally true, from the cognitive point of view. What distinguishes defeasibility theories from other theories that endorse that general intuition (e.g., causal theories, counterfactual theories à la Nozick, reliabilist information transfer theories like Dretske's, and Plantinga's proper function theory) is that the defeasibility account holds that the notion of an "accidentally" true belief should be explicated in terms of defeating evidence that the potential knower lacks. The general defeasibility theory holds that S is warranted in believing that p just in case S's belief that p is properly grounded and there is no true proposition (counterevidence) such that if it is added to S's beliefs, S would not be justified in believing that p. I use "properly grounded' to include both those types of beliefs that the reliabilist would hold are warranted because the belief states containing them are reliably produced as well as those types of beliefs for which we have adequate evidence. Thus the defeasibility theory can recognize that some beliefs are warranted, in part, because the belief states containing them are reliably produced and that other beliefs are warranted, in part, because they are adequately justified. It is important to note that the defeasibility theory does not entail that S is justified in believing that p in the absence of the defeating proposition; it leaves open the possibility that S might not have adequate reasons for believing that p and p still be warranted.[26] It does, of course, hold that if there is sufficiently strong evidence against p which S cannot "explain away," then p isn't known by S.

Let me point to one immediate advantage of this view over Plantinga's. Since, on his view, nothing, in principle, precludes a belief from being warranted and false, counterexamples like the case of Lucky Ms. Jones can rather easily be formulated. The general recipe for those cases, what I have called the Generalized Gettier Problem, is to locate a false but warranted belief, and by appealing to some version of a warrant transfer principle, transfer the warrant from the false belief to a true belief. (A version of the familiar closure principle will do if it applies to warrant.) The true belief will be warranted, but it will not be knowledge because, from the cognitive point of view, the belief is accidentally true. The defeasibility theory is not vulnerable to that type of potential counterexample since on this account a belief could not be warranted and false. If p were false, ~p would be a true, genuine defeater (see below for a discussion of what makes a defeater genuine), and hence p, if false, could not be warranted.

But there is, nevertheless, a well-known problem with the general defeasibility theory. Let us turn to it.

A Sketch of the The Corrected General Theory

I wrote in the immediately preceding section that the general defeasibility theory holds that S knows that p only if there is no true proposition such that if it is added to S's beliefs, S would not be justified in believing that p. That condition is designed to capture the intuition that a belief is accidentally true from the cognitive point of view if there is defeating evidence such that had we become aware of it at the same time or prior to believing p, we would not be justified in believing that p (if we were "aiming at the truth" to use Plantinga's expression). However, as has been pointed out in many papers, that condition is too strong as it stands because it excludes too many cases. There can be true propositions which ought not to disqualify S's belief as knowledge even though were S to come to believe them, S would not be justified in believing that p.

Consider the Grabit Cases.[27] In the first case, S sees what he takes to be Tom Grabit stealing a book from the library. But, unbeknownst to S, Tom has an identical twin, a kleptomaniac, who was in the library on the day in question. Thus the proposition "Tom has a kleptomaniac identical twin who was in the library on the day in question" is a genuine defeater of S's belief that Tom stole a book because S would not be justified in believing that Tom stole the book if the genuine defeater were added to S's beliefs. So far so good.

Now modify the case, so that S sees and believes exactly what he saw and believed in the previous case, but add that Tom's mother sincerely avows that "Tom has a kleptomaniac identical twin who was in the library on the day in question." Add further that Tom's mother is crazy and, in particular, has delusions about having had twins. There never was a twin of Tom. Unfortunately, the general theory is too strong, for in this case S does know (at least that is the commonly accepted intuition) but there is a proposition, namely, *Tom's mother sincerely avows that "Tom has a kleptomaniac identical twin who was in the library on the day in question,"* which if added to S's beliefs would be such that S is not justified in believing that Tom stole the book.

So, something must be done to weaken the condition. I want to consider a way to weaken it that has been advocated by some philosophers and show that this approach, though initially plausible, is unacceptable because it would, for example, mishandle the first Grabit case and one of the original Gettier cases. Then I want to suggest the appropriate way to handle these cases.

Consider the misleading Grabit Case. It could be pointed out that the defeating effect of the proposition *Tom's mother sincerely avows that "Tom has a kleptomaniac identical twin who was in the library on the day in question"* is removed when it is placed in the total relevant evidence set. Thus, one might require that even though there is a defeater of the proposition in question, if the defeater is itself defeated by further propositions in the total relevant evidence set, the original defeater is misleading. Call this view the "total relevant evidence set" view.[28]

Though such an approach might seem initially plausible, it cannot distinguish between genuine and misleading defeaters. Consider one of the original Gettier cases: S is justified in believing that the person sitting across the room from him has ten coins in his pocket and will get the job. Hence, if some appropriate justification transfer principle is correct, S is justified in believing that the person who will get the job has ten coins in his pocket. As luck would have it, S has arrived at a true existential generalization. However, it is not the person across the room but some other person who will get the job and has ten coins in his pocket. Suppose that person is Harold. The total relevant evidence set view would not exclude this as a case of knowledge since there is a restorer in the total relevant evidence, namely, *Harold has ten coins in his pocket and Harold will get the job*. Indeed, since one of the necessary conditions of knowledge that p is that p is true, there will always be a restorer in the total relevant evidence set, namely p. Thus this approach does not correctly distinguish between misleading and genuine defeaters.

This problem could be handled, however, by the defenders of the total relevant evidence set view. For they might define a genuine defeater as follows: a defeater of p is genuine just in case its defeating effect remains after removing p, anything entailing p, and anything providing a new justification for p from all of the relevant evidence. That suggestion will solve the problem discussed above because "Harold has ten coins in his pocket and Harold will get the job" entails "the person who will get the job has ten coins in his pocket." But the revised position will still sanction too many beliefs as knowledge.

To see that, recall the first, nonmisleading Grabit Case in which S lacked knowledge because Tom did, indeed, have a kleptomaniac identical twin who was in the library on the day in question. The proposition "Tom has a kleptomaniac identical twin who was in the library on the day in question" is the paradigm example of a nonmisleading defeater; but in the context of the total relevant evidence (minus p and anything either entailing p or providing a new justification for p) its defeating effect is itself defeated. For the following proposition is in the total relevant set: "S did not see the identical twin." (That proposition does not entail or provide a new justification for the proposition that Tom stole the book.) Indeed, it is easy to see that there will often be such restoring propositions in the total relevant evidence set since something must explain away the defeating effect of the genuine defeater—because p is true. And that something need not entail p or provide a new justification for p.

So, if the "total relevant evidence" approach to distinguishing genuine and misleading defeaters will not work, what is the right way? I think that the correct way to account for these misleading cases is to distinguish between what I call the initiating defeater and the effective defeater.[29] In the misleading Grabit Case, the proposition "Tom's mother sincerely avows that Tom has a kleptomaniac identical twin" is true and if added to S's beliefs, S would not be justified in believing that Tom stole the book. But it is crucial to note that the reason this proposition is a defeater is simply that it provides S with a good reason to believe that Tom has a kleptomaniac identical twin. After all, his mother says he has such a twin. By way of contrast, if someone who S believes is not in a position to know about Tom's family were to say that Tom had an identical twin, such a claim would not have the same effect on the range of S's justified beliefs. S's belief that Tom stole the book would not be defeated. Put another way, it is only because the true proposition "Tom's mother avows that Tom has a kleptomaniac identical twin" provides S with a reason for thinking that Tom has such a twin, that the original belief is not justified.

What actually does the defeating in this case is the proposition that Tom has a kleptomaniac twin. If that weren't added to S's beliefs, S would still be justified in believing that Tom stole the book. That proposition is what I call the *effective defeater*. The *initiating defeater*, as I wish to call it, is the proposition "Tom's mother avows that he has a kleptomaniac identical twin." It is only because the initiating defeater provides evidence for the effective defeater that S's original belief is not justified once the initiating defeater is added to S's beliefs. Adding the initiating defeater also results in adding the effective defeater to S's beliefs. And, in this case, although the initiating defeater is true, the effective defeater is false. So we can say, roughly, that a defeater is genuine just in case it defeats without depending on a false proposition.[30]

To clarify the distinction between genuine and misleading defeaters, return to the original Grabit Case in which Tom does, indeed, have a kleptomaniac twin. In that case, even though the proposition that "Tom has a kleptomaniac identical twin . . ." does provide some evidence for the claim that the brother stole the book (and that is false), it is not *because* that proposition provides evidence for that claim that the initiating defeater is also an effective defeater. It is enough that there is a kleptomaniac identical twin in the library on the day in question to defeat the justification. In other words, although the initiating defeater might render plausible a false effective defeater, in this case, there is a true effective defeater because the initiating defeater and the effective defeater are the same.

We can put the distinction more precisely and say that a proposition, d, is an *initiating defeater of S's belief that p* and d* is an *effective defeater of S's belief that p* iff d is the first proposition in an inference chain, C, such that the last member of C, d*, is such that when d* is added to S's beliefs, p is not justified. By an "inference chain," I mean a set of propositions such that each member of the set is related to another member of the set by the "is a good reason for" relation.[31] Thus the initiating defeater, say d, is a good reason for some proposition, say d_1, which is a good reason for some proposition, say d_2, and d_2 is a good reason for d_3, and . . . is a good reason for d*. So we can say that an initiating defeater d *is genuine* just in case it is true and there is some inference chain C to an effective defeater d* and there are no false propositions in C.[32]

We can now say that the correct version of the defeasibility theory holds that a belief p is warranted for S just in case p is properly grounded and there is no genuine defeater of S's belief that p.

The Explanation of the Conflicting Intuitions in the Test Case

In the test case, the reliabilists will hold that Mr. Damage has knowledge; the proper functionists will hold that Mr. Damage lacks knowledge. Legitimate intuitions will clash and nothing can be settled by merely appealing to them.

But something can be learned from them. First, we can probe the basis for the conflicting intuitions a bit further and, second, we can develop accounts of warrant which are such that they are sensitive to the varying intuitions in such cases. The "right" account of warrant would be such that where intuitions genuinely clash, people with the diverging intuitions can point to some feature of the account and use it to explain the varying intuitions about such cases. Any account that can explain the varying, legitimate intuitions would gain some credibility over those that cannot account for the varying intuitions.

Neither the reliabilists nor the proper functionists can point to features in their accounts that explain the varying intuitions in the test case. A sufficient condition for knowledge is present according to the reliabilists; a necessary condition of knowledge is absent according to the proper functionists. Neither view can do justice to the contrary intuitions.

We can begin to see how the defeasibility theory can account for the conflicting intuitions in the test case by pointing out that there are many occasions when S's true belief fails to be certifiable as knowledge due to malfunctions in S's cognitive equipment. Consider three cases:

(1) S comes to believe, by looking, that there are two people standing before her. Even were there two people standing before her (one which doesn't visually affect her), if she is suffering from double vision, she does not know that there are two people before her.

(2) S comes to believe, by looking, that there is round tower a great distance away. Even if the tower is round, S doesn't know that it is round.

(3) S comes to believe, by looking, that there is a barn. Even if there is a barn, S does not know that there is a barn if S is in Phony Barn Country.

In each of these cases, I take it that it is clear that S fails to know the relevant proposition and that there are malfunctions of S's cognitive equipment as described by Plantinga. In Case 1, the equipment is damaged. In Case 2, the equipment is not being employed as it was designed to be employed because the tower is too far away. In Case 3, the circumstances in which the equipment is employed are not those in which the equipment typically produces truth. So far, so good for the proper functionist account.

But it is crucial to note that in each of these cases, there is a genuine defeater such that if added to S's beliefs, S would not be justified in continuing to believe the relevant proposition. The genuine defeaters are:

(1) S's double vision is likely to produce inaccurate representations of how many people are standing before S.
(2) The tower that S is looking at is at a distance such that S cannot distinguish, by looking, round from square towers.
(3) S is in Phony Barn Country.

Indeed, typically, whenever S fails to know and the belief was brought about by malfunctioning cognitive equipment, the proposition describing the malfunction is a genuine defeater.[33] It renders plausible a true effective defeater, namely, the process by which S arrived at the belief is not likely to result in true beliefs. So, when the proper function account of warrant *correctly* excludes a belief from those which are known, the defeasibility theory will do so as well, because there is a genuine initiating defeater.

But recall the case of Lucky Ms. Jones. I claimed that Plantinga's account resulted in incorrectly ascribing the knowledge that she owns a well-functioning Ford to Ms. Jones. That is because (1) Jones believes that she owns a well-functioning Ford and (2) it is true that she does and (3) the belief was brought about by properly functioning cognitive equipment. The defeasibility account provides the right answer since "The Ford that Jones was driving this morning is not well functioning" is a genuine initiating defeater. So here is a case in which the proper function theory yields the wrong verdict, but the corrected defeasibility theory gives the right verdict.

Now return to the Brain Damage Case. I claimed that in that case there will be conflicting intuitions about whether S does know that he is brain damaged. On the one hand, the proper functionists will claim that S does not know that he is brain damaged. On the other hand, the reliabilists will hold that Mr. Damage does know that he is brain damaged. How can we explain the conflicting intuitions?

Well, Plantinga's account cannot explain them. It is clear that the belief that he is brain damaged arose from a malfunctioning brain. So if Plantinga's account were correct, there would be no room for conflicting intuitions.

The same holds for the reliabilist account. The particular type of brain damage that afflicts Mr. Damage is such that although not generally reliable, it is reliable with regard to at least one proposition, namely, that S has brain damage. Thus, according to the reliabilist, because a sufficient condition of knowledge is fulfilled in this case, there is no room for conflicting intuitions.

But I take it that there are genuinely conflicting intuitions here. I think the conflicting intuitions can be explained by the corrected defeasibility theory. Within that theory the issue can be put this way: Is the proposition "S's belief that he has brain damage is the result of malfunctioning cognitive equipment" a genuine initiating defeater? Or is it merely a misleading defeater?

I think the answer to those questions depends on whether one thinks that such a proposition is also an effective defeater. Plantinga thinks it is. For he thinks that if I believe that a particular belief of mine is the result of a malfunctioning cognitive equipment, then I am not justified in holding that belief any longer. It doesn't have the proper credentials, so to speak. Hence, the proposition in question is a genuine defeater. Thus, S fails to know that he has brain damage.

On the other hand, the reliabilist will not think it is a genuine initiating defeater because its defeating effect depends on its providing a good reason to believe that the malfunctioning cognitive equipment in this case is likely to produce false beliefs about whether S has brain damage. That, by hypothesis, is false. This particular type of malfunctioning cognitive equipment is not at all likely to produce that false belief.

Thus the corrected version of the defeasibility theory is able to account for the conflicting intuitions. Each side can appeal the defeasibility theory's account of warrant to vindicate their intuitions. For the distinction between genuine and misleading defeaters can account for the conflicting intuitions in this case as well as many of the other rather penumbral cases (to use Plantinga's term, WPF, ix).

To sum up so far: First, we have seen that whenever the proper function theory is clearly correct that S fails to have knowledge because of some sort of malfunction of the cognitive equipment or some abnormality in the environment, the defeasibility theory gets it right, too, because there will be a genuine defeater. Second, there are cases (e.g., the Lucky Ms. Jones Case) in which S fails to have knowledge but the proper function theory incorrectly ascribes knowledge to S whereas the corrected defeasibility theory correctly withholds knowledge. Finally, there are cases in which it is not clear whether S's belief is warranted (the brain damage case, for example) which is such that only the defeasibility theory can account for varying views.[34]

Finally, it is important to see that in the clear cases discussed earlier in which we are not functioning properly but in which we have knowledge—the Pinocchio Case, the Garden of Eden Case, Radio/Filling Case, and the struck-by-lightning cases—the defeasibility theory makes the right judgment call. I do not think that there is a genuine defeater in any of those cases. For example, consider the Garden of Eden Case. It is true that we humans are not "functioning properly," given the intentions of the creators. But that is not a genuine defeater. It defeats only because it renders plausible the proposition that we are not likely to arrive at the truth (because our cognitive equipment is not functioning properly). But, of course, that effective defeater is false.

But *even* in these cases, if someone (say Plantinga) were to hold that defying the creator is likely to lead us into error, then the defeasibility theory gets it right since "we are not functioning properly" would be a genuine defeater because it renders plausible the proposition that we are likely to arrive at false beliefs in this case—and that would be held to be true by, say, Plantinga.

Hence, the defeasibility theory has the resources to explain the varying intuitions in the test case as well as both proper functionist and antiproper functionist intuitions in cases like the Garden of Eden Case.

The Last Objection to Defeasibility Theory

As far as I know, there is only one objection to what I have called the corrected defeasibility theory that has appeared in print which has not been answered. In the Appendix of WCD, Plantinga offers an objection to the defeasibility account. Although it is specifically aimed at John Pollock's account and I have already indicated why I think that specific defeasibility account does not work, the objection which Plantinga presents is sufficiently general that it would, if correct, apply to the account which I endorse. Indeed, a similar objection was developed against my account by Robert Shope. Here is what Plantinga says after expounding Pollock's view:

> I mention a small problem—one that probably requires no more than a little more Chisholming. Suppose P is a proposition that happens, (unbeknownst to me) to be true: Can I know (on this account) that I do not believe that P? (WCD, 220)

A striking similar counterexample was developed by Shope. But he took it to be much more significant than something solvable with a bit of Chisholming. Here is what he says:[35]

Suppose that S refrains from believing that r and knows that he does. Thus, S knows that S does not believe that r. But, if r is true, then if r were added to what S believes, S would no longer be justified in believing that S does not believe that r.

In other words, if this counterexample were correct, r would be what I called a genuine defeater and it would prevent S from knowing that he does not believe that r. Does this present a problem for the corrected defeasibility theory? I think the answer is clearly "no."

Presumably, when S believes that S does not believe that r, S believes that of himself at a particular time (or for all times—the result is the same). The time when S believes that of himself could be earlier, later, or the same time that S does not believe that r. Thus, there are implicit time parameters in the propositions. Adding those time parameters, we get: At t_j S knows that S does not believe r at t_i. If the times are different, that is, if S believes of himself that he didn't believe r at some earlier time or that he will not believe r at some later time, adding r to S's beliefs at t_j will not provide any grounds for defeating S's knowledge.

But let t_i be the same as t_j and things might look a bit different. But even this case presents no difficulties for the corrected defeasibility theory. Would adding r to S's beliefs at t_j defeat the justification of the belief that S doesn't believe that r at t_j? First, let me point out that r, alone, does not defeat S's justification for the proposition that S does not believe that r. Indeed, r, alone, provides no evidence against the proposition that S does not believe that r. There is no inference chain, however weak one makes the evidential links, from r to S believes that r. And even if, contrary to fact, there were such a chain, r would be the initiating defeater and "S believes that r" would be the effective defeater. But since "S believes that r" is false (remember this is a case in which S knows that he does not believe that r), r would be a misleading defeater according to what I have called the "corrected" version of the defeasibility theory. Hence, S's justification, if defeated at all, is defeated by a misleading defeater. In other words, S's knowledge, and hence the corrected defeasibility theory, is not threatened by this case.[36]

Conclusion

I hope that I have shown that warrant cannot be understood in terms of proper function. There are cases (e.g., Lucky Ms. Jones) in which a belief is accidentally true, from the cognitive point of view, but nevertheless it results from properly functioning cognitive equipment in an appropriate environment; and there are cases (e.g., the Radio/ Filling Case and the Garden of Eden Case) in which a belief is true and not accidentally so, from the cognitive point of view, but nevertheless it does not result from properly functioning cognitive equipment. In short, proper function is neither a sufficient nor a necessary condition of knowledge.

I have also given some reasons for thinking that the defeasibility theory is preferable to both the proper functionist account and the reliabilist account of warrant. The defeasibility theory gives the right verdict in some cases in which the proper function theory gives the wrong verdict and only the defeasibility theory can account for varying intuitions in some cases (e.g., the Test Case of Mr. Damage) which elude such treatment by the proper functionist or reliabilist accounts. Finally, there is a satisfactory response to the only hitherto unanswered objection to the defeasibility theory.

Notes

1. Throughout I refer to Alvin Plantinga's two books, *Warrant: The Current Debate* and *Warrant and Proper Function*, (New York: Oxford University Press, 1993), abbreviated "WCD" and "WPF."

2. Edmund Gettier, "Is Justified True Belief Knowledge?" *Analysis*, 23 (1963), 121–23. Plantinga's discussion of the Gettier cases includes, among other things, the claim that the moral to be drawn from them is that a purely internalist account of warrant is bound to fail. He is right. I discuss that later in this paper. See WPF, pp. 33ff.

3. Emphasizing the nonaccidentality of true beliefs in the explication of knowledge is not original with me. I first discussed this in "A Proposed Definition of Propositional Knowledge," *Journal of Philosophy*, 67 (1971), 471–82. For other explicit treatments see Peter Unger, "An Analysis of Factual Knowledge", *Journal of Philosophy*, 65 (1968), 147–70; and Ernest Sosa, "Propositional Knowledge," *Philosophical Studies*, 20 (1969), 33–43; and Ernest Sosa "How Do You Know?" *American Philosophical Quarterly*, 11 (1974), 113–22. Although Sosa and I would not give the same account of all of the cases he discusses, his *APQ* paper addresses many of the same issues discussed in this paper.

4. There are passages in Plato that suggest the nonaccidentality of true beliefs has a much longer tradition. See *Meno*, 97–98, and *Theaetetus*, 210B.

5. This passage comes from Meditation 4 in *The Philosophical Works of*

Descartes, eds. Elizabeth S. Haldane and G. R. T. Ross (Cambridge: Cambridge University Press, 1911; reprint New York: Dover, 1955), Vol. I, p. 176.

6. The passage is from *An Essay Concerning Human Understanding*, ed. A. C. Fraser (New York: Dover, 1959), IV, xvii, 24, pp. 413–14.

7. Epistemologists have been known to change their minds about the appropriate answer to that question.

8. See especially Chapters 11 and 12 in WPF.

9. By "strict reliabilist accounts" I mean to be referring to those reliabilists who do not include a justification condition in the analysis of knowledge.

10. I think this case is first mentioned by Sosa, "Propositional Knowledge," op. cit., esp. p. 39. Plantinga discusses it in WCD (195) and WPF (29). In Sosa's original case, the brain damage causes hypochondria which in turn causes S to believe that he has brain damage. Intuitions will vary in this case as well. But the distinction between misleading and genuine defeaters discussed later is sufficient to account for the varying intuitions. Specifically, does the proposition "Mr. Damage's belief that he has brain damage arose from malfunctioning cognitive equipment" defeat only because it renders plausible the false proposition "Mr. Damage's belief that he has brain damage is not reliably produced from the cognitive point of view"? If so, then it is a misleading defeater—and Mr. Damage has knowledge as the reliabilists would say. If not, then it is a genuine defeater—and Mr. Damage does not have knowledge as the proper functionists would say. That will become clear, I hope, after the introduction in Part III of the distinction between genuine and misleading defeaters.

11. L. S. Carrier reacts to this case in the way I think a reliabilist should. See his "An Analysis of Empirical Knowledge," *Southern Journal of Philosophy*, 9 (1971), 3–11. Unger, op. cit., discusses some similar cases and gives the analysis I think a reliabilist should give.

12. Plantinga employs the Brain Damage case explicitly against Fred Dretske's reliabilism (WCD, 195–97). Dretske has not written about this particular case, but in my correspondence with him he has agreed that if the case of Mr. Damage were presented in a way that made clear (1) that Mr. Damage possessed the information that he has brain damage of a specific sort and (2) that the originating cause of his possessing that information is his brain damage of that sort, then, ceteris paribus, Mr. Damage has knowledge that he has brain damage of that sort. I chose to present the test case without using Dretske's technical notion of "information" so that I could underscore the distinction between reliabilism, in general, and Plantinga's account of proper function. But, by following the constraints just mentioned, the case could be presented in a way that accords with Dretske's particular form of reliabilism. See Fred Dretske, *Knowledge and the Flow of Information* (Cambridge: MIT Press, 1981).

13. Peter Unger, op. cit.

14. I should point out that Plantinga's use of "defeater" is not the same as

mine. Defeaters for Plantinga include beliefs that S possesses which override an otherwise warranted belief. I use "defeaters" to refer to propositions that are not part of S's beliefs.

15. Plantinga sometimes adds that the belief must be held with sufficient conviction for it to be counted as warranted. See WPF, p. 194 and p. 19, for example, where he says that the more firmly S believes a proposition that is the result of properly functioning cognitive equipment, the more warrant p has for S. For our purposes we can ignore that. It doesn't play a major role in his account. And that is a good thing, too, since if warrant does come in degrees, there seem to be many cases where the degree of warrant is very high, but S does not have a very firm conviction, if only out of sheer epistemic timidity.

16. The hypothetical, that *if* warrant is transferable, then warrant entails truth emerges from an examination of "Warrant Entails Truth" by Trenton Merricks in *Philosophy and Phenomenological Research*, 55 (1995), 841–855, and a reply to it by Sharon Ryan in *PPR*, 56 (1996), 183–92.

Merricks argues that warrant must entail truth because if it didn't, what I have called the Generalized Gettier Problem would be unavoidable. For suppose that a belief p can be false and warranted. Transfer the warrant (via a valid warrant transfer principle) to a true belief q. Thus, q is true, warranted, and believed. But given that warrant is whatever has to be added to true belief to yield knowledge, this generalized Gettier argument would require that warrant entail truth, since q would be accidentally true from the cognitive point of view.

But Ryan has pointed out that there are accounts of warrant which would block an unrestricted use of a warrant transfer principle. In particular, as she argues, some accounts of warrant would block the transfer of warrant from a false belief to a true belief because the true belief would be accidentally true and, as I have been urging here, a warranted belief must be non-accidentally true.

Nevertheless, I think whether warrant entails truth remains unclear. What is clear is that *if* warrant is transferable under certain knowledge-preserving inferences (implication, for example), then warranted beliefs must be true. Further, since "warrant" is a term of art and not some sophisticated counterpart of "justification," we cannot appeal to a well-formed set of intuitions about what constitutes warrant. Put another way, we are relatively free to characterize warrant in whatever way we think works best to fill the gap between true belief and knowledge. And I think there is a good reason for holding that warrant is transferable under knowledge-preserving inferences because otherwise it will be difficult (but not impossible) to explain why knowledge is closed under such inferences.

It is worth noting at this point that the defeasibility theory has the result that a warranted belief, say p, is true, since if it were false, ~p would be a true, nonmisleading defeater of p. (See my paper "A Proposed Definition of Propositional Knowledge," *Journal of Philosophy*, 68 (1971), 471–82, and the main text below.) Misleading defeaters are discussed in the main text. Thus, the defeasibility theory has the advantage of not forcing one to deny the validity of all warrant transfer principles. That seems highly desirable to me since if a theory can accommodate at least some warrant transfer principles, there are fewer possible reasons for rejecting the theory.

17. I want to thank Jonathan Kvanvig for his help with the points under discussion here. Indeed, he gave me very valuable comments on many points in this paper.

18. See Michael Clark, "Knowledge and Grounds: A Comment on Mr. Gettier's Paper," *Analysis*, 24 (1963), 46–48.

19. See Robert Shope, *The Analysis of Knowledge* (Princeton: Princeton University Press, 1983) for a full treatment of the Gettier problem and various attempts to resolve it.

20. I think Keith Lehrer was the first to point this out. See his *Knowledge* (Oxford: Oxford University Press, 1974), pp. 20–21. Shope, op. cit., discusses this case and others, see especially pp. 22–25.

21. See note 16 for a further discussion of this point.

22. I have an acquaintance whose hobby is collecting old tools. In some cases, their proper function cannot easily be determined by inspecting them. The best way of discovering their proper function is to find old newspaper tool advertisements or old tool catalogs that contain pictures or descriptions of the tools along with accounts of their intended uses.

23. Plantinga considers and rejects such nontheistic, naturalistic accounts of proper function. See his Chapter 11, WPF.

24. See my book, *Certainty: A Refutation of Scepticism* (Minnesota: University of Minnesota Press, 1981) for such a full-blown account, especially pp. 137–66. Note, however, a modification of that account mentioned in note 26.

25. See Shope, op. cit., pp. 52, 71, 201. This criticism was first developed by him in "The Conditional Fallacy in Contemporary Philosophy", *Journal of Philosophy*, 75 (1978), 397–413.

26. Thus, I think there is an accommodation that should be made in the face of persistent reliabilist intuitions. But even if we grant that some propositions are known without adequate evidence that provides a justification of the proposition, it does not follow that evidence cannot be employed to defeat those propositions. Thus the telepathist would have knowledge because his or her beliefs are reliability produced and there is no defeating evidence for the beliefs. This can also help to account for the "deviant" causal chain problem (and thus the generality problem) encountered by reliabilism. For example, Goldman's Phony Barn case [Alvin Goldman, "Discrimination and Perceptual Knowledge," *Journal of Philosophy*, 73 (1976), 771–91] and some versions of the Grabit cases (discussed later in the main text) show that there is defeating evidence even in those cases in which the causal chains which bring about a belief are those which, typically, bring about beliefs which are not accidentally true. In those cases, S sees a real barn or S sees Tom Grabit stealing a book,

but because there is relevant defeating evidence (S is in Phony Barn Country or Tom has a kleptomaniac, identical twin who was in the library) unknown by S, it is a felicitous coincidence, from the cognitive point of view, that S's belief is true. With the caveat soon to be mentioned, very much the same holds for cases in which the belief state containing the proposition in question is reliably caused and not justified.

I should note, just for the record so to speak, that this represents a change in my view. I used to think that a defeasibility theory was forced to maintain that knowledge entails justification because central to its account of nonaccidentally true beliefs was the claim that S knows that p only if there is no proposition that defeats S's justification for p. (See *Certainty*, op.cit.) But that is not required by the central intuition motivating the defeasibility theory and it seems to preclude making any accommodations to the reliabilist's intuitions. All that is *required* is merely that there is no evidence that if added to S's beliefs would make it such that S is not "close enough" to being justified in believing that p. It does not follow that p is justified for S prior to adding the defeater to S's beliefs. So an important accommodation can be made to reliabilism.

But, to use Plantinga's term (cited later in the text), a bit of "Chisholming" is needed here. For suppose that a proposition is reliably produced and not justified (as in the telepathist case). That is, S's evidence is such that it is not adequate to justify p. Any true and irrelevant proposition, say d, would be such that if added to S's evidence for p, p would not be justified. That is so, because p isn't justified before adding d. Thus no genuine accommodation to reliabilism has been made, since S would not know that p if p were not justified. Put another way, any proposition that is not justified would automatically be defeated.

I think the best way to handle this problem is to recall that there are three possible justificatory situations relative to any given proposition, say p. S can be justified in believing that p, S can be neither justified in believing p nor justified in denying p, and S can be justified in denying p. Those various conditions can be located along a continuum corresponding to the evidence S has for and against p. Now, if S's belief state that contains p is reliably caused and p is not justified for S, presumably if the denial of p is justified, then S doesn't know that p. (Accommodation to reliabilism, yes; but I'm not willing to completely surrender!) So the issue becomes this: How are we going to characterize defeaters (whether misleading or not) when p is grounded for S because the belief state containing it is reliably produced and S is neither justified in believing that p nor justified in denying p? I think the accommodation can be made by saying that if p is grounded and neither it nor its denial is justified, then there is no defeater when there is no true proposition which if added to S's beliefs is such that it moves p "too far" from being justified.

I don't think there is a precise way to characterize that distance. Of course, if it moves p's status all the way to its denial being justified, then clearly it is accidental, from a cognitive point of view, that S's belief is true. But more precision isn't desirable. It is not desirable, since "how far from being justified" the defeater must move p's justificatory status in order for it to be accidental that S's belief is true, is inherently vague. Adding precision would distort the subject under analysis.

For ease of presentation, the complication required in the account of defeaters in order to accommodate but not surrender to reliabilism will be ignored in the main text. So whenever I write "There is no defeater d such that adding d to S's beliefs is such that p is not justified," that should be understood as shorthand for "There is no defeater d such that either (1) if p is justified for S, adding d to S's beliefs is such that p is not justified, or (2) if p is not justified for S and the belief state containing p is reliably produced, then adding d to S's beliefs moves p's justificatory status too far from p's being justified." Of course, as we will see, the defeater must be a genuine one as well.

27. I think these cases were first introduced by Keith Lehrer and Thomas Paxson in "Knowledge: Undefeated Justified True Belief," *Journal of Philosophy*, 66 (1969), 225–37. There is a full discussion of them in Shope, op. cit., esp. 45–51.

28. John Pollock develops this view in his book, *Contemporary Theories of Knowledge* (Totowa, N.J.: Rowman and Littlefield, 1986), especially pp. 188ff. Plantinga cites Pollock's defeasibility account rather approvingly in WCD, pp. 218–21. The only objection Plantinga considers is the one that I will discuss near the end of Part III. I believe the total relevant evidence account of misleading defeaters was first developed by John Barker in "What You Don't Know Won't Hurt You?" *American Philosophical Quarterly*, 13 (1976), 303–8. I give substantially the same criticisms of that account mentioned here in "Misleading Evidence and the Restoration of Justification," *Philosophical Studies*, 37 (1980), 81–89.

29. I discuss the distinction between initiating and effective defeaters in some detail in *Certainty*, op. cit., especially pp. 146–56. This is not the place to rehearse all of the various caveats required to state the view clearly. Here I am just interested in the general form of the distinction in order to show how it can be employed to account for the most clear cases and how it can account for those cases in which there are varying intuitions, as I believe there are in the Brain Damage Test Case discussed earlier.

30. This account of the distinction between misleading and genuine defeaters was criticized by Steven R. Levy in "Misleading Defeaters," *Journal of Philosophy*, 75 (1978), 739–42. I replied to it in "Misleading 'Misleading Defeaters'," *Journal of Philosophy*, 76 (1979), 382–86.

31. Note that "is a good reason for" is not transitive. If it were, every true initiating defeater would also be a true effective defeater. Thus there would be no viable distinction between genuine and misleading initiating defeaters. To see that it is not transitive, consider this case: Suppose I have a good reason, r_1, for thinking f, that some object before me is fool's gold. The proposition f

is a good reason for thinking r_2 that the object in front of me looks just like gold. And r_2 is a good reason for thinking g, that some object before me is gold. Letting "R" stand for "is a good reason for" then you have r_1Rf and fRr_2 and r_2Rg; but r_1 is not a good reason for g.

32. There are some further complications that would need to be introduced regarding the ways in which members of the chain C can combine with S's beliefs to produce an effective defeater, but they are not relevant here and the discussion of them would take us too far afield. See *Certainty*, op. cit., especially pp. 143–48.

33. I should point out that some of these genuine defeaters do confirm or render plausible false propositions which are effective defeaters. But that does not make them misleading initiating defeaters. They also defeat on their own; it is not necessary to go through a false proposition in order to arrive at an effective defeater. For example, in the double vision case, it is rendered probable by the initiating defeater (S's double vision is likely to produce inaccurate representations of how many people are standing before S) that there are not two similar objects before S. But the initiating defeater defeats on its own without going through that proposition. In parallel fashion, as I have already argued, in the genuine Grabit Case, the initiating defeater "Tom has a kleptomaniac identical twin who was in the library on the day in question" renders plausible the false proposition that S saw the identical twin (rather than Tom). But there is an evidence chain that terminates in an effective defeater which does not contain a false proposition, namely the chain in which the initiating defeater (Tom has a . . .) and the effective defeater are the same proposition.

34. I have discussed other penumbral cases elsewhere. Specifically, contrast my discussion of the Harman Civil Rights Worker Case (*Certainty*, op. cit., 158) with Plantinga's account (WPF, 34).

35. This is given in Shope, op. cit., pp. 52, 71, 201.

36. What Shope and Plantinga might have in mind it this: If r were added to S's beliefs, then S would have the belief state containing r, and then (by introspection) S could tell that S believes that r. So, perhaps the "effect" of adding r to S's beliefs is that S is not justified in believing that S does not believe that r. But to take "S's beliefs" in the sentence "there is no genuine defeater which if added to *S's beliefs* is such that S is no longer justified in believing that S does not believe that r" to refer to S's *belief states* is a mistake. I grant that "S's beliefs" is ambiguous. It can refer to S's belief states or it can refer to the propositional content of those states. In the sentence under scrutiny here, "S's beliefs" refers to the propositional contents of S's belief states. To paraphrase, the sentence means that there is no true proposition which if added to the propositions which S believes is such that it makes p not justified for S. Thus when one "adds r," one adds r to the propositions that S believes; one does not add the belief state containing r to S's other belief states. Put another way, if Shope and Plantinga were to be

asking what would happen if one adds the belief state whose content is r to S's other belief states, then, of course, S would have the belief state whose content is r. But that is not a test of the claim made by the defeasibility theory (in the sentence under scrutiny) because "S's beliefs" refers to the *contents* of S's belief states—not to the states themselves. More importantly, adding the belief state whose content is r to S's belief states at t_j is contrary to the hypothesis under consideration. That hypothesis includes the fact that S does not believe that r—that is, the belief state with r as its content is not among S's belief states at t_j.

7

Warrant Versus Indefeasible Justification

Marshall Swain

According to Alvin Plantinga, *warrant* is some "quantity or quality enough of which, together with truth and belief, is sufficient for knowledge."[1] Since his main concern is to provide an analysis of warrant, this locates his epistemological work squarely within the contemporary discussion of knowledge and justification, much of which is devoted to providing analyses of the concepts in this family. Plantinga's two-volume work on warrant is, however, much more than just another attempt to provide an analysis of knowledge. It is, as well, a rich and varied discussion of a wide variety of epistemological topics. Even so, the connection between warrant and knowledge featured in the opening quotation is never very far from the surface in any part of these volumes. For example, as Plantinga considers the positions that he takes to be competitors of his notion of warrant, the reasons given for rejecting them often rely heavily on intuitions concerning knowledge.[2]

One particularly important role that the "warrant analysis of knowledge" (as I shall call it) plays in Plantinga's work has to do with positions he wants to establish that go well beyond the realm of epistemology. In the larger context, Plantinga is arguing for a theistic worldview, in which we humans have been designed in accordance with a plan (or plans) and in which it makes sense to talk of ourselves as functioning properly in accordance with that plan. His strategy in arguing for this picture includes roughly the following steps. First, knowledge is preanalytically characterized as warranted true belief (as in the opening quotation above). Second, contemporary theories of justification, whether internalist, externalist, foundationalist, or coherentist, are rejected as being neither necessary nor sufficient for warrant. Third, an account of warrant which does not incorporate the notion of justification is given in terms of properly functioning faculties. Fourth, it is argued that an adequate account of properly functioning faculties ultimately requires a supernaturalistic ontology, since no naturalistic ontology can support an account of proper function. And then, fifth, it is concluded that if one accepts the claim that we have warranted true beliefs (i.e., knowledge), then one should be driven to the conclusion that the supernaturalistic picture is correct. If you don't want to be a skeptic, you'll have to be a theist.

In this discussion, I want to focus on a key step in Plantinga's overall argument, namely, his apparent contention that only his account of warrant in terms of properly functioning faculties can ultimately provide a successful account of knowledge. I shall argue, in the end, that this view is not supportable, since the account of knowledge in terms of warrant is not as good an explanation of our intuitions about knowledge as other views in the epistemic marketplace. In particular, I shall argue, the theory that knowledge is ultimately undefeated justified true belief (the defeasibility theory, hereafter) is superior to Plantinga's version of the warranted true belief view (the warrant theory, hereafter) as an account of knowledge.[3] For one thing, the defeasibility theory does at least as good a job, and in some cases a better one, as the warrant theory in accounting for relevant examples. For another, the defeasibility theory does not commit us, or even threaten to commit us, to the idea that our faculties must function in accordance with some design plan, which is the feature of Plantinga's view of warrant that leads to supernaturalism. Putting these things together, we have an argument in favor of the defeasibility theory as the better overall explanation of our intuitions about knowledge.

Warrant versus Indefeasible Justification

Plantinga's theory of warrant is a species of externalism. There are vestiges of reliabilism in his account, as evidenced in the requirement that a belief is warranted only if it is produced by a properly functioning faculty in a truth-conducive manner. The version of reliabilism that is closest to Plantinga's view is the reliable indicator theory, advanced in various forms by David Armstrong, William Alston, and me.[4] The official analysis of warrant may be summarized in the following way: S's belief B is warranted if and only if:

(1) B is produced in S by a properly functioning cognitive faculty; alternatively, B is produced in S by a cognitive faculty which is functioning in accordance with its design plan;

(2) B is produced in a cognitive environment that is fitting for this kind of cognitive faculty; that is, the environment must be the one, or very similar to the one, for which it is designed to function in the way in which it is functioning;

(3) The segment, or module, of the design plan governing the production of B is aimed at the production of true beliefs (rather than at survival, pleasure, or some other goal);

(4) The segment of the design plan governing production of B must be well designed, or truth-conducive; alternatively, there must be a high objective (statistical) probability that beliefs produced by this faculty in such an environment will be true.[5]

Throughout most of his discussion, Plantinga is officially neutral concerning the intertwined notions of a design plan and proper function. Neutral, that is, between a naturalistic account of the notion of function and a supernaturalistic account. The required design plan could, he is initially willing to allow, be produced either by the forces of evolution or by an intentioned designer. This neutrality comes to an abrupt end in the final chapters of *Warrant and Proper Function*, when (as noted above) Plantinga provides arguments against naturalism and in favor of supernaturalism.

One especially important thing to note about this account of warrant is that justification plays no role in warrant. Knowledge is true belief which is warranted in the above sense; whether such a belief is justified or not is, so far as I can tell, irrelevant to whether it is an example either of knowledge or of justified belief. This is, of course, in sharp contrast with the more traditional contemporary discussions of knowledge, in which it is assumed that justification of a belief is a necessary condition of its being a case of knowledge. But, this should come as no surprise, given that Plantinga devotes a major portion of *Warrant: The Current Debate* to arguing against any strong connections ("necessary for," "sufficient for") between warrant and justification. As I will argue later, this feature of the notion of warrant, and the associated account of knowledge, leads to some serious problems.

By contrast, the notion of indefeasible justification is very much a part of the traditional approach to the analysis of knowledge. Based on an analogy with the legal and ethical concept of a defeasible obligation, epistemic defeasibility was introduced into epistemology as an ingredient in one of the main strategies for dealing with Gettier cases. In these cases, an individual's justified true belief fails to count as knowledge because the justification is defective as a source of knowledge. According to the defeasibility theory, the defect involved can be characterized in terms of evidence that the subject does not possess which overrides, or defeats, the subject's prima facie justification for belief. This account holds that knowledge is indefeasibly justified true belief. It has significant advantages over other attempts to modify the traditional analysis of knowledge in response to the Gettier (and other) examples.

Care must be taken, however, in the definition of defeasibility. The most successful versions of this theory are careful to note that the defeating effect of unpossessed evidence on a justification is sometimes merely misleading, and is itself subject to defeat. These versions endeavor to provide an account of knowledge in terms of "ultimately undefeated" justification or in terms of justifications undefeated by merely misleading evidence.[6]

It is important to note that the indefeasibility strategy is not essentially linked with any particular account of epistemic justification. One can be an internalist, or an externalist, with respect to the nature of justification and still hold that knowledge is indefeasibly justified true belief. Similarly, one can be a foundationalist or a coherentist. Virtually all of the theories of justification considered and rejected by Plantinga as neither necessary nor sufficient for warrant could, with appropriate modifications, provide the analysis of justification required for the defeasibility account of knowledge.

For the sake of argument in this paper, I am going to assume (what I believe to be true in any case) that some version of the defeasibility account of knowledge is superior to any other "traditional" (i.e., justification-based) account. This assumption is not strictly necessary. If some other justification-based account should turn out to have the advantage, then, I believe, the points that I want to make about the adequacy of the warrant theory can probably be recast in the framework of that account. My goal here is not so much to defend the defeasibility theory (I've done that elsewhere), but rather to show that Plantinga's warrant theory is not the best, or even the best kind of account of knowledge available to us. Since it isn't, we need not be stuck with any of its (purported) metaphysical consequences.

Some Critical Cases

One of the things that a proposed analysis of knowledge must do is yield an acceptable set of results in preanalytically clear cases of knowledge (or, lack of it). Given the enormous amount of attention paid to this problem over the past few decades, there is no shortage of examples available for the purpose of testing an account of knowledge. The defeasibility theory has, of course, already been pretty well tested. But, the warrant theory has not. In this section, I shall compare the two accounts with respect to a relatively small set of examples, chosen because they represent, in my view, the primary kinds of scenarios that tend to be critical in the evaluation of accounts of knowledge.

The Gettier Cases

I shall begin with the well-known Gettier cases[7] since, at a minimum, any account of knowledge worth its salt will have to give a clear account of how it is that the subjects in such cases fail to have knowledge, even though they have justified true belief. Moreover, it is clear from Plantinga's discussion that he considers the Gettier cases to be of critical importance in his defense of the theory of warrant. He says, for example, that contemporary work on justification, particularly the internalist theories, is best viewed as an attempt to provide an account of warrant (where warrant is characterized as in the opening quote of this paper). He says, more specifically, "Internalism in epistemology goes hand in hand with the idea that warrant is really *justification*. More exactly, what it goes with is the idea that justification is necessary and *nearly* sufficient for it [i.e., warrant]; what is required in addition is only a fillip to mollify Gettier" (WPF, v–vi). In his rejection of various accounts of justification, both internalist and externalist, Plantinga typically argues that they are not nearly sufficient for warrant, with the implied assumption that they would fail to be so even with "a fillip to mollify Gettier." By contrast, his own account of warrant, unlike any of the rejected theories of justification, easily handles the Gettier examples with no additional "fillips" required.

This characterization of justification theories is both inaccurate and misleading. I know of very few justification theorists who would agree with it. Although it is generally assumed that justification is a necessary condition for knowledge, it is not generally assumed that it is "nearly" sufficient for it. Indeed, it is precisely the Gettier examples that originally caused justification theorists to see that there is a significant gap between justified true belief and knowledge, hardly the sort of gap that can be filled with a mere fillip. Instead, I believe, most justification theorists would argue that only a major addition to an account of justification (or, replacement of it, as in some externalist theories) can be sufficient to provide an account of what Plantinga calls "warrant." The defeasibility theory, as characterized above, is among the chief examples of an attempt to provide such a concept.

Gettier cases have a familiar structure. An individual has a justification for some true belief that h, but this justified true belief is not knowledge because the justification is defective in a particular way. In all such cases, the individual has arrived at the justified true belief by reasoning which depends on an essential intermediate premise which, though justified, is false. Were the falsity of this essential intermediate premise brought forth as additional evidence, the resulting conjunction of this evidence with the individual's initial evidence would no longer justify the proposition h. For the defeasibility theorist, the situation is characterized by saying that the justification the individual has (in a Gettier case) is ultimately defeasible, and this is taken to explain why the individual does not have knowledge.

This will be illustrated by considering a specific example, introduced by Keith Lehrer.[8] Suppose Smith correctly infers h that someone in his class owns a Ford from some true evidence e that justifies the false belief q that a student, Mr. Nogot, owns a Ford. It so happens that another student in Smith's class, Mr. Havit, does own a Ford, but Smith has no evidence one way or the other for this proposition. Smith's justification for h, which consists of e and his inference to h through the false but justified proposition q that Mr. Nogot owns a Ford, is nevertheless rendered defeasible by the true proposition e', which asserts that "Nogot does not own a Ford." Because Smith's justification is defeasible, he does not know that someone in his class owns a Ford. All Gettier cases have essentially the same structure as this one, and so the defeasibility account provides a general solution to the problem posed for the traditional analysis of knowledge by such cases.

Plantinga's account of warrant also provides a general solution to such cases. In these examples, as Plantinga points out, "it is merely *by accident* that the justified true belief in question is true" (WPF, 33). In the case described above, it is merely by accident that someone in Smith's class other than Nogot owns a Ford, at least relative to the evidence that Smith has. But, of course, we want to know what is meant by saying that such things are true "merely by accident," and Plantinga's account gives an intuitively satisfying answer:

> The basic idea is simple enough: a true belief is formed in these cases, all right, but not as a result of the proper function of the cognitive modules governed by the relevant parts of the design plan. The faculties involved are functioning properly, but there is still no warrant; and the reason has to do with the local cognitive environment in which the belief is formed. . . . Our design plan leads us to believe what we are told by others. . . . But it does not work well when our fellows lie to us or deceive us in some other manner, as in the case of [Nogot], who lies about the Ford. . . . (WPF, 33–34)

The true beliefs arrived at in most Gettier-style examples fail to be warranted, and hence fail to count as knowledge, because the environment in which the individual is functioning is a hostile one, cognitively speaking. In the example at hand, the environment is not the sort in which accepting what others tell us is a reliable way of getting at the truth. That we do manage to get at the truth in such a case is accidental:

> Credulity is designed to operate in the presence of a certain condition: that of our fellows knowing the truth and being both willing and able to communicate it. In the absence of that condition, if it produces a true belief, it is just by accident, by virtue of a piece of epistemic good luck: in which case the belief in question has little or nothing by way of warrant. (WPF, 34–35)

Since most Gettier-style cases have this feature, namely, that the subject has arrived at a true belief in an environment in which his or her faculties cannot function reliably, the warrant theory provides a general solution to the Gettier problem.

It would appear, then, that the defeasibility and warrant theories provide roughly equivalent results in the infamous Gettier examples. Moreover, they focus on similar features of such examples in providing a solution. For the defeasibility theorist, the source of defeating counterevidence in Gettier cases is the fact that the environment is unexpectedly abnormal with respect to the evidence and the proposition believed. The defeaters, in such cases, describe these abnormalities: "Nogot does not own a Ford," "Nogot is lying about the Ford," etc. And, it is these same environmental abnormalities that render the subject's belief unwarranted, as explained in the above quotes from

Plantinga. These two accounts are explanatorily very similar, at least in Gettier cases.

There are, however, other examples in which the two accounts do not seem (to me, at least) to be equally plausible as explanations of the failure of a subject to have knowledge, and it is here where I find the defeasibility theory to have a clear advantage. I shall turn now to a consideration of several such examples.

Goldman's Discrimination Cases

Another class of counterexamples to the justified true belief account of knowledge is at least as well known in the literature as the Gettier examples, but in these cases the problem presented has a somewhat different structure. I have in mind some examples raised by Alvin Goldman in his paper "Discrimination and Perceptual Knowledge."9 In one of these, a subject, Henry, is imagined to be driving through the countryside, observing familiar objects, such as barns. He perceives a barn at a particular location, comes to believe that it is a barn on the basis of so perceiving it, and is correct about what he sees. So, given his background evidence about barns, it would seem that he knows there is a barn at that location. However, unknown to Henry, there are also present in the neighborhood a number of barn facsimiles, consisting of barn façades propped up by sticks from behind. To a casual passerby, these facsimiles look just like barns and would be taken for barns. All else being equal, the ordinary passerby would not be able to *discriminate* the façades from real barns. It seems generally agreed that the subject, in these circumstances, does not have knowledge.

Just as in Gettier cases, there is an element of accidentality involved in these discrimination cases. The subject could just as easily have seen a barn façade as a real barn, and would have believed it to be a barn either way. The primary difference between these cases and the original Gettier cases lies in the fact that the subject does not, in the discrimination examples, reason through any false lemmas, nor are any false propositions essential to his being justified. Otherwise, they create much the same kind of problem for the traditional analysis as do the Gettier examples.

The defeasibility analysis provides a fairly straightforward explanation of why the subject does not have knowledge in these examples. The subject's justification is defeated by unpossessed evidence about the presence of barn façades. Perhaps an example of a genuine defeater would be the proposition "there are present in this area a number of barn façades that look just like barns," or perhaps "some of the items you have been perceiving are barn façades, and not real barns." The subject's justification is ultimately defeated; or, alternatively, there is available some genuinely defeating counterevidence, which is not merely misleading.

How does Plantinga's account hold up? No better than the defeasibility account, and perhaps not as well, it seems to me. In these cases, the subject's faculties of recognition are functioning just as they should, in accordance with their design plan, and have in fact lead to a true belief in pretty much exactly the way they were designed to (all assuming, of course, that they were designed at all). If anything in the account of warrant could be singled out as not satisfied, it would (as in the Gettier examples) have to be the environment. And, indeed, Plantinga includes the barn façade example in the broad class of examples that he calls Gettier cases, indicating that the solution in this kind of case is, for him, essentially the same as in Gettier cases. Here is more of what Plantinga says, couched this time in the broader context of the debate between internalists and externalists:

> in the typical Gettier case, the locus of the cognitive glitch is in the cognitive environment: the latter is in some small way misleading. (WPF, 34)

But, in a larger context,

> in all these Gettier cases, the cognitive glitch has to do with what is *not* accessible to the agent in [the sense required by internalists] . . . there is conformity to the design plan on the part of the *internal* aspects of the cognitive situation, but some feature of the cognitive situation external (in the internalist's sense) to the agent forestalls warrant. (WPF, 36)

For the defeasibility theorist, even those who are externalists, this analysis of the situation is pretty much on target; the justification is defeated by features of the cognitive situation that are external to the agent (in the internalist's sense). But how precisely are these features to be characterized, on Plantinga's view?

In the barn façade example, specifically, how does Plantinga's account get us the right result? The environment, we shall have to say, is not the sort for which our faculties of perception and recognition were designed. It is not optimal, or paradigmatic of the intended environment. In "the case of the fake barns . . . the local cognitive environment deviat[es] in some more or less moderate fashion from the paradigm situations for which the faculty was designed." If this is the right answer, then we should be able to specify what sort of environment is the right one. Is it only an environment in which there is nothing at all present such that the subject might have confused that thing with the thing he actually sees? Presumably that would be too strong, for we would certainly claim to have knowledge in many cases where we might have been misled. If we are perceiving someone who is well known to us, and that person has a twin who is in town but not too close by, then it is possible that we might have perceived the twin instead, and might have confused the one with the other, but this need not prevent us from having knowledge that our friend is present. Shall we then say that the appropriate environment is one that is free from perceptual equivalents that are *close by*, "directly threatening" our belief system? Or is it only the fact that the perceptual equivalents have been purposefully placed in our presence by someone who is trying to deceive us that makes the environment inappropriate for warrant production?

For Plantinga, the answers to such questions will ultimately depend on a more precise characterization of the notion of an optimal design plan. This complicates the attempt to find the answers, because we are no longer relying solely on intuitions about knowledge. I, for one, have no very clear intuitions about optimal, or paradigmatic, environments or design plans, and I suspect that I am not alone in this deprived state. Because of this, I find Plantinga's theory to be too vague to be of service in dealing with the discrimination examples.

But in fairness, it must be noted that the defeasibility theory also needs to answer hard questions about the differences among the various scenarios suggested above. In which of these is the potentially undermining counterevidence genuinely defeating, and which not? This is the problem of relevant alternatives, and is one of the chief difficulties for the defeasibility theory. But, at least, in attempting to answer these questions, the defeasibility theorist needs deal only with intuitions about knowledge. I take this to be a slight, but not decisive, advantage.

I conclude that, in the discrimination cases, the defeasibility theory provides at least as good an explanation of the epistemological facts as does Plantinga's warrant theory, and perhaps better. I move now to yet another kind of example, in which I find the defeasibility theory to have an even clearer advantage.

Merely Misleading Defeaters

There is another well-known class of examples, which superficially appear to mimic the Gettier and discrimination cases, but in which, unlike those cases, the subject does have knowledge. Perhaps the best-known representative of this class is the Grabit example, originally introduced by Keith Lehrer and Thomas Paxson.[10]

> Suppose [Smith sees] a man walk into the library and remove a book from the library by concealing it beneath his coat. Since [Smith is] sure that the man is Tom Grabit . . . [he] reports that [he] knows that Tom Grabit has removed the book. However, suppose further that Mrs. Grabit, the mother of Tom, has averred that on the day in question Tom was not in the library, indeed, was thousands of miles away, and that Tom's identical twin brother, John, was in the library. Imagine, moreover, that [Smith] is entirely ignorant of the fact that Mrs. Grabit has said these things. The statement that Mrs. Grabit has said these things would defeat any justification [Smith has] for believing that Tom Grabit removed the book . . . until we finish the story by adding that Mrs. Grabit is a compulsive and pathological liar, that John Grabit is a fiction of her demented mind, and that Tom Grabit took the book. . . . (p. 150)

In this example, it is generally agreed, Smith does have knowledge that Tom stole the book, even though there is available to him some potentially undermining counterevidence. On the defeasibility account, such examples are handled in one of two basic ways. On one version, it is argued that the potentially defeating counterevidence ("Tom's mother says . . . ") is merely misleading, and hence is not genuinely defeating. For a justification to be defeated, on this version, there must be available some undermining evidence which is not merely misleading. On the other version, it is argued that the potentially defeating effect of the (misleading) counterevidence is itself defeated by further relevant evidence, namely, that Tom's mother is insane. To guard against such cases, according to this version, we must require that a genuine defeater be one that is ultimately undefeated by further evidence. I do not want to argue the merits of one of these versions of the defeasibility theory over the other in this paper. Rather, I want to note that, on either version, Smith's justification for believing that Tom stole the book remains undefeated, because either (a) the only potential defeaters are merely misleading or (b) they are ultimately defeated. On the defeasibility account, then, we get a clear explanation of this kind of example.

The same cannot be said for Plantinga's view, in my opinion, for it does not seem that the warrant theory has any obvious way of accounting for misleading defeaters in an environment. Presumably, Plantinga will want to say that the subject, Smith, has belief-forming faculties that are functioning properly. Smith comes to be believe in a perfectly nonproblematic way (on the basis of seeing him, being acquainted with him, etc.) that Tom stole the book. But what about the environment in which he forms this belief? Is it the sort of environment in which such a faculty is designed to function? Even more than in the discrimination cases, I find it very difficult to answer this question in the case at hand. Let us suppose that the faculty in question is roughly characterized as the one that is operating when we come to believe that we recognize someone we know. Under what conditions is this faculty designed to function in a reliable manner? Presumably, when the individual really is the one we know, not a stand-in or hologram image, or an image projected through trick mirrors. And, presumably, when the ambient atmosphere is such that we can see the individual clearly. All of these conditions are met in the Grabit case. But, if there is a designer with an optimal plan in mind, should that designer not rule out environments in which people are telling misidentification lies about the individual whom we see? Would an environment in which people around us have been misled into thinking that the individual we see is someone else count as appropriate ones? I do not mean these questions to be merely rhetorical; I just don't know what the answers are, nor do I find in Plantinga any clear indication of what the answers *should* be. Moreover, it seems to me that the answers in the Grabit-style cases should be the same, in principle, as those that would be given in the discrimination cases. In the Grabit example, there is a "glitch" in the environment, just as in the discrimination cases. But, this time, the glitch does not prevent the subject from knowing. I see nothing, however, in the warrant theory that enables us to distinguish between warrant-killing glitches and harmless glitches.

Perhaps there are some clear answers to such questions, and perhaps they have to do with Plantinga's discussion of the various "tradeoffs and compromises" that would be required in the construction of a design plan.[11] It must be recognized, as well, that not all cases will admit of precisely specified parameters for the specification of appropriate environments, just as it's not going to be clear in all cases whether a justification is ultimately defeated or undefeated. But, in the

Grabit-style examples, it *does* seem quite clear that the justification is ultimately undefeated, and quite unclear whether it is warranted.

BonJour's Examples

I want, finally, to consider a type of example that has not received much discussion in the context of the analysis of knowledge, but rather in the context of current debate between internalists and externalists with respect to the analysis of justification. I introduce this kind of example because I find that it illustrates another facet of the failure of Plantinga's warrant theory as an analysis of knowledge; this time the problem has to do with Plantinga's wholesale rejection of the concept of justification as an essential ingredient in knowing.

I have in mind some examples introduced by Laurence BonJour in his attack on externalist theories of justification.[12] BonJour's examples are all variations on a single thought experiment, which is the supposition of completely reliable clairvoyant power in an individual, with the variations expressing differing degrees and respects in which the individual in question possesses or lacks information concerning this clairvoyant ability. The general thrust of the examples is that one can satisfy the conditions of an externalist analysis of justification (such as the reliabilist account) even though one is completely unjustified in one's beliefs. Plantinga's account is an externalist one, very closely allied with the reliability theory, and so it would not be surprising to find that BonJour's examples present a threat to the adequacy of this account.

The most challenging of the examples provided by BonJour involves Norman, and is described as follows:

> Norman, under conditions which usually obtain, is a completely reliable clairvoyant with respect to certain kinds of subject matter. He possesses no evidence or reasons of any kind for or against the thesis that he possesses it. One day Norman comes to believe that the President is in New York City, though he has no evidence either for or against this belief. In fact, the belief is true, and results from his clairvoyant power under circumstances in which it is completely reliable. (p. 41)

BonJour claims, and I think most of us would agree, that Norman is only irrational in his belief, that his belief is completely unjustified. Since his belief is, however, a completely reliable sign that the President is in New York City, this belief appears to qualify as an instance of justified belief on a reliability theory of justification, and on other externalist accounts as well.

BonJour generalizes on this result to conclude that there is a fundamental problem for all externalist theories: no set of externalist conditions can be sufficient for justification if the satisfaction of those conditions cannot be established by the believer. BonJour would grant justification to Norman's belief, for example, only if Norman knows about his clairvoyant ability. BonJour summarizes the situation as follows:

> We are now face-to-face with the fundamental—and obvious—intuitive problem with externalism: *why* should the mere fact that such an external relation obtains mean that Norman's belief is epistemically justified when the relation in question is entirely outside his ken? (p. 42)

Even if one does not agree (as I do not) with BonJour about the problems with externalism, it seems fairly clear that examples of this type present a serious problem for Plantinga.[13] Norman has a faculty of clairvoyance (unusual, perhaps, among humans), presumably as part of his design plan. On the occasion in question, his faculty is functioning properly, and it would appear that the environment is of the type in which it is designed to function, and the beliefs formed by such a faculty are highly reliable. All the conditions of Plantinga's account would appear to be satisfied, and so we should conclude that Norman knows the whereabouts of the President. But, this is an unfortunate conclusion, for Norman knows no such thing.

For the defeasibility theorist, this case presents no problem at all, but this time the explanation does not depend on the facts of defeasibility. In this case, Norman's belief is simply unjustified, and so his belief fails to count as knowledge for that reason alone. And this illustrates an important difference between the defeasibility theory and the warrant theory. Plantinga rejects the various accounts of justification that have been offered on the grounds that none of them is anywhere near sufficient for warrant, and also argues that most of them fail even to be necessary for warrant. Even if we grant that his examples establish these conclusions, it does not follow that justification (of some appropriate sort) is not necessary for knowledge. The BonJour examples illustrate precisely the relation among these various concepts. Norman's true belief is warranted (in Plantinga's sense), but not justified (so justification is not necessary for warrant); but it is not a case of knowledge (so warranted true belief is not sufficient for knowledge).

The indefeasible justification account clearly has the upper hand in this kind of example, because it recognizes that justification is an essential part of the conditions for knowing.

Conclusions

If we want to use the term "warrant" as the third term in a tripartite analysis of knowledge, then Plantinga's account of warrant appears to be deficient. Although it works nicely in the original Gettier cases, it fails to give clear results in more subtle cases (such as the barn and Grabit examples), and it gives clearly incorrect results in still others (the clairvoyance examples). It would, I suggest, be better to define warranted belief as indefeasibly justified belief, since this will better serve us in the analysis of knowledge. Or we can keep the term "warrant," defining it as Plantinga does. But then we should reject the idea that knowledge is warranted true belief. Either way, a key premise in Plantinga's larger argument for theism is blocked. We need not assume that we have been designed by anyone just because we have knowledge of the world around us.

Notes

1. See Alvin Plantinga, *Warrant and Proper Function* (New York: Oxford University Press, 1993), p. v. *passim*. Hereafter, this volume will be referred to as WPF.

2. Most of this discussion takes place in the volume *Warrant: The Current Debate* (New York: Oxford University Press, 1993), the companion volume to the one referenced in the previous note. Hereafter, this volume will be referred to as WCD.

3. An alternative way of characterizing my conclusion is to say that the notion of indefeasible justification is a *better* way of defining warrant than is Plantinga's own proposed definition, if warrant is to be that which gives knowledge when added to true belief.

4. See David Armstrong, *Belief, Truth, and Knowledge* (Cambridge: Cambridge University Press, 1973); William Alston, "An Internalist Externalism," in his *Epistemic Justification: Essays in the Theory of Knowledge* (Ithaca: Cornell University Press, 1989), originally published in *Synthese*, 74 (1988), 265–83; and Marshall Swain, *Reasons and Knowledge* (Ithaca: Cornell University Press, 1979).

5. These conditions are presented in several places. See, for example, *Warrant and Proper Function*, p. 19.

6. For examples of the "ultimately undefeated" version of a defeasibility theory, see my *Reasons and Knowledge*, op. cit., Chapter 5, and Keith Lehrer, *Theory of Knowledge* (Boulder: Westview Press, 1990), Chapter 7. The best defense of the "merely misleading" defeasibility theory that I am aware of is found in Peter Klein, "Misleading Evidence and the Restoration of Justification," *Philosophical Studies* (37.1, 1980), 81–99, and in his *Certainty: A Refutation of Skepticism* (Minneapolis: University of Minnesota Press, 1981), pp. 137–70. See also David Annis, "Knowledge and Defeasbility," *Philosophical Studies* (24, 1973), 199–203; reprinted in George S. Pappas and Marshall Swain, *Essays on Knowledge and Justification* (Ithaca: Cornell University Press, 1978).

7. So-called because of the famous paper "Is Justified True Belief Knowledge?" by Edmund Gettier, which first appeared in *Analysis* (23, 1963), 121–23. This paper has been reprinted in a great many anthologies, far too many to list here.

8. See Keith Lehrer, "Knowledge, Truth, and Evidence," *Analysis* (25, 1965), 168–75, and *Theory of Knowledge*, op. cit.

9. See Goldman, "Discrimination and Perceptual Knowledge," *Journal of Philosophy* (73.20, 1976), 771–91, reprinted in Pappas and Swain, op. cit.

10. See Keith Lehrer and Thomas Paxson, Jr., "Knowledge: Undefeated Justified True Belief," *Journal of Philosophy* (66.8, 1969), 225–37; reprinted in Pappas and Swain, op. cit.

11. See WPF, 38–40.

12. See Laurence BonJour, *The Structure of Empirical Knowledge* (Cambridge: Harvard University Press, 1985), Chapter 4.

13. This has been pointed out by others, as well. See, for example, Louis Pojman, *What Can We Know?* (Belmont: Wadsworth Press, 1995), Chapter 9.

Part III
Naturalism

8

Science, Materialism, and False Consciousness

Bas C. van Fraassen

As activity, science has become a large-scale cultural phenomenon. As product, it is drawn on by industry, agriculture, and medicine, thus affecting not only the scene of its activity but all the rest of the world as well. Western philosophy has always harboured a tradition which regards scientific inquiry as a paradigm for rational inquiry in general. Yet almost every philosopher in that tradition has pointed to limits of this paradigm and its scope.

Every philosophy provides a different lens through which to view this object of common admiration. In this essay I shall reflect on two views of science which are at first glance inimical to each other. The first is Pierre Duhem's, who saw science as neutral on all issues of metaphysics, theology, and religion. The second is exemplified by Paul Feyerabend, who called for alternate research programs guided by rival metaphysics, and argued that such rivalry has always been a driving force in science. I will argue that Duhem is right, in the main, though our picture of science must be leavened by the insights of the contrary point of view. This will not be an archaeological inquiry into those thinkers' thought; I will make it mainly an independent reflection on these same issues.[1]

A Challenge to Duhem[2]

Pierre Duhem walked a tightrope. Today we accept much of his critique of certain views of science as correct. But in his own day he was accused of allowing his religious and metaphysical views to enter his physics in an improper way. Duhem contended that science describes but does not explain—at least in the sense in which metaphysicians want explanation. This leaves room for metaphysicians (and therefore, theologians) to add their explanations to science, whether as foundation or as supplement. Is this view of science not simply the philosophical dodge of someone who tries to make the world safe for religion? In response Duhem articulated his view of science as truly neutral on all metaphysical questions. The *correct* or *proper* way to pursue physical theory requires this neutrality. Why so? Without this neutrality, he says, the disagreements that run riot in metaphysics will ingress into physics. As a result, physics would not be an activity we can all work at *together*, regardless of our metaphysical views. Science is to be a common ground, where all can join in a common enterprise, regardless of creed, worldview, religion, or metaphysical beliefs.

On this fundamental point there is no real agreement today. Some do indeed hold that neutrality in this sense is part of the objectivity that characterizes scientific inquiry. Others point to the far-reaching assumptions with which famous scientists have approached their subject.[3] Some, perhaps especially philosophers in the scientific realist camp, frankly approve of this, and take some metaphysical assumptions to be beneficial or even indispensable to science. Others, such as Marxist, feminist, social constructivist, and religious critics attempt to expose the bias which crept into scientific theories due to the scientists' unacknowledged background opinions.[4] Duhem could rest easy with such views if they are understood as asserting defects in extant science.[5] But not all are thus; indeed, some advocate that science be pursued under the aegis of certain worldviews or of presumed knowledge come by extra-scientifically.

The most weighty challenge posed for Duhem's view of science is, I think, this: if metaphysical assumptions can make a difference to science, who is to say that science will not be more successful if it is less neutral? Is this not also an empirical question?

Philosophical positions, and specifically those embodied in metaphysical systems, normally identify themselves through their theses. Those theses can certainly have empirical implications, even when they are not first and foremost empirical hypotheses. What happens, exactly, if a scientist begins with or draws on such a position? I have two answers. My first answer (in the next section) is this: if assumptions have some non-metaphysical, empirical content, then once admitted into science the implied empirical hypotheses will, as it were, *forget their origins*. They can play a role, but not one that will offer comfort to the original motives or extra-scientific orientations that brought them in.

However, there is more to a metaphysical thesis than its empirical implications. Will the remainder, the metaphysics advanced as "underpinning" for science, not play a much more significant role? My answer to this (in the third section of this chapter) is that in fact, metaphysical assumptions do not in themselves—apart from any empirical implications—make a difference to science. I cannot pretend to prove this very general contention, but I shall try to support and illustrate it with the central example of science's 'presumptive materialism'. There is indeed a way in which materialism can play a role in shaping science, as I shall try to show: not through the content of its theses, entering as assumptions, but through attitudes for which these theses are mere codes. That is, I shall ascribe the true effect of metaphysics on science as a case of false consciousness.

Scientific Inquiry and Its Presuppositions

Just how can a metaphysical standpoint contribute empirical hypotheses to science? To examine this, we need to look at the senses in which science is and is not presuppositionless. At any given historical stage, science includes a large body of putative knowledge about nature, that is, the currently accepted theories and facts classified as evidence. This body is quite obviously not neutral with respect to empirical hypotheses. The willingness to stand on the shoulders of our past is the very basis prerequisite for progress; but it may hinder progress as well. As Feyerabend and Kuhn have shown so convincingly, progress in science depends crucially on the exploration of rival empirical hypotheses. Would it not *therefore* be a very good thing if there could be more and larger scale rivalries? Such diversity could come from science being guided in different research communities by various systems of metaphysics. Feyerabend advocated such proliferation, for exactly that reason.

The Argument for Proliferation

If we agree, are we not led to a further conclusion? For then, exactly to the extent that these large scale rivalries are *in fact absent*, science is not neutral after all between the metaphysical systems under whose guidance empirically differing sciences *could* be developed. In this way, the admission of non-neutrality with respect to empirical hypotheses seemingly entails non-neutrality with respect to metaphysics.

This argument insinuates a good deal more than it establishes. It would be a very interesting argument if some or all of the following suppositions were true. Behind these lies some deeper supposition, about how metaphysical positions contribute empirical hypotheses to science, which I shall take up below. That apart, three suppositions are subliminally at work here:

(1) if an empirical hypothesis has its origin in something outside of science, then this origin makes a difference once it enters science. (For example, hypotheses with a common origin would be related in some way which is both due thereto, and of importance within science.)
(2) questions answered in the course of exploring a hypothesis have some bearing on that origin, other than coincidentally;
(3) the value of introducing a hypothesis for exploration is intimately linked with opening up the possibility that it is true (in the sense of eliminating or suspending the acceptance of theories contrary to that hypothesis.)

It seems to me that all of these are mistaken.

Presuppositions

The idea that science is, or even can be, presuppositionless is rightly dismissed today as incorrect. But there is a distinction to be made.[6] In one way, it cannot be: every empirical inquiry has its presuppositions. The investigator approaches his subject with specific questions or with a specific way of asking questions and so the very design of the inquiry involves some preliminary idea of that subject matter. In another way, however, science must be presuppositionless if it is to be science at all. No rational inquiry may 'beg the question' by presupposing the results of that inquiry.

Every inquiry has presuppositions, exactly because it is defined in part by specific questions or a specific way of asking questions. These questions, and to that extent the subject matter of the inquiry, are delimited in part by a class of 'relevant' features—the parameters in which the subject and its problems are to be stated. Whether or not those features alone are relevant to other concerns we might have, it is they which discipline and focus the inquiry. This is a crucial point which Kant saw as the revolution that initiated modern scientific method. He took it to be one necessary condition of fruitful science: that the inquirer decide on and strictly determine as a preliminary which questions he will put to nature.

When Galileo caused balls, the weights of which he had himself previously determined, to roll down an inclined plane . . . a light broke upon all students of nature. They learned that reason has insight only into that which it produces after a plan of its own . . . (*Critique of Pure Reason*, preface to the second edition, B xiii.)

But does this procedure, perhaps a crucial prerequisite for scientific progress as Kant maintains, not open science up to the charge of biasing all its inquiries from the outset?

If an inquiry turns out to have presupposed any part of its results from the beginning, then it was flawed—isn't that so? Such a flaw is in principle detectable by anyone, including by those who engage in the inquiry. Detection of such a presupposition, however, does not automatically invalidate the results. Quite the contrary—the obligation not to beg the question means simply that when the presupposition comes to light, it must be turned into an acknowledged assumption. As example take the aberration in starlight, to allow for which astronomers have to point their telescopes away from the star to be observed, at an angle which varies with the seasons. From this it was concluded that the aether is motionless with respect to the stars, and is not e. g. dragged along by the Earth. This conclusion followed in a context in which certain presuppositions were in force. In retrospect we reinterpret this finding: one conclusion properly stated is that if light be a wave travelling through a material medium, the aether, then . . . etc. With the wave theory of light triumphant perhaps there seemed to be no point in rendering that "if" explicit. Nevertheless, this acknowledgment of previously tacit assumptions, once laid bare, is required for science to be scientific.

Prior probabilities provide a more difficult example of the ubiquity of initial presuppositions. Historically it is clear that they play a role in theory choice and research design. Perhaps the opposition within science and orthodox statistics against the role of prior probabilities derives exactly from the sense that they are to some extent a presupposition of results of the inquiry. If I investigate hypotheses A and B with the prior opinion that A is ten times as likely as B, am I not going someways toward the assumption that the outcome is to be that A is true? If those prior probabilities enter experimental design, is that not a flaw of the same sort, even if not to the same degree, as a design that ensures the outcome in certain respects? Exactly the same point is to be made here as above: the disclosure of such partial presuppositions does not disqualify the research, but once disclosed or challenged they are to be fully acknowledged in the announced research results. There is a flaw only if the researcher begs his own question. Prior probabilities, however, are not theses but propositional attitudes. They cannot be removed by listing them in the antecedent, though some "explicitating" response is possible.[7]

The simple idea that presuppositions in science are examples of flaws in design is therefore not tenable. The unearthing, bringing to light, laying bare of presuppositions is an *unendliche Aufgabe*. The hidden assumptions form a potential infinite; for every one we uncover, there will be (in some platonic sense) another. To this aspect of our finitude we must be resigned: consciousness is not transparent to itself.

The inevitability of presuppositions and the consequent need for proliferation in theoretical research are no objection to Duhem's concept of the neutrality of science. The question is, however, whether this gives purchase to religious or metaphysical interests, which may insinuate themselves by contributing empirical presuppositions to science. Again, as a purely historical or psychological point about the origin of hypotheses, Duhem cannot be understood to have denied this. The Duhemian point must be that if this happens, it does not matter to science—that these origins provide neither credentials to hypotheses nor guidance to inquiry. In this he would be right, I think. To make that point we must look a bit further into that way in which science is not presuppositionless.

Questions and Parameters of Inquiry

The passage I cited from Kant is famous. It marks the historical recognition of the sense in which science is not presuppositionless. But it does not make sufficiently explicit exactly how Galileo and his peers set about this new way to study nature. Scientific inquiry is an *objectifying* procedure.[8] This is in the main a 'European' rather than 'Anglo-Saxon' way of putting it. What it denotes is a specific way in which presuppositions enter into scientific inquiry, a way in which scientific inquiry is delimited in a certain way beforehand.

A science, or a research project within a science, has a domain. It is tempting to think of its initial delimiting as specifying a set of things; e.g. "this will be a study of frogs." But that is not accurate, since the central subject matter will inevitably have to be connected with other things. Even an anatomical study of frogs will inquire into, for example, the rate of coagulation of frog blood when exposed to air, and the air is not part of a frog. The more accurate way of delimiting such a domain is in terms of the quantities which will be allowed to figure in the description of the phenomena to be studied. Under quantities I include here properties and relations; "quantities" is the more inclusive term, since we can think of properties as two-valued quantities, and so forth.

So the first step in setting up the scientific inquiry is to select the *relevant* quantities. All questions to be broached must be questions formulable in terms of these quantities. The next step will be to describe the phenomena solely in terms of these quantities. This description must be systematic; the result will be a 'data model', which can be studied to discern patterns in the phenomena. The further step of framing and investigating hypotheses, which will stand or fall depending on their fit (in various ways) to these data models, will be equally constrained in terms of admissible quantities (though these may include "theoretical" quantities not used in the construction of the data models).

The paradigm example of this procedure is Galileo's list of primary qualities for physics: physical description was to proceed solely in terms of these qualities, no others to be admitted. Of course, Galileo's proposal was extreme: he wished to lay down the list of relevant quantities for the scientific description of nature once and for all. All quantities not on the list were to be the subject of reductive or eliminating analyses. We do not have to think of the objectifying procedure either as delimited once and for all or as necessarily linked to a reductionist thesis. Such a thesis may appear as a completeness claim for a certain theory, produced as science-as-product by the inquiry. In the case of theories of frogs, it will be less likely to come along than in the case of fundamental physics. In Galileo's case, the claim was definitely premature, as it was again in the case of Descartes's physics which admitted only kinematic quantities. A more recent instructive example is the methodological innovation attempted by behaviorism in psychology. The attempt to set up a well-delimited and well defined scientific inquiry is one thing; the shortlived completeness claims associated with it are another.

Such a clearly delimited inquiry may face radical failure, namely if questions formulated in its own terms cannot be answered in its own terms. The result is a "crisis in the foundations" of the particular science. The science in question must then augment or revise either its list of relevant parameters or its range of questions to be addressed. If for instance it is asked how current values of a certain quantity depend functionally on its preceding values, and/or current or preceding values of other quantities, there may be no answer. Then the modifications introduced to escape this crisis may indeed revise or extend the list of admissible 'relevant' quantities. This describes exactly the transition from Cartesian to Newtonian physics. It is not the only way: alternatively one might admit statistical modes of description that still utilize only the 'old' quantities. There is a recurrent trade-off in the history of science between determinism and 'hidden variables'.

Could revisions in the set of descriptive parameters shift science into the metaphysical, or occult? It could, in the sense that the new parameters were earlier on excluded exactly on the basis that they were 'occult'. This is illustrated very well by the Cartesian reaction to Newton's mass and force as being a reintroduction of the 'occult' qualities which had been banished by the mechanical philosophy. It is equally illustrated in the 'orthodox' Newtonians' attitude in the 18th century to aether and subtle fluid theories, as precluded by Newton's *vera causa* rule.

But we must be careful not to generalize too shallowly on this point. First of all, even if occultism or alchemy had inspired the introduction of those new parameters, their role in scientific inquiry once introduced robbed them of all connections with those 'disciplines' whence they 'came'. But secondly, science has a 'shell' structure which imposes strict discipline on how the list of relevant parameters can be revised. Each scientific project lives in an environment created by larger projects, past and present, on which it draws, and with which it needs to stay in harmony. The set of parameters is revisable; it is not fixed in stone. But an alteration in the set of 'relevant' parameters 'revolutionizes' the project, engenders an heir-project so to speak. The revolution may be more or less radical depending on how high up in the 'shell' structure the alteration or augmentation of parameters occurs. So the study of frogs, and indeed of animal physiology generally, was definitely revolutionized when Volta did his experiments in which static electricity made frog-legs move. But notice that the new parameter in the description of the physiological phenomena belongs to a higher shell, physics. Physics itself and everything in between physics and physiology felt the effects of this revolutionary move. Only a narrow frog specialist would refer to it solely as a scientific revolution in the theory of frogs.

The crucial point—about the revolutionary character of alteration in the set of relevant parameters, due to the 'shell' structure of science—is the difference between possibility in principle and historical feasibility. Imagine a judge in an American court sentencing a thief to have his hand cut off. It is true that our values, laws, and beliefs can be revised so as to incorporate those operative in whatever other culture you care to mention, *in principle*—but that does not mean that such an alteration is now feasible.

Empirical Hypotheses Forget Their Origin

I will use a single example to illustrate two points which are closely related to this delicate interplay of assumption and disclosure. The first point is that an empirical hypothesis introduced into science for reasons, and perhaps with putative credentials, coming from outside that science, will so to speak *forget its origins*—as I said above—so that its fortunes within science will soon have little or nothing to do with those origins. What this means is that within science the suggested empirical hypothesis will have none of the significance it had in its extra-scientific context, nor need there be any relation to other hypotheses with the same origin.

Examples of this sort of thing must necessarily be fanciful. Imagine the introduction of the following hypothesis of a paranormal phenomenon: horses did not evolve from lower forms of life, they appeared on earth quite separately at some definite time in the past.[9] Suppose that some community of biologists admits this hypothesis as basis for research, but is in other respects like our biological research community in every way. That means: the set of questions that defines their inquiry would still be the same. Therefore the origin of the hypothesis, possibly in contexts outside scientific inquiry, would not play any role. Only the description of the paranormal phenomenon within the parameters of biology and its parent sciences (physics, chemistry) would be 'relevant'.

It would become crucial for them to theorize about the hypothetical introduction of the horse. When does the first horse exist in the world? Did it grow from a baby horse to a mature horse? What animal does it mate with? Did many 'first' horses come into existence at the same time? In addition, in either case, there needs to be an inquiry into the survival rate of these new babies, and whether many of them are created so as to counteract attrition by exposure etc. or whether they always come to be in conditions that allow them to survive till they have offspring.

These questions within biology and paleontology lead to questions for physics. What exists just prior to the existence of the first horse, in the location where the first horse first appears, whether as baby or as mature specimen? This latter question is itself circumscribed by the questions that define the background of biological inquiry: the 'what' refers to physical conditions, the configuration of the matter at that location. Was energy, mass, momentum conserved in this transition that marks the appearance of the first horse? What, if any, of the matter located there immediately beforehand, is part of that first horse?

The second point, which may at first look tangential to this but is not, concerns the curious notion one sometimes sees of "science stoppers."[10] For example, it is sometimes suggested that paranormal hypotheses, such as the existence of ghosts or hypotheses of special creation of different animal species, stop science in its tracks if admitted. But there cannot be such a thing as a true 'science stopper' at all.

Some of the questions raised in our example may be answered in unorthodox ways, but the inquiry does not, cannot come to a stop. Suppose the theory developed is that the first instance of every natural kind just springs into being, at its moment of entry into history, always on top of some mountain.[11] Then all the conservation laws I mentioned are violated, very many times, so physics has to be carefully but radically revised so as to allow for these phenomena. Moreover, answers have to be sought to what happened to the air in that place: exactly what is the distribution of additional momenta imparted to the air molecules so as to move them out of the way? Can this be described deterministically or only in terms of irreducible probabilities? Alternatively, of course, the answer hypothesized may be that the organic and inorganic matter present changed into a baby of the new species. The exact process of change would then become the topic of inquiry. The research program for such a biology *seriously pursued* is vast. If the community of biologists in question did not proceed in this way, but treated the hypothesis as a "science stopper," then its pursuit would not be scientific.

To support this conclusion, let me take up two putative objections.[12] The first is that someone might proceed quite differently from the above, so as to preserve most of extant science while maintaining the hypothesis, by restricting prior theory to "normal" as opposed to "exceptional" occurrences. The intuitive idea would be that the paranormal phenomena occur very rarely or perhaps even only once in the distant past, while science only formulates regularities that hold 'in general'. There are two reasons why this is not possible without disengaging oneself from science. The first is that the theory cannot be maintained unmodified however small or large the "area of exception" is chosen. If for example the initial creation is of many horses (to prevent rapid extinction), then the general predator-prey balance is upset, with consequences for the evolution of other species. If instead the initial creation is of few, then there must be a compensating hypothesis, such as of rapid mutation, to offset the damaging effects of inbreeding. The hypothesis might be more insulated from counterevidence the larger in time and space we mark out the area/epoch of exception, and the farther it is placed in the past. But that does not remove the problem in principle. In addition, quite apart from the questionability of manoeuvres designed to eliminate possibilities of refutation, they weaken science by curtailing its treatment of *other* phenomena in that epoch/area.

The second reason is more important. When the theory is thus restricted, we change it from an assertion of form *A* to one of form *A, unless X*. Now *X* cannot be something like *A miracle occurs*; it must be formulated in terms of the parameters demarcating the domain of the theory. But *X* must also be genuinely informative, otherwise the 'restriction' becomes something like *A, unless not A*. This would be less of a problem for someone who held that in the whole history of the universe, only the appearance of horses was such an exceptional, paranormal occurrence. It becomes a serious problem if this manoeuvre is suggested as a general way to proceed in science, i.e. to formulate theories for 'normal' developments with 'exceptional areas/epochs' in which science is silent. Now, describing the areas of exception in terms of the relevant parameters is as challenging a task as any outlined above. Moreover, if the motivation is a belief in agencies properly outside the domain of all science, that belief itself may imply that the task is impossible. But then the 'restriction' would leave us only with a 'science' asserting that certain regularities always hold except when they are violated. That is an empty assertion. The proposed policy would therefore certainly stop science for those who adopt it; but that is why I say that adopting it involves disengaging oneself from science altogether.

The second putative objection is that the inspiration which suggested this hypothesis may turn out to make a great difference to science, whether for benefit or harm. The reason would be that scientists not strongly motivated by beliefs contrary to evolution will not pursue biological theories that would require such radical revisions in physics and chemistry. Therefore, the credit or blame for the effects on science of this new direction in research belong in that case to the extra-scientific inspiration.

Note well: the putative reason offered is a psychological hypothesis about the private life of scientists who explore hypotheses contrary to current accepted scientific opinion. Such a thesis may always be able to take refuge somewhere between the subjects' behaviour and their rhetoric. But on the face of it at least, as we will see below, the actual history of science does not seem to support the hypothesis.

Exploration of Rival Empirical Hypotheses

Science is very clearly not neutral with respect to empirical hypotheses. Equally clearly, rival empirical hypotheses are explored in science, and should be. Duhem could not possibly have meant to deny that, given how eloquently he wrote on these very matters. So his reason for advocating neutrality with respect to metaphysics cannot simply be the need for agreement and unity. Yet the one danger he mentions explicitly is that

> to make physical theories depend on metaphysics is surely not the way to let them enjoy the privilege of universal consent. . . . A physical theory reputed to be satisfactory by the sectarians of one metaphysical school will be rejected by the partisans of another school.[13]

Can these really be the words of a physicist so engaged in polemics and controversy with the scientific orthodoxy of his day?

Some reflection on Duhem and Feyerabend's own examples will bring us to a more palatable view of the matter. General agreement on a large body of background theories and data can go hand in hand with exploration of possibilities that would overturn them—indeed, that is exactly how it is in science!

To see this, consider how the call for exploration of rival hypotheses fits in with the point of developing science in the first place. Unlike pure philosophy, science is not a purely academic exercise. Science fails to attain its goal if it does not produce some such thing as the 'body of science', 'accepted scientific opinion', science-as-product to function as guide to practical life. The end is to come up with theories that meet science's criteria of success, and having thus succeeded can be drawn upon for the many needs for which we value the success of science. This requires a certain unity and agreement within science—the science that science is building is one—which, a little paradoxically, derives its value exactly from its emergence out of disagreement and disharmony.

Everyone is free to design his own inquiry; a scientific community will do so in its own way, and hope to be vindicated in its choices. Kuhn and Feyerabend have amassed impressive historical evidence for the crucial role in scientific progress of alternatives to accepted theories, developed while the evidence was still overwhelmingly against the alternative.[14] On the other hand, the economics of scarcity that govern all human life applies here as well, and random pursuit of alternative theories would be as unproductive as experimentation not guided by any theory. Anyone basing advocacy of specific departures in scientific research on Feyerabend's sorts of grounds must, it seems to me, also submit to Feyerabend's harsh response to the "But then anything goes!" objection:

> the distinction between the crank and the respectable thinker lies in the research that is done once a certain point of view is adopted. The crank usually is content with defending the point of view in its original, undeveloped, metaphysical form, and he is not at all prepared to test its usefulness in all those cases which seem to favor the opponent. . . . It is this further investigation . . . which distinguishes the 'respectable thinker' from the crank. The original content of his theory does not. (1981, p. 199)

Feyerabend's own examples show that even 'mainstream' science is the constant scene of exploration of rival hypotheses and replete with controversies over alternative theoretical approaches. Moreover, there is a quite distinct and often lively area of marginal 'foundational' research in which those engaged in 'normal' science participate along the way. Feyerabend complained at great length of the dominance of the Copenhagen school of thought in quantum mechanics. But not only was he able to point to alternatives under investigation by such eminent physicists as de Broglie and Bohm, we have since seen ample energy devoted to testing the predicted violations of Bell's inequalities, developing the many-worlds interpretation beloved of cosmologists, and the dynamic reduction program (GRW model), to mention a few.[15] Each of these passes Feyerabend's criterion quite handsomely—in contrast to such examples as Velikovsky or Dianetics, which do not belong even to the margins of science at this point, by that criterion.

This is well illustrated with aspects of science which Duhem himself brought to light in the history of science. Specifically, Newton's development of his theory of the heavens, without preserving consistency with Kepler's laws of planetary motion or Galileo's law of fall, was a clear case of proliferating rival hypotheses in the teeth of the evidence.[16] Thus, the value of proliferation in science has a form compatible with Duhem's claim of neutrality for science; indeed, actual science already recognizes that value and gives it its due.

The advocacy of proliferation would reach absurdity if carried to its logical extreme. Even if we were immortal and had unlimited resources, we could not have an alternative research project going on for every definable set of parameters and questions, and every set of prior probabilities for the answers. However, the mere thought of this impossible fancy forces us to consider a distinction with respect to introduction of hypotheses. If there were a research project going for every set of hypotheses and every allocation of probabilities thereto, then would science as a whole imply nothing at all? Would accepted scientific opinion consist only of tautologies?

Clearly that does not follow, since we can distinguish (1) formulating a hypothesis and designing research to tease out or test its implications, and (2) ceasing to accept theories that imply its falsity. Indeed, Feyerabend's most dramatic examples of the value of exploring new hypotheses which are in conflict with the evidence, *sub specie* accepted scientific opinion, are of exactly the former sort. It follows therefore, contrary to what Feyerabend seems to imply, that if science is not neutral on some hypothesis, the creation of a rival research project to explore it does not engender neutrality. There is a need for proliferation in theoretical research, but not a need to suspend acceptance of current science while we proliferate.

The cases examined by Feyerabend, in which exploration of rival hypotheses and indeed whole cosmologies turned out to be of crucial and indispensable help in unseating unsatisfactory older theories, illustrate this very well. They do not turn on that ('suspension' or 'non-acceptance') sense of exploration! In each case we see scientists exploring hypotheses which are admittedly and often blatantly counter to the accepted evidence as well as accepted scientific opinion. Since Feyerabend himself illustrates this abundantly, it is surprising that he does not see the corollary: *inconsistency with accepted science and lack of positive prior probability does not prevent exploration of rival empirical hypotheses within science.* On the contrary, many great advances in science provide counterexamples to such a view. There is a second corollary: the remedy for a perceived paucity of such exploration need in general not come from scientists who do have positive probabilities for alternative hypotheses or who reject the accepted theories in extant science.[17] Who knows what motives are needed? Intellectual playfulness, fascination with the long shot or with the role of rebel, who knows?

The view we must associate with Duhem is realized if there is agreement on what is to be accepted combined with free exploration of alternative theories and experimental inquiry suggested by those alternatives (to the extent that our scarcities permit). In that case there can be great diversity, but there will not be the sorry spectacle of a science that never comes to any conclusion because physical theories "reputed to be satisfactory by the sectarians of one metaphysical school will be rejected by the partisans of another".

Presumptive Materialism

The more important question confronting Duhem's concept of science is therefore whether science starting from certain metaphysical beliefs might be—because of the way the world is, not because of the historical context of inquiry—more successful than science which is neutral with respect to metaphysics.

One popular plea for metaphysics rests on the idea that for the good of science, scientists must start with provisional realism—there are unobservable causes for all observable phenomena or some such thesis—and presumptive materialism—matter is all there is, so those causes are all material mechanisms of some sort.

This thesis certainly sounds debatable: surely it must be either so or not so. . . . But appearances are deceiving. Genuine debatability presumes understanding of what the suggestion actually means. A much more basic presupposition is at stake: do provisional realism and presumptive materialism *in this sense* make any difference to science at all? By "in this sense" I mean, in the sense of assumptions, theses, factual claims about what there is and what there is not, apart from the implied empirical consequences which we discussed in the preceding part. Let us look specifically at presumptive materialism.

What Is Matter?

Does the thesis that *matter is all there is* rule out at least some kinds of theories, so that they are not even candidates for scientific exploration? I will argue that this is quite illusory. There may however be a certain attitude, orientation, or stance associated with this thesis, which does affect science as well as practical and intellectual life generally, and for which this thesis functions as code. If that is so then materialism may be a prime example of false consciousness in philosophy. For in that case materialists may take themselves to be maintaining a theory while they are in reality merely expressing attitudes, in ways which lend themselves to such expression only under conditions of confusion and unclarity.

This is not simply an indictment of materialism. I offer this diagnosis in part as explanation of something which materialism has in common with other hardy perennials of philosophy. That is: there is besides the theses on which the day's materialists take their stand, and which vary with time, also such a thing as the 'spirit of materialism' which never dies. False consciousness can be avoided in two ways: (1) the philosopher may lack that spirit and be genuinely concerned solely with certain definite views on what there is, or (2) the philosopher may have that spirit and not confuse its expression with any particular view of what the world is like. The latter, however, has to my knowledge never yet been instantiated.

To begin, it certainly sounds as if *matter is all there is* (briefly, the *Thesis*) is a substantive factual claim. Does it not rule out Descartes's mind-body dualism, Aquinas's souls, spirits, entelechies, cosmic purpose? Well, it genuinely rules those out only if each can be made clear enough so that the denial has some genuine content; and even then it may not.[18] Now, if the Thesis is the important part of materialism, then materialists will not rest till the distinction between matter and what is not matter has been made so clear that the Thesis is clearly a factual claim, which can clearly be either true or false. But if they do not, then by *modus tollens* I conclude. . . .

What would count as something that is not material? Descartes said that matter is extended and mind is not; mind thinks. But if that is not a stipulative definition, it is certainly wrong. Else we would have to say that Hertz's massive point particles, if they exist, are not material. Equally we would have to say that Hartry Field denies materialism when he claims that space-time points are real, concrete individuals. And finally, we would have to conclude that Alvin Plantinga either does not think or is not incarnate, both of which are clearly false, to an extraordinary degree, given his subtlety and size.

It may be unfair to take Descartes as our whipping boy. But more recent putative statements of materialism do not, it seems to me, fare much better. Typically they start from some version of received scientific opinion, perhaps with some anxiety about being up to date. They will not say that elementary particles are all there is, since they know that there are trees, persons, and rocks as well. But they will say that everything is composed solely of elementary particles. If we take this seriously we shall, I wager, once more land in an untenable historical parochialism. When Newton introduced forces in addition to bodies, did he deny the Thesis? Forces are not composed of particles. When Huyghens's waves-in-the-aether theory defeated Newton's particle theory of light, was that a set-back for materialism? Surely not, although the aether was a continuous medium, not particulate. When a recent article in a physics journal bore the title "Particles do not exist", was that a denial of materialism? The author's argument was that particle number is not relativistically invariant, so that how many particles there are is as *relative* as left/right, up/down, rest/motion. If that is so, does materialism bite the dust? Surely not. But if materialism were really, purely and simply, some such thesis as that everything is composed of elementary particles, I could not so readily say "Surely not"!

Two Moves for Materialists

Soi-disant materialists have certainly taken cognizance of this difficulty, that their most important terms seem to lack content. In response, they have opted for one of two moves. Some have attempted to formulate very specific theses relating to the putative subject matter of psychology, argued that these are empirical, and offered the results as a specific version of materialism. (By "empirical" I mean here "having some empirical implications"; it does not preclude other implications concerning the unobservable.) Others have nailed the Thesis down by nailing it to a specific science, by means of a completeness claim for that science. It seems to me—and I will try to show—that neither move leaves us with materialism as an identifiable substantive thesis.

The First Move: Materialism as Scientific Hypothesis

U.T. Place argued that it is tenable to say that certain events and processes traditionally classified as mental (for example, sensation) are identical with events and processes in the brain.[19] That this is indeed so he labelled as *materialism*, and argued that it is in fact a scientific hypothesis. In response to Smart he agreed further that the conditions required for the assertability of such a hypothesis— conditions under which alone such an identity statement can be true— are subject to philosophical debate rather than empirical testing.[20] But once such conditions are specified, the remaining question is empirical. For the described 'mental' events and processes have a certain complexity, which brain events and processes may or may not have. The name "materialism" is also given to this or closely similar claims about the psychological e.g. by David Armstrong.[21]

There are three preliminary questions to be raised. First of all, not every replacement for what I have called the Thesis can be accepted as the 'real' materialism—can this one? Since the main question before us is what exactly the materialist's main thesis could be, we should perhaps accept any seriously offered contender. But if we could identify certain familiar psychological events and processes with physiological ones in some not too weak sense, we would hardly be finished with the traditional concerns of materialism. That a person has a *purpose*, for example, does not consist in any specific type of occurrent event or process; nor that her sins are forgiven, that she is in a state of grace, or that she is precious beyond rubies. And these are only examples about persons; what else may there not be between heaven and earth never dreamt of in materialist philosophy? I don't want to be fanciful, but merely establishing that sensations are brainstates seems hardly more than a drop in the bucket for the materialist. The virtue of such a ringing Thesis as "Matter is All" was to settle the hash of all such stuff once and for all.

Second preliminary question: does the description of the 'mental' or the psychological in terms of which the replacement thesis is formulated, do justice to its intended concern? Armstrong was rather more conscious than Place of the second preliminary question when he was debating Malcolm, a Wittgensteinian. Today he would also have to contend with putative failures of functionalism, arguments that no computational theory of consciousness could even in principle be successful, and demonstrations that truth conditions for belief attributions must have historical and social parameters outside the believer.

But leave these debates aside. Third question: supposing the empirical claim is false, or is scientifically investigated and found wanting, will there or will there not be a fall-back position to call 'the real materialism after all'? It would be a poor game if after much scientific strife, the loser could say "that's not it at all, that is not what I meant at all." Well, what if we accept Place's or Armstrong's formulation, and their empirical claims are found wanting? Suppose, for example, that no neurological process can be identified which can even in principle predict human decisions reached simultaneously or at the exact end of that process. The next empirical question would be what probabilities can be assigned to the (neutrally described) actions being decided upon, conditional on the states of the central nervous system. If these probabilities cannot even in principle be made as near *zero* and *one* as we like, is that the end of materialism?

Think of the exact parallel: no quantum state will predict the exact time of radioactive decay. Is that the end of materialism? It is not; and neither would materialism come to an end if what humans do could be related only probabilistically to their brainstates. A favorite belief of the materialists would have to be relinquished, but they would all know how to retrench. For the spirit of materialism is never exhausted in piecemeal empirical claims.[22]

The Second Move: Whatever It Takes

If you press a materialist, you quickly find that the most important constraint on the meaning of the Thesis is that it should be compatible with science, *whatever science comes up with*. This is contrary to what some of them *say*. If, they say, certain phenomena could not be explained purely in terms of material factors, then the scientific thing to do would be to give up materialism. But, holding the Thesis, they make the bold conjecture that this will never happen. That *what* would never happen?

If that question cannot be answered with a precise and independent account of what material factors are, there is still one option. That is to nail a completeness claim to science, or to a specific science such as physics. The instructive example here is J.J.C. Smart, who begins his essay "Materialism" with an offer to explain what he means:

> By 'materialism' I mean the theory that there is nothing in the world over and above those entities which are postulated by physics (or, or course, those entities which will be postulated by future and more adequate physical theories).[23]

He quickly discusses some older and more recent postulations in actual physics, which make that 'theory' look substantive. But of course the parenthetical qualification makes that discussion *completely irrelevant*!

Smart may believe, or think that he believes, the 'theory' here
formulated; but if he does, he certainly does not know *what* he
believes. For of course he has no more idea than you or I of what
physics will postulate in the future. It is a truly courageous faith, that
believes in an 'I know not what'—isn't it?

Indeed, in believing this, Smart cannot be certain that he believes
anything at all. Suppose science goes on forever, and every theory is
eventually succeeded by a better one. That has certainly been the case
so far, and always some accepted successor has implied that the
previously postulated entities (known, after all, only by description)
do not exist. If that is also how it will continue, world without end,
then Smart's so-called theory—as formulated above—entails that *there
is nothing*. Let's not be too quick to celebrate this demonstration of
clear empirical content (about what the future of physics will not be
like). Most likely Smart did not notice this implication and would have
preferred to rephrase if he had.

In a clear indication that he is at least subliminally aware of the
problem, Smart quickly adds some extra content. Not content with his
initial formulation once he realizes that it is compatible with emergent
properties, holism, and the irreducibility of biology to physics, he says

> I wish to lay down that it is incompatible with materialism that there
> should be any irreducibly emergent laws or properties, say in biology or
> psychology. . . . I also want to deny any theory of 'emergent
> properties'. . . . (ibid. pp. 203–204)

We should read this as an amendment of the above definition of
materialism, for the 'theory' formulated above does not fit this bill. We
must wonder how Smart knows that it is not adequate. Is he perhaps
telling us that either physics will forever eschew emergent properties,
or else materialism is false? Since quantum physics provides, at this
point, a clear example of holism, should we conclude that materialism
has already come to an end?

Of course not. Faced with the consequences of the stance that
materialism should be whatever it takes to be a completeness claim for
physics, Smart started backpedaling. Everything that is "repugnant"
to him (to use his phrase) may be incorporated in future physics. So he
adds, in effect, that physics will be false if that happens. But faced
with that consequence, no materialist will stick by him if he sticks by
that. They'll point out, quite rightly, that he was of a 'classical' mind,
and like so often happens with the older generation in physics itself,

quite unable to assimilate new visions of the structure of the *material* world.

Materialism as False Consciousness

So is it all just a matter of scientific reactionaries with their self-trivializing theses dressed up as uncompromising metaphysical constraints on science? No, it is not. For all this effort to codify materialism bespeaks something much more important: *the spirit of materialism*. Materialism is a hardy philosophical tradition, which appears differently substantiated in each philosophical era. Each instantiation has its empirical as well as its non-empirical claims, which interpret for that era, in its own terms, the invariant attitudes and convictions which I call here the 'spirit of materialism'.

How shall we identify what is really involved in materialism? Our great clue is the apparent ability of materialists to revise the content of their main thesis, as science changes. If we took literally the claim of a materialist that his position is simply belief in the claim that all is matter, as currently construed, we would be faced with an insoluble mystery. For how would such a materialist know how to retrench when his favorite scientific hypotheses fail? How did the 18th century materialists know that gravity, or forces in general, were material? How did they know in the 19th century that the electromagnetic field was material, and persisted in this conviction after the aether had been sent packing?

Of course it is possible to *measure* certain quantities. But that cannot provide the criterion needed. Just think again of the transition from Cartesian to Newtonian physics. Newton identified forces as the causes of changes in states of motion. Accordingly, if you measure the direction and rate of change of momentum, you obtain a description of that cause in terms of its effects. (The recipe for measuring force direction and magnitude is exactly to measure those effects.) But it could be added consistently that these causes are immaterial, spiritual—even mental, if Mind does not need to be someone's mind. If instead the forces are said to be material just like the extended bodies so classified before, the materialist must seemingly have some rather mysterious type of knowledge: a *knowledge-that* the newly introduced entities have the *je ne sais quoi* which makes for materiality.

But what is it then, in this metaphysical position, that guides the change in content, which it would be pedantic to signal with a change in name? If the "physicalist" or "naturalist" part of this philosophical position is not merely the *desire* or *commitment* to have metaphysics guided by physics—i.e. something that cannot be captured in any thesis or factual belief—then what is it? This knowledge of how to retrench cannot derive from the substantive belief currently identified as the view that all is physical. So what does it derive from? Whatever the answer is, *that*, and not the explicit thesis, is the real answer to what materialism is.

Hence I propose the following diagnosis of materialism: it is not identifiable with a theory about what there is, but only with an attitude or cluster of attitudes. These attitudes include strong deference to science in matters of opinion about what there is, and the inclination to accept (approximative) completeness claims for science as actually constituted at any given time.[24] Given this diagnosis, the apparent knowledge of what is and what is not material among newly hypothesized entities is mere appearance. The ability to adjust the content of the thesis that all is matter again and again is then explained instead by a *knowing-how* to retrench which derives from invariant attitudes. This does not reflect badly on materialism; on the contrary, it gives materialism its due.[25] But it does imply that only the confusion of *theses held* with *attitudes expressed*, which yields false consciousness, can account for the conviction that science requires presumptive materialism.

I mean this as a diagnosis of materialism, not a refutation. Its incarnation at any moment will be some position distinguished by certain empirical consequences, and these will either stand or fall as science evolves. But whether they stand or fall, materialism as general philosophical position, as historical tradition in philosophy, will survive. Given this, however, there can—for that very reason—be no question of regarding materialism as an assumption at the foundations of science. There is no 'presumptive materialism' which constrains scientific theories to consistency with certain determinate factual theses. For even materialism itself is not so constrained, and it survives by changing so as to accommodate the new sciences.

Naturalism, Materialism, Scientism: Where Does Science End?

Duhem conceived of science as neutral on all issues of metaphysics and religion. It seems to me that, properly understood, science is thus automatically. No special effort is needed to make science be this way, or to prevent it from becoming otherwise. But this holds only for the process of scientific inquiry and its products, scientific findings and theories. The practice of science may, as many other good and much-needed work, be attended by collateral damage to other spheres of life. As paradigm of rational inquiry, for example, it may be extrapolated from what that literally means to a paramount guide to life. There may be psychological reasons for such effects of scientific education. But if science does take on this additional status, it can only be through mediation by certain attendant attitudes and stances which are in no way inherent in science itself.

Satisfaction with Objectifying Inquiry

Scientific inquiry is the paradigm of 'objectifying' inquiry, in the sense I explained. It is possible to be satisfied—or think that one is satisfied—with such inquiry as sole cognitive approach to the conditions of our existence. This is an attitude, which may be expressed rhetorically as "What else is there to be found out, except what can be found out in this way? What more is there to understand, once we have all the information needed to provide the missing pieces in our theoretical puzzles?" Given this attitude, all wonder ends once scientific curiosity has been satisfied.

Several writers have taken this attitude to be the characteristic of secular life.[26] On that premise, there is at least a logical possibility of being at once *not* secular and yet a committed (lay or professional) participant in the scientific enterprise. For after all, that attitude is not part of science itself, but circumscribes a role it can have in our existence.

However, this sort of satisfaction with science, which preempts wonder when scientific curiosity is satisfied, singles out at best one subclass of the secular. It does not charaterize any who seek meaning or significance outside objectifying inquiry. Such a quest may focus on art, poetry, aesthetic experience of any sort, nature apprehended as the Romantics taught, or on understanding through emotion, empathy, meditation, kinesthesis. . . . The varieties of religious experience too are so diverse that each of the above shades into them without any sharp break. Moreover, with the recognition of non-theistic religions, spiritual disciplines such as Zen and yoga, and the fervor of certain kinds of social ideals, we must almost speak of secular religions, so blurry is the borderline. This is not to say that there is no difference, but that we should probably be content only to chart certain important forms of secular orientation. It may be a mistake to try and draw an exact boundary that could be recognized as such from both sides.

Naturalism and Scientism

"Naturalism" is today a much more popular term among philosophers than "materialism". Epistemology has been naturalized by Quine, philosophy of science by Ronald Giere; Putnam has spoken to deaf ears with his "Why reason cannot be naturalized". Even to diagnose what it is to naturalize something is far from easy. To identify what naturalism is, apart from something praiseworthy, I have found nigh-impossible. Perhaps it is just the materialism I have been discussing here, under a different name. Alvin Plantinga recently offered a critique of naturalism, but says only that it entails that God does not exist nor any other supernatural being. Obviously this cannot be taken as definition, on pain of the circularity involved in characterizing "natural" in terms of "supernatural". I will not stop to analyze the texts of recent and current *soi-disant* naturalists and naturalizers to the extent that I have here scrutinized "Australian materialism". Yet I venture to assert: we see here too a position that only purports to be a factual thesis. Most likely it can not be identified with any factual thesis at all, but derives all its strength and support from attitudes that engender affinity with certain theses at each historical stage.

If this is correct, no such argument as Plantinga has recently given against naturalism can succeed. For this argument hinges on reflections on the probability of certain events on a supposition which includes philosophical naturalism. That makes sense only if naturalism is an identifiable thesis, a factual assertion. Even if the argument is internally correct, therefore, it is no more effective against naturalism than points about quantum field theory are against materialism—they affect only a some temporary tradeable asset of the position.[27]

Another term that comes to mind here is "scientism". The term was originally devised for philosophical attempts to cast science itself as a metaphysical system or as ideology, but also came to mean something like "science-idolatry". It should be sharply distinguished from positivism, even in its original form, though Comte (and later Ayer) certainly did not disentangle the two. Part of scientism is that very satisfaction with science (or more generally, objectifying inquiry) alone, such that wonder is preempted and no questions remain at all once scientific curiosity is satisfied. If this is combined with faith in the possibility of, or a felt need for, traditional philosophical system building then of course science must include any viable metaphysics. Absent such faith or need, the attitude can only be combined with positivism of one sort or another. With this stance, no questions remain at all once science has answered *its* questions.[28] For those having this stance, there is certainly nothing to be apprehended or understood outside this sort of inquiry taken as a whole.[29]

Neither metaphysics nor any sort of positivism or empiricism need carry such an attitude or cluster of attitudes, orientation, approach to life, or way of being in the world. That should be, it seems to me, a comforting point to all. The discomfort will be, I hope, that of losing the analogue to the naturalistic fallacy in this domain: the idea that such attitudes can ultimately be justified by advancing factual theses, whether empirical or non-empirical.

That said, let us now compare scientism with materialism as I characterized it earlier. Materialism purports in the first instance to be a thesis about what there is: *all is matter*. But sympathy with science, with its ever-striving, endless enterprise then poses a dilemma. Horn One: the thesis can be given the form of a specific scientific hypothesis. In that case it cannot be proposed as basis for a lasting philosophy. To be scientific, it must be yoked to science in progress, and so be hostage to the fortunes of future experience and future scientific development. This implies for every empirical thesis the prospect of being given up eventually, however well-grounded it may be in present science. Horn Two: the thesis can be given the form of a completeness claim for a specific science, say physics. But completeness claimed for today's science reduces to the previous case. Aiming the completeness claim at science in the long run empties it of content, since no one today can know what science will eventually be like.

We already saw J. J. C. Smart uncomfortably straddling the horns of this dilemma. Quite instructive here is Paul Feyerabend's essay on materialism (1963, with 1980 postscript). At the outset we find:

> The crudest form of materialism will be taken as the basis of argument. If *it* can successfully evade the objections of some philosophers, then a more refined doctrine will be even less troubled.
>
> Materialism, as it will be discussed here, assumes that the only entities existing in the world are atoms, aggregates of atoms and that the only properties and relations are the properties of, and the relations between, such aggregates. A simple atomism such as the theory of Democritos will be sufficient for our purposes. (*op. cit.* (1981), p. 161)

This suggests that any materialist thesis takes the form of a completeness claim for a certain scientific description of the world. It also suggests that philosophical disputes concerning materialism are entirely independent of the *content* of the thesis in question. If both suggestions are correct, there is already a serious question whether there is any such thing as materialism, the philosophical position construed as thesis.

Feyerabend gives several of the arguments found in various forms in Place, Smart, Lewis, and Armstrong, though without evident awareness of those discussions. (Feigl appears to be a common source with Smart.) He also allows for the possibility that no form of reduction of 'folk' psychology to physics is possible, in which case he favors eliminative materialism. But in the note added in 1980 he arrives at something like the conception of materialism as stance:

> It may well be that a materialistic language . . . is richer in cognitive content than commonsense. . . . But it will be much poorer in other respects. For example, it will lack the associations which now connect mental events with emotions, our relations to others, and which are the basis of the arts and the humanities. We therefore have to make a choice: do we want scientific efficiency, or do we want a rich human life of the kind now known to us and described by our artists? The choice concerns the *quality of our lives*—it is a *moral* choice. Only a few modern philosophers have recognized this feature of the strife about materialism. (*Ibid.*, pp. 162–63, n. 1)

The point is that the completeness claim for physics (at whatever stage) is indeed a factual claim (that physics answers all the questions that it is designed to answer, all that can be formulated in its terms) but its role in philosophy is not just that. The factual claim conveys, in some 'Gricean' way, the satisfaction with the restriction to these questions and the dismissal of any wonder not thereby addressed.

Thus materialism shades into scientism. If materialism continues to be officially identified through the content of its theses, and yet gains significance through this intellectual stance, it is—as I said—a matter of false consciousness. If instead it is an acknowledged avowal, then arguments surrounding its theses are mere byplay. No wonder they are independent of the specific contents of those theses—they serve only to remove some apparent obstacles! Feyerabend's choice of Democritean atomism as sample incarnation of the materialism he wanted to defend shows his characteristic courage, in displaying openly and exactly those weaknesses left out of the limelight. Materialism, the philosophical position, is in the main a stance that rests entirely on endorsement, avowal, and dismissal of certain approaches to life.[30]

Conclusion: The Relation of Metaphysics to Science

At this point I would like to express my own, empiricist point of view. Firstly, there is no empirical claim which may not be contradicted by the eventual content (product) of science. Therefore, to accept the scientific enterprise at all, as one of rational inquiry to which we are committed, is to adopt an attitude of detachment with respect to any and all empirical claims. All such claims are to be readily surrendered as hostages to the fortunes of future experience. Therefore, it seems to me that they cannot and should not be part of any philosophical position. This goes for 'materialist' theses, but also of course, for 'anti-materialist' theses, whether about psychological functioning, physiological evolution or conservation of matter/energy.[31]

Secondly, there is no non-empirical claim which matters at all to the process of science. The illustration of materialism generalizes to all metaphysics. I include here also theist, dualist, and idealist metaphysics, if any of these be coherent. Suppose some scientist wishes to write something to the effect that there is no God on the first page of his notebook. This may of course simply express some anti-religious sentiment. He could however intend it to be a metaphysical thesis with which all his scientific theories are to be compatible. Then he may write something like "Matter is all there is; God does not exist" and adds something equating God with the Omnipotent, Omnipresent, Omniscient Being as understood in metaphysical debates. (For contrast recall Pascal's amulet text "The God of Abraham, Isaac, and Jacob, not the God of the philosophers"!). When this scientist comes to the end of that notebook, he'll find that the thesis made no difference after all. At least, its *content*—as opposed to its emotive force—played no role. The same thing would have happened if he had written its negation down instead.[32]

Perhaps metaphysics has not always been, and perhaps it is not always even now an attempt to provide foundations or extensions of science, purportedly forged in the same mold as science itself, and thus in uneasy balance between rivalry and apologetics with respect to science. Perhaps, if wonder remains once scientific curiosity is satisfied, philosophy still harbors some response thereto; or perhaps, it too must then pack its bags and leave the field for other kinds of play. I do not know. But the picture of science deeply imbued with metaphysics, permeated by presumptive materialism and naturalism and thereby impervious to exploration of rival empirical hypotheses—that picture is not accurate. In the main, Duhem's view of science is right.

Notes

This essay is a labor of love, to honor Alvin Plantinga, a philosopher with whom I deeply disagree yet to whom I am indebted much more than I can say. I admire especially the directness which enables him to cut straight through to the heart of every philosophical matter, always preserving his gentle irony and good humor. While I admired Plantinga from afar since my student days, his friendship during this past decade has sustained me when hanging by my fingertips, both on rocks and in other senses.

1. The way in which I proceed will be, in various obvious ways, a reaction to Alvin Plantinga's essays in which he introduced the terms "Duhemian" and "Augustinian" for views of science which fall into these two camps: "Methodological Naturalism?" (forthcoming in J. van der Meer (ed.) *Facets of Faith and Science*. Lanham, Md.: University Press of America) and "Science: Augustinian or Duhemian?" (ms., 1994). This paper is written so as to be self-contained, and will not take Plantinga's (or Feyerabend's) specific ideas as target, but I will indicate connections with those papers in the notes. I wish to thank Ric Otte for helpful comments on an early draft.

2. My first paragraph is almost the same as a passage in Alvin Plantinga, "Science: Augustinian or Duhemian?" section 4.

3. Witness for example E. A. Burtt, *Metaphysical Foundations of Modern Science*. London: Routledge and Kegan Paul, 1924, 1932; republished by the Humanities Press, 1952.

4. To these belong Plantinga's critical analyses of certain parts of science in the papers mentioned above.

5. Provided, that is, the purported defects are of a sort that could be effectively criticized within science, from any point of view, even if it tends to take a partisan of some particular point of view to spot the defect. I won't bore the reader by repetition of the point that scientists' limitations imply a potential benefit in outsiders criticisms, be they Christian, Marxist, feminist, atheist, etc., in origin. The critique of which insiders are equally capable may not occur to them without prodding. That was well argued by Feyerabend in *Against Method* (London: Verso, 1988) and elsewhere, though that was far from his most interesting point about scientific inquiry.

6. This is the distinction which opens Rudolf Bultmann's "Is Exegesis without Presuppositions Possible?" pp. 145–53 in his *New Testament and Mythology* (Philadelphia: Fortress Press, 1989).

7. Two options are to list assumptions of statistical frequencies corresponding to those prior probabilities, or to redesign the experiment so as to be more "robust," that is, to be equally telling, in the same way, for a large range of prior probability functions.

8. I take this term also from Rudolf Bultmann (op. cit. pp. 45–46, 49, 131–32, 142) who drew heavily on the philosophy of Sartre and Heidegger which dominated certain parts of continental philosophy at that time. Bultmann broaches the question of what science is in the context of the further questions whether theology is or can be a science, how history differs from natural science, and how scientific questions differ from historical questions. The origin of his ideas are fairly clear; see especially Husserl's description of what he calls the natural attitude or natural orientation, and his discussion of the character of the Galilean and Cartesian demarcation of scientific theorizing in *The Crisis in European Sciences and Transcendental Phenomenology* (tr. D. Carr. Evanston, Ill.: Northwestern University Press, 1970). The contrasts drawn, however, are not the same.

9. Two remarks are in order here. First, the word "paranormal" is as context-dependent as "normal", referring to the currently accepted description of nature in the context of utterance. Second, while I do not want at all to enter the debate over evolution and so-called creation science, it is clear that some of the motivation for Plantinga's discussions of methodology came from that debate, and my discussion of this similar example may therefore (indirectly) provide a further point of contact.

10. Plantinga appears to accept this idea, if only for purposes of argument, in the papers mentioned above.

11. Notice that even if some other beliefs concerning paranormal phenomena or supernatural agencies had suggested the hypothesis, those would play no important role here. The reason is that they would not answer any of the questions pursued in biology and physics. (If a fuse blows when I press the light switch, it may be true and of incredible significance to my life that I pressed the switch in utter despair, yearning even for the artificial comfort that a little table lamp could bring, but it is irrelevant to the electrician's inquiry.) The participants in the inquiry must get on with their proper work, which is defined by the way the inquiry defines itself, namely in terms of the questions asked.

12. Thanks to Ric Otte for suggesting these.

13. *The Aim and Structure of Physical Theory* (tr. P. P. Wiener. Princeton: Princeton University Press, 1954), Appendix. This passage is quoted and discussed by Plantinga in "Science: Augustinian or Duhemian?" sect. 4.

14. Alvin Plantinga has suggested the name "Augustinian science" for what might be the realization of Feyerabend's dream of science consisting of many research communities guided by diverse metaphysical positions, held with firm commitment. Plantinga's contrasts this with "Duhemian science"; his advocacy of non-Duhemian (Augustinian) science sounds at times like a

repetition of Feyerabend's call for proliferation of theories. Note that Feyerabend credits recognition of the value of such proliferation to Mill, Popper, and Lakatos; see Feyerabend's "Problems of Empiricism" pp. 145–260 in R. Colodny (ed.) *Beyond the Edge of Certainty* (Englewood Cliffs, N.J.: Prentice Hall, 1965). See also his *Realism, Rationalism, and Scientific Method. Philosophical Papers*, vol. 1 (Cambridge: Cambridge University Press, 1981).

15. Nor is it difficult to find similar rival explorations in biology in general or evolutionary theory in particular; think of such hypotheses as group selection and the controversies over sociobiology. It does not follow that the "creation science," which my students from North Carolina tell me is taught there in high schools, is the sort of thing Feyerabend advocates.

16. Feyerabend notes this in "Problems of Empiricism," p. 168 and n.101, with reference to Duhem, op. cit., Chs. 9 and 10.

17. Plantinga has detailed certain motivations expressed by scientists explaining why they opted for one hypothesis rather than another in their own work, which suggest an entrenched resistance against the sort of exploratory research in question here. Feyerabend too chronicles such sentiments, expressed whenever "normal" science is in progress. But as Feyerabend's studies show (sometimes *malgré lui*, as he fulminates against conservativism) is that alternatives are being explored and developed, not far underground, even when the accepted theories are triumphantly marching on. Those alternatives are waiting in the wings for crisis, but also capable of evoking crisis when they become interesting enough in their own right. For this and many other reasons I conclude that on such issues we should not pay too much attention to scientists' reflections on how they proceed.

18. Eleonore Stump, "Non-Cartesian Substance Dualism and Materialism without Reductionism" (*Faith and Philosophy*, forthcoming) is very instructive here. Aquinas's doctrine on souls is at least not a mind-body dualism (if either is coherent—which I doubt).

19. U. T. Place, "Is Consciousness a Brain Process?" *British Journal of Psychology* 47 (1956), 44–50.

20. J. J. C. Smart, "Sensations and Brain Processes," *Philos. Review* 68 (1959), 141–156 (with later version reprinted in J. J. C. Smart, *Essays Metaphysical and Moral* (Oxford: Blackwell, (1987), 189–202); U. T. Place, "Materialism as a Scientific Hypothesis," *Philos. Review* 69 (1960), 101–4.

21. See, e.g., his half of D. M. Armstrong and Norman Malcolm, *Consciousness and Causality* (Oxford: Blackwell, 1984), and his *A Materialist Theory of Mind* (London: Routledge and Kegan Paul, 1968; revised edition with new preface, New York: Routledge, 1993).

22. Not to be forgotten, in this connection is *eliminative materialism*, which is an option even if the logical structures of psychological and physicalist discourse are so mismatched as to preclude any form of reduction or supervenience! That was a great insight of Feyerabend, Wilfrid Sellars, Richard Rorty, and Paul Churchland who did not care to play for such "small" stakes as

Place. Armstrong, however, says that if he were to be convinced of the irreducibility he would reluctantly become a dualist. I wonder if this means that he knows of a coherent and at least minimally adequate mind-body dualism?

23. "Materialism," Ch. 16 of his *Essays Metaphysical and Moral*; the paper was originally published in 1963. The passage just quoted could be, for greater clarity, followed by David Lewis's acknowledgment that as physics changes, so must any such thesis: "[Materialism] was so named when the best physics of the day was the physics of matter alone. Now our best physics acknowledges other bearers of fundamental properties. . . . But it would be pedantry to change the name on that account . . ." (David Lewis, "Reduction of Mind," pp. 412–31 in S. Guttenplan (ed.), *A Companion to the Philosophy of Mind*. Oxford: Blackwell, 1994; quote from p. 413). This is at the same time the continuation of Lewis's "An Argument for the Identity Theory," *Journal of Philosophy* 63 (1966), 17–25; reprinted with additions in his *Philosophical Papers*, vol 1. (Oxford: Oxford University Press, 1983) which clearly belongs to the tradition of "Australian materialism" we are here examining.

24. The attitudes described here contrast with those I take to be typical of empiricism, of deference to or admiration for science as a paradigm of rational inquiry, characterized by mutual and self-criticism. The empiricist attitude does not imply deference to science in matters of opinion, but a certain epistemic detachment with respect to the content of current or even ideal science.

25. What exactly is the spirit of materialism? I will try to say a little more in the last section. However, the making explicit of materialism in the sense of a perennial philosophy, or support for the conclusion that it can exist without false consciousness, is properly a task for the materialists themselves.

26. Emil L. Fackenheim, *God's Presence in History: Jewish Affirmations and Philosophical Reflection* (New York: New York University Press, 1970); M. Buber *The Eclipse of God: Studies in the Relation between Religion and Philosophy* (New York: Humanities Press, 1988); R. Bultmann "Science and Existence", pp. 131–144 in Bultmann, op. cit.

27. See the last chapter of *Warrant and Proper Function* (New York: Oxford University Press, 1993) and "Naturalism Defeated" (ms., 1995). Thanks to Jonathan Kvanvig for helping me to make this explicit.

28. There is one important qualification to this: the phrase "has answered" is overly simplistic. For any subject at all admits of endless varieties of objectifying inquiry, each with its own selection of 'relevant' parameters and range of 'relevant' questions.

29. I am not excepting theology here; included in objectifying inquiry is all *Wissenschaft*. This is another blurring of the religious/secular boundary, that theology once made "positive" can be pursued equally well (in principle) by the secular. For if pursued on a theoretical level it too 'forgets its origins'.

30. In a less sympathetic vein, R. G. Collingwood wrote similarly about materialism in modern philosophy, which he described as heir to Renaissance

pantheism: "To the very end it retained the impress of its pantheistic origin. . . . The phenomenon is so uniform that . . . we can recognize a materialist author by his habit of using the traditional forms of Christian piety in speaking about the material world. . . . Scientifically speaking, on the other hand, materialism was from first to last an aspiration rather than an achievement. . . . [T]he scientific credit of materialism was maintained by drawing very large cheques in its own favour on assets not yet to hand" (*The Idea of Nature*, New York: Oxford University Press, 1960; pp. 104–5).

31. For the religious, perhaps any presumed empirical knowledge should be treated as earthly riches in general: to be enjoyed, in all their fragility and radical uncertainty, with a certain detachment. (I must say "perhaps", for there are whole spectra of genuinely religious attitudes.) For discussion of the epistemic "detachment" involved in a commitment to science, see further my "Against Transcendental Empiricism" in T. J. Stapledon (ed.), *The Question of Hermeneutics* (Dordrecht: Kluwer, 1994) and "The World of Empiricism" (in Jan Hilgevoort (ed.), *Physics and Our View of the World*, Cambridge: Cambridge University Press, 1994 pp. 114–34).

32. I.e. still on the assumption that the content is what matters. Obviously the results of his theorizing would be different if he had certain attitudes triggerable by beliefs of that sort. An example might be someone who wishes and intends to do what God wants if God exists. Beliefs about God might then trigger wishes, desires, intentions, and eventually actions. Still, the *theses* in question do not affect science; if we consider *only* the content of these theses, they play no role at all.

Bibliography

Armstrong, D. M. *A Materialist Theory of Mind*. London: Routledge and Kegan Paul, 1968; rev. ed. with new preface, New York: Routledge, 1993.

Armstrong, D. M. and Norman Malcolm, *Consciousness and Causality*. Oxford: Blackwell, 1984.

Buber, M. *The Eclipse of God: Studies in the Relation between Religion and Philosophy*. New York: Humanities Press, 1988.

Bultmann, R. *New Testament and Mythology*. Philadelphia: Fortress Press, 1989.

Burtt, E. A. *Metaphysical Foundations of Modern Science*. London: Routledge and Kegan Paul, 1924; republished by the Humanities Press, 1952.

Collingwood, R. G. *The Idea of Nature*. New York: Oxford University Press, 1960.

Duhem, P. *The Aim and Structure of Physical Theory*. Tr. P. P. Wiener. Princeton: Princeton University Press, 1954.

Fackenheim, E. L. *God's Presence in History: Jewish Affirmations and Philosophical Reflections*. New York: New York University Press, 1970.

Science, Materialism, and False Consciousness   181
Feyerabend, P. K. *Against Method*. London: Verso, 1988.

Feyerabend, Paul K. "Problems of Empiricism", pp. 145–260 in R. Colodny (ed.), *Beyond the Edge of Certainty*. Englewood Cliffs, N.J.: Prentice Hall, 1965.

Feyerabend, Paul K. *Realism, Rationalism, and Scientific Method: Philosophical Papers*, vol. 1. Cambridge: Cambridge University Press, 1981.

Husserl, E. *The Crisis in European Sciences and Transcendental Phenomology*. Tr. D. Carr. Evanston, Ill.: Northwestern University Press, 1970.

Kant, I. *Critique of Pure Reason*. Tr. N. K. Smith. New York: St. Martin's Press, 1965.

Lewis, D. K. "An Argument for the Identity Theory", *Journal of Philosophy* 63 (1966), 17–25; reprinted with additions in his *Philosophical Papers*, vol 1. Oxford: Oxford University Press, 1983.

Lewis, D. K. "Reduction of Mind", pp. 412–31 in S. Guttenplan (ed.), *A Companion to the Philosophy of Mind*. Oxford: Blackwell, 1994.

Place, U. T. "Is Consciousness a Brain Process?" *British Journal of Psychology* 47 (1956), 44–50.

Place, U. T. "Materialism as a Scientific Hypothesis", *Philosophy Review* 69 (1960), 101–4.

Plantinga, Alvin. "Methodological Naturalism?" forthcoming in J. van der Meer (ed.), *Facets of Faith and Science*. Lanham, Md.: University Press of America.

Plantinga, Alvin. "Naturalism Defeated" (ms., 1995).

Plantinga, Alvin. "Science: Augustinian or Duhemian?" (ms., 1994).

Plantinga, Alvin. *Warrant and Proper Function*. New York: Oxford University Press, 1993.

Smart, J. J. C. "Sensations and Brain Processes", *Philosophy Review* 68 (1959), 141–56 (reprinted with revisions, pp. 189–202) in his *Essays Metaphysical and Moral*. Oxford: Blackwell, 1987.

Stump, Eleonore. "Non-Cartesian Substance Dualism and Materialism without Reductionism", *Faith and Philosophy* (forthcoming).

Van Fraassen, Bas C. (1987). "Against Naturalized Empiricism," pp. 68–88 in P. Leonardi and M. Santambrogio (eds.), *On Quine*. Cambridge: Cambridge University Press, 1995.

Van Fraassen, Bas C. "Against Transcendental Empiricism," in T. J. Stapledon (ed.), *The Question of Hermeneutics*. Dordrecht: Kluwer, 1994.

Van Fraassen, Bas C. "The World of Empiricism," pp. 114–34 in Jan Hilgevoort (ed.), *Physics and Our View of the World*. Cambridge: Cambridge University Press, 1994.

9

Plantinga's Naturalism

Earl Conee

Alvin Plantinga proposes an original and ingenious theory of warrant.[1] "Warrant" is Plantinga's term for a magnitude that suffices for knowledge when a high enough degree of it characterizes a true belief. Plantinga's theory of warrant in a sentence: A belief is warranted for someone when the person has the belief as a result of the "proper functioning" of a cognitive mechanism that is aimed at producing true beliefs and operating in an "appropriate environment," as long as being such a result makes it objectively highly probable that the belief is true. The theory explains the "proper functioning" of our cognitive system, and the system's "appropriate environment," by reference to God's design.

Thus Plantinga's theory of warrant—"proper functionalism" for short—invokes God, the epitome of a supernatural entity. Amazingly, Plantinga nonetheless regards his theory of warrant as a naturalistic proposal. He is quite open about this. He explicitly advocates a supernatural ontology for a naturalistic epistemology (p. 46).

Is that coherent? I think not.

Pre-Plantingan Naturalism in Epistemology

"Naturalism" is a rather freely applied term. "Naturalistic epistemology" does not refer to any clear definite category. But a common theme can be discerned in work that is so classified by observing that work from a broad and softly focused overview. Using broad and blurry terms, the theme can be said to be that of locating the epistemic within nature and finding epistemic topics to be suitable for investigation by scientific methods.

Sympathetic observers of naturalism in epistemology seem to concur that these are its central characteristics. In a survey of naturalistic epistemology, James Maffie writes, "Naturalists are united by a shared commitment to the continuity of epistemology and science."[2] In a survey of recent work in epistemology and the philosophy of science, Philip Kitcher characterizes naturalistic epistemology by its rejection of two assumptions: first, that epistemology is to be pursued apsychologistically, and second, that epistemological findings are instances of a priori knowledge.[3] In the introduction to a collection of essays in naturalistic epistemology, Hilary Kornblith identifies naturalistic epistemology as the view that questions about how we ought to arrive at our beliefs cannot be answered independently of questions about how we do arrive at our beliefs.[4] Thus what these commentators unite in seeing as a naturalistic approach is a directing of epistemological research toward facts about nature using methods appropriate for discovering such facts. They do not say that a commitment to a supernatural entity disqualifies a view from being naturalistic. But they may well think that this goes without saying, since it is difficult otherwise to see why the methods of natural science in general, and psychology in particular, would be ways to discover the epistemic facts.

Recent history of naturalistic epistemology aside, needless confusion ought to be minimized. A doctrine known as "naturalism" ought to place some sort of dominant emphasis on something worth calling "nature." Otherwise the title is pointlessly misleading. Plantinga remarks that "naturalistic epistemology is ill-named" (p. 46). That remark is remarkably puzzling, and Plantinga's further comments do not clarify it. He begins to support it by making the stunning assertion that naturalistic epistemology is "quite compatible with supernaturalistic theism" (p. 46). This seems quite doubtful. If naturalistic epistemology is what it appears to be—an application of a naturalistic world view and methodology to epistemic topics—then it is incompatible with any sort of supernaturalism.

Plantinga continues to address his claim that naturalistic epistemology is ill-named by asserting that the most plausible way for a theist to think about warrant is from the perspective of naturalistic epistemology.[5] This clearly does not tell us what he takes the naturalistic perspective to be.

Finally, by way of commenting on his stunning compatibility claim, Plantinga asserts that he will in later chapters defend the view that naturalism in epistemology "requires supernaturalism in anthropology" (p. 46). But the later chapters to which he is referring offer no general characterization of an ill-named naturalism. Those chapters consist in arguing that "proper functioning" as Plantinga construes it has no good naturalistic interpretation (Chapter 11), and that "metaphysical naturalism," described only as a metaphysics without God that is exemplified in the writings of Bertrand Russell, W. V. Quine, and David Armstrong (p. 220), is not rationally acceptable (Chapter 12).

Thus, the work of these later chapters still leaves us wondering: What *is* the ill-named category called "naturalistic epistemology," beyond something that includes Plantinga's own theory of warrant? In particular, what renders *naturalistic* the view that Plantinga is claiming to be best for theists to take of warrant, and which requires a supernatural person? Or is "naturalistic" what is supposed to be *wrong* with the name, and if so, why? What does unite the theories that are so-called? As far as I see, Plantinga never says. One thing is clear. On pain of inconsistency the ill-named naturalism that Plantinga recommends to theists cannot be the naturalism the literature suggests to me, since that consists in a purely natural godless ontology and a scientifically oriented methodology.

So much for the application of the expression "naturalistic epistemology." More substantially, the broad drift of thinking that the above commentators find in the naturalistic approach has two prima facie virtues. Natural science has been conspicuously and spectacularly successful in its predictions and convincing in its explanations. It is reasonable to suppose that this success has a methodological origin. Thus it is reasonable to suppose that to the extent that the questions of epistemology are accessible to the methods of science, the potential for progress toward answering epistemological questions increases. And second, the natural world appears to provide an epistemically safer ontology than do platonistic and supernatural realms. Thus, to the extent that epistemic truths are taken to be wholly about nature, they appear to be more defensibly located.

Again, both of these are prima facie virtues, perhaps ultimately overridden. But they are at least apparent assets, and they are available to naturalism in virtue of the characteristics that the above commentators and I find in it. A "naturalism" that deviates substantially from this perspective risks the loss of these strengths. We will see that this is the fate of Plantinga's theory of warrant.

Plantinga's "Naturalistic" Theory

As we have observed, Plantinga's view of what is in the category of naturalism is strikingly novel. Naturalism is seen to include proper functionalism, a theory that invokes God. God is as supernatural as anything could be. What good reason could there be to regard proper functionalism as naturalistic?

Plantinga offers reasons. Let us examine them carefully.

Mild Naturalism

Plantinga takes a naturalistic theory of warrant at its "mildest" to consist in denying that warrant has a deontological analysis, i.e., an analysis in terms of epistemic duty fulfillment (p. 45). As Plantinga observes, his theory of warrant is naturalistic in this "mild" sense. The most obviously evaluative terminology in the theory—"proper function" and "appropriate environment"—is explained in terms of God's design and not in terms of duty.[6]

But this is no sense of "naturalism" at all. A denial of a deontological analysis is not sufficient to place Plantinga's theory in the category of any sort of naturalism, however mild. A truly naturalistic account cannot use evaluative primitives of any sort, deontological or otherwise, unless they are shown to be naturalistically legitimate.[7] A theory of warrant with a teleological primitive, or an aesthetic primitive, or a primitive expression of moral right or entitlement, would be as non-naturalistic as a theory with a deontological evaluative primitive. A naturalistic account also cannot use any other non-natural ontological or methodological equipment, such as the defense of a conclusion by the authority of a scriptural citation. In any such way a theory could have a non-natural component.

Arguably, proper functionalism has another non-natural component in addition to its reliance on God, one that it shares with the most widely touted candidate for a naturalistic epistemological theory, reliabilism. In reliabilist theories, the relevant sense of "reliability" is explained as some sort of conduciveness to *truth*. Yet the property of being true is not a topic of any current or prospective natural science. It is unclear why primitive employment of a truth predicate does not disqualify reliabilism as a naturalistic proposal, just as would a primitive appeal to good reasons or coherence. If so, then Plantinga's theory of warrant would be likewise disqualified. It makes primitive use of "true" in describing the aim of a mechanism that must function according to its aim in order for a belief to be warranted.

Whatever the naturalistic status of a theory making primitive use of "true," there remains the general point that on any credible interpretation of naturalism, merely denying that an epistemic concept has a deontological analysis does not imply that the theory is naturalistic. So Plantinga's denial of a deontological analysis of warrant does not imply that proper functionalism is any recognizable sort of naturalism.[8]

Moderate Naturalism

Plantinga distinguishes two other grades of naturalistic involvement, and he classes proper functionalism in both grades. His second and "moderate" grade of naturalism in epistemology is an affirmation of a weak version of Kornblith's defining naturalistic thesis that was presented above. The weak version, without going as far as the previous Kornblith citation by claiming that questions about how we ought to arrive at our beliefs "cannot be answered independently" of questions about how we actually arrive at our beliefs, affirms that questions about actual belief formation are "relevant" to questions of how we ought to arrive at beliefs. Plantinga takes it that his theory of warrant "surely" affirms this much of a naturalism, at least to the extent that the "ought" is construed as asserting "the normativity that goes with warrant," and "actually arrive at" is construed as "actually arrive at when there is no cognitive malfunction" (p. 46). Plantinga claims that when these questions are construed in this way, the question of how we ought to arrive at our beliefs is according to his theory "identical" to the question of how we do arrive at our beliefs (p. 46). He infers that his theory is naturalistic in the moderate sense (p. 46).

These contentions seem thoroughly erroneous. Even going along for the moment with Plantinga's interpretation of "actually arrive at" as meaning "actually arrive at when there is no cognitive malfunction," his theory of warrant still does not identify the resulting question of how we "actually arrive at" our beliefs, so construed, with the question of how we arrive at warranted beliefs. The theory implies that a warranted belief must be produced by something much more specific than the lack of a cognitive malfunction. A warranted belief must be produced by a process governed by a segment of the design plan for our cognitive capacities which is "aimed at the production of true beliefs" (p. 46). This segment is not always operative when there is no cognitive malfunction.

For instance, Plantinga claims that there need not be any cognitive malfunction when someone is taken in by a mirage, although the resulting beliefs are not warranted. The reason for the lack of warrant is said to be that the resulting belief acquisition is not governed by the segment of the design plan for our cognitive faculties that is aimed "directly" at the production of true beliefs (p. 40). Likewise, there can be what Plantinga counts as a properly functioning cognitive system that results in a belief stemming from an optimism that is needed to recover from a serious illness, and such a belief is not warranted according to Plantinga's theory no matter how well it meets the theory's other conditions. This is to be true because that optimistic segment of the design plan is not aimed at truth (p. 16).

Even a belief produced by the proper functioning of a directly truth-directed portion of our cognitive system need not be warranted according to Plantinga's theory. It is separately required that a warranted belief be produced "in a cognitive environment that is appropriate" for the believer's cognitive mechanisms (p. 46).

Finally, it is further separately required by the theory that "there is a high statistical probability that a belief produced under [the other required] conditions is true" (pp. 46–47).

Thus, on Plantinga's theory the "ought to arrive" question is identical to the "actually arrives" question only if "ought to arrive" is construed as "arrives with warrant," and "actually arrives" is construed in the following way: "actually arrives *when the belief is produced by the segment of the design plan for our cognitive system which is aimed directly at producing true beliefs, and the system is operating in an appropriate environment, and all of that yields a high statistical probability that such beliefs are true.*" This interpretation of "actually arrives" is well beyond far-fetched. A utilitarian might as well say that the question of how we ought to act is identical to the question of how we do act, interpreting "how we do act" as meaning "how we act *when we maximize utility.*"

Given that Plantinga's theory does not, on any reasonable interpretation of Kornblith's questions, render them identical, it is also clear that proper functionalism confers on our actual processes of belief production no special relevance to warranted belief production. In any case where we have a belief that is warranted when we arrive at it, the way that we arrive at the belief is a way to arrive at a warranted belief.

If Plantinga's theory implies any such belief not to be warranted, then it is wrong. If it correctly classifies all such beliefs, then it is right about them. That much about actual belief production does not distinguish Plantinga's theory from anything. It is analytic.

If we get evidence about what warrants belief from our knowledge of our actual belief production, then we can use that evidence to test Plantinga's theory, just as it can test any other. No thesis about how we actually arrive at beliefs, or about what proportion of our actual beliefs are warranted, is implied by Plantinga's theory of warrant on its own. It says nothing about how often our cognitive mechanisms function normally, or about how often during their normal function the truth-directed segment of their design plan governs belief production, or about how often when all of this happens we are in an appropriate environment, or about how often, when all of this is so, it is sufficiently statistically probable that the resulting beliefs are true. The nature of the actual mechanisms of belief production neither confirms nor disconfirms Plantinga's theory. Adding further, definitely epistemic claims about which of our actual beliefs are warranted, or what proportion of them are warranted, results in assertions that are of obvious relevance to the accuracy of Plantinga's theory, and to that of any other theory of warrant as well. But such epistemic claims cannot be reasonably counted as simply answering questions of how we actually arrive at our beliefs.

There is no good reason to think that proper functionalism makes actual belief production "relevant" to warranted belief production in any way that distinguishes proper functionalism from overtly thoroughly non-naturalistic theories of warrant. Thus there is no good reason to think that the theory is an example of Kornblith's moderate naturalism.

Radical Naturalism

The third and "radical" grade of naturalistic involvement distinguished by Plantinga is attributed to Quine. This is initially identified as the proposal that traditional epistemology be "replaced" by descriptive psychology (p. 45). But by use of an argument that we will examine immediately below, Plantinga concludes that a certain sort of normativity "runs riot" (p. 46) in descriptive psychology itself. And he claims that this is the very sort of normativity involved in warrant (p. 46). These thoughts lead him to assert that Quine's radical naturalism is "presumably" the view that the only sort of normativity appropriate to epistemology is the sort found in descriptive psychology (p. 46). Plantinga infers that his theory of warrant is naturalistic in the radical Quinean sense, as long as his theory holds that being warranted is *identical to*, rather than merely *supervening on*, the property of being produced by properly functioning faculties in the right sort of environment (p. 46).

Plantinga argues as follows that the normativity involved in warrant runs riot in descriptive psychology. He asserts that descriptive psychology typically delivers functional generalizations of the form "When human organism O is in state S and conditions C obtain, there is a probability *p* that O will go into S*." He holds that such generalizations "taken neat" are false, since they do not hold of humans "who have just been attacked by sharks, or transported to Alpha Centauri, or suffered a stroke" (p. 46). From this he infers that the functional generalizations of descriptive psychology are to be understood to include an implicit qualification: "When a *properly functioning* human organism *in an appropriate environment* is in state S, then . . ." (p. 46). Plantinga asserts that these qualifications express the sort of normativity that his theory implies to be involved in warrant (p. 46).

There are two main problems with this argument. Let us consider Plantinga's last claim first, the claim that an implicit qualification of functional generalizations in descriptive psychology introduces the very sorts of evaluative properties that are, according to his theory, involved in warrant. This is clearly not so. Even assuming for the moment that Plantinga's suggested "proper-functioning-in-an-appropriate-environment" clause formulates a qualification that is implicit in typical psychological generalizations, this could not express the same evaluative properties that Plantinga invokes in his theory of warrant. Their extensions are different. For instance, Plantinga claims that if almost all of us were left nearly blind by some nuclear disaster, "the new style visual system would not be functioning properly" (p. 201). Yet it is clear that an accurate postdisaster descriptive human psychology would include functional generalizations that are true of the nearly blind majority, just as an accurate descriptive piscine psychology includes functional generalizations that are true of cave fish with degenerate visual systems. Any implicit qualification of those functional generalizations thus would not exclude the disaster victims, though their eyes would be "improperly" functioning in Plantinga's sense. So any senses of "proper" and "appropriate" that enter into an implicit qualification of the functional generalizations in descriptive psychology cannot be the senses that Plantinga employs in his theory of warrant.

It is plausible that functional generalizations in psychology are somehow implicitly qualified. But their qualification seems to be best understood as some sort of ceteris paribus clause, or whatever is the best way to understand the laws allowing exceptions that appear in all of the special sciences.[9] The other special sciences show that whatever the implicit qualification is exactly, it is not normative. For instance, a chemical law governing the dissolution of a salt is clearly not subject to any implicit normative qualification, merely because the process does not continue according to the law when, for example, the molecules involved are disintegrated by a nuclear blast. Despite having such exceptions, it is clear that there is no qualification in the chemical law that might reasonably be expressed by saying that a "properly functioning" dissolution in an "appropriate environment" proceeds as the law specifies. Neither the process nor the environment "malfunctions" when a blast interrupts them.

A better idea seems to be that one usefully distinguished kind of causal process is that of processes governed by chemical forces. The laws of chemistry describe what happens by natural necessity when chemical forces are operative. Chemical laws are true ceteris paribus. There are exceptions to them "taken neat," because more basic physical forces can interfere. But chemical forces are decisive often enough to make practicable the distinct theoretical science of chemistry.

The same considerations argue that it is not plausible to suppose that the exceptions to psychological generalizations that arise from nonpsychological factors such as biological disintegration imply a need for any normative qualification of the generalizations. Rather, accurate psychological generalizations say no more than what must happen in sentient organisms when the distinct kind of causal process that is governed by psychological forces is operative. Such laws do not say anything suggesting that it is "proper" for such forces to be operative. The intended qualification of psychological laws just sets aside other potential influences, nonpsychological factors that must be at least controllable in their impact if theoretical psychology is to be practicable.

If anything like this is the correct account of the exceptions to psychological generalizations, then it is a mistake for Plantinga to use the fact that psychological generalizations are false when "taken neat" to defend the conclusion that there is something normative about psychological laws. Much less does it follow that they are implicitly qualified by the very normative characteristics employed in his theory of warrant. There is nothing radically naturalistic about proper functionalism.

Methodological Naturalism

We have now reviewed Plantinga's defense of the naturalistic character of his theory of warrant. As has been emphasized, proper functionalism invokes God in accounting for the requisite truth-directedness of an operative cognitive mechanism when a belief is warranted. The theory is thus ontologically supernaturalistic. But, as just discussed, Plantinga argues that the sort of normativity that his theory employs also appears centrally in empirical psychology. Plantinga's adverting to empirical psychology might be thought to suggest that his approach to warrant is somehow guided by empirical science. If so, then the approach would exemplify the method that naturalists employ according to the commentators cited above. Indeed, we have seen that Maffie, Kitcher, and Kornblith seem to favor some such methodological characterization of what constitutes naturalism in epistemology. So perhaps Plantinga's work on warrant, while not naturalistic for reasons he articulates, is in fact naturalistic in an important methodological sense.

A closer look at Plantinga's claims about proper function shows that they are not empirically guided to any significant extent. His approach to the nature of warrant employs traditional analytic philosophical methodology.[10]

Plantinga does cite biological and psychological sources in defense of the claim that an appeal to proper functions is "deeply embedded in science" (p. 5). But when it comes to the particular psychological function that plays a role in proper functionalism, no scientific support is mentioned. In an effort to identify a first approximation to the particular sort of proper functioning that his theory ultimately requires, Plantinga asserts an overall function for our "cognitive faculties."[11]

> The purpose of the heart is to pump blood; that of our cognitive faculties (overall) is to supply us with reliable information: about our environment, about the past, about the thoughts and feelings of others, and so on. (p. 14)

Plantinga asserts without support that our cognitive mechanisms have this overall purpose. Even assuming that "purpose" here has a scientifically legitimate reading, this particular purpose is not inevitable. Yet no empirical work is cited on behalf of this claim. So the claim gives no appearance of being scientifically guided theorizing.

It might be thought that this claim about cognitive purpose should count as methodologically naturalistic in virtue of its being a sufficiently obvious consequence of the familiar facts of evolutionary biology. After all, the relevant faculties evolved in our ancestors under environmental pressures. It might seem that it is eminently reasonable to infer that this occurred because the faculties supply us with reliably accurate information about subject matters concerning which the faculties are usually employing in belief formation. So evolutionary forces sustained the faculties for this "purpose."

Anyone who finds persuasive the inference just made from evolution to reliability would be well advised to consult the final chapter of *Warrant and Proper Function*. In that chapter Plantinga explains no fewer than five rival hypotheses about how we might have evolved our actual cognitive mechanisms without their being reliable, and he argues that we have no good empirical basis for regarding the rival hypotheses as improbable (pp. 222–28).

The present methodological point does not turn on the merits of Plantinga's arguments in his final chapter. The point is that Plantinga's assertion that the overall purpose of our cognitive mechanisms is the acquisition of reliable information is certainly not based on any evolutionary reasoning, since he argues at length for the inadequacy of such reasoning. The assertion of purpose is made without any methodologically naturalistic basis.

Plantinga's theory of warrant does not finally rely on construing proper function in terms of this alleged overall purpose for our cognitive faculties. This purpose is taken up in a preliminary way, on route to a more specific relation between truth and the proper functioning that is held to be crucial for the theory of warrant. Plantinga allows that our cognitive mechanisms can function properly while beliefs are produced by wishful thinking or optimism (p. 16). These are not warranted beliefs. In an effort to accommodate his theory to this intuitive fact, Plantinga writes:

> Not all aspects of the design of our cognitive faculties need be aimed at the production of true belief; some might be such as to conduce to survival, or relief from suffering, or the possibility of loyalty, or inclination to have more children, and so on. What confers warrant is one's cognitive faculties working properly, or working according to the design

plan *insofar as that segment of the design plan is aimed at producing true beliefs*. (p. 16; emphasis in the original)

The theory thus does not finally require warranted beliefs merely to result from proper cognitive functioning in general, which can occur during wishful thinking and the like. Rather, it requires that the production of any warranted belief be governed by what Plantinga later characterizes as a "directly" truth-aimed segment of the design plan for the cognitive mechanisms involved (p. 40).

This language in terms of which the requisite psychological function is described—"aim" and "design plan"—literally applies only to things that are planned with some aim in mind. Natural science makes no claim that any capacity in sentient organisms originated from a literal design plan that was literally aimed to accomplish some end. So it is clear that science could not be a source for the hypothesizing of such a capacity.

Plantinga also describes the requirement in different terms. He characterizes it as the requirement that "the cognitive processes that produce the belief have the production of true belief as their purpose . . ." (p. 38). Making use of this formulation, we can also suppose that this notion of the "purpose" of a cognitive process can receive a satisfactory scientifically acceptable interpretation, perhaps in terms of an evolved function.[12] Then the idea that some belief forming processes have as their purpose the production of true beliefs is not so easily disqualified from having support from natural science. But there is still nothing methodologically naturalistic about the way that this functional proposal is made. Plantinga does not rely on science here. He cites no empirical evidence for the existence of any psychological process the function of which is true belief production. Rather, when he postulates the need for such a process to have a warranted belief, he does so purely on the basis of a traditional analytic philosophical consideration. He argues that this requirement avoids intuitive counterexamples (pp. 16–17, 38–40).

Neither the merits of this analytic method nor the success of this employment of it are at stake here. The point is only that it is Plantinga's method. His early mention of a scientific role for proper functions does not show that his approach to the nature of warrant is methodologically naturalistic. Where he specifies the particular function to which his theory appeals, there is no guidance from natural science at all. There is no other evidence that Plantinga employs any recognizably naturalistic method in developing his theory of warrant.[13]

Conclusion

There is nothing worth counting as naturalistic about Plantinga's theory of warrant. Including God in the theory initially appears to disqualify it as a version of naturalism, and Plantinga's efforts do not supply us with anything that overrides this appearance.

Perhaps in the end Plantinga does not intend to be taken completely seriously in arguing in the ways that we have reviewed that his theory of warrant is a naturalistic theory. After counting his theory as a radical naturalism, he makes the following lighthearted comment: "[S]triking the naturalistic pose is all the rage these days, and it's a great pleasure to be able to join the fun" (p. 46).

I take no pleasure in spoiling anyone's fun. But it would be too costly to allow this recreational endeavor to go unchallenged. Stretching our interpretation to accommodate proper functionalism in the category of "naturalistic epistemology" would so distort the meaning of the phrase as to ruin it for those who are earnestly trying to mean something natural by it.[14]

Notes

1. *Warrant and Proper Function* (New York: Oxford University Press, 1993). All subsequent references are to this volume, unless otherwise noted.

2. "Recent Work on Naturalized Epistemology," *American Philosophical Quarterly* (1990), p. 281.

3. "The Naturalists Return," *Philosophical Review* (1992), pp. 57–58.

4. Introduction, *Naturalizing Epistemology,* 2nd ed., Hilary Kornblith, ed. (Cambridge: MIT Press, 1994), p. 3.

5. This issue is said in a footnote to be pursued in a paper by Plantinga, "Justification and Theism" (*Faith and Philosophy* (1987) pp. 403–26). But nothing that is mentioned in that paper is described there as naturalistic epistemology. Instead, the paper defends a previous version of proper functionalism. It is formulated in the same apparently non-naturalistic terms, describing the "proper functioning" of cognitive faculties in an "appropriate environment," where God's design determines the relevant proprieties. There is no appearance that naturalism of any kind is discussed in the paper.

6. Not all of the naturalistically suspect language of the theory is so explained, though. See the discussion of truth below.

7. Plantinga argues that his use of certain normative terms, "proper function" and "appropriate environment," is naturalistically acceptable. That argument is criticized in the *Radical Naturalism* section below.

8. The denial of a deontological analysis is also not necessary for a

naturalistic account, whatever the details of what is required to count as naturalism. A deontological analysis of some epistemic terms is compatible with there being an ultimate analysis of the deontological language in naturalistically acceptable terms. This is not an idle theoretical possibility. A naturalist in ethics, for instance, might quite reasonably proceed by first giving an explicitly deontological analysis of some ethical judgments, e.g., ones framed in terms of moral "rights" or moral "oughts". If successful, this would have the benefit of effecting a conceptual reduction within the ethical domain. Such a proposal could be rendered naturalistic by going on to offer a naturalistically acceptable account, whatever exactly that turns out to require, of the deontological expressions employed in the initial analysis. One way that this might be done would be by taking the view of some contemporary moral realists that the deontological expressions in the initial analysis have their reference causally determined, and that this reference turns out to be to acknowlegedly natural properties. Some epistemic terms might well likewise have an initial deontological analysis within what is ultimately a naturalistic theory by anyone's lights—although Plantinga argues at length that in the case of his primitives, "proper function" and "appropriate environment," no ontologically naturalistic analysis is possible (Chapter 11).

9. Jerry Fodor has long championed this sort of position. See, e.g., his "You Can Fool Some of the People All of the Time, Everything Else Being Equal," *Mind* (1991), pp. 19–34.

10. If anything, Plantinga's work on warrant engages in a priori psychology more than that of most analytic epistemologists, by dint of its empirically ungrounded assertion of an overall purpose for our cognitive mechanisms. See immediately below.

11. In a completely responsible scientific inquiry, empirical substantiation would be needed for asserting that we have capacities that manage to achieve cognition, before going on to specify a purpose for mechanisms that do this for us. At the outset these faculties would be less prejudicially called something like "apparent capacities for belief acquisition." At a minimum, we should not be lured into thinking that reliable information acquisition must be the function of certain faculties that we have, simply because it is taken for granted that they are *cognitive* faculties.

12. Though again, Plantinga himself explicitly argues that this cannot be correctly done (Chapter 11).

13. In fairness it should be repeated that Plantinga never claims to employ a naturalistic methodology.

14. I am very grateful for comments on previous drafts of this paper from Richard Feldman, Carlo Penco, and Edward Wierenga.

Part IV

Warrant, Justification, and Expert Knowledge

10

Plantinga, Gettier, and Warrant

Richard Feldman

Alvin Plantinga begins his book *Warrant: The Current Debate* with the statement:

> My topic is warrant: that, whatever precisely it is, which together with truth makes the difference between knowledge and mere true belief. More specifically, my topic is contemporary views of warrant.[1] (1993a, p. 3)

In this paper I will discuss three points about Plantinga's work, all tracing in one way or another to the way Plantinga sets up his topic. First, I will examine Plantinga's use of the term 'warrant' and argue that, given what he means by it, the contemporary views he examines are not theories of warrant in his sense. Roughly, the reason is that theories of warrant must be theories that purport to solve the Gettier problem. The theories he discusses don't. Second, Plantinga is eager to refute internalist views about warrant, but I will argue that his objections to internalism miss their mark, partly because he mistakenly takes those theories to be theories of warrant. Finally, I will examine and criticize Plantinga's claims about the way his own theory handles Gettier cases.

Warrant and Justification

Early in his book Plantinga says, "I propose to begin my study of contemporary views of warrant by examining some *internalist* theories of warrant . . .'' (1993a, p. 5). According to Plantinga, "The basic thrust of internalism in epistemology . . . is that the properties that confer warrant upon a belief are properties to which the believer has some sort of special epistemic access'' (1993a, p. 6). As examples of internalist theories he cites versions of foundationalism defended by Roderick Chisholm (1966, 1977, 1982), coherentism as defended by Laurence BonJour (1985) and others, evidentialism as defended by Earl Conee and me (1985), as well as several other views. At the end of his survey of the current debate, Plantinga concludes that "Internalism, therefore, is quite insufficient; for an account of warrant we must look elsewhere'' (1993a, p. 183).

In my view, approximately no recent nonskeptical epistemologists have been internalists about warrant. In particular, the contemporary philosophers Plantinga takes as characteristic internalists have not been internalists about warrant. They have been internalists about something else—justification—but not about warrant. There's good reason for this, since internalism about warrant is plainly unacceptable, given any plausible account of what internalism is and given what Plantinga means by "warrant." Plantinga's rejection of internalism thus rests partly on a misinterpretation which, I believe, stems in part from his attitude toward the Gettier problem. The matter is complicated by the fact that Plantinga in some places seems to acknowledge just the point that I want to make here, but elsewhere he overlooks it or minimizes it.

The general point I want to make about all the philosophers whose views I'm about to discuss is this: while they defend internalist accounts of epistemic justification, they say that what's needed for knowledge is justified true belief plus something else. That something else is what's needed to deal with Gettier cases. And, in every case, that something else is something external. So, all these philosophers may well be internalist about justification, but none is internalist about warrant, where warrant is whatever must be added to true belief to get knowledge. For all these philosophers, warrant is justification plus something else such as "undefeated justification" or "justification dependent upon no falsehood" or the like. These are externalist notions.

Chisholm figures prominently in Plantinga's scheme. What Plantinga dubs Chisholm's "classical" view is the view about *warrant* that Chisholm defends in the first two editions of *Theory of Knowledge* and in *The Foundations of Knowing*. The details of Chisholm's theory don't matter for present purposes. Chisholm holds that a person knows a proposition only if the person believes it, it is true, and it is *evident* for the person. Being *evident*, which is Chisholm's way of expressing what others might express by saying that a proposition is justified for a person, is clearly an internalist notion. So, Chisholm is an internalist about evidence (or justification).

However, Chisholm's view is *not* that if a proposition is evident for a person, then that proposition (or belief in it) is warranted for the person. That is, Chisholm does not hold that being evident is all that must be added to true belief to get knowledge. His account of what else is needed evolved over time, but in all cases the something else was something externalist in character. In the first edition of *Theory of Knowledge* he says that a person knows *h* only if something that justifies *h* justifies no falsehoods (p. 23). This is no internalist condition, since two worlds internally exactly alike could be such that in one a justifier justifies no falsehoods while in another it does justify a falsehood. In the second edition of that work, Chisholm added a similar condition to get around the Gettier cases. There he required that a known proposition be "nondefectively evident," where this means roughly that it have a basis "which is not a basis of any false proposition" (p. 109). Again, this is an externalist constraint, since it depends upon the actual truth values of the proposition supported by the basis. He defends a similar, but somewhat more complex, idea in *The Foundations of Knowing* (p. 48). So, Chisholm does not defend an internalist account of warrant.

Similar remarks apply to other theorists Plantinga discusses. In *The Structure of Empirical Knowledge* Laurence BonJour defends a coherentist account of epistemic justification. He makes it clear that he is defending an internalist account of justification, but not of warrant. In one of the very few passages in which he mentions Gettier cases, he says of an example, "Of course, for the sort of reason suggested by Gettier examples, his beliefs would presumably not count as knowledge even if they happened fortuitously to be true, but it is only justification which is presently at issue" (p. 150).

Plantinga describes the theory John Pollock defends in *Contemporary Theories of Knowledge* as "quasi-internalist." But Pollock holds that knowledge requires that one's belief be "objectively justified." A person S is objectively justified in believing P provided that, roughly, S is subjectively justified in believing P and there is no truth such that, if it were added to S's beliefs, then S would no longer be justified in believing P (p. 185).[2] Again, this is a plainly externalist requirement, since it depends upon which propositions actually are true.

This establishes, conclusively I think, that the theorists Plantinga discusses are not internalists about warrant. They may be internalists about something, perhaps justification, but they are not internalists about warrant. They all do contend that a certain sort of internalist condition is necessary for warrant and thus for knowledge. It is consistent with all I've said that they are mistaken in thinking that any such condition is necessary for warrant. Whether they are or not, it is misleading to present them as being internalist about warrant.

In addition to misleadingly suggesting that internalist epistemologists are internalists about warrant (in his sense), Plantinga makes unjustified assumptions about the nature of warrant. For example, he says:

> Finally, warrant comes in degrees. Some of my beliefs have more by way of that quantity for me than others. . . . Initially, then, and to a first approximation, warrant is a normative, possibly complex quantity that comes in degrees, enough of which is what distinguishes knowledge from mere true belief. (1993a, p. 4)

He faults several theories for failing to capture the "obvious" fact that warrant comes in degrees (p. 110, p. 160).[3]

Now, it is obvious that there are things in the neighborhood of warrant that come in degrees—evidential support and reliability, for example. However, it is far from clear that *warrant* comes in degrees. Suppose warrant is "undefeated justification" or "justification that depends upon *no* falsehoods." These are not things that come in degrees. While Plantinga may have some perfectly telling objections to some or all of the theories he criticizes, his assumption that warrant comes in degrees is unsupported, and objections dependent upon that assumption fail. Similarly unjustified is the assumption that there is *any* quantity such that having enough of it, together with true belief, is sufficient for knowledge.

The internalist philosophers discussed earlier abandon internalism about warrant in response to the Gettier problem. Plantinga clearly sees the very point they all saw. He says that "what the Gettier examples really show . . . is that internalist accounts of warrant are fundamentally wanting; hence the added epicycles, so long as they appeal to only internalist factors, are doomed to failure" (1993b, p. 32). Exactly. But all the philosophers under discussion saw just that point and consequently added externalist epicycles to their accounts of knowledge. So there is no disagreement among Plantinga and his targets on this point.

Plantinga sometimes acknowledges that the theorists he describes don't really offer their theories as theories of warrant. However, he suggests that what others have thought needed to be added to deal with the Gettier problem is a minor detail. Consider the following passages:

> After 1963 the justified true belief account of knowledge was seen to be defective and lost its exalted status; but even those convinced by Gettier that justification (along with truth) is not *sufficient* for knowledge still mostly think it *necessary* and *nearly sufficient* for knowledge: the basic shape or contour of the concept of knowledge is given by justified true belief, even if a quasi-technical fillip or addendum ("the fourth condition") is needed to appease Gettier. (1993a, p. 6)

> The most interesting question, of course, is whether the twentieth-century received tradition is correct here; can warrant (apart, perhaps, from a fillip to mollify Gettier) be explained in terms of justification? (1993a, p. 29)

> I had thought that justificationists think justification necessary and (with true belief) *nearly* sufficient, so to speak, for warrant; the basic idea or basic picture is that knowledge is justified true belief. True: this turns out not to be exactly right; a codicil must be added to take care of annoying little counterexamples of the type Gettier proposed; but the main structure of knowledge is given by justified true belief. (1993c, p. 70)

These passages, and several others like them, suggest that Plantinga takes internalists to hold that an internalist condition—justification—is "nearly sufficient" for warrant, that the clause added to deal with the problem brought on by Gettier's "annoying little counterexamples" is a technical detail, a "quasi-technical fillip" or a mere "addendum" or a "codicil." This suggests that whatever is added to the justified true belief analysis to deal with the Gettier problem is a relatively minor detail, one that does not change the character of the analysis in any significant way.

This, however, is a seriously misleading picture. All the philosophers under discussion added to an internalist condition something externalist as a fourth condition. Perhaps the significance of that was lost on those writing before the internalist/externalist controversy came to the forefront of epistemological debate. Nevertheless, it significantly understates the role of the fourth condition to characterize it in the terms Plantinga does. It portrays all these philosophers who are externalists about warrant as internalists.

In the places in which Plantinga acknowledges that epistemological internalists aren't really internalists about warrant, he attributes to them the view that justification is "nearly sufficient" for warrant or the view that justified true belief is "almost" knowledge. And it is surely true that some epistemologists do speak this way. BonJour's remark that the justified true belief analysis of knowledge is "at least approximately correct" (1985, p. 3) is not atypical. Plantinga takes this to mean that the internalists think that being justified makes one "almost warranted" and that cases of justified true belief are very close to being cases of knowledge. As I will argue at the end of the next section, this is a misinterpretation of assertions such as BonJour's.

Plantinga's Objections to Internalism

Plantinga raises a series of objections to allegedly internalist accounts of warrant. Many of the objections take the form of examples designed to show that the conditions advanced by internalists are not necessary or are not sufficient for warrant. Evaluation of many of these objections is complicated by the fact that defenders of the theories in question did not think of their conditions as sufficient for warrant. Nevertheless, it will be instructive to examine in some detail one of Plantinga's examples. The result will be a clearer appreciation of the problems the justified true belief analysis of knowledge is susceptible to. Whether the result is put by saying that there are many different sorts of Gettier cases or that there are objections to that analysis other than the sort raised by Gettier is largely a terminological issue deserving scant attention.

Many of Plantinga's examples concern people suffering from serious delusions or diseases who believe what seems obviously true to them. I've argued in an earlier paper that the examples Plantinga uses to reject internalist theories are, in at least some cases, Gettier examples (1993, pp. 35–40). They are examples that defenders of internalist theories would take to be examples of justified beliefs that fail the fourth condition for knowledge. Plantinga replied that the examples are not like Gettier examples and that they do illustrate the failure of internalist theories (1993c, pp. 69–71). I want to examine his reply in this section.

As the target internalist theory, let us consider my favorite view, evidentialism. This is the view that a belief is justified to the extent that it is supported by the believer's evidence. The central example of Plantinga's reply concerns a patient at the Pine Rest Christian Psychiatric Hospital

> who complained that he wasn't getting the credit he deserved for inventing a new form of human reproduction, "rotational reproduction" as he called it. This kind of reproduction doesn't involve sex. Instead, you suspend a woman from the ceiling with a rope and get her rotating at a high rate of speed; the result is a large number of children, enough to populate a city the size of Chicago. As a matter of fact, he claimed, this is precisely how Chicago *was* populated. He realized, he said, that there is something churlish about insisting on getting all the credit due one, but he did think he really hadn't got enough recognition for this important discovery. After all, where would Chicago be without it? (1993c, p. 69)

Plantinga's claim about this example is that the man's beliefs may well fit his evidence, since everything internally available to him supports it. So on internalist standards, or at least internalist standards defended by evidentialists, his belief is warranted.

In my earlier paper (1993), I argued that in numerous cases Plantinga's objections to internalist theories failed. The examples are typically underdescribed. When they are filled out, they either are (1) cases of unjustified (and unwarranted) belief that fail to satisfy evidentialist conditions, and hence they are not counterexamples to evidentialism, or (2) Gettier-like cases of justified belief that are not knowledge. Examples of type (2) would show that evidentialist conditions are not sufficient for warrant. But that, of course, is no problem for evidentialists since they agree that internalist conditions are not sufficient for warrant.

I think that exactly these problems affect Plantinga's rotational reproduction example. The question for evidentialists is whether the belief that Chicago was populated by rotational reproduction fits the man's evidence. It's hard to see why we should think that it does. Indeed, it is difficult to see what in the example is supposed to be any evidence at all for that belief. Plantinga, however, thinks evidentialists are forced to say that the mere fact that a belief seems true to a person provides the person with evidence sufficient to justify the belief. He works himself into this position in the following way (1993c, pp. 67–69).

Epistemologists sometimes think that all evidence is propositional evidence. But that, Plantinga thinks, is surely insufficient for evidentialist purposes. An adequate theory must also recognize sensory or phenomenal evidence of the sort involved in the justification of our perceptual beliefs and other beliefs about the things around us. Plantinga also thinks evidentialists will have to appeal to the "felt attractiveness" of some beliefs and say that such attractiveness provides impulsional evidence (1993c, p. 68). Since the victim of the delusions feels strongly that Chicago was populated via rotational reproduction, he has impulsional evidence in favor of that belief. The belief therefore fits his evidence and is evidentially justified. But, Plantinga says, it obviously isn't warranted.

This argument goes wrong in at least two places. First, evidentialists need not say that mere felt attractiveness provides evidence in support of the believed proposition. Rather, they can hold that it combined with other evidence can provide supportive evidence. Thus, for example, the typical person has information about her general reliability in certain domains. I know, for example, that my beliefs about the names and specializations of my colleagues are generally right. In contrast, I know that my beliefs about which movies I've seen over the past few years are highly unreliable. When the name of a recent movie comes up in conversation, my assertions about whether I've seen it are often eventually shown to be wrong. Since I know this about myself, feeling in myself some attraction to the belief that I have (or have not) seen a particular movie is of little or no evidential value.

Furthermore, even in cases in which one does have evidence about one's reliability and thus an inclination to believe does enter into something like what Plantinga describes as impulsional evidence, any such evidence can be overridden by other evidence. I might be inclined to believe something in a domain in which I know myself to be reliable. Still, I might have and neglect to heed strong counterevidence that undermines the support that inclination to believe provides.

There is little reason to think that in Plantinga's rotational reproduction example the man has any evidence supporting his general reliability about methods of reproduction (or any other category in which we might include his belief). Even if there is some such evidence, it is likely that he has encountered strong counterevidence, such as incredulous stares or ridicule or reasoned counterargument from those whom he has told about rotational reproduction. Thus, there is little reason to think that the belief is justified on evidentialist standards.

Perhaps it is possible to revise the example so that the belief is supported by the evidence. Perhaps the man's companions at Pine Rest tell him he is right. Perhaps they produce books seeming to verify his belief and they help him figure out a coherent explanation for the failure of his theory to gain popular acceptance. Perhaps he doesn't meet with people who explain the physical impossibility of his theory. It's hard to imagine all this in detail, but it is possible. Is this trouble for evidentialists?

I don't think so. Evidentialists are not committed to the conclusion that the belief is *warranted*. In this rather far-fetched example, the belief is unlikely to satisfy the fourth condition for knowledge. There are, for example, other truths about the origin of the people of Chicago that would defeat his justification. Exactly how this works out depends upon the details of the additional condition for knowledge (and warrant) but, however that goes, it is likely to rule out this case. Evidentialists may be committed to the conclusion that the belief is justified, but I don't see anything wrong with that.

As originally formulated, the example is not much like a typical Gettier case since the belief in rotational reproduction is not true or justified. As revised, it is still not true. But we can, just possibly, imagine a case in which the man's belief about rotational reproduction is true. However, if the idea then is that the belief is true for reasons unconnected to the man's belief, then the example seems to be a clear Gettier-style example. It will fail any adequate fourth condition for knowledge.[4] Plantinga says that examples such as his don't appear to be Gettier style examples. He writes:

> examples of this kind—examples involving insanity, or brains in vats, or people deceived by Cartesian evil demons—don't seem much like Gettier's original example of the person who lies to you about a Ford, which turns out, unbeknownst to him, to be true, so that your belief is both justified and true. (1993b, p. 70)

It is true that Plantinga's example isn't much like the original Gettier cases. It is also true that brain-in-a-vat cases aren't much like the original Gettier cases. Of course, all those examples are examples in which the belief in question is false. Moreover, in Plantinga's example, on their most natural construal it strikes me as implausible to charge evidentialists with the conclusion that the beliefs are justified. But when you make the example one in which the delusional belief actually is a truth supported by the man's overall evidence, then it is relevantly like Gettier cases. They are evidentially supported true beliefs, but they are true for reasons in some sense unconnected to that evidence.

Plantinga makes a further claim about what he thinks his examples show, a claim that brings out clearly what he thinks internalists are committed to. He says of his examples:

these examples show that justification (construed evidentially) isn't any-where *nearly* sufficient for warrant. Consider again the man in Pine Rest who thought he had discovered rotational reproduction: he might very well be both deontologically and evidentially justified; but his beliefs don't come anywhere near having warrant. (1993c, p. 70)

Plantinga thinks that internalists hold that satisfying their conditions makes one at least come close to having warrant, that having adequate evidence, for example, is almost sufficient for warrant. He thinks that his examples falsify such claims since the insane or deceived people in his examples don't come anywhere close to being warranted. But I think Plantinga's objection here is based on a misunderstanding of internalism.

Internalists may well hold that in the vast majority of cases, a person with a justified true belief will have knowledge and a person lacking knowledge will not have a justified true belief. The justified true belief analysis of knowledge is almost right in that it evaluates almost all cases properly. There may be something slightly odd about saying that it gets almost all cases right, given that there are an infinite number of possible Gettier-like cases that it gets wrong. Still, I think we can make clear sense of the idea that it gets almost all cases right, that it gets wrong only cases that are in a certain way (or ways) unusual. Similarly, I think that in most cases evidentially justified beliefs are warranted.

Points such as those just described do not imply that having a justified true belief makes it the case that one "almost knows" the proposition in question, that the case is very similar to a case of knowledge. Internalists need not think that having a justified belief makes one "almost warranted."

It makes good sense to say that a person comes close to knowing when the person's evidence for a truth falls just a little short of what's required for knowledge. But that's not what goes on in Gettier cases. In those cases, the person's evidence is strong enough. It's not at all clear to me that in the standard Gettier cases, the person almost knows the proposition in question. For example, I'm not at all inclined to say, in the familiar examples, that Nogot comes close to knowing that someone in the office owns a Ford or that there's a sheep in the field. The way in which the person falls short of knowledge is not that she comes up short along some scale such that, had she only been a little farther along on the scale, she would have had knowledge.

When Plantinga argues that his examples show that "justification (construed evidentially) isn't anywhere *nearly* sufficient for warrant," it's clear that he must have in mind the sort of thing I just said internalists need not say. Plantinga is encouraged to think this way by his characterization of Gettier examples as "annoying little" examples requiring only minor technical adjustments in the analysis of warrant. But here he's arguing against something internalists ought not, and do not, say. What internalists may say, that most evidentially justified beliefs are warranted, is not called into question by his examples.

I conclude that Plantinga's rotational reproduction example does not cast any doubt on any internalist or evidentialist thesis. I believe that his other examples fail for similar reasons, but I will not go into them here.

Plantinga's Theory and the Gettier Problem

Plantinga provides the following summary statement of his account of warrant:

> A belief has warrant for me only if (1) it has been produced in me by cognitive faculties that are working properly (functioning as they ought to, subject to no cognitive dysfunction) in a cognitive environment that is appropriate for my kinds of cognitive faculties, (2) the segment of the design plan governing the production of that belief is aimed at the production of true beliefs, and (3) there is a high statistical probability that a belief produced under those conditions will be true. Under those conditions, furthermore, the degree of warrant is an increasing function of degree of belief. (1993b, pp. 46–47)

Although this passage says only that the three stated conditions are necessary for warrant, Plantinga's other statements of his theory make it clear that he intends to claim that these conditions are both necessary and sufficient for warrant (1993b, p. 19). The third condition is intended to state a general reliability requirement. It amounts to the claim that, in general, when the cognitive system functions as designed in a proper environment and a segment aimed at truth governs the production of a belief, the system produces a true belief.[5]

The Gettier Problem

Gettier cases pose a problem for Plantinga's theory. They are examples in which one's cognitive system functions perfectly well. Moreover, it forms a true belief. Thus Plantinga's conditions for knowledge apparently are satisfied. Yet these are not cases of knowledge. It will be helpful to have an example for consideration throughout this section. One of Gettier's original examples will serve perfectly well (1963). As Plantinga describes it:

> Smith comes into your office bragging about his new Ford, shows you the bill of sale and title, takes you for a ride in it, and in general supplies you with a great deal of evidence for the proposition that he owns a Ford. Naturally enough you believe the proposition that he owns a Ford. Acting on the maxim that it never hurts to believe an extra truth or two, you infer from that proposition its disjunction with *Brown is in Barcelona* (Brown is an acquaintance of yours about whose whereabouts you have no information). As luck would have it, Smith is lying (he does not own a Ford) but Brown, by happy coincidence, is indeed in Barcelona. (1993b, p. 32)

I'll refer to this example as 'the Barcelona case'. There is no malfunction of your faculties in this situation. You properly hear what Smith has said, you draw just the inductive conclusion you should from his testimony, and then you make a perfectly good deduction from that conclusion. So, clause (1) of Plantinga's account seems to be satisfied. Furthermore, if any segments of our cognitive system are aimed at the truth, the segment responsible for this belief would seem to be one of them. We might have parts of our cognitive system that incline toward excessive caution or optimism. Such things may have survival value, and the beliefs they produce may result from functioning as designed. But the goal in such cases is not truth and clause (2) is not satisfied. Nothing of the sort is operative here. The inductive and deductive systems at work do seem to be aimed at truth. Finally, we can assume that the general reliability condition of clause (3) is satisfied.

It appears, then, that you have a warranted true belief that either Smith owns a Ford or Brown is in Barcelona. Given that warrant is whatever must be added to true belief to get knowledge, it appears that Plantinga's theory implies, incorrectly, that you do have knowledge in this case. Since this example is typical of Gettier cases, it seems that Plantinga's theory does not properly deal with the Gettier problem.

Plantinga's First Response

Plantinga says two rather different things about Gettier cases. One response has to do with the environments in which the beliefs are formed. Plantinga says that in Gettier cases, "(t)he faculties involved are functioning properly, but there is still no warrant; and the reason has to do with the local cognitive environment in which the belief is formed" (1993b, p. 33). A little later he says,

> The locus of infelicity, in these cases too, is not the cognitive faculties of the person forming the justified true belief that lacks warrant; they function just as they should. The locus is instead in the cognitive environment; it deviates, ordinarily to a small degree, from the paradigm situations for which the faculty in question has been designed. . . . What we have in Gettier situations is a belief's being formed in circumstances differing from the paradigm circumstances for which our faculties have been designed. (1993b, p. 35)

Plantinga applies this idea to the Barcelona case. The example involves a process, *credulity*, "whereby for the most part we believe what our fellows tell us" (1993b, p. 33). Plantinga writes:

> Still, credulity is part of our design plan. But it does not work well when our fellows lie to us or deceive us in some other manner. . . . It does not work well in the sense that the result of its proper operation in *those* circumstances does not or need not result in true belief. More exactly, it's not that *credulity* does not work well in these cases—after all, it may be working precisely according to its specifications in the design plan. It is rather that credulity is designed, we might say, to work in a certain kind of situation (one in which our fellows do not intend to mislead us), and designed to produce a given result (our learning something from our fellows) in that situation. But when our fellows tell us what they think is false, then credulity fails to achieve the aimed at result. (1993b, p. 34)

A reasonable interpretation of this passage is that in the Barcelona example: (a) the cognitive system generally, and the credulity segment in particular, does function properly, (b) this segment of the design plan is aimed at truth, but it fails to achieve this result when it produces the belief that Smith owns a Ford, and (c) the environment is not a suitable one, it is not "appropriate for [your] kinds of cognitive faculties" (1993b, p. 46). Plantinga's contention, then, seems to be that in the Barcelona case clause (1) of his definition is not satisfied because your faculties were not designed to function in the environment of that example.

Now this is a surprising contention. For one thing, you can know a lot of things in the environment in which the example takes place. You can know that Smith is talking, that Smith said he owns a Ford, that Smith took you for a ride in a Ford, etc. So, in general, this environment must be one that is "appropriate" for your cognitive faculties. If it isn't, then Plantinga is committed to the conclusion that you can't know anything in this environment, an obviously absurd conclusion. Furthermore, to the extent that we can talk about the circumstances in which you are designed to function, this surely is such a circumstance. That is, your cognitive design does cover this sort of situation and it does dictate what you should believe: that Smith owns a Ford (and it permits believing that Smith owns a Ford or Brown is in Barcelona). So, arguing that the situation of the Barcelona case, and Gettier cases generally, is not appropriate for human cognitive faculties is false and, if true, would yield the conclusion that we know too little.

Plantinga might reply that his contention about the Gettier cases is not that their circumstances are in general ones for which our cognitive faculties are not suited. Rather, the specific faculty operative in them is not designed for the circumstances of the example. In the Barcelona case, for example, the operative faculty is *credulity* and it is not designed to function in the presence of liars. Other faculties, such as perception, are designed for those very circumstances and so we can gain perceptual knowledge in the presence of liars. Plantinga can thus avoid the objection just raised.

The reply just suggested on Plantinga's behalf turns on untestable and implausible assumptions about the circumstances for which our cognitive faculties were designed and on equally questionable assumptions about the individuation of our cognitive faculties. As Plantinga notes, we sometimes learn to become more discriminating about which of the things we hear are worthy of belief (1993b, p. 33–4). Imagine a sophisticated believer who detects a liar and disbelieves the liar's testimony. What faculty produced that warranted belief and what circumstances is it designed for? If *credulity* produced the belief, then *credulity* is, contrary to what Plantinga says, designed to work in the presence of liars. Perhaps, then, we should say that the faculty at work is not *credulity* but rather *incredulity*, which is designed to function only in the presence of liars. Such a view may save the theory, but it is distressingly ad hoc.

Other examples make matters worse. Plantinga mentions Bertrand Russell's example in which you see a stopped watch that coincidentally shows exactly the present time. You form a true belief about the time, but lack knowledge (1993b, 33). Plantinga must say your belief is not warranted. Following the line of thought currently under consideration, he must say that the faculty responsible for the belief is not designed to function in the presence of stopped watches. But notice that you do gain some knowledge from looking at the watch: you learn that there is a watch there and you learn what time it stopped. So, the faculties responsible for these beliefs must be designed to function in the presence of stopped watches, but the faculty responsible for the belief about the time must not be designed for that circumstance. Plantinga could make up some faculties to get the right results. He could say that we have a watch-identifying faculty, a watch-reading faculty, and a time-determining faculty, each designed for different circumstances. Such contentions, however, are entirely arbitrary and unsupportable.

More generally, one can simply decide whether a case is a case of knowledge or not and then identify an operative faculty and the circumstances in which it is intended to operate so that we get the desired result. Perhaps we cannot decisively refute such a theory. It's quite apparent, though, that there's little by way of a general theory and nothing that is illuminating or informative about why there is no warrant in Gettier cases.

Plantinga's Second Response

Plantinga goes on to elaborate on the significance of the Gettier cases, and when he does his explanation of the way his theory is supposed to deal with them turns out to be rather different from what we've just seen. Some Gettier cases involve perceptual illusions (e.g., laundry draped over a rock so that, from a distance, it looks like a sheep) or false testimony (e.g., the Barcelona case). The person who believes the testimony of a liar, or of his senses, functions properly but still lacks warrant. Plantinga explains:

> consider these perceptual illusion cases, and for definiteness imagine that our faculties have actually been designed; and then think about these matters from an engineering and design point of view. The designer aims at a cognitive system that delivers truth (true beliefs), of course; but he also has other constraints he means or needs to work within. He wants the system to be realized within a . . . humanoid body . . . in a certain kind of world, with certain kinds of natural laws or regularities. . . . He also wants the cognitive system to draw an amount of energy consonant with our general type of body, and to require a brain of only modest size . . . . So the designer's overall aim is at truth, but within the constraints

imposed by these other factors; and this may require trade-offs. (1993b, pp. 38–39)

The idea here is that although the larger system is aimed at truth, designing a system to achieve true beliefs in certain circumstances conflicts with other goals, such as speed, efficiency, and brain size. The overall design of the system results from a compromise among these various factors. Plantinga takes this to mean that some parts of the system are directly aimed at truth, while others have other ends or are included only to keep the overall system efficient and workable.

The relevance of all this to the Gettier cases, according to Plantinga, is that in the Gettier cases the beliefs are produced by segments that are part of the best compromise, but are not directly aimed at truth. Since his theory holds that "a belief has warrant for you only when it is produced by a segment of the design plan directly aimed at truth" (1993b, p. 40), he claims that his theory correctly implies that the beliefs in the Gettier cases are not warranted. Applied to his summary statement of his theory, the idea in this section is that clause (2) is not satisfied in Gettier cases.

The claim that the segment governing the production of the beliefs in the Gettier cases is not aimed at truth is puzzling. The element of the design system operative in the Barcelona case was said to be *credulity*. This, Plantinga said, is aimed at the truth. But now he's apparently claiming that it isn't. I believe that what Plantinga has in mind is that the specific "segment" of the design plan involved in producing the belief that Smith owns a Ford is not something so general as *credulity*. Rather, it is the very specific thing operative in this situation. In some places, Plantinga refers to segments as triples, consisting of a circumstance, a belief, and a purpose (1993b, p. 22). So, as Plantinga is thinking of things, in the Barcelona case, the segment of the design plan governing the production of the belief that Smith owns a Ford is a triple that we might display as follows:

<dishonest testifier, belief that Jones owns a Ford, efficiency>

This belief therefore does not have warrant, since it does not satisfy clause (2) of his account. Beliefs deduced from it also lack warrant, although the basis for that claim is not entirely clear. Perhaps the idea is that each of the segments responsible for the production of the beliefs leading up to a belief must be aimed at truth.

In contrast, when in the presence of an honest person, the triple might be:

<honest testifier, belief that p, truth>

So, in such cases one can get a warranted belief and knowledge.

There is something to the idea that in some Gettier cases a more complex belief-forming system might have enabled the believer to tell that there was something wrong in the situation. Perhaps a more acute perceptual system would enable people to distinguish genuine barns from facsimiles. Perhaps a better ability to evaluate people would enable us to distinguish liars from honest folks more reliably. Such abilities may come at a cost, either deficiencies elsewhere in the system or larger heads. It is arguably better that we lack those heightened abilities. So, invoking trade-offs and compromises to explain some Gettier-style examples may be acceptable. However, as a general account of those examples, it is unacceptable.

The claim that the segments of our design plan that get us knowledge are "directly" aimed at the truth while the segments responsible for the beliefs in Gettier cases have other aims is rather implausible. It is, however, distressingly difficult to refute, largely because there are so few constraints on what one might say about the "direct aims" of various segments of our design plan. Because there is so little to restrict what one says about the aims of the segments of the design plan that govern the production of our beliefs, it is possible for a defender of Plantinga's theory to say what's necessary to defend the theory from potential counterexamples. However, what one has to say becomes increasingly implausible. I'll describe some examples that illustrate those implausibilities.

First, notice how fine-grained the segments of the design plan have to be. Perhaps it is plausible to think that we have a "credulity module" and perhaps it is reasonable to think that it is aimed at getting us true beliefs. Maybe the same can be said of our perceptual system. In contrast, we might have other elements designed to bring us comfort or pleasure, even at the expense of false belief. So, maybe it is plausible to think that there are a variety of modules or elements of our cognitive design plans, only some of which are aimed at truth. But Plantinga's theory, as currently spelled out, has a seemingly unlimited supply of triples, with each situation and belief having its own aim or goal. That there is such specificity in our design plan is difficult to accept.

Furthermore, what determines the aims in each of these segments is extremely mysterious. It makes some sense, perhaps, to say that the whole system and some of its larger components have aims. But there is no clear basis for saying that the aim of the segment that makes me believe what you say is one thing, while the aim of the segment leading me to believe what some other person says is something else entirely. Assigning these specific ends in the way Plantinga must is quite arbitrary. No evolutionary account of the aims of our cognitive system could plausibly make such fine-grained assignments of "direct" aims to segments of the cognitive system.

Next, consider a variant of the original Barcelona case. In this variant Smith is telling the truth and does own a Ford. Your belief that Smith owns a Ford is warranted and you do know that he owns a Ford. It is, in other words, an entirely normal case. Imagine that, from your internal perspective, this revised case and the original Barcelona case are exactly alike, the cognitive processes occurring in the two cases are exact duplicates of each other. Plantinga's response to the Gettier problem implies that the segments governing the production of the beliefs in the two cases differ in their aims. One is aiming at the truth; the other is aiming at something else, efficiency perhaps. However, the cognitive processes are exactly the same. It is difficult to see any basis for distinguishing the aims of the segments of the design plan governing these two beliefs.

Consider finally a slightly different example. You are reading the sports section of the newspaper. There is a list of the scores of last night's basketball games. You believe that each game did have the outcome reported in the paper. Suppose there is a misprint in one of the reports. Following the pattern of Plantinga's account of the Barcelona case, his theory would have it that the goal of the segment governing the false belief was not truth, while the goal of the segments governing the other beliefs is truth. This seems wildly ad hoc, but it is a response forced on Plantinga. (If he were to say that the segment responsible for the false belief is aimed at truth, then consider the belief that disjoins that falsehood with the truth that Brown is in Barcelona. That disjunctive belief would be a truth produced by a segment aimed at the truth. The theory would then imply, incorrectly, that the disjunction is known.)

One wonders what basis a defender of Plantinga could have for thinking that the various segments of the design plan have the aims they must have if the theory is to work out properly. After all, one could equally well (or, better) say that the segment of the design plan operative in these similar cases is exactly the same. Perhaps the aim is truth. But then the theory fails, so Plantinga is forced to distinguish their aims. The resulting theory, while perhaps not decisively refuted, merits rejection.

A Theistic Defense

Plantinga may see things from an entirely different perspective. After all, he thinks that God is the designer of our cognitive system. Given God's perfections, if he designed our system to yield true beliefs, it would yield true beliefs. Others of us can think that an imperfect Mother Nature "designed" our systems with the aim of true belief, but things failed to work out as planned. That can't happen within Plantinga's theistic framework.[6] So, we can ask ourselves, thinking of things from Plantinga's perspective: "Why would God design our cognitive system so that we believe that Smith owns a Ford in the original Barcelona case?" The answer can't be, "So that we would have a true belief." It can't be because we don't achieve that end, and so God couldn't have been aiming at it. Thus, we conclude that God must have had something else in mind. And perhaps goals having to do with simplicity and efficiency are part of the answer. In contrast, in the revised Barcelona case, where there is no deception, we can again ask, "Why would God design our cognitive system so that we believe that Smith owns a Ford in this case?" And here the answer, "So that we would have a true belief" is at least not ruled out. So, maybe Plantinga has a rationale for his answers, even if it is not going to appeal to anyone lacking his theistic background beliefs.

There are other Gettier-style examples that undermine this defense of Plantinga.[7] These are cases in which one does not reason through any false belief. Consider again your evidence concerning Smith's Ford ownership. Suppose that Smith is one of your coworkers. You know the following proposition:

Smith, who is one of my coworkers, drives a Ford, says that he owns a Ford, etc.

You existentially generalize on this, deriving the conclusion:

There exists one coworker of mine who drives a Ford, says he owns a Ford, etc.

This, too, is something you know. From this you conclude that

One of my coworkers does own a Ford.

Let us suppose that this is also true, but it is true not because of Smith who does not own a Ford, but because another coworker, of whom you are ignorant, does own a Ford. You don't know that one of your coworkers owns a Ford. But that is a true belief. So, to defend his theory, Plantinga must say that it is not warranted. So, we ask ourselves, "Why did God design your cognitive system so that in this case you'd believe that one of your coworkers owns a Ford?" The answer "So that you'd get a true belief" is *not* ruled out. After all, you did get a true belief. But to avoid the counterexample, Plantinga must exclude that answer and provide another one.

The only answer that will work for Plantinga that I can think of goes like this: He can say that the goal in that case was not truth, but rather simplicity or efficiency, just as in the other Gettier cases. It's true that Plantinga can *say* this. But there's something obviously unsatisfactory about his saying it. For what's clearly the case is that the only rationale for saying it is that it saves the theory. The reasoning goes from the fact that there is no knowledge, to the conclusion that the goal of the segment producing the belief is not truth. Given that we have no independent way to assign goals to the segments of the design plan, we have no way to establish that Plantinga is wrong. But we also have no reason to believe that he is right or that his theory provides any enlightening account of what goes on in Gettier cases.

Conclusion

I conclude that Plantinga's work goes seriously wrong in several ways all having to do with the Gettier problem. The internalists whose views he criticizes are not internalists about warrant, although they are internalists about justification or other important epistemological notions. The examples Plantinga uses to criticize these theories, at least the one example discussed in detail here, fail to refute those theories because they are, at best, variations of Gettier cases. As a result, they are examples of justified beliefs that fail to be knowledge because they fail some additional, externalist, condition for knowledge. Finally, Plantinga's own account of warrant incorrectly deals with standard Gettier-style cases. The appearance to the contrary is brought about only by making arbitrary and implausible claims about the identity and purposes of the segments of our cognitive design plan.[8]

Notes

1. Plantinga reports that a typo led to the occurrence of both "truth" and "true belief" in his first sentence.

2. This ignores details of Pollock's theory that are irrelevant here.

3. Peter Markie argues that Plantinga's own theory fails to explain adequately degrees of warrant. See his paper, "Degrees of Warrant," in this volume.

4. If the belief is true and the man has good reasons for it that are properly connected to its truth, then it's not so clear that he lacks knowledge.

5. I misunderstood the intent of clause (3) when I wrote "Proper Functionalism." Some of my claims in that paper rely on the assumption that (3) requires just the reliability of the specific segment of the design plan rather than the reliability of the whole system. Correspondence with Plantinga helped me to see this point.

6. I ignore here the possibility that we freely go wrong. That seems to have nothing to do with the Gettier problem.

7. I discussed this sort of example in "An Alleged Defect in Gettier Counterexamples" (1974).

8. I am grateful to Earl Conee, Jonathan Kvanvig, Peter Markie, Ted Sider, and the students in my spring 1994 epistemology seminar for helpful discussions of drafts of this paper and related topics.

References

BonJour, Laurence, 1985: *The Structure of Empirical Knowledge*, Cambridge: Harvard University Press.

Chisholm, Roderick, 1966: *Theory of Knowledge*, Englewood Cliffs, N.J.: Prentice Hall.

——, 1977: *Theory of Knowledge* (2nd ed.), Englewood Cliffs, N.J.: Prentice Hall.

——, 1982: *The Foundations of Knowing*, Minneapolis: University of Minnesota Press.

Feldman, Richard, 1974: "An Alleged Defect in Gettier Counterexamples," *Australasian Journal of Philosophy* 52: 68–69.

——, 1993: "Proper Functionalism," *Nous* 27: 34–50.

Feldman, Richard and Earl Conee, 1985: "Evidentialism," *Philosophical Studies* 48: 15–34.

Gettier, Edmund, 1963: "Is Justified True Belief Knowledge?" *Analysis* 23: 121–23.

Markie, Peter, 1996: "Degrees of Warrant," this volume.

Plantinga, Alvin, 1993a: *Warrant: The Current Debate*, New York: Oxford University Press.

———, 1993b: *Warrant and Proper Function*, New York: Oxford University Press.

———, 1993c: "Why We Need Proper Function," *Nous* 27: 66–82.

Pollock, John, 1986: *Contemporary Theories of Knowledge*, Totowa, N.J.: Roman and Littlefield.

11

Degrees of Warrant

Peter J. Markie

Alvin Plantinga clears the ground in *Warrant: The Current Debate*, examining and rejecting several accounts of epistemic warrant; he builds anew in *Warrant and Proper Function*, developing an account of his own.[1] Yet, epistemic renewal is a risky business just like its political and social counterparts—the new may retain problems that made us want to reject the old—and Plantinga's theory is a case in point. It has one of the major weakness he finds in Laurence BonJour's coherence theory, John Pollock's quasi-internalism, and Alvin Goldman's reliabilism. It does not adequately explain what makes some warranted beliefs more warranted than others.[2]

Plantinga's Theory and the Degrees of Warrant Problem

Offering that our concept of warrant "is too complex to yield to analysis by way of a couple of austerely elegant clauses," Plantinga seeks the "necessary and sufficient conditions for the central paradigmatic core" of the concept [*WPF*, ix]. He finds the following.

> [A]s I see it, a belief has warrant for me only if (1) it has been produced in me by cognitive faculties that are working properly (functioning as they ought to, subject to no cognitive dysfunction) in a cognitive environment that is appropriate for my kinds of cognitive faculties, (2) the segment of the design plan governing the production of that belief is aimed at the production of true beliefs, and (3) there is a high statistical probability that a belief produced under those conditions will be true. [*WPF*, 46–47]

221

I shall assume that each of Plantinga's three conditions is familiar enough to need no special explanation.[3] Although he only states his conditions as necessary ones here, he claims their joint sufficiency elsewhere [*WPF*, 19], so I shall take them to be both necessary and sufficient, at least for "the central paradigmatic core" of the concept of warrant. I'll call their statement as necessary and sufficient conditions the Warrant Principle. Since Plantinga offers the Warrant Principle as capturing "the central core of our concept" [*WPF*, 47], I shall assume he takes it to be a necessary truth.

Now what about degrees of warrant? If a theory says that beliefs are warranted by virtue of having some characteristic C, it is at least initially reasonable to expect it to explain degrees of warrant directly in terms of degrees of C: one belief is more warranted than another insofar as it is has more of C than the other. Some of Plantinga's warrant conditions do come in degrees. An epistemic faculty can function more or less properly, in a more or less appropriate environment and with greater or less reliability.[4] So it is at least initially reasonable to expect that on Plantinga's theory a belief's degree of warrant will be the degree to which it is formed by the proper function in an appropriate environment of a cognitive faculty that is aimed at truth and reliable. Yet this is not how the theory works. Plantinga explains degrees of warrant in a different way, and for good reason: warranted beliefs can differ in their degree of warrant without differing in the extent to which they meet his three conditions.

Suppose that Paul sees a maple tree a short distance in front of him and a cardinal in a tree a bit farther away. He is quite knowledgeable about trees and birds, his vision is functioning perfectly well, it's a clear day, and there are no obstructions in his line of sight. His belief in the maple and his belief in the cardinal are both warranted. He is also more warranted in his belief about the maple than in his belief about the cardinal, given the differences in distance and object size and the fact that his vision is generally less reliable over greater distances and smaller objects. Nonetheless, there need be no corresponding difference in the extent to which Paul's beliefs meet Plantinga's three conditions for warrant.

Paul's beliefs equally satisfy Plantinga's second and third conditions (being formed by a faculty aimed at the truth and being formed by a reliable faculty). Each belief is formed by the same faculty (vision), so each is just as much formed by a faculty aimed at the truth and each is formed by an equally reliable faculty. Plantinga himself calls our attention to the fact that so long as the same faculty is involved in such cases, we cannot explain degrees of warrant by degrees of faculty reliability.

> [T]he problem will be that some of Paul's vision-induced beliefs will have a good deal more warrant than others; his beliefs about what he sees up close in good light will have more warrant than what he sees in a dim light at some distance; and then it can't be that what determines the degree of warrant of one of Paul's vision-induced beliefs will just be the overall reliability of his vision. So if we try to explain degree of warrant in terms of concrete faculties or powers such as vision, we run into a dead end. [*WCD*, 209]

Paul's beliefs are also on a par relative to Plantinga's first condition (being formed by a cognitive faculty functioning properly in an appropriate environment). The design plan for Paul's vision determines the extent to which it functions properly and the extent to which the environment is appropriate. His vision functions properly insofar as it functions as it was designed to function [*WPF*, 16]; it functions in an appropriate environment insofar as it functions in an environment similar to the one for which it was designed [*WPF*, 11]. The design plan for Paul's vision does not seem to support a distinction in propriety of function or in appropriateness of environment in the formation of his two beliefs. The close-up vision involved in Paul's first belief and the moderate-distance vision involved in his second fall equally within his vision's design plan. Environments where the perceived object is very near and large, as in the case of his first belief, and ones where it is moderately far and small, as in the case of his second, fall equally within the sort of environment for which his vision is designed. As we shall see, Plantinga assumes that the design plan for Paul's vision mandates some differences in belief intensity. Paul is to be more convinced of the maple than of the cardinal. Yet this does not imply that his vision functions more or less properly in one case than in the other or that the environment in one case is more or less appropriate; indeed, it is to assume that Paul's vision is designed for each environment and functions according to its design in each. In each case, his vision produces a belief and the beliefs differ in degree, but it functions with equal propriety in equally appropriate environments.

Of course, I may have misunderstood the design plan for Paul's vision. Perhaps it does provide for a difference in propriety of function or appropriateness of environment. It is hard to be sure without a clear specification of the plan itself. Yet the actual provisions of the design plan are not really to the point. Even if the actual plan for Paul's vision treats the two cases differently in terms of propriety of function or appropriateness of environment, it is still possible that it treat them the same. Paul could be designed so that the plan for his vision does not distinguish between the two cases in terms of proper function or environmental appropriateness, but his vision remains less reliable over the moderate increase in distance and the decrease in object size. The difference in degree of warrant between Paul's beliefs does not necessitate that they differ in the extent to which they meet Plantinga's first condition. Some may say that Paul's beliefs are formed by different faculties of different degrees of reliability so that they differ after all in the extent to which they meet Plantinga's conditions. Paul's belief about the maple is formed by his fairly reliable faculty of near, large-object vision; his belief about the cardinal by his less reliable faculty of moderate-distance, small-object vision. Plantinga himself points out a problem here.

> Of course, there are subfaculties as well as faculties: and just as vision is a subfaculty of perception, so there may be subfaculties of vision. Perhaps there are subfaculties narrow enough so that all of their outputs have the same degree of warrant. . . . Perhaps there are subfaculties as narrow as all that—but then again perhaps there are not. We can't just make up subfaculties and organs. . . . We can't gerrymander concrete processes or mechanisms just any way we want. [*WCD*, 209–210]

The subfaculty strategy is ad hoc, for we have no basis for claiming that distinctions between degrees of warrant are matched by distinctions between subfaculties.

In short, Plantinga's theory cannot explain degrees of warrant directly in terms of the degree to which its three warrant conditions are met. Undeterred, Plantinga tries another way. Let's now consider it.

Plantinga's Response to the Degree Problem

To save his own theory from the criticism he levels against BonJour, Pollock, and Goldman, Plantinga claims that degrees of warrant, which we have seen are not directly correlated with degrees of the complex property he thinks makes for warrant in the first place, are directly correlated with degrees of a different property: intensity of belief. After he presents the Warrant Principle, he adds the following to his account of the central core of our concept of warrant.

Under those [the Warrant Principle's] conditions, furthermore, the degree of warrant is an increasing function of degree of belief. [*WPF*, 47]

Plantinga also puts his point in terms of necessary and sufficient conditions.

[I]f both B and B* have warrant for S, B has more warrant than B* for S iff S believes B more firmly than B*. [*WPF*, 9; see too *WPF*, 19]

I shall call this the Degrees of Warrant Principle. It is meant to capture part of the core of our concept of warrant, so I shall assume that it is offered as a necessary truth.

We need to be cautious here. Not just any relation between warranted beliefs that is necessarily correlated with differences in warrant will provide an adequate explanation of what makes some warranted beliefs more warranted than others. Just as we cannot solve the degrees of warrant problem within Plantinga's theory by simply making up subfaculties with varying degrees of reliability, so too we cannot solve it by just picking any property of beliefs that necessarily varies with degrees of warrant. Consider an analogous case. If we want to explain what it is for one set to be larger than another, it won't do to pick just any relation between sets that is necessarily correlated with the larger-than relation. Perhaps one set's being larger than another is necessarily correlated with its being believed by God to be larger than the other— necessarily, S is larger than S* if and only if S is believed by God to be larger than S*—but the fact that a set is believed by God to be larger is hardly an adequate explanation of what makes it larger. An adequate explanation must ultimately refer to what determines each set's size. God's beliefs belong in a successful explanation only if God's beliefs somehow help determine a set's size. So too, even if differences in warrant are necessarily correlated with differences in belief intensity, a mere difference in intensity does not itself explain a difference in warrant. An adequate explanation must ultimately refer to the qualities that are the basis for warrant. Differences in belief intensity are relevant only if they are somehow tied to what warrants beliefs in the first place. If the Degrees of Warrant Principle is to be part of an adequate account of what makes one warranted belief more warranted than another, it must be based in the Warrant Principle's account of what makes beliefs warranted per se.[5] Plantinga does not clearly say how the Degrees of Warrant Principle is based in the Warrant Principle, but some of his remarks suggest a plausible line of reasoning. At one point, he compares his belief that $7 + 5 = 12$ with his belief that forty years ago he had a red bike with balloon tires.

> I believe the former [that $7 + 5 = 12$] more strongly than the latter [that forty years ago, I owned a red bike with balloon tires]; this is correlated with the fact that the former has more by way of warrant for me than the latter. I therefore conjecture that when my cognitive establishment is working properly, then in the typical case, the degree to which I believe a given proposition will be proportional to the degree it has warrant—or if the relationship isn't one of straightforward proportionality, some appropriate functional relationship will hold between warrant and this impulse. When my faculties are functioning properly, a belief has warrant to the degree that I find myself inclined to accept it; and this (again, if my faculties are functioning properly and nothing interferes) will be the degree to which I do accept it. [*WPF*, 9]

Plantinga conjectures that when his cognitive faculties function properly the intensity of his beliefs is directly proportional to their warrant. He might, then, base the Degrees of Warrant Principle on the Warrant Principle as follows.

Argument A:
1. If the Warrant Principle is true, then when a belief is warranted, it is the result of the proper functioning of a cognitive faculty aimed at truth.
2. If a cognitive faculty aimed at truth is functioning properly, it leads us not only to believe a particular proposition but to believe it with a particular degree of belief and, if the belief is warranted, that degree of belief is proportional to its degree of warrant.
3. Hence, if the Warrant Principle is true, then whenever two beliefs are warranted for us, each one's degree of warrant is directly proportional to the degree to which we believe it.
4. Hence if the Warrant Principle is true, the Degrees of Warrant Principle is true.

The Degrees of Warrant Principle is indeed an extension of the Warrant Principle, if Argument A is sound.

The crucial premise in Argument A is, of course, the second, that if our cognitive faculties are functioning properly, we hold beliefs with an intensity proportional to their warrant. This premise must be necessarily true for Argument A to establish the Degrees of Warrant Principle as an necessary implication of the Warrant Principle. Why should we take it as a necessary truth, let alone a contingent one?

The premise seems to be based on three assumptions Plantinga makes. First, he assumes that for a cognitive faculty to function properly is for the faculty to function in accord with its design plan [*WPF*, 13–14]. Second, he assumes that the design plan for each cognitive faculty dictates that the beliefs formed by that faculty have a certain degree of belief; as he puts it, "the design plan dictates the appropriate degree or firmness of a given belief in given circumstances" [*WPF*, 15]. Third, he assumes that the degree of belief dictated by a faculty's design plan is directly proportional to the degree of warrant possessed by beliefs produced by the faculty ("when my cognitive establishment is working properly, then in the typical case, the degree to which I believe a given proposition will be proportional to the degree it has warrant" [*WPF*, 9]). His rationale for the second premise in Argument A, thus, seems to be the following.

Argument B:
1. If a cognitive faculty functions properly, it functions in accord with its design plan.
2. The design plan for each cognitive faculty dictates a degree of belief for each belief formed by that faculty.
3. The degrees of belief dictated by the design plan for any faculty, insofar as the design plan is aimed at producing true beliefs, are proportional to the degrees of warrant the beliefs formed by the faculty will have if warranted.
4. Therefore, if a cognitive faculty aimed at the truth functions properly, it leads us not only to believe a particular proposition but to believe it with a particular degree of belief and, if the belief is warranted, that degree of belief is proportional to its degree of warrant.

Each premise in Argument B must be necessarily true to establish the necessity of the conclusion. Let's grant Plantinga the first two premises. Each epistemic faculty must have a design plan and each faculty's design plan must mandate not only what beliefs are formed in response to what stimuli, but also the intensity of each belief. What about the third premise? Why should we think that it is a necessary, or even a contingent, truth that the design plans for cognitive faculties aimed at the truth all dictate degrees of belief proportional to the degrees of warrant had by the beliefs they produce? Plantinga's account begins to unravel with this question.

Problems for Plantinga

The third premise in Argument B clearly is not a necessary truth. Some designer might have given one of our cognitive faculties a degree of belief that is epistemically too low. The designer might, for example, have made us just the way we are, except for one small change. The degree of belief specified for the epistemic faculty by which we form such beliefs as that $7 + 5 = 12$ is decreased. When this faculty functions properly (that is, as it is designed to function), we believe simple mathematical propositions with no more intensity than we hold such memory beliefs as that in our youth we had a red bike with balloon tires, these memory beliefs being formed just as they in fact are now. Under these possible circumstances, Plantinga's belief that $7 + 5 = 12$ is still warranted for him, and it is still more warranted for him than his belief that he had a red bike with balloon tires as a youth, but his design plan does not call for the belief to have an intensity directly proportional to its warrant. Indeed, that is just why the design plan is flawed and the creator epistemically mistaken; its mandated level of belief does not coincide with the level of warrant possessed by the beliefs it produces.

Consider too, Plantinga's warranted beliefs that Homer was born before 800 b.c. and that New York is larger than Cleveland. He admits that he might mistakenly believe the former with the intensity epistemically appropriate to the latter [*WCD*, 4]. This malfunction of his memory as currently designed can certainly be part of his memory's proper function under an epistemically incompetent designer's alternative plan. In that case, the design plan for Plantinga's memory will assign his belief in Homer a degree of confidence out of proportion to its degree of warrant.

Plantinga might say that situations like these cannot happen, but it is hard to see what the source of the impossibility could be. Couldn't we be designed just as we are except that the intensity of our simple mathematical beliefs is reduced to the intensity of our memory beliefs? Couldn't we be designed just as we are except that the intensity of our belief in Homer's birthdate is increased to the intensity of our belief in the size of New York relative to Cleveland? If, as Plantinga acknowledges [*WPF*, 17, 28], Humean subdeities could give us less reliable faculties than the ones we have, they could surely make design mistakes with regard to the intensity of our beliefs. Plantinga might, of course, admit that we can be designed in the ways indicated but claim that in such a possible world the warrant of our beliefs continues to match their intensity. In the possible world in which we are designed just as we are except that we believe that $7 + 5 = 12$ with the same intensity as we in fact believe that we had a red bike in our youth, our mathematical belief is no more warranted than our memory belief. Yet this is to ignore the fact that the change in our design extends only to degrees of belief. In the possible world contemplated, the faculty behind our mathematical belief is still more reliable by design than our memory. The mathematical belief is more likely to be true in just the nonaccidental way that suffices to give it a greater warrant.[6]

Moreover, the Degrees of Warrant Principle itself is open to actual world counterexamples. Suppose that I am diagnosed with cancer and, after consulting several specialists and various medical reports, I form a series of beliefs about my illness and my likelihood of survival. I believe that a certain treatment will most likely slow the cancer's progress and that, even with the treatment, I will most likely die from the disease within two years. Both beliefs are equally based in my evidence; both are equally warranted. Nonetheless, while I believe that the treatment will slow the cancer's progress with an intensity appropriate to my warrant, I am unable to be so confident of my death. I have equally warranted but unequally held beliefs. The Degrees of Warrant Principle is false. Similar cases are easy to construct. I see my son and one of his friends commit an armed robbery; my identification of each is equally warranted, and while I believe that each is guilty, I believe that about his friend more strongly than I believe it about him. My beliefs are equally warranted but unequally held.

Plantinga might again respond that these sorts of cases just cannot happen. If I don't hold the belief that I will die in two years with the confidence that I hold my equally well evidenced belief that the proposed treatment will slow the cancer, then I am not giving the former belief the confidence it epistemically deserves. This means one of two things. Perhaps my belief about my death is formed by a properly functioning faculty aimed at an end other than the truth, say, personal comfort. In this case, the belief is not warranted.

> What confers warrant is one's cognitive faculties working properly, or working according to the design plan insofar as that segment of the design plan is aimed at producing true beliefs. But someone whose holding a certain belief is a result of an aspect of our cognitive design that is aimed not at truth but at something else won't be such that the belief has warrant for him; he won't properly be said to know the proposition in question, even if it turns out to be true. [*WPF*, 16].

Alternatively, my belief about my death is formed by a faculty that is aimed at the truth but malfunctioning. The belief again has little or no warrant.

[T]he design plan dictates the appropriate degree or firmness of a given belief in given circumstances. You read in a relatively unreliable newspaper an account of a 53-car accident on a Los Angeles freeway; perhaps you then form the belief that there was a 53-car accident on the freeway. But if you hold that belief as firmly as, for example, that $2 + 1 = 3$, then your faculties are not functioning as they ought to and the belief has little warrant for you. [*WPF*, 15]

On either alternative, if I don't believe with appropriate confidence that I will die in two years, my faculties are not functioning properly with regard to seeking the truth, and my belief has little or no warrant for me. Since it has less warrant than the belief that the proposed treatment will slow my cancer, we do not have a case of equally warranted but unequally held beliefs.

This response has two problems. First, it implies that my belief in my death has little or no warrant, even though I have and can readily produce a great deal of evidence for it. Indeed, I can produce just as good evidence as I can for my belief about the proposed treatment, and when asked, I will assert the belief and explain its basis. I just do not hold it as intensely as my belief about the treatment. Second, it is clearly epistemically inappropriate for me to hold the belief about my death with as little confidence as I do, but if that belief really has little or no warrant, as Plantinga's position implies, I am actually giving it more confidence than it epistemically deserves.

We can now see a further problem with the Degrees of Warrant Principle. Besides assessing beliefs as warranted or unwarranted, we also assess levels of belief as being epistemically appropriate or inappropriate. As Plantinga puts it, "we may hold a belief more or less strongly, more or less firmly; we appraise not only the belief itself, but also the degree to which it is accepted" [*WCD*, 4]. A belief's degree of warrant determines whether its intensity is epistemically appropriate. If, to use one of Plantinga's examples [*WCD*, 4], we believe that Homer was born before 800 b.c. with as much confidence as we properly believe that New York is larger than Cleveland, our degree of confidence about Homer is epistemically excessive. It is excessive just because it is more than the belief's degree of warrant merits. So too, if we believe that New York is larger than Cleveland with no more confidence than we properly believe that Homer was born before 800 b.c., our degree of confidence about New York is epistemically insufficient. It is insufficient just because it is less than the belief's degree of warrant merits.

Plantinga's theory does not allow for cases of warranted belief in which the degree of belief is epistemically inappropriate. Consider first the cases in which our confidence is too low, those in which we are warranted in believing p but believe p with less intensity than is called for by its degree of warrant. According to Plantinga's theory, since our degree of belief is inappropriate, our belief is not the result of a properly functioning cognitive faculty aimed at the truth, in which case our belief is unwarranted and our degree of belief is not epistemically insufficient after all. Plantinga's theory thus precludes the existence of warranted beliefs in which the belief level is too low. Now consider the cases in which our confidence is inappropriately high, those in which we are warranted in believing p but believe p with more intensity than is called for by its degree of warrant. Once again, according to Plantinga's theory, since our level of belief is inappropriate, our belief is not the result of a properly functioning faculty aimed at the truth, in which case it is unwarranted and our degree of belief is excessive, not because it is more than the belief's positive degree of warrant deserves, but because the belief has no warrant at all. Plantinga's theory thus precludes the existence of warranted beliefs in which the belief level is too high.

So Plantinga fails to explain degrees of warrant. The Degrees of Warrant Principle is not adequately based in the Warrant Principle, so that, even if it were necessarily true, it would not adequately explain what makes one belief more warranted than another. The Degrees of Warrant Principle is open to actual world counterexamples. It also prevents Plantinga from allowing for cases of warranted belief in which the level of belief is epistemically inappropriate.

Possible Adjustments in Plantinga's Theory

Can we fix Plantinga's theory so that it better explains degrees of warrant but still retains its basic insights? Two possibilities suggest themselves. Each is problematic.

We might try to explain degrees of warrant in terms of degrees of reliability. Consider again Paul's vision-based beliefs in the maple and the cardinal. It is certainly plausible to think that the reason his first belief has more warrant than the second is that vision is more reliable with regard to large, near objects than small, moderately distant ones. Consider Plantinga's belief that $7 + 5 = 12$ and his belief that forty years ago he had a red bike with balloon tires. It is plausible to think that the reason the first has more warrant than the second is that it stems from a more reliable faculty.

We have, of course, seen that Plantinga's theory does not immediately lend itself to this approach. His theory treats reliability as a property of faculties, and there is no reason to believe that the divisions between our faculties correspond to the differences in warrant between our beliefs. Paul's unequally warranted beliefs about the maple and the cardinal may just as well be formed by the same faculty as by faculties of different reliability. We can slide past this problem, however, if we switch our attention from faculties to cognitive process types, at least for the purpose of explaining degrees of warrant. As Plantinga points out, there are distinctions between process types even when there are none between faculties.

> So we can't be at all sure that there are concrete faculties or subfaculties of the right narrowness; and just here is where types are handy. We can make up types ad libitum (more realistically, any type we might find useful is already there). [*WCD*, 210]

Even if Paul's beliefs in the maple and the cardinal are both formed by the same faculty, the visual process leading to his belief in the maple is an instance of one type (visual identification of a familiar, large, and near object), while that leading to his belief in the cardinal is an instance of another (visual identification of a familiar but small and moderately distant object), and the first process type is more reliable than the second.

So let's leave Plantinga's account of warrant per se just as it is in the Warrant Principle, so that warrant is understood in terms of the proper functioning of cognitive faculties, but explain degrees of warrant in terms of the reliability of relevant associated process types. We might adopt something like the following: Where B and B* are both warranted for S, B has more warrant than B* for S if and only if, where P and P* are, respectively, the process tokens by which B and B* are produced by properly functioning cognitive faculties, the relevant process type exemplified by P is more reliable than that exemplified by P*. Paul's beliefs in the maple and the cardinal are produced by the same properly functioning faculty, but the process by which the first is produced is an instance of a more reliable relevant process type than that by which the second is produced.

This approach does not reduce Plantinga's theory a form of reliabilism.[7] Warrant per se is still explained in terms of the proper functioning of cognitive faculties rather than the reliability of cognitive process types. Plantinga may continue to avoid some of the standard problem cases for reliabilism—e.g., brain lesions that cause subjects to believe they have a brain lesion when they have no supporting evidence—by claiming that the beliefs involved lack warrant. He may still say that, "Although such belief-producing processes are in fact reliable, the beliefs they yield have little by way of warrant; and the reason is that these processes are pathologically out of accord with the design plan for human beings" [*WPF*, 14]. If Paul has a brain lesion that causes him to believe that he has a brain lesion, his belief-forming process may be an instance of a very reliable process type, but it does not represent the exercise of a properly functioning cognitive faculty.

Nonetheless, Plantinga's theory will now encounter another problem he frequently raises for reliabilism: the generality problem. Every process is a token of many types of varying degrees of reliability, so which type(s) are relevant to a belief's degree of warrant and why? Consider how Plantinga poses the generality problem for Goldman's reliabilism.

> What determines the degree of justification, according to Goldman, is the degree of reliability of the relevant process type. But then the relevant process type, the one that determines the degree of warrant of the belief in question, must be a very narrow type: it must be such that all the beliefs in its output have the same degree of warrant. (It couldn't be a broad type like *vision*, say, because the outputs of processes exemplifying this type will have many different degrees of warrant: perceptual beliefs resulting from examining a middle-sized object from ten feet in bright and sunny conditions, obviously, will have more warrant than beliefs arising from distant vision on a dark and foggy night.) So suppose we take relevant types narrowly enough so that all the beliefs in the output of a relevant type have the *same* degree of justification or warrant: then first, it will be extremely difficult to *specify* any relevant type. Indeed, if, as Goldman suggests, the relevant type must be specified in psychological or physiological terms, we won't be able to specify any such types at all; our knowledge is much too limited for that. [*WCD*, 198–99]

These remarks will apply equally well to Plantinga's theory, if he explains degrees of warrant in terms of the reliability of belief process types.[8]

A second way to revise Plantinga's theory is to deny that there are degrees of warrant in the first place. Our warranted beliefs are never such that some are more or less warranted than others. What comes in degrees is the intensity with which we are warranted in believing a particular content. When Paul forms his vision-based beliefs about the maple and the cardinal, he is warranted in believing in the maple with more confidence than he is warranted in believing in the cardinal, but each belief, with its different degree of intensity, is equally warranted for him. So too, Plantinga is warranted in believing that $7 + 5 = 12$ with more confidence than he is warranted in believing that forty years ago he had a red bike with balloon tires, but each belief with its different degree of intensity is equally warranted. If Plantinga takes this approach, he will no longer have to account for degrees of warrant. He will instead have to account for the varying intensities with which beliefs may be warranted. He can approach this task in terms of proper function. Since he believes that the design plan for each faculty mandates the intensity with which each belief is held, he might adopt something like the following.

(I) A belief B has warrant for S if and only if S is warranted in believing the content of B with some degree of intensity.

(II) S is warranted in believing the content of B with degree of intensity D if and only if S's belief in that content with degree of intensity D (1) has been produced in S by cognitive faculties that are working properly in a cognitive environment that is appropriate for S's kinds of cognitive abilities, (2) the segment of the design plan governing the production of S's belief is aimed at the production of true beliefs, and (3) there is a high statistical probability that a belief produced under those conditions will be true.

There are no degrees of warrant relative to (I). Each warranted belief is equally such that the subject is warranted in believing the content with some intensity or other. According to (II), a belief of a particular intensity is warranted just when the belief is formed with that intensity through the proper function in an appropriate environment of a cognitive faculty that is aimed at the truth and reliable.

This approach is also problematic. Consider again the case in which, although I have equal evidence that treatment will slow my cancer's progress and that I will die in two years, I do not believe the latter with the same intensity with which I appropriately believe the former. How are we to understand this case relative to (I) and (II); what exactly is my epistemic error? It is not that I fail to believe in my death with a degree of belief appropriate to its degree of warrant; for warrant, as now understood, does not come in degrees. Presumably, my error is that I fail to believe in my death with all the intensity with which I am warranted in believing in it. The following are true.

(1) I believe I am likely to die from cancer in two years with a degree of intensity no greater than D.
(2) I am warranted in believing I am likely to die from cancer in two years with degree of intensity D*, which is greater than D.

Yet, according to (II), (2) is true only if the proper functioning of my epistemic abilities leads me to believe with degree of intensity D* that I am likely to die in two years, and that is just what I do not do. Plantinga's theory needs to cover cases in which beliefs are actually held with less confidence than is warranted. Perhaps it can do this, but something more subtle than (II) is required.[9]

There's a second problem as well. Consider again a possible world in which our cognitive faculties are just as they in fact are except that a lower degree of belief is mandated for the epistemic faculty by which we believe that $7 + 5 = 12$. When this faculty functions as designed, we hold such simple mathematical beliefs with no more confidence than we hold such memory beliefs as that we had a red bike in our youth, these memory beliefs being formed as they are now. The proper functioning of our redesigned faculties leads us to believe that $7 + 5 = 12$ with the same intensity as we believe that we owned a red bike in our youth. Yet, since our faculties are otherwise unchanged, we are actually warranted in holding the mathematical belief with more confidence than the bike belief; for we are more likely to be right about that bit of mathematics than about that bit of our past. The faculty behind our mathematical belief continues to be more reliable than our memory, and the difference in reliability is not accidental but a result of differences in cognitive design. As noted in the previous section, Plantinga might claim that situations like this cannot happen, but it is difficult to see why that should be the case.[10]

Conclusion

In its current form, Plantinga's theory fails to account for degrees of warrant. The Degrees of Warrant Principle does not explain what makes one belief more warranted than another. It is open to actual world counterexamples. It prevents Plantinga from allowing for cases of warranted belief in which the degree of belief is epistemically inappropriate. There are at least two ways to revise Plantinga's theory. One is to explain degrees of warrant in terms of degrees of process type reliability, but the theory then encounters the generality problem, which Plantinga claims to avoid. The other is to trade degrees of warrant for degrees of warranted belief intensity, but the theory then encounters the problem of accounting for beliefs that are held with less confidence than is warranted, as well as the problem of accounting for the fact that our cognitive faculties might have been designed so that the mandated intensity of a belief is not always epistemically appropriate. When it comes to degrees of warrant, Plantinga has yet to improve on the theories he rejects.[11]

Notes

1. Alvin Plantinga, *Warrant: The Current Debate* (Oxford: Oxford University Press, 1993), hereafter referred to as *WCD*; Alvin Plantinga, *Warrant and Proper Function* (Oxford: Oxford University Press, 1993), hereafter referred to as *WPF*.

2. Plantinga's main discussion of degrees of warrant relative to BonJour's coherence theory is at *WCD* 109–10, relative to Pollock's quasi-internalism at *WCD* 169, and relative to Goldman's reliabilism at *WCD* 198–99. Since my primary concern is Plantinga's own account of warrant, I shall not evaluate his attempt to show that each of these theories fails to account for degrees of warrant.

3. Take note of one point, however. Plantinga's third condition may be interpreted as applying to the believer's cognitive system as a whole and requiring its reliability or as applying to the cognitive faculty involved in the production of the belief at hand and requiring its reliability. Richard Feldman, for one, reads Plantinga in the first way and tells me he bases his reading in part on conversations with Plantinga. I read Plantinga in the second way. I find the second reading most in keeping with Plantinga's statements in his books and subsequent publications. Consider Plantinga's clarification of his third condition at *WPF* 17: "Even more exactly, the module of the design plan governing its [the belief's] production must be such that it is objectively highly probable that a belief produced by cognitive faculties functioning properly according to that module (in a congenial environment) will be true or verisimilitudinous." Consider too his remark in "Why We Need Proper Function," *Nous*, 27:1 (1993), p. 73, when he considers whether his third condition is met in a particular case described by Feldman: "And is there a high objective probability that a belief produced by these faculties (the ones involved in the production of Feldman's belief) functioning properly in an appropriate cogni-

tive environment will be true?'' Examination will reveal that my criticisms of Plantinga's theory are independent of this issue.

4. I, for one, am unsure whether a cognitive faculty can be more or less aimed at the truth as Plantinga intends that condition to be understood.

5. Plantinga might respond that the Degrees of Warrant Principle is not intended to explain what makes one warranted belief more warranted than another. Yet, surely we need an explanation, and no other part of his theory even comes close to providing one.

6. Plantinga might claim that the situations I have described are impossible because God necessarily designs every cognitive faculty aimed at the truth so that its design plan mandates a degree of belief proportional to the degree of warrant had by the beliefs it produces. (I owe this suggestion to Jon Kvanvig.) This reply will, of course, be lost on those who do not share the requisite theology. Those who are unsure of whether the situations I have described are possible should consider whether they are at least what Ernest Sosa has termed ''opposing counterexamples'': they are not clearly impossible and they clearly entail that the third premise in Argument A is false, thus making that premise less than clearly necessary. See Ernest Sosa, ''Proper Functionalism and Virtue Epistemology,'' *Nous*, 27:1 (1993), pp. 54–55. See too Plantinga, ''Why We Need Proper Function,'' pp. 76–77.

7. For a discussion of the relation between Plantinga's theory and reliabilism, see Richard Feldman, ''Proper Functionalism,'' *Nous*, 27:1 (1993), pp. 40–49, and Plantinga's reply in ''Why We Need Proper Function,'' pp. 71–76.

8. Plantinga goes on to claim that a narrow specification of relevant types also prevents Goldman's reliabilism from accounting for such examples as the brain lesion case. As already noted, Plantinga can avoid such cases so long as he requires that only beliefs formed by properly functioning cognitive faculties are warranted. Given this, Plantinga might claim that the generality problem is not a serious difficulty for this theory even when it is revised as I have suggested. He seems to believe that the most serious difficulty represented by the generality problem is not that we don't have an adequate specification of relevant process types but that any specification will be open to the brain lesion types of counterexamples. Consider his remarks at *WPF* 29: ''[T]he problem is not incompleteness, but something much more debilitating: we can see that no matter which level of generality we select, the [Goldman] analysis will give us the wrong results.'' See too his remarks at *WCD* 198–99.

9. What is required is a treatment of the distinction between (i) S's believing p with intensity D being warranted and (ii) a belief in p with intensity D being warranted for S. The former entails that S believes p with intensity D, while the latter does not. Principle (II) gives necessary and sufficient conditions for (i) but not (ii). To explain my epistemic error, Plantinga needs to give us an account of (ii), for my error lies in the fact that a belief in the proposition that I am likely to die in two years with intensity D* is warranted for me but I only believe that proposition with intensity D.

10. Plantinga could claim that if the two faculties mandate the same intensity of belief, then the phenomenological experiences involved in each are the same in that each belief just seems right to the same extent, and if this is true, then the beliefs are equal in warranted intensity. Yet this would be to claim that the similarity phenomenological experience is sufficient for sameness in warranted belief intensity. It would, thus, be to ignore the important difference in faculty reliability based in differences in cognitive design.

11. Jon Kvanvig and Richard Feldman provided quite helpful comments on an earlier version of this paper.

12

Experts, Knowledge, and Perception

George S. Pappas

People who qualify as experts in some field or subject matter present interesting case studies for both the psychologist and the epistemologist. Such individuals often employ methods or procedures for acquiring knowledge which are quite different from those used by more ordinary cognizers or by novices in the field. In some cases these expert methods involve special kinds of calculation or reasoning; in others it seems that something other than reasoning is operative, perhaps something along the lines of pattern recognition. In the latter cases, the expert procedure is rather like a finely honed skill, in a sense more like knowing how to do something than anything we might consider reasoning from additional premises or beliefs.

I will present a few examples of each sort of case. My aim ultimately is to suggest that ordinary cognizers are often very much like experts in some cases. The ordinary cognizer often acquires new knowledge, that is, by utilization of methods which closely match those employed by some experts. This suggestion, I think, is one that easily fits in with the account of warrant and knowledge which Alvin Plantinga has proposed.

Strategy-Experts

In one sense of the term, an expert is just a person with a great deal of knowledge in some subject area. A person who knows much of what there is to know about Balkan history, we tend to think, is an expert in that field. In another sense of the word, an expert in subject S is a person who is able to use her knowledge in S in effective ways. So we often call on experts to make identifications, diagnoses, prognoses, and the like. Legal and medical experts are but two of the familiar cases of individuals who are able to make special use of their abundant knowledge in these domains. Of course, one has the ability to make effective use of one's stock of knowledge in subject S only if one has that knowledge. But it is clear that there need be no connection running in the opposite direction. That is, a person who possesses much knowledge in S may be quite poor at making good use of this knowledge in concrete situations. So these two notions of an expert in subject S are distinct.

Persons who are experts in the use of their considerable knowledge in subject S often have an important additional skill; namely, they are able to easily and quickly acquire new knowledge in S. Persons who are experts in this sense seem to mobilize special strategies for the acquisition of new knowledge in S, strategies that a novice in the field cannot access. I will call such individuals strategy-experts. These are individuals who typically have a great deal of knowledge in a subject S, and who are also able to utilize special methods of obtaining new knowledge in S, methods which are generally closed at least in subject S to other individuals.

In this paper I will focus attention on strategy-experts. I do not aim to canvass all that might be said on the topic, however, for there are just too many unusual strategies which such individuals employ. Rather, I will concentrate on a few significant examples, for they are ones which raise interesting epistemological matters.

A strategy-expert is generally a person who has already acquired a store of knowledge in subject S, usually of diverse sorts, and who has methods or strategies for acquiring new information or knowledge in S, methods which are quite different from what others typically follow in the same area. Moreover, the strategy-expert differs from ordinary cognizers in S in the speed with which she acquires new knowledge. Perhaps as a novice the strategy-expert went through a sequence of steps, a prescribed bit of learned reasoning that led to early knowledge in S. But now, as an expert, she no longer relies upon that set of routines. Something else is operative in many cases in which strategy-experts acquire new knowledge in relevant subject areas.

To illustrate this point we may consider a case of strategies employed in solving physics problems. In two different studies,[1] researchers concentrated on how experts and novices approached the problems.

One of their findings concerned how the experts conceived the problems. They would categorize many seemingly different problems in the same way, because they noticed that they all could be solved using conservation of energy principles. Novices, on the other hand, placed the various problems in many different categories, depending on which physical features were mentioned in the statement of the problem.

How the problems are initially characterized seems to be very important. Doing so in terms of basic physical principles (such as conservation principles), according to Chi et al,[2] prompts activation in the experts of specific schemata that will help determine which equations are to be used to solve the problems. This procedure typically enables them to solve the problem quickly and efficiently, with a minimum of calculation. Novices, though, lack these schemata concerning relevant basic physical principles, and so they choose equations which describe or contain the goal (that which was to be solved for in the statement of the problem) and then work backwards towards the information contained in the statement of the problem, choosing a sequence of equations that might be utilized to solve for unknowns mentioned in the statement of the problem. This done, they then reversed the procedure, and stated the entire solution to the problem.

The number of inferences used by the novice is far greater, because there is so much calculation. Solution time, then, is also far greater for the novice than it is for the experts. All of this is due, in turn, to the quite different strategies employed by the experts and novices.[3]

Other examples come from studies of certain mathematical experts. Alexander Aitken, a professor of mathematics at Edinburgh for many years, enjoyed great fame as a mathematical calculator. Here is Aitken commenting on how he turned the fraction 1/851 into a decimal equivalent:

> The instant observation was that 851 is 23 times 37. I use this fact as follows: 1/37 is 0.027027027027 . . . and so on repeated. This I divide mentally by 23 [23 into 0.027 is 0.001 with remainder 4] . . . in a flash I can see that 23 into 4027 is 175 with remainder 2 and into 2027 is 88 with remainder 3, and into 3027 is 131 with remainder 14, and even into 14,027 is 609 with remainder 20. And so on like that. Also before I ever start this, I know how far it is necessary to go in this manner before reaching the end of the recurring period: for 1/37 recurs at three places, 1/23 recurs at twenty-two places, the lowest common multiple of 3 and 22 is 66, whence I know that there is a recurring period of 66 places.[4]

In this case, Aitken's method for solving the problem amounted to first converting 1/851 to 1/23 times 1/37; then he changes into decimal form the fraction with the shortest period of repetition—in this case, it is 1/37, whose period of repetition is 027; then he multiplies this decimal by the remaining fraction of 1/23, though he does so by the equivalent procedure of dividing the decimal by 23, thus reaching the result of 0.001175. This procedure is Aitken's description of his calculating method after the fact. In actual operation, he came up with the correct result in an extremely short time, so quickly that it seemed virtually instantaneous to nonexpert observers.

In these cases from physics and mathematics the experts do reason or calculate, and they do draw relevant inferences. Moreover, they can typically recall and recount what the reasoning was, even if they did not go through their inferences self-consciously. What makes them different from novices is the kind of reasoning used, the principles appealed to, the diminished degree of calculation, and the speed with which solutions are achieved. There are other cases, however, in which strategy-experts do not seem to do any calculation or reasoning, though they apparently acquire new knowledge nonetheless.

Mathematical cases, especially those involving prodigies, are once again instructive. Recent research has tended to divide some mathematical prodigies who can perform amazing feats into those who "see" mathematical results, and others who "hear" such results. In the former case is the story of the interviewer who was speaking with twin brothers who, though somewhat retarded in certain intellectual spheres, were mathematically gifted in some areas of mathematics. In the interview, a box of wooden matches was accidentally knocked onto the floor and the matches spilled out. The brothers looked at the heap of matches and instantly and in unison asserted "111." They then looked at each other, smiled, and in unison said "37." On further questioning, the twins claimed to see the number 111 in the heap of matches, and also to see the factor 37 (3 × 37 = 111).[5]

Other mathematical prodigies say that they "hear" numbers, even that they sometimes "feel" them. Louis Fleury was one of the latter individuals.

He said that he "felt the outlines of imaginary cubarithms passing beneath his fingers," that is to say the embossed counting symbols used by blind people. "When he was carrying out an operation," wrote Dr. Desruelles, who studied Fleury at the asylum in Armentieres, "his fingers moved with extreme rapidity. With the right hand he grasped the fingers of the left hand one after another; one represented hundreds, another tens, a third units. He moved his fingers feverishly over the lapel of his jacket and it was curious to watch him using these tactile images to obtain sensations correspondingto those he would have had in touching cubarithms.'"[6]

In Fleury's case, it is clear that he is doing some calculations. He is merely calculating differently from the way others would, and more rapidly. However, in the twin brothers case calculation does not seem to be a factor. They claim to see their results, and to reach them nearly instantaneously, without having to work them out.

The same seems to be true in other mathematical cases. Writing of another prodigy named Langdon, Bernard Rimland observed:

My hunch is that when this dramatic, quantum change took place (when his calculating suddenly became unconscious and extremely rapid), the site of the processing had migrated from the left hemisphere of the brain—which specializes in logical, sequential, step-at-a-time processes—to some other area, quite possibly in his right hemisphere—which grasps patterns of information all at once. Whether my hunch is correct or not, it does become clear that a very complex set of calculations can be automated if repeated often enough, and can be done in what is, apparently, a simultaneous rather than a sequential fashion.[7]

Rimland's hunch about the right hemisphere is controversial, of course, but it also seems to be independent of the claim about the instantaneous nature of Langdon's cognitive achievement.

Langdon's skill was that of being able to tell, given a specific date, the day of the week on which that date fell. He was similar to another set of twins, Charles and George, who could do the same.

One of the twins, Charles, was completely accurate only for this century, but his brother George made correct day-date identifications in centuries ranging from 4,100 B.C. to 40,400 A.D.[8]

We can understand what Rimland is suggesting for Langdon, and by implication for twin George, by reflecting on the ordinary competent number user who early in life mastered the multiplication tables up to 12. She encounters a situation in which she must multiply 7 by 9. She immediately reaches the result "63" but not by counting or calculating. Her answer, using Rimland's term, is instantaneous. Perhaps it is retrieved from long-term memory. Or maybe it is something more like pattern-recognition. Whatever the psychologically correct story, what seems clear is that in reaching her result she does not and need not engage in any calculation. The same is true of Langdon, and of twin George. It is also true of Aitken, though in a different context from that discussed earlier. In addition to his great calculating skills, Aitken was able to take any number up to 1,500 and quite automatically say whether it was prime or not and, if it was not prime, to give all of its factors. In this situation, Aitken is apparently relying on an expanded repertoire of mathematical facts, but as a psychological process it seems no different from that of the ordinary person who tells at once that 7 times 9 is 63. That is, in these cases Aitken did not calculate or work out the solutions, but instead instantly retrieved the results from long-term memory.

However, it might be thought that there are also important differences in the cases. Langdon and twin George acquire new knowledge of sundry calendar dates, while the woman reaching the result that $7 \times 9 = 63$ does not, and neither does Aitken with numbers up to 1500. The woman already knows that 7 times 9 equals 63. Perhaps this alone, secondly, is reason to believe that she retrieves an item from long-term memory, while George and Langdon do something else. These differences aside, they are all the same in the sense that George and Langdon no more calculate than does the woman doing the multiplication of 7 and 9.

There is a sense, however, in which even the woman multiplying 7 and 9 may be said to acquire new knowledge. If she is doing some arithmetic problems, and at one stage in the problem she is to multiply 7 and 9 before proceeding to other operations, perhaps she can be said to acquire new knowledge that 63 is the correct result for that line in the problem. She comes to know, that is, that 63 goes here, where here is the line or stage of the specific problem calling for that multiplication. If so, then she may also acquire this knowledge without going through any sort of mathematical calculation.

Another factor is operative in some of the examples discussed thus far, namely long familiarity and repetition. The woman who learns the multiplication tables as a child practices them, perhaps reciting them and writing them out. She also uses them over many years. At some point, her familiarity with these operations is so strong that she no longer has to pause and think about a given product; the product 63, for instance, comes into her mind immediately on being given the factors. Rimland suggests the same for Langdon, as we have seen, and no doubt much the same story will hold in a modified form for the physics experts. They acquire their special talents after much exposure to problems suitably similar to those presently encountered.

Nonmathematical cases are also important, including those found in studies of expert chess players. In these studies A. de Groot[9] found that chess experts were able to study a board for ten to fifteen seconds, and then recall the positions of the various pieces better than novice players could do, and even better than veteran players could do, in the same setting. This result has been interpreted as indicative of different perceptual activities in the expert versus the other nonexperts. The expert, according to de Groot, has stored in long-term memory a series of organized configurations of pieces. His superior chess playing ability, then, is held to depend on a perceptual response specific to chess and pieces arrayed. The chess experts "picture" the board to themselves in some way, and then make appropriate moves. What they typically do not do, de Groot reports, is calculate numbers of moves ahead and likely countermoves, something the ordinary player generally does. Their expert ability derives instead from their capacity to picture a great number of board configurations and match the current perceived scene to one such picture. What the expert does, on this view, is more like this: recognize the picture presented, whence this move. Pattern recognition is most likely what is being indicated by de Groot for the chess experts.

What has been noted about experts thus far carries over to individuals we might not reckon as experts in any sense. Consider the many persons who are long-time users of elementary logic; they regularly use modus ponens and other simple inference rules and have been doing so for quite some time. That some sequence of lines allows of a modus ponens inference is often not something these individuals figure out or calculate. Instead, they recognize at once that the relevant structure is present and draw the inference. These persons are experts, I want to say, in a very circumscribed domain, namely, a few elementary inference rules utilized on relatively simple sentential structures (even modus ponens is a bit difficult to effectively use in contexts where the formulas are exceedingly complex). It is reasonable to so regard them, I think, because they have reached a stage at which they achieve new knowledge in this domain—for example, that this sequence admits of modus ponens detachment—without the need to rely on rules which describe permissible moves when formulas have specific structures. No doubt when they first learned elementary logic they needed to fall back on the rule, perhaps recalling to mind what the rule was and then carefully noting that a given sequence falls under the rule. But now, after so much experience in logic, they recognize relevant contexts immediately, without rehearsing the rule or calling it to mind and with no need to do such things.

Of course, if such a logic user were challenged or questioned about the inference drawn, she could easily settle the matter by calling on the needed rule. But this fact about what she would do or say in such contexts does nothing to show that she relies on and uses the rule when making the inference.

Another simple example is illustrative of the same point. Imagine a person who works on an assembly line where his job is to sort buttons coming down the conveyor belt and place them in various slots: red button here, blue there; round buttons in slot two if they are red, but in slot three if they are blue, and so on. As a beginner, this person doubtless learns and memorizes a set of rules concerning button placement. Moreover, he will typically rehearse the rules to himself as he works. Often these same rules will be posted near by or kept handy for ready consultation. A veteran button-man on this line, however, need not consult the written rules, nor run them over in his mind as each piece comes down the belt. He seizes each piece as it comes down the belt and places them in appropriate slots, all with no apparent reasoning at all.[10]

A final reasonably familiar example concerns those individuals who are very good at picking out regional accents. At one time I could easily recognize and distinguish eight or nine different Philadelphia accents. I could tell from which part of town the speaker hailed just by listening to him or her speaking in normal conversational situations (as opposed to, say, performance situations), and I was very accurate in my judgments on this matter. Other individuals are much more successful. For instance, there have been cases of people in England who can so accurately pick out an accent as to be able to tell from which village in a section of England a person comes, even to the point of picking out different individuals from neighboring villages.

These cases are instructive for several reasons. First, accent-experts are plainly focusing upon certain speech features and sound patterns or rhythms. In some cases they notice certain idioms that only a speaker from a given place would use. For example, native Philadelphians say "I'm going down the shore." Nearly everyone else would signal their beach destination by saying something such as "I'm going to the shore" or, perhaps more likely, "I'm going to the beach." But just as often it is accent which really counts, especially when all of the speakers use the same idiomatic expressions. Further, secondly, accent-experts are generally unable to describe which features they are attending to and which accent-features correlate with which places. In this respect, then, they are not following rules for selecting places to go with different accents even if there are some rules which govern their selection-behavior. For these accent-experts typically have no beliefs about rules they might be following when they make place selections. Despite this, third, accent-experts are quite accurate in their place selections and, I would say, often acquire knowledge of appropriate place selections as a result of their judgments about accents.

To sum up thus far: strategy-experts are those persons who have a good bit of knowledge in some area and are especially adept at acquiring new knowledge in that area. Their acquisition techniques are varied. Some, such as Aitken and other mathematical experts, are master calculators who carry out these processes with great ingenuity and remarkable speed. Others, as in the mathematical prodigies cases and the chess players example, do not seem to calculate or reason at all, but arrive at results from the exercise of a skill which is apparently perceptual, most likely involving pattern recognition of various sorts. The same seems to be true, I suggested, for the button-man, modus ponens, and accent cases. In each of these examples, subjects acquire new knowledge without the need to calculate or rely on rules which may govern their activities. In this respect they qualify as strategy-experts in their respective very limited domains.

Everyone an Expert?

Certain cases of perception by quite ordinary cognizers can be seen to be quite similar to cases of strategy-experts in relevant ways. I will restrict attention to very modest perceptual cases, such as picking out a seen item as a red and circular object, rather than identifying the seen object as, e.g., a tomato.

So imagine a person who has had long familiarity with red and circular (actually: spherical) objects, and who is not drugged, drunk, or otherwise visually or mentally impaired. If she is attentive to her visual surroundings and is looking at a red circular object, she will likely form the belief that there is a red circular object there.[11] Moreover, this belief will not typically arise as a result of any inference she draws or reasoning in which she engages. Instead, the belief that there is something red and circular there generally arises as an immediate response to her perceptual experience.

It is perhaps true that in these circumstances, something appears red and circular to her, in that sense of "appears" which is phenomenological and descriptive rather than, in Roderick Chisholm's terms, hedging or epistemic.[12] However, in all but rare cases a person will not have beliefs about how something then appears, and so will not reason from appearance-beliefs to the belief that there is something red and circular there.[13]

In these restricted perceptual situations it seems clear that normal cognizers are similar to some of the strategy-experts discussed earlier. That is, the ordinary cognizer acquires these perceptual beliefs[14] not via reasoning or inference from beliefs about how something then appears, nor as a result of following rules which govern belief-forming behavior. Rather, these perceptual beliefs are formed as a direct causal result of the having of the perceptual experience.

Moreover, in the case of the strategy-experts it is natural to think that they acquire fresh knowledge in their respective fields of expertise. The mathematical prodigies who claim to see or otherwise perceive numbers are so frequently correct in their judgments without relying on or needing to rely on calculation or mathematical principles or rules. So it is quite reasonable to suppose that when they are correct in these judgments, they have knowledge. Just so in the restricted perception cases. There, subjects are usually correct in their perceptual beliefs; they do not need to rely on reasoning from other beliefs to arrive at their perceptual beliefs, nor do they so rely. They thus acquire new perceptual knowledge, as a result of their perceptual experiences, when their perceptual beliefs are correct.

It is clear that these results apply to legions of ordinary cognizers in restricted perceptual situations. It is for this reason that it is reasonable to classify these many individuals as strategy-experts in these restricted domains, even if they are not experts in much of anything else.

These contentions regarding perception, perceptual beliefs, and perceptual knowledge match fairly well with Plantinga's view on the matter. He agrees that the restricted perceptual beliefs arise as a direct result of one's perceptual experiences.[15] A perhaps insignificant difference is that he describes these experiences adverbially, speaking of being appeared to in different ways, where I have used the terminology of appearing. We thus agree that in these perceptual domains subjects do not reason or infer from beliefs about how they are appeared to, to beliefs about the perceived objects. Nor, I have said, need subjects so reason if they are to have well-founded perceptual beliefs, beliefs which often count as knowledge. In this, I surmise, Plantinga would concur.

I have not argued in this paper, with Plantinga, that the restricted perceptual beliefs constitute immediate, noninferential knowledge (what Plantinga refers to as basic beliefs), though I have elsewhere defended this view.[16] Where there may be an area of disagreement between us concerns the grounds for thinking that people have knowledge in these perceptual cases. I have suggested that this is partly a matter of their not needing to rely on reasoning from other beliefs in order to have what Plantinga would term a warranted perceptual belief. I have not followed Plantinga in claiming that it is in virtue of the fact that one is perceptually functioning properly that one has a warranted belief which constitutes immediate knowledge.[17]

Notes

1. M. Chi, P. Feltovich, and R. Glaser, "Categorization and Representation of Physics Problems by Experts and Novices," *Cognitive Science*, Vol. 5, 1981; M. Chi, R. Glaser, and E. Rees, "Expertise in Problem Solving," in R. Sternberg, ed., *Advances in the Psychology of Human Intelligence* (Hillsdale, N.J.: Erlbaum, 1982).

2. Ibid.

3. Other studies of problem solving have proposed essentially the same sort of account of what the experts are using as strategies. See, e.g., D. Simon and H. Simon, "Individual Differences in Solving Physics Problems," in R. Siegler, ed., *Children's Thinking: What Develops?* (Hillsdale, N.J.: Erlbaum, 1978).

4. Quoted in Steven B. Smith, *The Great Mental Calculators* (New York: Columbia University Press, 1983), pp. 20–21. Smith's quote is taken from I. M. L. Hunter, "Mental Calculation," in P. C. Wason and P. Johnson-Laird, eds., *Thinking and Reasoning* (Middlesex, England: Penguin, 1968). The words in brackets are Hunter's.

5. PBS television program on prodigies, October 1994.

6. Steven B. Smith, *The Great Mental Calculators*, op. cit., p. 20.

7. Ibid., p. 33.

8. Ibid., p. 29.

9. A. de Groot, *Thought and Choice in Chess* (The Hague: Mouton), 1965.

10. I have discussed cases such as these in a related context in "Non-Inferential Knowledge," *Philosophia*, Vol. 12, 1982. See also Steven Reynolds, "Knowing How to Believe with Justification," *Philosophical Studies*, Vol. 64, 1991.

11. Here I assume that seeing a red circular object does not consist in or

250 *George S. Pappas*

include as a component the acquisition of a belief that there is a red circular object there. But the assumption has had its detractors; e.g., G. Pitcher, *A Theory of Perception* (Princeton: Princeton University Press, 1971). Plantinga sides with me on this matter, in his *Warrant and Proper Function* (New York: Oxford University Press, 1993); see p. 92, and note 4.

12. R. Chisholm, *Perceiving* (Ithaca: Cornell University Press, 1957).

13. J. Pollock, *Contemporary Theories of Knowledge* (Totowa, N. J.: Rowman and Littlefield, 1986), p. 63.

14. By a perceptual belief I do not mean a belief about perceiving itself, but rather a belief which is about items perceived and which is acquired in perception of those items.

15. A. Plantinga, *Warrant and Proper Function*, op. cit., pp. 92–93.

16. See "Non-Inferential Knowledge," op. cit., and for related arguments, "Lost Justification," *Midwest Studies in Philosophy*, Vol. 5, 1980.

17. I do not mean to suggest that what I have claimed is inconsistent with Plantinga's account of proper function; he may well want to use the latter account as an explanation of why reliance on reasoning from other beliefs is not needed.

Part V

Virtue Epistemology

13

Proper Functionalism and Virtue Epistemology

Ernest Sosa

Comprehensive and packed, Alvin Plantinga's two-volume treatise defies summary. The first volume, *Warrant: Current Views*, is a meticulous critical survey of epistemology today. Many current approaches are presented and exhaustively discussed, and a negative verdict is passed on each in turn. This prepares the way for volume two, *Warrant and Proper Function*, where a positive view is advanced and developed in satisfying detail. The cumulative result is most impressive, and should command attention for years to come.

Here I cannot possibly do justice to the scope and richness of Plantinga's accomplishment. Given the limitations imposed by the occasion, I will discuss only what seem the most important and original proposals, and will compare them with some relevant alternatives.

A. Paradigm Reliabilism Refuted and Replaced

"Paradigm reliabilism" is Plantinga's label for Alvin Goldman's early reliabilism.

> *Paradigm reliabilism*: first of all, belief B is "justified" if and only if B is produced by a reliable belief-producing causal process; and, secondly, the justification of the belief varies in direct proportion to the reliability of the process that produces it.

253

A serious problem afflicts this view:

(A1)   Any given belief B is a result of many "type processes" of different degrees of generality. Thus a belief may be a result of vision, of shape vision, of shape vision in good light, of shape vision in good light arm's length away, etc.

(A2)   Take such a process to be broadly general—say, vision; then the beliefs produced by it will *not* all have the same degree of justification, which contradicts paradigm reliabilism.

(A3)   Take then the other alternative: take the processes narrowly enough to make it likely that all beliefs produced by such a narrow process *will* be equally well justified. Now the consequence is that some narrowly defined process types seem to yield truth reliably enough but still *without* justification.

One such counter example is the "Case of the Epistemically Serendipitous Tumor," used by Plantinga in several places, in one of which he formulates it as follows:

> Consider, for example, the person whose belief that he has a brain tumor is caused by his brain tumor. There is a rare but specific sort of brain tumor, we may suppose, such that associated with it are a number of cognitive processes of the relevant degree of specificity, most of which cause its victim to hold absurdly false beliefs. One of the presses associated with the tumor, however, causes the victim to believe that he has a brain tumor. Suppose, then that S suffers from this sort of tumor and accordingly believes that he suffers from a brain tumor. Then the relevant type, while it may be hard to specify in detail, will certainly be highly reliable: but surely it is not the case that this belief—the belief that he has a brain tumor—has much by way of positive epistemic status for S.[1]

In view of this, Plantinga's own proposal tries to do justice to reliabilist intuitions while going beyond them in escaping the brain lesion objection. Here is a sketch of the proposal:

Plantinga's Proper Functionalism: Belief B on the part of subject S has warrant if B is a result of S's faculties functioning properly in an appropriate environment according to a design plan that successfully aims at truth acquisition.[2]

('Warrant' here means that quantity enough of which, together with true belief, is sufficient for knowledge. As for 'design plan', the core notion involves *conscious* design aimed at some aim.)

A Reliabilist Response and Plantinga's Rejoinder

Goldman answers that Plantinga himself needs to face the problem he raises for reliabilism, since "... a little reflection should make it clear that cognitive faculty individuation is no trivial matter."[3] Isn't there a reliable "brain lesion faculty" that yields the victim's belief in his own faculty? How then are we to rule out the victim's being warranted in that belief? Plantinga's main response allows the reliability of the process that yields belief in the brain lesion, but alleges the reliability of that process to be merely an accident. The reliability of that process is said to be accidental *from the point of view of the design plan of the believer.* This design plan does not call for any faculty of brain tumor detection connecting the presence of the tumor to apprehension thereof, a faculty successfully aimed at the truth and designed to operate in the circumstances of the actual belief in question.

Here is the way Plantinga seems to reason:

(B1)   There is a concept of "proper functioning" common to both theists and atheists, one that applies just as much to refrigerators as to the human heart, and one that does not obviously require reference to any conscious design.

(B2)   It is this concept that is appealed to in the account of warranted belief as belief deriving from the operation of a properly functioning faculty that is: (i) successfully aimed at yielding truth, and (ii) designed to operate in the circumstances present in the case of the given belief.

(B3)   According to this account of warrant, therefore, we may deny that the victim of the brain lesion has a warranted belief, since we may deny that his belief derives from a properly functioning faculty *present in the design plan.*

The notion of design plan is hence crucial for proper functionalist strategy, since the design plan is what enables us to discriminate between mere causal processes that do not constitute or reflect faculties working properly, such as the lesion/belief-in-lesion mechanism, and the more August causal processes that do represent such faculties through their presence in the imposed "design plan."

A Further Problem for Proper Functionalism: The Swampman

Consider again our statement of proper functionalism:

(PF)   Belief B on the part of subject S has warrant if B is a result of S's faculties functioning properly in an appropriate environment

according to a design plan that successfully aims at truth acquisition.

And note that Plantinga is willing to allow for the sake of discussion
that the designer of the design plan be some impersonal natural process
such as evolution through random mutation and natural selection.

An example constructed by Donald Davidson in another connection
now proves troublesome for proper functionalism. I mean the case of
the chance Swampman:

> Suppose lightning strikes a dead tree in a swamp; I am standing nearby.
> My body is reduced to its elements, while entirely by coincidence (and
> out of different molecules) the tree is turned into my physical replica. My
> replica, The Swampman, moves exactly as I did; according to its nature
> it departs the swamp, encounters and seems to recognize my friends, and
> appears to return their greetings in English. It moves into my house and
> seems to write articles on radical interpretation. No one can tell the
> difference. But there *is* a difference.[4]

For present purposes a modified example is also interesting, one
where the lightning creates not an adult but a very small baby, which
is later found by a hunter who raises it in the normal way until it is an
adult to all appearances perfectly normal. As an adult, Swampbaby
surely knows a lot of things, and hence has much warranted belief. Yet
he is not designed by any external agent or process, whether personal
or impersonal. The problem for proper functionalism is then this: PF
takes it to be impossible that there be someone with warranted belief
who has no design plan imposed by any agency or process that
designed him. But it seems possible for Swampbaby to exist and to
reach adulthood full of warranted beliefs without having been designed
either by God or by evolution. Indeed it even seems logically possible
for the original Swampman to have warranted beliefs not long after
creation if not right away.[5]

From his published response to a related objection, we can infer
how Plantinga would respond to this proposed counter example.
Stripped down to its essentials his argument would be this:

> The Swampman is not clearly enough metaphysically possible, and hence
> not clearly a counter example to proper functionalism. Therefore, the
> most one should allege on the basis of the example against proper
> functionalism is that there is a state of affairs S such that if proper
> function is analyzed in terms of design by some conscious agency or

some impersonal process, then proper functionalism implies that S is impossible, where it is not clear that S is impossible.

And about this Plantinga would add that he does *not* ". . . see this as much by way of an objection to an analysis or account."[6]

A Methodological Excursus

Plantinga's response raises an interesting methodological question for analytic philosophy in general. Consider the following response to any proposed counterexample: "You should not be so sure that your example is really possible. We can certainly turn out wrong even about the most plausible *a priori* assumptions. Remember Frege!" Could one not always attack any proposed counter example as not clearly a real possibility; and to the extent that this is plausible would one not be within one's epistemic rights in rejecting the example as no refutation?

In order to evaluate this response we need to consider what is involved in a philosophical counter example. A purported counter example is offered as something that goes against a target philosophical thesis T of the form; *P is a necessary truth*. What relation must there be between C and T for C to count as a successful counter example to T? Here is one main possibility:

Refuting Counterexample. If C is clearly possible and C clearly logically implies Not-P, then P is clearly not necessary, and the philosophical thesis T is thereby refuted, in the sense that we can now be sure that P is not a necessary truth.

But that is not the only way in which C can successfully counter the philosophical thesis that P is a necessary truth. For there is also the following:

Opposing Counterexample. If C is not clearly impossible and C clearly logically implies Not-P, then P is *not* clearly necessary, and P is less clearly necessary the less clear it is that C is impossible.[7]

(Where all attributions and comparisons of clarity are to be understood as relative to us at the time in question—what is, really, clear to S may, after all, be unclear to S', etc.) If this principle is right then what do we need for C to be, at t, an "opposing" counter example to the thesis that P is necessary? All we need is that C be *both* clearly incompatible with P and the thesis that P is necessary? All we need is that C be *both* clearly incompatible with P and *not* clearly impossible. If C combines those two features at a time t, then P cannot be clearly necessary at t (all, again, for a given subject S). And when C does combine those two features at t, it will then do "epistemic damage" to the thesis that P is necessary (thesis T), at least in the sense that the possession of those two features by C ensures that T is less clear than it might be. Suppose it to be *extremely* clear that C is incompatible with P. In that case C will be more "epistemically damaging" to the thesis T, that P is necessary, the less clear it is that C is impossible, in the sense that T will be less clear the less clear it is that C is impossible. While a refuting counter example constitutes a particularly resounding defeat for a philosophical thesis, a merely opposing counter example also does epistemic damage, the extent of the damage being inversely proportional to the degree to which it is clear that C is impossible. Every refuting example is an opposing example, but not every opposing example is a refuting example.

The Swampman Again

Against a proposed counter example similar to the Swampman case, Plantinga replies as follows:

> I haven't any reason to think this possible [meaning the proposed counter example]. I'm not positive that it is impossible; but I am inclined to think it is, and hence don't consider it a counter example to my account. To put it another way, the . . . case isn't at all clearly possible; so I don't mind if my account implies that it isn't possible.[8]

But the fact that the proposed counter example is not at all clearly possible shows only that it is not a *refuting* counter example. It might still be an *opposing* counterexample. Plantinga himself is sensitive to this, as may be seen in his further comments:

> It is true, I think, that one has *some* inclination to think it possible that a being capable of warranted belief should pop into existence "by chance" or by virtue of an incompetent agent's trying to create something quite different. This needn't be thought of as casting doubt on my account of warrant, however—maybe instead it casts doubt on the idea that proper

function requires a reasonably successful and not wholly incompetent designer.[9]

The important point for our purposes is that a counter example that is less than clearly possible can still serve to cast doubt on a philosophical thesis, and will do so to the extent that it is both clearly incompatible with the thesis and less than clearly impossible. Of course, if the philosophical thesis is complex and composed of several subtheses, it may not be immediately clear which of the subtheses, if any, one should protect, and which of the subtheses, if any, will be appropriate targets of the new doubt. But one thing is clear: the complex as a whole will suffer epistemically from attack by such a counter example.

Care is required, however, in stating exactly what seems intuitively plausible about the original Swampman. It seems plausible to attribute to him the following: beliefs in great profusion; true beliefs about his present state and circumstances, soon after his appearance in the swamp; and plenty of true general beliefs as well. It is also plausible that he is massively in error about his past (having had none). What shall we say once we go beyond mere true belief, however, on to properties epistemically more interesting? What might he know, for example? What is he justified in believing? What is he "warranted" in believing?

The Swampman is plausibly regarded as a match for Davidson in the justification of their respective beliefs. After all, there is no internal difference between them. Whatever reasons, memories, inferences, or experiences might have justified Davidson in holding any belief will be matched exactly by corresponding counterparts in the Swampman. Indeed the Swampman is strikingly similar to the victim of the Cartesian evil demon: just as the Cartesian victim is so circumstanced as to be massively wrong about his surroundings, past, present, and future, so the Davidsonian Swampman is so circumstanced as to be massively wrong about his past. Each is a match for any of us, however, in the internal coherence and justification of his body of beliefs. Suppose now the Swampman is right in a particular belief, about the past, present, or future. His belief is then both true and justified. Does it amount to knowledge? This is much less clear. Compare the corresponding question about the Cartesian demon's victim, Suppose he happens to be right in some one particular belief about his surroundings. His belief is then both true and justified, but surely does not amount to knowledge. In some sense the victim is just right by accident and good luck, and not because he really knows. What then shall we say of the Swampman's warrant for believing the various things that he believes?

If along with Plantinga we are defining "warrant" as just whatever quantity is sufficient for knowledge when (in sufficient measure) added to true belief, then obviously we must grant that the Swampman lacks warrant for many of his beliefs. However, even if we grant that the Swampman lacks warrant for much of what he believes, is it not plausible that he does know at least some things, and does have warrant for corresponding beliefs? If warrant required design by God or evolution, as proper functionalism would have it, then the Swampman could have warrant for *none* of his beliefs.[10]

Accordingly, to the extent that at the present moment it is unclear to you that a Swampman with warranted beliefs is impossible, to that extent it should be unclear to you that warrant necessarily derives from faculties functioning according to their design plans, etc. Actually, that is so *assuming* it is very clear that the Swampman's faculties could not function according to their design plan, since the Swampman, being a creature of pure chance, does not have faculties that function according to *any* design.

But this last assumption is also one that Plantinga questions. He is inclined to object that if it is possible that a being capable of belief come into existence by chance, then it is also possible that a believing being complete with *design plan* come into existence by chance. But here my understanding of the proposed notion of design plan gives out. If a "design plan" might fall into place independently of any sort of conscious or unconscious design, then I lose my grip on the meaning of the locution "design plan."

I am myself strongly inclined to believe that the Swampman is logically and metaphysically possible. But how confidently we may accept the account of warrant as requiring design is surely to be determined by how well it compares with alternative accounts in its ability to fit our pretheoretic intuitions and other pertinent beliefs. And so we should consider what alternatives there are to the proper functionalism which views *functioning properly* as "functioning in accordance with imposed design."

Two Alternatives to Proper Functionalism

According to a more explicitly developed proper functionalism, my belief B is warranted only if

(1) it has been produced in me by cognitive faculties that are working properly (functioning as they ought to, subject to no cognitive dysfunction) in a cognitive environment that is appropriate for my kinds of cognitive faculties, (2) the segment of the design plan governing the production of that belief is aimed at the production of true beliefs, and (3) there is a high statistical probability that a belief produced under those conditions will be true.[11]

In seeking an alternative to proper functionalism, let us try to understand "working properly" without appealing to notions like "design" or "design plan" or "Divine design" or even "evolutionary design." What then might it mean to say that something is "working properly"? According to a very weak and basic notion of "working properly," all that is required for something to work properly relative to goal G in environment E is that it be ø'ing where ø'ing in E has a sufficient propensity to lead to G. In line with this, the fuller account above might well be replaced by the following simpler account:

(W)   My belief B is warranted only if it is produced in me by a faculty F in a cognitive environment E such that F is working properly relative to the goal of truth acquisition and error avoidance in environment E.

Account W reduces to a form of "reliabilism," in a broad sense,[12] but one which requires one's warranted beliefs to derive from the operation of "faculties."

Against examples like that of the brain lesion, one can now argue that they involve belief-producing processes, but nothing that could properly be called a "faculty." And we can leave for later work the problem of how to define the concept of a "faculty." This is analogous to solving our problems by appeal to "properly working faculties" and leaving it for later reflection to determine the definition of "properly working faculty." What is more, the problems involved in giving an account of what it is to possess a faculty seem rather less forbidding than those that stand in our way to a clear view of what it is to possess a *properly working* faculty.

"True enough," it may be responded, "it is not so hard to get an account of what it is to have a faculty or an intellectual virtue. But once we have the account it is not at all clear why the brain lesion does not give its victim a faculty, a rather restricted and specialized faculty, but nonetheless a faculty." How are we to preclude such "faculties" from providing warrant? Proper functionalism would require the faculty in question to be part of the design plan, whereas the brain lesion "faculty" is said not to be part of the design plan. But this does not solve the problems we have found with proper functionalism. And there is the further problem that it is not really clear that the brain lesion could not be part of the victim's design plan (newly acquired through the accident or whatever it is that causes the lesion). Insofar as it is unclear that the victim's belief B that he has a brain lesion is *not* caused by a faculty that functions properly, therefore, and insofar as that is *not much more clear* than the claim that B is *not* caused by a "faculty" at all, where's the gain in the move from the simpler requirement to the more complex? Why move from simply requiring that a belief must be caused by a reliable faculty if it is to have warrant to requiring more elaborately that the belief must be caused by a faculty that is not only reliable but is functioning properly in some sense that involves design by conscious agent or impersonal process?

That is just a comparative point, however, and the account of warrant in terms of reliable faculties still lacks a convincing explanation of why the belief in the brain lesion does not derive from the operation of a reliable "faculty." It is small consolation to know that an alternative, more elaborate account still faces a similar problem. We may, nevertheless, compatibly with the simpler account, have the resources to solve our problem, and more generally the generality problem, with no need to appeal either to a theological or to an evolutionary account of faculties and their proper working. Let us now explore some ideas toward such a solution.

In a recent paper,[13] Goldman returns to the debate with Plantinga on reliabilism, and he now offers an account of justified belief ". . . that is in the reliabilist tradition, but departs at a crucial juncture from other versions of reliabilism." The main idea of this new account is that of intellectual virtue, and the approach is hence a version of what might well be termed "virtue epistemology." Here is how it is used by Goldman in response to Plantinga's brain lesion counter example and similar examples. About such examples, Goldman now has this to say:

> These include processes engendered by a brain tumor, radiation-caused processes, and the like. In each case Plantinga imagines that the process is reliable, but reports that we would not judge it to be justification conferring. My diagnosis [is as follows:] . . . At a minimum, the processes imagined by Plantinga fail to match any virtue on a typical evaluator's list. So the beliefs are at least non-justified. Furthermore, evaluators may have a prior representation of pathological processes as examples of

cognitive vices. Plantinga's cases might be judged (relevantly) similar to these vices, so that the beliefs they produce would be declared unjustified.[14]

In some of Plantinga's cases, it is further supposed that the hypothetical agent possesses countervailing evidence against his belief, which he steadfastly ignores.

[This] added element would strengthen a judgment of unjustifiedness according to our theory, because ignoring contrary evidence is an intellectual vice.[15]

Goldman's answer to Plantinga rests on four main components, and I quote from Goldman's paper in each case.

Goldman's New Approach

(1) The basic approach is, roughly, to identify the concept of justified belief with the concept of belief acquired through the exercise of intellectual virtues.[16]

(2) The . . . epistemic evaluator has a mentally stored set, or list, of cognitive virtues and vices. When asked to evaluate an actual or hypothetical case of belief, the evaluator considers the processes by which the belief was produced, and matches these against his list of virtues and vices.[17]

(3) Belief-forming processes . . . are deemed virtuous because they (are deemed to) produce a high ratio of true beliefs. Processes . . . are deemed vicious because they (are deemed to) produce a low ratio of true beliefs.[18]

(4) To sum up the present theory, . . . it depicts justificational evaluation as involving two stages. The first stage features the acquisition by an evaluator of some set of intellectual virtues and vices. This is where reliability enters the picture. In the second stage, the evaluator applies his list of virtues and vices to decide the epistemic status of targeted beliefs. At this stage there is no direct consideration of reliability.[19]

The proposal might then be formulated briefly as follows (V):

(Va) [X is an *intellectual virtue* $\rightarrow$ X produces a high ratio of true beliefs]

(Vb) [B is a justified belief $\exists$ B is a belief acquired through the exercise of one or more intellectual virtues][20]

However, there are at least two main ways to interpret Vb, one of which is this (where w ranges over possible worlds):

J1   (∀w) [B is justified in w ∃ B is acquired in w through the exercise
       of one or more intellectual virtues that are virtuous in w]

The problem with J1, as Goldman well knows, is the "new evil
demon problem," namely the problem that Descartes's evil demon
victim is not deprived of *ordinary* justification, in some straightforward
sense; he still derives his beliefs from sources that we all recognize as
justification-conferring: namely, sense experience, memory, et cetera.
The environment changes radically, but the victim retains his repertoire of intellectual virtues. True, because the environment of the
victim is so radically abnormal and wrong for his normal virtues, his
virtues may not qualify as virtuous *relative to that environment*. But,
according to Goldman, despite J1 the fact remains that for ". . . most
epistemic evaluators . . . the victims' beliefs are justified." And this
seems quite right, again in some relevant sense of "justification." So
J1 does not provide an adequate explication of Goldman's new approach nor does it promise a full and illuminating enough account of
all that is conveyed by ordinary "epistemic justification." Here now is
an alternative:

J2   (∀w) [B is justified in w ∃ B is acquired in w through the exercise
       of one or more intellectual virtues that are virtuous in our *actual*
       world a]

This is not open to the objections lodged above against J1. However,
against this Goldman objects that ". . . there is no evidence that "the
folk" are inclined to relativize virtues and vices to this or that possible
world." And it is mainly for this reason that Goldman would reject
both J1 and J2. His own proposal is much more modest, and has two
main parts, as follows.

Goldman's Preferred "List" Proposal (L)

(La)   As evaluator one acquires a list of virtues. These are belief-forming
       processes or mechanisms that one deems reliable or truth-
       conducive.

(Lb)   Actual or hypothetical beliefs are then assessed as justified if
       and only if they derive appropriately from virtues on the list of
       the evaluator.

Surprisingly, this new account does not reveal what is involved in
the notion of epistemic justification itself. One might conceivably think

that there *is* no such notion, and adopt a prescriptivist or noncognitivist stance here, as does Richard Rorty in his recent writings,[21] but this raises problems. How, for example, could we make sense of the following examples?

(Ea)   I wish I had only justified beliefs.

(Eb)   Someone has justified beliefs.

(Ec)   Anyone who knows that p has a justified true belief that p.

The vocabulary of justification functions quite smoothly in contexts—such as Ea, Eb, and Ec above—where it cannot coherently function in prescriptivist fashion. The prescriptive aspect of that vocabulary cannot be all or nearly all there is to it, therefore, in contrast to vocabulary such as 'Hurray'; and we still wonder what is involved in a belief's being epistemically justified. Of course, the "list" proposal, L above, gives us an account of how an evaluator properly goes about evaluating a belief as epistemically justified. And it even includes an account of why an evaluator includes certain virtues or faculties on her preferred list. But it still does not tell us what it is for a virtue or faculty to be virtuous, and what is involved in a belief's being epistemically justified—*not just what is involved in an evaluator's evaluating it as justified. N.B., but what would be involved in its actually being epistemically justified.*

Let V1 and V2 be the relativistic principles that combine Va with J1 and J2, respectively. Thus they amount to the following:

V1   ($\forall$w) [B is justified$_1$ in w $\exists$ B derives in w from the exercise of one or more intellectual virtues that in w virtuously produce a high ratio of true beliefs]

V2   ($\forall$w) [B, in w, is justified$_2$ $\exists$ B derives in w from the exercise of one or more intellectual virtues that in our actual world a virtuously produce a high ratio of true beliefs]

It is a virtue of V1 and V2 that they explain and make sense of the content of the "list" proposal.[22] This also enables one to deal with cases Ea—Ec just above, and with other such cases that seem at least initially problematic for account V. So let's have a closer look at the problem that Goldman charges against our V1 and V2 proposed as accounts of respective concepts of epistemic justification.

The problem is supposed to arise when V1 and V2 are regarded as conceptual analyses of epistemic justification. If one thinks of "conceptual analysis" as just *a priori* reflection leading to certain conclusions, then there are two sorts of such conceptual analysis worth distinguishing. First, meaning analysis, which leads to conclusions that one would reject only if one failed to understand one or another of the constitutive concepts. Secondly, substantive analysis, which leads to conclusions that are *a priori* and necessary all right, but which are difficult enough that one could certainly make a mistake without that mistake evincing just a failure to understand the words or concepts involved. Meaning analysis might thus lead to a proposition such as: A sister is a female sibling. Substantive analysis, by contrast, might lead to a proposition like: X is a right action if X is optimific. One can easily reject a result of substantive analysis, while understanding what one rejects and the constitutive concepts; whereas this does not seem possible with regard to the results of meaning analysis. Note also, finally, that either sort of analysis might lead to propositions that are not necessary biconditionals, such as the following: (a) Abortion is wrong. (b) One ought always to treat people as ends. (c) $Kp \rightarrow Bp$. (d) There are universals, and these exist necessarily.

Presumably V1 and V2 are offered as substantive analyses. We need to keep this in mind when we consider Goldman's claim that there is no evidence that the folk are inclined to relativize virtues and vices. Compare: "X is far from here," as applied to Alpha Centauri; to San Francisco. "She is tall," as applied by a Pygmy; by a Watusi. "It is 5 p.m.," as said in New York; as said in Tokyo. Or take "It is raining." Where do we check for falling water? The point with all these examples is that often enough we relativize necessarily and automatically through contextual features, even if those features are not present to the consciousness of the speaker(s). Might this not be how it is with regard to the relativization proposed by VI and V2? Might it not be that the folk are relativizing after all, but in the automatic, context-driven way in which we constantly relativize when we use indexicals, as in the examples above? If so, then we can after all accept V1 and V2.

The main point is now that V1 gives us at least a partial account of "justification" (or of something close to warrant, perhaps, or of aptness), one which offers an alternative to proper functionalism, and one secure against the New Evil Demon Problem.

Actually, my own preferred alternative to proper functionalist epistemology would supplement Goldman's list account (L). I would add not only principles V1 and V2, with their respective senses or sorts of "justification," but also the following reflections on knowledge and its relations to belief, truth, and faculties.

If a faculty operates to give one a belief, and thereby a piece of direct knowledge, one must have some awareness of one's belief and its source, and of the virtue of that source both in general and in the specific instance. Hence it must be that in the circumstances one would (most likely) believe P iff P were the case—i.e., one (at least probabilistically) tracks the truth (which is part of what is involved in the source's operating virtuously in the specific instance). And that' must be so, moreover, because P is in a field of propositions F and one is in conditions C with respect to P, such that believing a proposition in field F, while one is in conditions C with respect to it, would make one very likely to be right. And, finally, one must grasp that one's belief non-accidentally reflects the truth of P through the exercise of such a virtue. This account therefore combines requirements of *tracking* and *nonaccidentality*, of *reliable virtues* or *faculties*, and of *epistemic perspective*.

Even if such an account is right for object-level beliefs and direct knowledge, however, more needs to be said about the sort of doxastic ascent apparently required. It would be absurd to require at *every* level that one must ascend to the next higher level in search of justification. Yet it seems no less absurd to allow a meta-level belief B' to help justify or warrant an object level belief B even though B' is itself unjustified or unwarranted. Perhaps we need to require sufficient comprehensive coherence in a body of beliefs for the justification and aptness of its members. Perhaps such a comprehensively coherent body of beliefs would need to include meta-beliefs concerning object-level beliefs and the faculties that give rise to them, and the reliability of these faculties. Nevertheless, we surely would need also to allow that, at some level of ascent, it will suffice for the justification and aptness of a belief that it be non-accidentally true because of its virtuous source, and through its place in an interlocking, comprehensively coherent system of beliefs, *without* needing to be in turn the object of higher-yet beliefs directed upon it. That sketches my preferred alternative to proper functionalism, but this is not the place to lay it out in detail.[23]

Irenic Conclusion: Three Forms of Virtue Epistemology.

The disagreement among the two Alvins and myself is actually relatively minor when compared with our large areas of agreement. My agreement is especially extensive with Alvin Goldman, as he has also remarked. Indeed, almost all of his recent paper I find acceptable and more. But, for the reasons given, I prefer to interpret it in line with the general account VI rather than *just* the "list" proposal L. I can even accept the "list" proposal L, and indeed I do. Our disagreement therefore boils down to this: should proposal L be supplemented with accounts V1 and V2, which would give us a general account of two sorts of epistemic justification, enabling us to explain a cognitivist (and not just prescriptivist) "justification," and which, moreover, would also enable us to explain and support Goldman's "list" proposal? The only objection lodged against adopting V1 and V2 is that "there is no evidence that the folk are inclined to relativize virtues and vices." But this is outweighed by the fact that the pertinent rela-tivization may be contextual and implicit.

As for Alvin Plantinga, we agree that "internal" factors are insufficient to give us an account of knowledge or even of warrant; that we must appeal also to the operative faculties; that for knowledge it is required that such faculties be "operating properly" in a way that is truth conducive; that these faculties must not only "operate properly" in general, relative to the pertinent environment of the subject vis-a-vis the sort of proposition involved, but that, further, they must *not* be misfiring or malfunctioning in the specific instance, and giving knowledge only by accident. However, Plantinga and I disagree in our accounts of what is involved in such "proper functioning," since he wishes to explain this in teleological terms, and ultimately (for the "core" cases, anyhow) in theological terms; whereas my own conception of a faculty that functions properly is very weak indeed, and requires only that such a faculty be generally reliable in the environment that is pertinent, and be virtuous in the specific instance as well, ensuring that the subject would (most likely) believe that p, as he does, if and only if it were the case that p.

Since our disagreements seem *relatively* small when compared with the large areas of agreement, it seems appropriate to view the three approaches as varieties of a single more fundamental option in epistemology, one which puts the explicative emphasis on truth-conducive intellectual virtues or faculties, and is properly termed "virtue epistemology."[24]

Notes

This paper was part of a symposium on Alvin Plantinga's Warrant and Proper Function at the APA Pacific Division meetings of March 1992.

1. "Positive Epistemic Status and Proper Function," in *Philosophical Perspectives 2, Epistemology*, ed. James Tomberlin (Atascadero: Ridgeview, 1988), p. 30. Goldman's earlier proposal to account for propositional knowledge by requiring one's true belief to be causally connected with the fact believed had already elicited the following objection: "Suppose . . . that a certain very serious brain damage causes me to be a hypochondriac and this in turn eventually leads to my belief that I have a seriously damaged brain. If I have no evidence for my belief, then surely I do not know what I believe." See p. 39 of my "Propositional Knowledge," *Philosophical Studies* XX(1969): 33–43. Goldman's account is in "A Causal Theory of Knowing," *Journal of Philosophy* 64(1967): 357.72. The generality problem for reliabilism just explained is pointed out already by Goldman in "What Is Justified Belief," in George Pappas, ed., *Justification and Knowledge* (Dordrecht: Reidel, 1979); and it is developed convincingly by Richard Feldman in "Reliability and Justification," *The Monist* 68(1985): 159–174.

2. Alvin Plantinga, "A Reply to James Taylor," *Philosophical Studies* 64(1991): 203–17; p. 203. (What I have given here is actually a close paraphrase of Plantinga's own sketch.)

3. Plantinga reports this response in *Warrant and Proper Function*, where Goldman is said to have made it in a symposium on warrant at meetings of the APA Central Division in St. Louis in 1986.

4. Donald Davidson "Knowing One's Own Mind," *Proceedings and Addresses of the APA*, 1986, pp. 443–44.

5. Compare the similar objection made by James Taylor in "Plantinga's Proper Functioning Analysis of Epistemic Warrant," *Philosophical Studies* 64(1991): 185–203.

6. Alvin Plantinga, "A Reply to James Taylor," *Philosophical Studies* 64(1991): 203–17; p. 208.

7. Perhaps it will help to put the principle somewhat differently by contraposing as follows: "If P is clearly necessary and clearly incompatible with C, then C is clearly impossible; and C is more clearly impossible the more clear it is that P is necessary."

8. Ibid., p. 206.

9. Ibid.

10. Independently of proper functionalism, it is anyhow an interesting question why the Swampman lacks warrant for many of his beliefs, as does the victim of the evil demon. If he is "right" in a certain belief and that belief is quite apt and highly justified, deriving as it does from the exercise of excellent cognitive faculties, what then can be missing that denies it the title of knowledge? As Gettier cases already show, a justified, true belief is not necessarily knowledge; nor need a belief be knowledge even if true and generated by excellent cognitive faculties. At a minimum we must distinguish between faculties that generate apt beliefs without depending on other beliefs and faculties that do depend on other beliefs. We may infer deductively or

inductively in excellent fashion, and that may yield justified and apt beliefs, but these will not constitute knowledge if our premises were justified and even apt but still false! A given belief may be justified and apt if a member of a comprehensively coherent body of beliefs, but it will amount to knowledge thereby only if excising any false members will leave a sufficiently comprehensive and coherent body of beliefs. This is obviously a requirement the Cartesian victim cannot satisfy for the vast majority of his beliefs, and a similar problem afflicts the Swampman.

11. Alvin Plantinga, *Warrant and Proper Function* (New York: Oxford University Press, 1993), Ch. II.

12. One that does not require the warrant for one's beliefs to be systematically aligned with the reliability of the causal processes, even the internal causal processes that lead to them.

13. "Epistemic Folkways and Scientific Epistemology," in his collection, *Liasons: Philosophy Meets the Cognitive and Social Sciences* (Cambridge, Mass.: MIT Press/Bradford, 1991).

14. Ibid., p. 159.

15. Ibid., p. 160.

16. Ibid., p. 157.

17. Ibid.

18. Ibid., p. 160.

19. Ibid., p. 163.

20. Note that Goldman's "justified belief" is very close to Plantinga's "warranted belief" and to my own "apt belief." Such Goldmanian "justification" hence goes beyond mere internal "rationality" and the satisfaction of doxastic obligations, etc.

21. "For the pragmatist . . . 'knowledge' is, like 'truth,' simply a compliment paid to the beliefs which we think so well justified that, for the moment, further justification is not needed" (from R. Rorty, "Solidarity or Objectivity?" in volume 1 of his collected papers, *Objectivity, Relativism, and Truth* (Cambridge, U.K.: Cambridge University Press, 1991), p. 24).

22. The sense of "justification" captured by V2 (Va plus J2) is that involved in saying that the evil demon victim retains justification for perceptual beliefs, etc. Nevertheless, there appears also a concept of epistemically justified (or apt) belief that corresponds to VI (Va and J1). This would be the concept to use in attributing justification to a superior form of life in another possible world, where they flourish epistemically through faculties that would be useless in our earthly habitat.

23. The approach is developed further in my *Knowledge in Perspective* (Cambridge, U.K.: Cambridge University Press, 1991); especially in Part IV.

24. Though this last must eventually be qualified in Plantinga's case to make room for the role of design, and in my own case to make room for the role of *epistemic perspective*. And of course virtue epistemology is itself a type of generic reliabilism. But generic reliabilism comes in a great variety of types, most of which are clearly unacceptable.

14

Postscript to "Proper Functionalism and Virtue Epistemology"

Ernest Sosa

I welcome this opportunity to continue an exchange with Alvin Plantinga prompted by his two volumes—*Warrant: The Current Debate* and *Warrant and Proper Function*—a major contribution to the long tradition that it joins with impressive thoroughness, vigor, and depth.

In his response to my paper, Plantinga takes up two main issues that I wish to discuss further in what follows:[1]

Whether we can accomplish many of the epistemic purposes of his notion of properly functioning faculties (as I, ES, have argued) with the apparently simpler notion of a faculty (period, whether properly functioning or not)—which would put in question the need for the more complex notion in epistemology.

Whether the sort of more streamlined virtue epistemology that I prefer is subject to certain simple and decisive counterexamples.

I

One believes oneself tumor-afflicted, let us suppose, with a belief that derives not from evidence or reasoning but only from cognitive malfunction caused by a brain tumor. What reason can proper functionalism provide against counting as knowledge that tumor-derived belief? Such a belief is said to fall short for a very simple reason: because it does not derive from a properly functioning faculty—i.e., because it derives *not* from a faculty that functions in keeping with its design plan, but only from a brain tumor.

Is there not, however, a simpler answer that works equally well: namely, that the belief in question derives from no faculty (period)? Why the extra complexity imported by the appeal to design?

Typically ingenious is Plantinga's response: the differential complexity is said to be an illusion, since the very notion of a faculty *already* involves the notion of functioning properly, and, hence, in turn, the notion of working in accord with design. But how plausible is this claim of conceptual involvement?

According to the combined wisdom of several dictionaries, a faculty is an ability, capacity, or power to do something. But this is obviously too broad if we allow full scope to these supple terms. Suppose that wherever one is "able" to do something, one has a corresponding ability. In virtue of the tumor, then, one is able to believe correctly about whether one has a tumor, as shown by the fact that (in virtue of the tumor) one *does* believe correctly. By the latitudinarian dictionary account, therefore, the tumor confers upon one a faculty after all. But this is absurd.

We must go beyond the dictionary. A faculty can't be just any ability, power, or capacity. At best only a special sort of ability, etc., can count. What sort? Is Plantinga perhaps right in suggesting that it must be an ability that can "function properly," and thus "in accord with its design plan"?

A faculty is, first of all, an ability, etc., *of a whole person*. The heart does *do* something. It pumps blood. But neither that nor its corresponding ability confers upon it any "faculty."

Second, an ability, etc., does not count as a faculty unless it is an ability *to "accomplish" a sort of thing normally desirable*. Most of us are able to stumble, or at least capable of doing so, but there is no corresponding faculty.

Third, if an ability to accomplish a certain sort of thing is to count as a faculty, the sort of thing in question must not only be normally desirable, but must also lie at *a certain level of generality*. Thus there is no *special* faculty of running a marathon, though one might speak more smoothly of a faculty of running or, more smoothly yet, of a faculty of locomotion.[2] Here we are already approaching respects in which we need not follow ordinary language slavishly, but might well bend and stretch it to our purposes: e.g., by speaking of "sub-faculties" as we find need to descend to lower levels of abstraction.

Consider now such an ability, power, or capacity to accomplish a desirable sort of thing. Necessarily allied to that is the notion of "functioning," i.e., of performing a "function," a special, distinctive activity that is desirable or at least desired.[3] And the notion of "functioning *properly*" is not far to seek. In none of that, however, do I see a need to import any notion of design, either theological or merely teleological.

As far as logic, narrow or broad, is concerned, and as far as metaphysical possibility is concerned, it is hard to see anything to prevent a possible world in which some intelligent beings either come about by chance or are always in existence.[4] Such beings owe their existence and workings to no design. If they nevertheless function properly, therefore, it must be on a conception of such functioning that is design-independent. Suppose them to have the usual complement of humanoid faculties—or anyhow of abilities to acquire true beliefs by the familiar use of eyes, ears, etc., widespread among humans. These powers might systematically serve them well in yielding a multitude of indispensable true beliefs. And this, I contend, suffices to make of such powers (abilities, capacities) *faculties*, each with its function of producing a distinctive yield of true beliefs (of shape and color, of pitch and volume, etc.), and each functioning properly, i.e., performing its distinctive function adequately well. In none of this, again, do I see any metaphysical or broadly logical need to implicate any sort of design, theological or teleological.

I conclude that we can enjoy an illuminating conception of what a faculty is by appeal merely to abilities, powers, or capacities, and their apt functioning—e.g., in helping us grasp the truth and avoid error—absent any requirement of design.

Of course we still need some account of what it is for a faculty to "malfunction." In my paper I tried to sketch such an account without using any notion of design. Plantinga's response also raises some problems for this part of my proposal. The following section discusses his objections prior to developing my sketched proposal.

II

"There are further problems," says Plantinga:

> For example (as Sosa recognizes) if a belief is to be justified or warranted, then the faculty that produces it must be working properly *on the occasion of its production*. Of course Sosa hopes to avoid appeal to the

notion of proper function; he therefore suggests that "hence it must be that in the circumstances one would (most likely) believe P iff P were the case—i.e., one (at least probabilistically) tracks the truth . . . (p. 62 [of my paper])." So this tracking requirement is to do the work of the proper functioning requirement [or some of it anyhow] (p. 80).

Plantinga then argues that such a tracking requirement is too strong:

> Consider [says he, the] belief that
>
>> (1) I am not a brain in a vat on Alpha Centauri, serving as a subject in an experiment in which the experimenters give me the very experiences and beliefs I do in fact have just now.
>
> This doesn't satisfy Sosa's tracking requirement: it is not the case that probably, if it were false I would not believe it. (If it were false, I *would* believe it, since it is one of the beliefs I do in fact have just now.) But couldn't this belief have warrant for me? Note also that while (1) doesn't meet the tracking requirement,
>
>> (2) I am at home in Indiana and I am not a brain in a vat on Alpha Centauri, serving as a subject in an experiment in which the experimenters give me the very experiences and beliefs I do in fact have just now
>
> does. (If (2) were false, it would be because of the falsehood of its first conjunct, in which case I would not believe that conjunct or the whole proposition.) Can a view be right if it implies that I can know (2) but cannot know (1)?[5]

That objection is based essentially on misunderstanding, understandably so since what it overlooks is a subtlety I could not highlight in my paper to which it responds. Let me now do so.

Consider again the tracking requirement proposed in my paper:

(C)   S would believe P iff P were the case.

And compare that with:

(N)   If P̌ were the case, S would believe P; and
         If P were false, S would not believe P.

Plantinga's objection to my proposal treats C above (which I call "Cartesian" tracking) as essentially equivalent to N ("Nozickian" tracking). But there is a vast difference between the two, or so I will now argue.

First we need to distinguish two sorts of conditional, as follows.

$T(P) \rightarrow T(Q)$ P would be true only if Q were true as well. Or:
The only way P would be true is if Q were true as well.

$T(P) \Rightarrow T(Q)$ P could conceivably be true only if Q were true as well. Or:
The only conceivable way P could be true is if Q were true as well.

Thus someone might say, correctly: "There would be water out of this faucet only if the house's main valve were open (only if it should be open)." Or: "The only way there would be water out of this faucet is if the main valve were open." But it would not be true to say: "There could be water out of this faucet only if the house's main valve were open (only if it should be open)." Or: "The only conceivable way there could be water out of this faucet is if the main valve were open." After all, someone might *conceivably* have disconnected the pipes from the house's normal system of pipes and could conceivably be pumping water directly into the pipes with a private pump. It is just that, given the situation as it stands, no one in fact has the motivation or the opportunity to take the trouble to do all that. As the situation in fact stands, water would flow out of this open faucet only if the main valve were in fact open, allowing the city water to come into the house.

In terms of such conditionals (and omitting some refinements) Nozick's tracking account of knowledge is this:

NTA $K_S(P)$ IFFT   (P)
$B_S(P)$
$\sim T(P) \rightarrow \sim B_S(P)$
$T(P) \rightarrow B_S(P)$

The tracking requirement enables a proposed solution for the Gettier problem. In a Gettier case the subject has justified true belief but only accidentally, since what makes the belief true is *divorced* from the psychological basis that makes it justified. For this reason, even if the belief had not been true, that same psychological basis might easily have operated *anyhow*, and the subject might easily have believed just the same.

The tracking account is also used to deal with skepticism. The skeptic argues that one falls short because one cannot rule out skeptical scenarios known to be incompatible with one's ordinary knowledge. But one can "track" and thus know what one believes ordinarily (here is a hand, yonder a fire, etc.) even if one cannot track, and hence cannot rule out, such skeptical scenarios. Tracking is not closed under entailment, nor even under known entailment.

His tracking account thus leads Robert Nozick to a surprising combination of views. He is able to deal plausibly with Gettier cases, but his response to skepticism incurs some heavy costs. Here are some of its disadvantages:

d1 Swallowing that one might know that p and knowingly deduce that q, and believe that q on that basis, while still failing to know that q.

d2 Having to make an ad hoc exception for knowledge of necessary truths, since we get unpleasant results when we place the *negation* of a necessary truth such as $2 + 2 = 4$ in the antecedent of a subjunctive conditional. (Nozick hence proposes that his third condition be dropped for knowledge of necessary truths.)

d3 Having its so-called antiskeptical solution all too plausibly turned into a *reductio*, since it is most implausible that we should not know that we are not brains in a vat being fed normal experiences.

d4 Worse yet, there are many convincing counterexamples to Nozickian tracking as an account of knowledge. Here is a strikingly simple one. Consider: (a) p, and (b) I do not believe incorrectly (falsely) that p. Surely no one minimally rational and attentive who believes both of these will normally know either without knowing the other. Yet even in cases where one tracks the truth of (a), one could never track the truth of (b). After all, even if (b) were false, one would still believe it anyhow.[6]

Surprisingly, there is a minimal modification of Nozickian tracking that makes an enormous difference to its consequences. The new account, the Cartesian tracking account, is as follows:

CTA $\quad$ $K_S(P)$ IFF $\quad$ $T(P)$
$$B_S(P)$$
$$B_S(P) \rightarrow T(P)$$
$$T(P) \rightarrow B_S(P)$$

The difference comes with the third condition only.[7] The difference here is easily overlooked because it is easy to forget that subjunctive conditionals do not contrapose. In any case, once one focuses properly on Cartesian C-tracking, its differences from Nozickian N-tracking are striking.

First of all, CTA has advantages similar to those of NTA:

a1 It offers a similar solution to the Gettier problem.

a2 It answers the skeptic, now by arguing that we can know that we are not embroiled in a skeptical scenario, since, though we do not N-track, we *do* C-track that we are not in such a scenario. Thus it would be (remain) true that we were free of such a scenario only if we (still) believed it; and we *would* (still) believe we were free only if in fact we were free.

The most significant differences between the two tracking accounts emerge when we consider the disadvantages of Nozickian tracking (more strictly, of the Nozickian tracking account NTA).

Re d1: Cartesian tracking does not force us to reject the closure of knowledge under known entailment and deduction.

Re d2: Cartesian tracking need make no ad hoc exception for necessary truths. The same C-tracking required for knowledge of contingent truths is required also for knowledge of necessary truths.

Re d3: Cartesian tracking is *not* committed to the implausible view that we are in ignorance as to whether we are actually in some skeptical scenario where we are fed experiences artificially.

Re d4: Finally, Cartesian tracking is safe from the sort of counterexamples that we saw defeat Nozickian tracking. Consider again (i) p and (ii) I am not wrong in thinking that p. C-tracking here yields the right result, unlike N-tracking. Normally anyone minimally rational and attentive who believes both (i) and (ii) and C-tracks either also C-tracks the other.[8]

I have developed the contrast between Cartesian tracking and Nozickian tracking for two reasons: first, in order to explain why my proposal is not affected by the objection urged by Plantinga, whose examples counter Nozickian tracking but do not affect Cartesian tracking. In addition to that, there is a second reason for setting out that contrast and for the appeal to Cartesian tracking. Recall our main purpose in this volume: to explore the requirements of what Plantinga calls "warrant," of whatever it is that needs adding to true belief in order to constitute knowledge. I have argued that Cartesian tracking has an indispensable role to play in that regard, that it constitutes an essential component of such "warrant."[9]

Notes

1. My paper, "Proper Functionalism and Virtue Epistemology," *Nous* 27 (1993) 51–65, is referred to in what follows as PFVE. Plantinga's reply is "Why We Need Proper Function," *Nous* 27 (1993) 66–82. In that reply he also takes up a third main issue: Whether, in addition to the usual refuting counterexamples, there is also room for merely "opposing" counterexamples, as I suggested in my paper. The considerations adduced by Plantinga concerning this third issue are also well worth further reflection, and I intend to return to this whole issue elsewhere.

2. Even this, I feel, stretches the most usual sense of "faculty," which seems more aptly restricted to *cognitive* powers, or at least to more fully *mental* powers.

3. I do not say that *any* performance of such an activity is the performance of a function. Which are and which, if any, are not? That remains a question for further reflection.

4. "It is . . . possible that I . . . have popped into existence this very instant, complete with a complement of insistent but wholly false memory beliefs" (*Warrant and Proper Function*, p. 51). "Bertrand Russell is right: it is surely possible, in the broadly logical sense, that the world should have popped into existence five minutes ago, complete with all its apparent traces of the past—all its dusty books, decaying buildings, mature oaks, crumbling mountains, and apparent memories" (WPF, p. 62). Presumably, a world or a being that just "pops into existence" does not derive from design; anyhow, it does seem to me possible in any case, in the broadly logical or metaphysical sense, that a world such as ours, and especially that a being such as I am now, have popped into existence, as Russell supposes, unaided by design.

5. WPF, pp. 80–81.

6. So far as I know this consequence was previously undrawn. Can anyone find it acceptable?

7. It is this that accounts for the label "Cartesian," and not, of course, the strength of the conditionals involved. The conditionals remain ordinary subjunctive conditionals, and not the stronger "entailment" conditionals introduced earlier.

8. Two comparisons of N-tracking with C-tracking may be found in respective papers by Laurence BonJour and Steven Luper-Foy, both in Luper-Foy's collection, *The Possibility of Knowledge: Nozick and His Critics* (Totowa, N.J.: Rowman and Littlefield, 1987). BonJour perceptively compares the third condition of NTA ($\sim p \rightarrow \sim Bp$) with something approximately like the corresponding condition in CTA ($Bp \rightarrow p$). But he does not use that comparison

in the way suggested here. (He even writes that "it seems safe to treat the two conditions as amounting to at least approximately the same thing." Ibid., p. 302.) More similar to our own is Luper-Foy's approach. His proposed replacement for Nozick's third condition is this: "if my evidence were to lead me to believe that p is true, then p would be true" (which he calls the "contratracking condition"). Even he concludes, however, "that the tracking and contratracking conditions virtually never diverge in their assessments of putative cases of knowledge except when applied to cases about which our pretheoretic intuitions are unclear" (p. 235). But I cannot believe that many would find it pretheoretically intuitive that they do not know they are not just being fed normal experiences while envatted. In addition, Luper-Foy's condition applies only in cases where we believe something on the basis of some *evidence*. Finally, Luper-Foy does not consider the worst and most counterintuitive consequences of N-tracking: e.g., that I can well know that p even though I could never know that I am not wrong in thinking that p. It follows from the N-tracking account that I cannot possibly know the latter, but this does *not* follow from the C-tracking account. Are our "pretheoretic intuitions" here "unclear"? Can anyone find this at all credible?

9. Once clear on the contrast, one may see that Plantinga's objection to my tracking requirement as too strong depends crucially on confusing the two sorts of tracking. A further objection of his still remains standing, however. This objection depends on what he calls "the usual semantics for counterfactuals." But the element of that "usual semantics" on which the objection turns is also the main reason why I cannot accept that semantics.

On the usual semantics, as Plantinga observes, if P and Q are both true, it follows that $T(P) \rightarrow T(Q)$. But I cannot believe that just because one die will come up 3 and the other will come up 4, that therefore the one *would* come up 3 only if the other came up 4. So I must reject the "usual" semantics, and especially the very element of that semantics invoked essentially by Plantinga in his objection to my proposal.

Plantinga raises also a final objection to an aspect of my proposal that he draws from the following passage of my paper: "If a faculty operates to give one a belief, and thereby a piece of direct knowledge, one must have some awareness of one's belief and its source, and of the virtue of that source both in general and in the specific instance. . . . And, finally, one must grasp that one's belief nonaccidentally reflects the truth of P through the exercise of such a virtue. This account therefore combines requirements of *tracking* and *nonaccidentality*, of *reliable virtues or faculties*, and of *epistemic perspective*." But that final objection raised by Plantinga rests on a misunderstanding deriving from the fact that I could offer (in PFVE) only a very compressed sketch of my preferred alternative to the proper functioning conception of knowledge. My view is developed more fully in *Knowledge in Perspective* (Cambridge, U.K.: Cambridge University Press, 1991), esp. in Part IV; and it is defended further in the relevant respects in my "Virtue Perspectivism: A

Response to Foley and Fumerton," *Philosophical Issues* 5 (1994): 29–51; and in my "Reply to Dancy and BonJour," *Philosophical Studies* 78 (1995): 221–35. That fuller view distinguishes between animal knowledge and reflective knowledge (a distinction that I believe to be tantamount to Descartes's between *cognitio* and *scientia*—which may be found in his "Reply to the Second Set of Objections," e.g., on p. 39 of volume II of the Haldane and Ross translation published by Cambridge University Press as *The Philosophical Works of Descartes*). The requirement of reflection or of epistemic perspective applies directly only to reflective knowledge (*scientia*). But this application Plantinga seems inclined to grant: "the conditions Sosa mentions may well be required for certain kinds of knowledge—perhaps for wholly mature and self-conscious knowledge . . ." (p. 81). Here I can find no important disagreement between us, not yet anyhow, not on the basis so far provided.

15

Plantinga's Proper Function Account of Warrant

Jonathan L. Kvanvig

Alvin Plantinga offers a theory about one central epistemological concept, the concept of warrant.[1] He claims that warrant is that quantity enough of which, together with true belief, yields knowledge, and he argues that warrant is to be understood primarily in terms of proper function. To have a warranted belief, on this account, is to have a belief that results from cognitive equipment that is properly functioning, that is functioning as it was designed to function. Plantinga maintains that there is a design plan for various parts of our cognitive apparatus, and that such a design plan is a crucial component of an adequate theory of warrant.

Plantinga thus offers an approach to epistemology that begins by assessing the faculties or abilities of a cognitive system or agent. Once such an assessment is complete, the epistemologist is in a position to infer the epistemic status of the products of those faculties or abilities, e.g., beliefs. If the faculties are suitably virtuous or excellent, or deemed to be functioning in an ideal way or at least in an adequate way, the beliefs that result from the use of those faculties pass epistemic muster, they receive some type of positive epistemic evaluation. The crucial element of such a view is the primacy of evaluating the capacities of a system, and the derivative way in which epistemic concepts are applied. We might term such an approach "Aristotelian," for it is reminiscent of Aristotelian approaches in ethics, where the fundamental evaluation applies to persons and their characteristics, and derivatively to their actions. In the epistemological case, the derivative evaluation applies to the beliefs that are products of systems determined to have epistemically virtuous or adequate capacities.[2]

Plantinga formulates his theory as one concerning the epistemic notion of warrant, but I do not wish to pursue whether one should prefer this notion or other notions in an account of knowledge, notions such as justification, rationality, having the right to be sure, etc. Rather, I want to focus on a more general issue, an issue concerning where to begin constructing a theory of any of these epistemological concepts. As we shall see, Aristotelianism in epistemology offers a distinctive answer to the question of where to begin, an answer I will argue is incorrect.

To determine where to begin, we might first ask what kinds of things can have epistemic properties. Regarding the range of epistemic concepts that have been proposed, at least two answers are available: mental states or events themselves, such as beliefs or believings, sometimes receive epistemic support (warrant, justification, rationality, etc.), but propositions (sentences, statements) also sometimes receive such support (for a particular person in a particular situation). René Descartes's belief that he exists is epistemically supported for him, as is the claim (proposition) that he, Descartes, thinks, whether he believes it or not. The first kind I will call "psychological support," and the second kind "propositional support."[3]

This distinction is a common one in recent epistemology, and the argument for making the distinction is simple. Consider Sherlock and Watson, both of whom are in the same total epistemic situation regarding a particular case they are working one (i.e., each has shared all they know with the other about the case in question). As the case is drawing to a close, they may even share the same belief about who is guilty. Both believe, let us suppose, that the butler did it. There is a crucial difference, however. Watson holds the belief on the basis of a hunch he has that the butler did it; Holmes sees how the information he and Watson share shows that the butler did it. He has, as he is wont to say, "deduced" it.

Given the distinction between propositional and psychological support, we can express the difference between Holmes and Watson as follows. Both possess propositional support for the claim that the butler did it, but only Holmes's believing is psychologically supported. For Holmes believes that the butler did it because of, or on the basis of, the information they both possess. Watson believes only because he has a hunch, and so does not see how the information shows that the butler did it.

The argument for the distinction and its epistemological importance is thus straightforward, and once one notices the distinction, a natural question to ask is how the different applications of epistemic concepts are related. The Aristotelian viewpoint on the matter is that the fundamental application of epistemic concepts is to the products of epistemically suitable cognitive systems. This viewpoint falls directly out of the distinctive Aristotelian commitment that we begin epistemological inquiry by evaluating cognitive machinery. Once such evaluation is complete, the epistemic status of the products of that machinery, products such as beliefs, is determined by how adequate the equipment is. So, for the Aristotelian epistemologist, doxastic warrant has primacy over propositional support. Plantinga affirms this viewpoint by saying,

> According to the central and paradigmatic core of our notion of warrant (so I say) a belief B has warrant for you if and only if (1) the cognitive faculties involved in the production of B are functioning properly. . . ; (2) your cognitive environment is sufficiently similar to the one for which your cognitive faculties are designed; (3) . . . the design plan governing the production of the belief in question involves, as purpose or function, the production of true beliefs. . . ; and (4) the design plan is a good one: that is, there is a high statistical or objective probability that a belief produced in accordance with the relevant segment of the design plan in that sort of environment is true.[4]

The feature here that is important for my purposes is that according to Plantinga, "the central and paradigmatic core of our notion of warrant" is that "a belief B has warrant for you." In this regard, Plantinga is a paradigmatic Aristotelian in epistemology—he holds that the primary application of the concept of warrant is to beliefs, to the products of an adequate cognitive system.

Aristotelians in epistemology are not limited to beliefs as the primary recipients of epistemic evaluation. For example, the intentional attitude of withholding can be warranted, and an epistemological Aristotelian might consider the application of epistemic terms to withholdings to be as fundamental as is the application of such terms to beliefs. It is fair to say, however, that it is tempting for Aristotelians to focus primarily on beliefs when characterizing the kinds of mental states which partake of fundamental epistemic evaluation. Plantinga's proposal above does just this, as does a recent proposal by Alvin Goldman. In "What Is Justified Belief?" Goldman claims that the primary type of justification attaches to beliefs in virtue of having been produced by a reliable belief-producing mechanism.[5] Goldman, like Plantinga, puts the Aristotelian focus on beliefs; other mental states would seem to receive only derivative epistemic evaluation on their proposals.

Commitment to the derivative status of certain types of epistemic evaluation calls for some account of such status, and Goldman's proposal is interesting because he attempts to provide such an account. After clarifying what he considers to be the fundamental application of the concept of justification, he asks how we might understand talk of justification when it applies to propositions. Goldman argues that propositional justification can be understood in terms of doxastic justification, thereby defending a version of what I will call "doxasticism." Doxasticism is the view according to which the basic kind of justification is the kind that attaches to beliefs, and any other kind of justification, including that which attaches to propositions, can be defined in terms of the doxastic kind.

In the case of Plantinga, things are a bit more complicated. Given the above characterization by Plantinga of the fundamental notion of warrant, one might expect Plantinga to defend doxasticism as well. However, Plantinga's work on the concept of warrant includes no effort to characterize a notion of propositional warrant to supplement the notion of doxastic warrant on which he focuses, nor does he address the question of how the epistemic evaluation of other mental states is related to the epistemic status of beliefs. Goldman's proposal, to understand propositional justification in terms of doxastic, handles the latter issue indirectly, for we can explain, e.g., the epistemic status of withholding in terms of the epistemic status of the proposition regarding which the withholding occurs.

Plantinga, however, does not follow Goldman's lead here. In fact, there is some reason to think that Plantinga would deny that there is any such thing as propositional warrant at all, for Plantinga begins his study of warrant by claiming, "My topic is warrant: that, whatever precisely it is, which together with truth makes the difference between knowledge and mere true belief."[6] And in the preface to the second volume, he characterizes warrant as "this elusive quality or quantity enough of which, together with truth and belief, [that] is sufficient for knowledge."[7] If warrant is that which plugs the gap between true belief and knowledge, or if warrant is that which plugs such a gap when there is enough of it, then there will be no kind of warrant which is propositional in nature. For no amount of propositional support alone will be sufficient for plugging the gap between true belief and knowledge.[8]

This latter point may be missed if one thinks only of cases in which one has propositional support for claims one does not believe. In such a case, it may be tempting to think that if one believed the claim in question and there was enough propositional support for it, one would have knowledge. But one can have propositional support not only for claims one does not believe, but also for claims that one believes on the basis of something other than that which propositionally supports it. In such cases, knowledge is lacking precisely because of the failure to base one's belief on that which supports it epistemically. Because of this latter possibility, no amount of mere propositional support is sufficient to close the gap between true belief and knowledge.

Setting the issue of propositional support aside for a bit, there is still the issue of epistemic support for mental states other than beliefs. Here Plantinga explicitly endorses the possibility of such support. In circumscribing his topic, Plantinga not only claims that beliefs or believings are subject to epistemic appraisal, he also notes quite rightly that we appraise not only a person's beliefs "but also her skepticisms or (to use another Chisholmian term) her withholdings, her refrainings from belief. An unduly credulous person may believe what she ought not; an unduly skeptical (or cynical) person may fail to believe what she ought."[9] Such remarks indicate that the topic of Plantinga's work must take into account not only some property, complex or otherwise, that attaches to beliefs, but also some property, complex or otherwise, that attaches to things other than beliefs.

Unfortunately, we do not find in Plantinga's two-volume work any discussion of this further property. What we do find is an account of warrant on which it is a property of beliefs, leaving unaddressed the question of the nature of this property that attaches to something other than beliefs. At first glance, however, the supplementation looks simple. Warrant, we are told, is roughly the property a belief has when it is the product of properly functioning cognitive equipment in a suitable environment. This same property can attach to other cognitive attitudes as well, attitudes such as withholding. For example, a person's skepticism about a claim might be the result of properly functioning cognitive equipment in a suitable environment, and thus the withholding of belief in such a case would be warranted. The resulting view would then hold that warrant is a property that attaches not just to beliefs but also to other cognitive attitudes such as disbelief and withholding.

Such an approach is a broadened form of Aristotelianism. Instead of claiming that fundamental epistemic evaluation applies to beliefs, defenders of this view claim that it applies to intentional attitudes, at least to some that are not beliefs. On the proposal above, Plantinga is committed to such a view even if his explicit claims are that the fundamental concept of warrant attaches to beliefs. Furthermore, without embracing this broadened form of Aristotelianism, it is not clear how Plantinga could explain how withholdings or skepticisms could be warranted. Had he followed Goldman's lead and given a characterization of propositional support in terms of doxastic support, some defense would be available for his explicitly doxastic claims. Without following Goldman's lead, and given the feature of Plantinga's account noted above that might lead him to deny the existence of propositional warrant, we might need to attribute to Plantinga a version of Aristotelianism broader than doxasticism despite his explicit statements affirming the doxasticist viewpoint.

Independent of such hermeneutical details, there is a difference between doxasticism, which claims that fundamental evaluation applies to beliefs and that other kinds of epistemic evaluation must be understood in terms of this fundamental kind, and Aristotelianism, which claims that fundamental epistemic evaluation applies to intentional attitudes besides beliefs, and that any other kind of epistemic evaluation is to be understood in terms of the kind that applies to intentional attitudes. We might be tempted to think that nondoxasticist Aristotelians have some advantage over doxasticists, if only because they have less to explain. The nondoxasticist Aristotelian needs only to explain how any kind of propositional support that exists can be understood in terms of the epistemic evaluation that applies to intentional attitudes, whereas the doxasticist must be able to explain both propositional support and psychological support for some other mental states or events in terms of doxastic support. We might even find ourselves tempted to think that this nondoxasticist theory is able to handle much of what motivates the distinction between propositional and doxastic support. When there is propositional support for a claim a person does not believe, the nondoxasticist Aristotelian might claim that such support is to be understood in terms of the unwarrantedness of that person's withholding regarding that claim.

Unfortunately, things are a bit more complicated. Since withholding, disbelieving, and believing are all types of intentional attitudes, the above account of propositional support will fail. For it is simply false that we take one of these intentional attitudes toward every supported proposition whatsoever, for a necessary condition for taking any of these intentional attitudes toward a proposition is that one also conceive of that proposition. Since there are many propositions which we never conceive of, there are many propositions we never believe, disbelieve, or withhold concerning. Nonetheless, such propositions can be the recipients of epistemic support.

So the success of Aristotelianism in epistemology is not so easily secured. There are of course other options for the Aristotelian to try here, an obvious one being the counterfactual approach on which propositional support is to be understood in terms of some attitude that *would be* justified or warranted if it were held. We will consider such proposals later, but the point to note here is that some complications will have to be introduced in order for Aristotelianism to succeed. I believe, however, that the situation is worse, for I believe that Aristotelianism in epistemology cannot succeed. I believe, that is, that no version of Aristotelianism—the approach that begins by evaluating cognitive faculties and applies terms of epistemic appraisal to beliefs or other intentional attitudes on the basis of this evaluation of faculties—can succeed in explaining how terms of epistemic appraisal apply to propositions. Furthermore, I believe that an approach that claims that terms of epistemic appraisal apply fundamentally to propositions can explain the possibility of epistemic evaluation of beliefs and other intentional attitudes. I will give the name "propositionalism" to this view.

As stated, both the Aristotelian and the propositionalist agree that there is a fundamental kind of epistemic appraisal, and both seek to understand the other kind in terms of this fundamental kind. Of course, assuming interdefinability has its risks. The alternative view, that terms of epistemic appraisal are ambiguous between propositional and doxastic uses, is not initially attractive, however. For it seems quite easy to understand psychological uses in terms of propositional: doxastic justification, for example, is just propositional justification plus proper basing, i.e., propositional justification where one holds a belief on the basis of, or because of, that which justifies it or is epistemically relevant to it. It will not do, however, for Aristotelians to appeal to this definition, for it is a version of propositionalism—it defines doxastic support in terms of propositional support rather than the other way around. Nonetheless, the point remains that the interdefinability assumption is supported by this propositionalist proposal, for in order to defend the ambiguity thesis, one would have to argue against the plausibility of such accounts.

So the interdefinability position is quite attractive. Regardless of whether it is the most attractive or the least attractive, however, any complete epistemological theory should say what the relationship is between propositional and psychological applications of terms of epistemic appraisal. Plantinga does not address the question, and the quick proposal above to supplement his account by allowing warrant to apply fundamentally not only to beliefs but also to other propositional attitudes is not successful—it does not, for example, explain the possibility of support for propositions of which we have never conceived. Still, the propositionalist account above may offer hope to Plantinga and other Aristotelians, for if one can define X in terms of Y, one can often define Y in terms of X.[10] In this case, however, it cannot be done. I will argue that the basic kind of epistemic support cannot attach to beliefs or other intentional attitudes, as Plantinga and other Aristotelians maintain, and that if it is not the basic kind, the right conclusion to draw is that proper function is at best of ancillary interest to the epistemological project of understanding the terms of epistemic appraisal.

I will begin by considering the narrower view, doxasticism, and then extend the discussion to Aristotelianism more broadly. Before doing so, there is one messy situation from the above discussion that needs to be cleaned up. In the discussion that follows I will use Plantinga's favored term 'warrant', writing of both propositional and doxastic warrant, even though, as we have seen, Plantinga's explicit remarks about warrant imply that there is no kind of warrant that is propositional in character. I could avoid this problem by writing more circumlocutorily to avoid the appearance of violating Plantinga's usage, but there is little to be gained by it. Those more wedded to Plantinga's usage may feel free to interpret the relationship between Plantingian warrant—that which plugs the gap between true belief and knowledge—and propositional warrant akin to how we treat talk of Senators and former Senators. I do not care if one wants to insist that propositional warrant is not really a kind of warrant at all; what matters here is that terms of epistemic appraisal can apply to propositions, and I will speak of propositional warrant in discussing that phenomenon.

The Problem for Doxasticism

Consider how one might attempt to understand propositional warrant in terms of doxastic warrant. An initial difficulty is that sometimes one has warrant for things one does not believe; that is, propositional warrant can obtain without doxastic warrant. The way to proceed, however, is fairly obvious: in such cases, we imagine what things would be like were one to believe the claim in question. If things go well for the doxasticist, we will be able to say of the imagined situation that it is one where doxastic warrant obtains. So the place to begin is with a counterfactual: a particular propositional content is warranted for you, say, when you do not believe it, if you would have doxastic warrant for the belief had you believed that proposition.

Such an approach faces first the Problem of Cognitive Admirability. Consider the case of Sally the Scrupulous Scientist. Sally is scrupulous about scientific beliefs, so scrupulous that she would not hold such a belief unless it were warranted for her. Among the things she presently holds no belief about is whether superstring theory is correct. Since she is so cognitively admirable, she would not believe this claim unless believing it would be warranted for her. According to the simple counterfactual approach stated above, she thereby has propositional warrant for the claim that superstring theory is correct. For it is true of Sally that if she were to believe that superstring theory is correct, her belief would be warranted. Since she has no such warrant, the simple counterfactual approach does not specify a sufficient condition for propositional warrant.

This problem is easy to explain from a propositionalist's point of view, that point of view according to which the basic kind of warrant is propositional warrant. In the imagined counterfactual situation in which Sally believes that superstring theory is correct, Sally's total epistemic situation is radically different. Such a difference is implied by the description of Sally as unusually meticulous about conforming belief to evidence. Because of this difference, it is not surprising that her doxastic warrant in the counterfactual situation does not line up with what she actually has by way of propositional warrant.

If the doxasticist could make use of these claims, there would be a simple way to restrict the simple counterfactual approach. Instead of saying that propositional warrant obtains when and only when a person's belief in that proposition would be justified if held, the doxasticist could say that propositional warrant is to be understood in terms of having a doxastically warranted belief in counterfactual situations where one holds the belief in the same total epistemic situation, in that situation in which one's total evidence remains the same.

Unfortunately, this account is circular. Concepts such as the concept of evidence or total epistemic situation must be understood in terms of propositional warrant. One thing is evidence for another provided the former warrants the latter, and this warrant obtains in the presence of the former *whether or not one believes the latter*. Hence, the kind of warrant imparted is clearly propositional warrant. Similarly, two individuals are in the same total epistemic situation if and only if they have precisely the same evidence. So the problem raised for the doxasticist is to try to restrict the simple counterfactual approach to avoid counterexamples like the case of Sally without relying on notions like evidence and total epistemic situation that make the resulting account circular.

Here is how Goldman addresses this problem. Instead of restricting the counterfactual situation to those in which the person has the same evidence, he restricts it to those in which the person's *cognitive state* is pretty much the same as it presently is. He says a person S is propositionally justified in believing p "if and only if there is a reliable belief-forming operation available to S which is such that if S applies that operation to his total cognitive state at t, S would believe p at t-plus-delta (for a suitably small delta) and that belief would be [doxastically] justified."[11] Since the concept of a cognitive state can be specified without appeal to any epistemic concepts at all, it follows trivially that it can be specified without appeal to the epistemic concept of propositional warrant.

Of course, doxasticists cannot require identity of cognitive state in the proposed counterfactual situation, for such situations involve an added belief. Goldman is somewhat cavalier about the problems involved in specifying adequate overall similarity of total cognitive state. From the passage just quoted, all we are told about which counterfactual situations are relevant is that they are ones in which an "available" reliable belief-forming operation is applied to "one's present cognitive state." Such an approach hardly faces the problem. Some people hold beliefs in the face of direct perceptual information to the contrary. The "available" reliable belief-forming mechanism of perception has already been applied, and they've ignored it. Presumably, that implies that if it were applied, they would not have a doxastically warranted belief concerning what perception shows (because they would not have a belief).

Furthermore, if perception is always an "available" reliable mechanism in those who have the capacity to see, then when my eyes are closed, I have propositional warrant for the existence of everything around me within my range of vision. If I simply opened my eyes, the application of the belief-forming operation of perception would result, more or less immediately, in a doxastically warranted belief. But surely I do not always have propositional warrant regarding the existence of every visible thing around me, e.g., when I am sleeping or daydreaming.

My point, though, is not to try to argue that refinement which addresses these concerns is impossible, but only to show the difficulty of the task. In what follows, I will assume that the problems can be solved, and thus will assume that some doxasticist surrogate for total epistemic situation in terms of (sufficiently similar) total cognitive state can be found. For there are other problems that are deeper and more general.

One problem arises out of recent literature which shows that belief can undermine evidence or reasons for belief. One such case, due to Richard Foley, goes as follows. You are close enough to graduating that you know you will graduate if and only if you pass a final exam. You have no beliefs about the matter, but you do have evidence that you will pass. This initial description, then, is just another case in which you have fully adequate evidence, i.e., propositional warrant, for a claim you do not believe. Suppose, however, that your examiners have it in for you, and will change the exam to be so difficult you will not pass it should you come to believe that you will pass it (and they will change the exam at the precise instant of belief formation). Furthermore, you know that this is so. Then you are in a position where you have adequate evidence for the claim that you will pass the exam, but you also know that if you were to believe that claim, you would not rationally believe it.[12]

There are also propositional contents which themselves conspire to make doxastically warranted belief impossible. One can have propositional warrant, for example, for the claim that one has never considered the proposition that the square root of 625 is 25 (perhaps you have just begun learning about exponents and the like and you know you've not progressed past single-digit numbers). Believing the claim, however, would undermine the evidence you have for it, with the result that no one can be doxastically warranted in believing that they have never considered the proposition that the square root of 625 is 25.

What has not been noticed is the implication of such cases for doxasticism. In all these cases, the counterfactual analysis central to doxasticism fails. If you were to believe that you have never considered the proposition that the square root of 625 is 25, your belief would not be warranted. Yet you have propositional warrant to that claim. And if you were to believe you will pass the test, your belief would not be warranted, despite the fact that you now have warrant for the claim that you will pass.

The only way out for doxasticists is to deny that the relevant counterfactuals are false. How might they responsibly do so? They cannot do so by denying that one can have warrant for something one does not believe, nor can they responsibly deny that there are cases in which such warrant would be undermined by belief. What is left, then, is to focus on the antecedent of the counterfactual, which requires believing the proposition in roughly the same total cognitive state. The only possibility left open for doxasticists is to say that the cases in which believing undermines reasons for belief do not involve belief in roughly the same total cognitive state.

As already noted, the doxasticist cannot insist on identity of total cognitive state, for some changes have to occur for the belief to be added—minimally, adding the belief itself. The doxasticist idea is to minimize the changes in such a way as to be able to mimic the propositionalist's notion of total epistemic situation. The doxasticist idea then is to define what it is for total mental states to be *sufficiently similar* to each other, and hope to find such a definition which implies that the mental states cannot be sufficiently similar when adding a belief that undermines reasons for believing. If this result can be obtained, doxasticists can deny the falsity of the counterfactual by which they define propositional warrant in terms of doxastic warrant by appeal to the standard semantics for counterfactuals. According to the standard semantics, all counterfactuals with necessarily false antecedents are trivially true. Some object to this implication of that semantics, but the semantic theory is a very useful and powerful theory, and jettisoning a few intuitions because of these virtues may be worth the price. The result is that doxasticists may be able to rescue their view from counterexamples concerning belief which undermines warrant by taking refuge among standard semanticists regarding count-erfactuals.

This response opens doxasticism to further problems, however—problems that are irremediable. One problem concerns claims of the form *I have never considered the proposition that p* propositionally warranted, even when the claim is known to be false by the person in question. For the same reasons as those given above for thinking that it is impossible that one be in a cognitive state sufficiently similar to the actual one in which one believes that one has never considered the proposition that the square root of 625 is 25 will be reasons for think that there are no possible states sufficiently similar to the actual one in which one believes any proposition of the form *I have never considered p*. For to consider such a proposition is, transparently to all, to consider *p*; it is intrinsically the kind of proposition that would require radical alterations of our constitution to believe. So the reasons for claiming that the antecedent of the required counterfactual is necessarily false in the case of *I have never considered the proposition that the square root of 625 is 25* are also reasons for thinking that the required counterfactual is necessarily false for any proposition of the form *I have never considered p*. Obviously, however, some claims of this sort are propositionally warranted and some are not, despite the implication of this defense of doxasticism that all of them are propositionally warranted. For example, the proposition *I have never considered the claim that doxasticism is false* is not propositionally warranted for me.

Another problem for this defense of doxasticism arises from noting that cases in which believing undermines evidence are just the reverse of cases in which belief itself makes the content of the belief true or likely to be true. Believing that you will succeed makes success more likely, and knowing that this is so increases the warrant we have for the claim that we will succeed when we believe we will. In such cases, we will be unable to explain the degree of warrant a proposition has when not believed in terms of what degree of warrant it would have if it were believed.

Such cases raise problems for doxasticists similar to the problem raised by cases in which belief undermines warrant. Regarding the latter problem, doxasticists must say that it is impossible to come to hold a belief that undermines warrant in a cognitive state that is suitably similar to the actual state. Any reasons for saying so, however, will be reasons for saying the same thing about cases in which believing creates warrant. They will have to say that there is no possibility of holding the belief that success is imminent without making changes to one's total cognitive state that rule out the counterfactual total cognitive state as being sufficiently similar to one's actual total cognitive state. The implication of such a claim, however, is that the counterfactual in question will always be trivially true, yielding the result that we always have propositional warrant for thinking we will succeed at anything whatsoever. Robert Schuler or Norman Vincent Peale might think so, but they've apparently not thought about trying to put a Cadillac up your nose.

There is a deeper problem as well. I'll begin with some specific cases, and then discuss what they have in common. Consider the proposition that I do not exist. I doubt that I can believe that proposition, and if I cannot, then any doxasticist proposal resting on the standard semantics is bound to fail. For if I cannot believe that claim, any counterfactual having in its antecedent the requirement that I believe the claim will be trivially true according to the standard semantics.

Suppose, however, that I can believe that I don't exist. Even if I can believe that I don't exist, Plantinga (and anyone else committed to a traditional Western conception of God) is committed to the view that God cannot believe that he does not exist. Plantinga believes that God exists and necessarily so, and is essentially omniscient, and that eliminates the possibility of God being an atheist. If so, however, any doxasticist proposal resting on the standard semantics for counterfactuals will count the proposition *God does not exist* as being propositionally warranted for God. Perhaps there are theology departments that would welcome such as theological novelty rather than philosophical debacle.

Finally, suppose certain psychological states are self-presenting, implying that it is impossible to consider whether you are in such a state and be wrong about it. Suppose further that you are in some such state P, and consider the proposition *I am not in psychological state P.* Since there is no world in which I believe that proposition in the same total cognitive state I am presently in, any counterfactual whose antecedent stipulates that I believe that claim is a counterfactual with an impossible antecedent.

Each of these counterexamples illustrates the Problem of Essential Cognitive Admirability. A person of such a nature is essentially such that he or she would not believe any of some range of propositions without warrant, i.e., it is not possible for that person to believe any such proposition without holding a doxastically warranted belief. No counterfactual account of propositional warrant can be adequate to such possibilities if it accepts the standard semantics for counterfactuals. For no matter how one restricts the antecedent of the relevant counterfactual, the only situations in which such a person holds the belief in question are worlds in which the belief is warranted. This latter fact holds even for propositions that the person presently knows are false, as long as those propositions are within the range of propositions about which the person is essentially cognitively admirable.

Examples concerning essential cognitive admirability are especially telling against Plantinga, for he believes that there is an individual who is essentially cognitively admirable over the entire range of propositions. Since God is essentially omniscient, every proposition is such that God would believe it if and only if it were doxastically warranted for him. Given the doxasticist proposal that rests on the standard semantics for counterfactuals, this piece of theology together with doxasticism implies that every proposition whatsoever is propositionally warranted for God, even those known by God to be false.

The Problem of Essential Cognitive Admirability does not depend on appeals to omniscience, however. For we need not imagine cases in which a person is essentially cognitively admirable over all propositions in order to see the problem. More limited kinds of cognitive admirability are fully sufficient to show that such accounts must fail. The history of epistemology is rife with examples of theorists who claimed that human beings are essentially cognitively admirable over some range of propositions. For many epistemologists have thought that human beings are incorrigible or infallible about their own sensory states, or appearance states, or sense-data. Others have implied that we are essentially cognitively admirable about our own existence or the fact that we are a thinking thing. According to such epistemologists, humans are essentially such that they know the truth of certain claims if those claims are true and are believed to be true. Such epistemologists might be wrong, but it is surely possible that beings exist who are essentially cognitively admirable in these or other ways, and the mere possibility of such essentially cognitively admirable beings is sufficient to undermine doxasticism.

So what is a self-respecting doxasticist to do? In a word (actually two), give up. Clearly, no account of propositional warrant in terms of doxastic warrant is going to work. First, one has to get a belief into the picture when as things actually stand there is no such belief. To do so is to imagine a nonactual situation, thereby landing us in the domain of counterfactuals, and doxasticism is impaled on the horns of a dilemma concerning how to interpret certain counterfactuals. Doxasticists can either accept or reject the feature of the standard semantics that counterfactuals with necessarily false antecedents are trivially true. If they reject the semantics, their view founders on the problem of belief undermining reasons for believing; if they accept the semantics, their view founders on the problem of essential cognitive admirability and on cases in which belief itself creates evidence.

The Problem for Aristotelianism

The problems for doxasticism are easily generalized to Aristotelianism more broadly conceived. Recall that doxasticists claim that terms of epistemic appraisal apply fundamentally to beliefs, whereas Aristotelians are committed only the the application of these terms to cognitive states, some of which are beliefs but others of which are not. In particular, broader Aristotelians allow terms of epistemic appraisal to apply to withholdings or skepticisms in addition to believings. Such a broader view is of little help, however, in addressing the problems faced by doxasticists.

Broader Aristotelians may initially seem to have some resources that doxasticists lack. For example, suppose there is propositional warrant for a claim that one does not believe. If one takes the intentional attitude of withholding concerning that proposition, one might be tempted to think that the propositional warrant in question could be explained in terms of the psychological unwarrantedness of withholding. If such an account were successful, broader Aristotelians would have an advantage over doxasticists, for doxasticists are forced to apply some counterfactual analysis to such cases, and we have seen the difficulties that such analyses encounter already. The above suggestion is that broader Aristotelians could escape the need for a counterfactual analysis in such cases.

The appearance is misleading for two reasons. First, it is not clear that the above account is successful even for the kind of case in question. For withholding concerning a proposition would be unwarranted if either that proposition or its negation were warranted, so one cannot account for the warrantedness of a proposition solely in terms of the unwarrantedness of withholding. Furthermore, broader Aristotelians will not be able to avoid the need for a counterfactual analysis to handle this difficulty as well as difficulties arising from cases in which there is propositional warrant for a claim toward which one takes no intentional attitude whatsoever. Moreover, the problems for doxasticism concerning belief that undermines warrant, belief that creates warrant, and cases of essential cognitive admirability will constitute the same plague of death for broader Aristotelianism as they do for doxasticism. Broader Aristotelianism provides no haven in which to take refuge in the face of the problems for doxasticism.

What is left, then, is either to become a propositionalist, one who holds that the basic kind of warrant is propositional warrant, or to defend an ambiguity thesis about the relationship between propositional and psychological warrant. As we have already seen, however, the prospects for the ambiguity thesis are not good. For there is an obvious way to understand doxastic warrant in terms of propositional warrant:

DW: S's belief that p is doxastically warranted if and only if (i) p is propositionally warranted for S and (ii) S's belief is based on that which propositionally warrants it.[13]

Furthermore, this account of doxastic warrant is easily generalizable to other intentional attitudes capable of epistemic appraisal. In particular, a similar account can be given concerning the psychological warrant for withholding: withholding concerning a proposition p is psychologically warranted for S if and only if neither p nor ~p is warranted for S, and S's withholding concerning p is based on the information that implies that neither p nor ~p is warranted for S. So DW and generalizations of it to other attitudes provide a solid argument on behalf of the claim that there is only one sense of 'warrant', a sense which covers the application of the term both to propositional contents and to mental states capable of epistemic appraisal. Moreover, this propositionalist proposal is attractive in part because it handles with such ease the cases that are problematic for the Aristotelian. In cases in which belief undermines warrant, propositionalists can simply note that propositional warrant was present prior to the formation of the belief and absent after, yielding the appropriate result that the belief in question would not be doxastically warranted if formed. In cases in which belief itself is warrant-imparting, propositional warrant appears with the formation of the belief, allowing the result that no propositional warrant was present prior to the belief, but that the belief was doxastically warranted when formed. Finally, cases of essential cognitive admirability create no problem for the propositionalist, either. So DW presents an attractive alternative to Aristotelianism, one that provides a forceful argument against the ambiguity thesis needed to preserve Aristotelianism and one that is able to explain successfully the anomalies that plague its competitors.

The Lesson for Plantingian Epistemology

One is tempted at this point to begin applying the above discussion to Plantinga's epistemology by pointing out that he begins, as do all Aristotelians, with the wrong kind of warrant. The matter is more complicated than that, however, for Plantinga can defend himself here by claiming that he has defined warrant to be that quantity which fills the gap between true belief and knowledge. As we have seen, propositional warrant simply does not do that. Instead of focusing on the kind of warrant in question, I believe there is a more useful approach. As I see it, the heart of Plantingian epistemology is found in the claim that the central feature of an adequate account of knowledge, apart from the requirement of true belief, is the concept of proper function: we know only when our faculties are functioning properly, in accordance with their design plan. The lesson to be learned from the above difficulties faced by Aristotelianism is where in a full account of knowledge an appeal to proper function might be appropriate.

To approach this issue carefully, we must first distinguish between the third and fourth conditions for knowledge—the warrant condition, as I will call it (though I reject the Plantingian stipulation that warrant is what fills the gap between true belief and knowledge), from the Gettier condition. One place that an appeal to proper function might be appropriate is in giving an account of the Gettier condition for knowledge. Some of Plantinga's examples suggest just such a role. For example, in arguing against coherentism, Plantinga constructs the following counterexample:

> Perhaps I have been captured by Alpha Centaurian cognitive scientists, who make me the subject of a cognitive experiment; their aim is to give me a system of beliefs in which falsehood and coherence are maximized. They succeed in giving me a thoroughly coherent set of beliefs, but in a few cases they slip, giving me a true belief rather than a false one. . . . In such cases my beliefs may have a great deal of coherence, but they will have very little warrant. Those that are true, are true just by accident, and surely do not constitute knowledge for me.[14]

As an attempt to refute coherentism, such a counterexample invites the following reply. Coherentists can claim that they never intended their theory to fill the gap between true belief and knowledge, and that cases such as the above will be ruled out as cases of knowledge by an adequate response to the Gettier problem, leaving untouched the coherentist understanding of the third condition for knowledge.[15] The coherentist might agree with Plantinga, however, about the importance of an appeal to proper function in explaining why the above case is not a case of knowledge. So if proper function is central to knowledge, one way that might be true is for proper function to play a role in the fourth condition for knowledge, that condition aimed at solving the problem of accidentally true, but justified, belief made famous by Edmund Gettier.[16]

The concept of proper function might also play an important role in the third condition itself. Note first that propositional warrant is surely not all there is to such a third condition, even if we are convinced that it is the fundamental notion of warrant. For improperly based beliefs that have propositionally warranted contents are not cases of knowledge. So once we see the failure of Aristotelianism and the attractiveness of propositionalism, two quite different roles should be distinguished for the concept of proper function to play in the third condition. One might claim that the concept of proper function is central to an adequate understanding of warrant itself, or one might claim that it is central to the concept of proper basing. The first suggestion is just a version of Aristotelianism, a view sufficiently undermined by previous argument. The other option, that the concept of proper function is important in understanding the concept of properly basing a belief on that which warrants its content, is not affected by those arguments and has much to recommend it. On this latter alternative, for a belief to be properly based, it would need to result from properly functioning cognitive equipment.

If we find Plantinga's appeal to proper function persuasive and we pursue this line of thought, we might think of a proper function condition as a solution to the problem of deviant causal chains that plague causal theories of the basing relation. According to such theories, to base your belief on your evidence is for your awareness of the evidence to be causally responsible for your belief. The problem of deviant causal chains arises when one notices that awareness of evidence can cause belief in a variety of ways. For example, Watson may fall down the stairs as a result of the excitement upon being told the evidence for the claim that the butler committed the murder. The fall might induce an unshakable conviction that the butler did it, thereby yielding the result that awareness of the evidence was a cause of the belief in question. Sherlock's belief, however, is caused in a more straightforward way—namely, by Sherlock's coming to see that the evidence implies that the butler did it. Watson's belief, though caused by the evidence just as much as Sherlock's belief, is not caused in the right way. So the causal theory needs to be able to say what particular kinds of causal chains yield doxastically warranted beliefs, for not just any causal path from evidence to believe does that.

Perhaps Plantinga's proper function requirement can be of service to the causal theory by explaining what it means to say that Watson's belief is not caused in the right way whereas Sherlock's belief is. Sherlock's belief results from cognitive equipment functioning in the way it was designed to function, whereas Watson's does not, and, we might claim, it is this difference that explains why Sherlock's belief is properly based and Watson's is not.

I am not endorsing this proposal, but only pointing it out as a proposal worthy of further investigation. If the proposal is successful, it would explain some of the attractiveness of Plantinga's proposal to understand warrant in terms of proper function. For on the above proposal, there is a place for Plantinga's claims within a complete account of the third condition for knowledge. The result would be that proper function has an indirect connection with the fundamental concept of warrant, in that it would be a necessary condition for propositional warrant to transfer to belief.

It is easy to lose sight of the significance of the failures of Aristotelianism for Plantingian epistemology. For, it might seem, Plantinga *could* reply as follows:

> I am interested in that property, whether complex or simple, that fills the gap between true belief and knowledge. No doubt there are other epistemologically interesting properties that do not fill this gap and for which a proper function theory will not be adequate. But, if we understand 'warrant' to be that property that is sufficient for knowledge in the presence of true belief, no counterexamples have yet been given to a proper function account of that notion.[17]

This reply is correct as far as it goes; I have presented no counterexamples to Plantinga's theory. What I have done, instead, is to ask for a more thorough dig of an epistemological site. Such thoroughness would yield an awareness of the different kinds of things to which the terms of epistemic appraisal apply, and any theory proposed would need to explain and encompass this diversity. My complaint against Aristotelianism is that it lacks the resources to explain how terms of epistemic appraisal apply to propositions. As an instance of Aristotelianism, proper functionalism shares this weakness. Thus, I do not complain here that proper functionalism is subject to counterexample; I complain instead that it is not a deep enough theory. A theory could be deeper and yet retain an important place for the concept of proper function (as well as the other concepts Plantinga takes to be central to knowledge), but it could not be deeper without abandoning its Aristotelianism. Proper function may be central to knowledge by being central to the concept of psychological warrant, but a complete epistemology will have to posit the existence of a more fundamental concept of warrant, propositional warrant, that cannot be explained in terms of proper function or any other weapon in the arsenal of Aristotelianism. What exactly propositional warrant is I will have to postpone discussing (read: I wish I had a good theory of the concept). Such discussion will need to address whether propositional warrant is completely holistic or is a bit more molecular. If the latter, we will want to know whether it is a two-place relation, perhaps between propositions (or other informational chunks) but also perhaps between a proposition and an experience, or a three-place relation between propositions and an assumed background theory (or perhaps between a proposition, an experience, and a background theory). If the former, we will need something close to a molecular theory in order to understand the connection between propositional warrant and the theory of inference, though the molecular theory in question will no longer be formulated as one concerning propositional warrant itself, but rather as some special component of it.[18] In short, I do not have a good theory of propositional warrant, and the tasks involved are enormous. Nonetheless, the main point here is not what propositional warrant is, but that it is fundamental to any epistemology with any hope of providing a complete understanding of how we employ terms of epistemic appraisal. To put the point in a way especially relevant to Plantinga's project, a complete epistemology will simply have to deny that proper function is central to the fundamental concept of warrant, that concept in terms of which we can explain what fills the gap between true belief and knowledge.[19]

Notes

1. Alvin Plantinga, *Warrant: The Current Debate* and *Warrant and Proper Function* (Oxford, 1993).

2. Plantinga is not alone among contemporary epistemologists in favoring an Aristotelian approach to epistemology. Others include D. M. Armstrong, *Belief, Truth and Knowledge* (London, 1973); Alvin Goldman, *Epistemology and Cognition* (Cambridge, 1985); Robert Nozick, *Philosophical Explanations*, (Cambridge, 1981); Ernest Sosa, *Knowledge in Perspective: Selected Essays in Epistemology* (London, 1991). For a discussion of the Aristotelian approach of these and other authors, see Jonathan L. Kvanvig, *The Intellectual Virtues and the Life of the Mind: On the Place of the Virtues in Contemporary Epistemology* (Savage, Md., 1992).

3. I borrow this terminology from Roderick Firth. See his "Are Epistemic Concepts Reducible to Ethical Concepts?" in Alvin I. Goldman and Jaegwon

Kim, eds., *Values and Morals, Essays in Honor of William Frankena, Charles Stevenson, and Richard Brandt* (Dordrecht, 1978).

4. Plantinga, *Warrant and Proper Function*, p. 194.

5. Alvin Goldman, "What Is Justified Belief?" in George Pappas, ed., *Knowledge and Justification*, (Dordrecht, 1979), pp. 1–25.

6. Plantinga, *Warrant: The Current Debate*, p. 3.

7. Plantinga, *Warrant and Proper Function*, p. v.

8. I owe my grasping of this point to Trenton Merricks.

9. Plantinga, *Warrant: The Current Debate*, p. 4.

10. One cannot always define Y in terms of X when X is defined in terms of Y. One can define mathematical equality in terms of the relations of being strictly lesser than and greater than, but one cannot define either of these latter two in terms of equality. In general, if we define X in terms of Y plus other concepts, we have no guarantee that we can define Y in terms of X.

11. Goldman, "What Is Justified Belief?" p. 21.

12. Richard Foley, "Evidence and Reasons for Belief," *Analysis* 51.2 (March 1991), p. 99. Earl Conee discusses a similar case in "Evident But Rationally Unacceptable," *Australasian Journal of Philosophy* 65 (1987), pp. 316–26.

13. Definition DW is not quite what is needed. I have argued in "Coherentism: Misconstrual and Missaprehension," *Southwest Philosophy Review* 11 (1995), pp. 159–169, and in "Coherentists' Distractions," *Philosophical Topics*, forthcoming 1996, that one can offer an account of the basing relation which makes it out to be, not a relation between a belief and that which warrants it, but rather between a belief and that which is epistemically relevant to it (where x can be epistemically relevant to y without propositionally warranting it, or increasing its warrant status at all). It is relatively easy to see that this notion of epistemic relevance will itself be a concept of epistemic appraisal that applies fundamentally to propositions and not to beliefs, and since the issues raised by this complication would be far removed from the general issues of this paper, I will stick with the simpler, even though slightly misleading, formulation in the text.

14. Plantinga, *Warrant: The Current Debate*, p. 111.

15. As claims Laurence BonJour in *The Structure of Empirical Knowledge* (Cambridge, 1985), p. 150.

16. Richard Feldman further develops this complaint in "Proper Functionalism," *Nous* 72.1 (March 1993), pp. 34–50.

17. This reply put in the mouth of Plantinga stipulates an understanding of 'warrant' in an attempt to avoid certain problems. There is a tension in Plantinga's work between such a stipulative understanding and his first volume which treats the work of epistemologists such as Chisholm, BonJour, Lehrer, Goldman and other recent luminaries in epistemology as offering theories of warrant. It is clear, however, that none of the theories of justification these epistemologists offer is meant as a theory of warrant in the stipulated sense.

So relying on such a stipulation to carve off the epistemological terrain to be investigated runs the risk of making a straw-man argument out of Plantinga's first volume.

18. For an idea of what such a molecular theory might look like in the context of a holistic theory of warrant, see my defense of coherentism in "Coherentists' Distractions," *Philosophical Topics*, forthcoming 1996.

19. I wish to express my thanks to those who have commented on drafts of this paper: Colin Allen, Richard Feldman, Michael Hand, Peter Markie, Hugh McCann, Paul McNamara, and Scott Sturgeon.

Part VI

Alvin Plantinga Replies

16

Respondeo

Alvin Plantinga

My thanks to Jon Kvanvig and the other authors for these penetrating and illuminating essays; I have learned much from them. Replying to them is a privilege—a *scary* privilege. It is also a bit chastening. According to the Heidelberg Catechism, to live and die properly one must know the extent of one's sins and miseries: I find these essays very useful along those lines. I only wish I had read them *before* I wrote the Warrant volumes. But mostly I am delighted with new vistas and new ideas. Reading these essays has convinced me once again of the real importance of epistemology, and of its enormous *interest*. Those who proclaim the death of epistemology ought to read these essays—if this is what death is like, then Socrates was right: we (or epistemology) should be eager to die. It has also convinced me (once more) of the extreme difficulty of epistemology; with further insight, not only the answers but the very shape of the questions keep changing.

From a respondent's point of view the essays present an embarrassment of riches: it's hard to know where to start, which topics to address, how far to go with any topic. By way of compromise, my reply will have two parts. In the first I'll take the topic on which these essays have taught me the most, and try to say something of what I have learned. In the second I'll make specific replies to individual authors. I am not first of all interested in doggedly replying to every objection, even where I think I have a satisfactory reply; and (given the cornucopia of objections, ideas, suggestions) I won't be able to comment on nearly everything of importance. I've replied elsewhere to some of the objections raised here; where it still seems to me that my answer is apt, I'll simply refer the reader to that answer. I have also been obliged to shape my reply in such a way as to emphasize what I have to say that may be of interest: in many cases I unduly neglect contributions simply because I can't say much more than I already have. There is of course no proportion between the length of my reply to an essay and my judgment of its merit.

I: Rethinking Gettier

One of the really seminal developments in twentieth-century epistemology (its second half, anyway) was Edmund Gettier's three-page paper[1] presenting a couple of counterexamples to the Justified True Belief theory of knowledge. Of course the JTB account was so-called only *after* Gettier, and in fact it isn't really clear that it *was* the received view prior to Gettier.[2] But if the JTB theory had not existed, it would have been necessary to invent it, if only to provide occasion for Gettier and responses to him. I'm grateful to Peter Klein and Marshall Swain for calling to my attention a response to Gettier that I unconscionably neglected in the Warrant volumes: defeasibility theories. And I am grateful to Klein and Richard Feldman for making it crystal clear to me that my own treatment of what I called "quasi-Gettier" problems is defective. Others have expressed skepticism about my treatment, but (like the farmer who had to hit the bull over the head with a two by four to get his attention) Klein finally managed to get me to pay proper attention. I'll say something about defeasibility theories below (concluding that Klein's version, sophisticated and refined as it is, isn't successful as an account of warrant); but I'll begin by looking into Klein's complaints about my account of quasi-Gettier problems.

But first, what *are* Gettier problems? Suppose we quickly review the usual list.[3] First, there is Gettier's original Smith-has-a-Ford-or-Brown-is-in-Barcelona example; here you come to hold a true, justified but unwarranted belief (one that doesn't constitute knowledge) by inferring it from a false but justified belief. Second, there is the kind of example represented by Carl Ginet's[4] proud but impecunious Wisconsinites who erect all those barn facades to make themselves look more prosperous than they are; traveling through the area I see what is in fact a barn, forming the justified, true, but unwarranted belief *Now that's a fine barn*. Here there is deception on the part of those

Wisconsinites. Third, there is Bertrand Russell's pre-Gettier Gettier example of the clock that stops at midnight: you see it at noon and form the belief that it is noon; your belief is justified and true, but doesn't constitute knowledge. In this case there is neither deception nor inference from a false belief. In none of these three kinds is there failure of proper function on the part of the believer; but fourth, there are also examples where a cognitive glitch is involved. In Alexius Meinong's example as reported by Roderick Chisholm, an aging forest ranger suffers hearing loss and can no longer hear his wind chimes; he also develops tinnitus, sometimes hearing chime-like sounds due to no external stimulus; this sometimes occurs just when the wind chimes are in fact sounding, thus producing in him the justified, true, but unwarranted belief that the wind is up. Still another kind of example, one involving no malfunction, deception, or inference from a false belief: you are a desert tyro and seem to see an oasis about three-quarters of a mile away, forming the belief that there is an oasis near by. As it happens, you are the victim of a mirage, but in fact there is an oasis near by; your belief is justified and true, but does not constitute knowledge.

One feature these examples have in common, of course, is that they are cases of justified true belief that do not constitute cases of knowledge; hence they refute JTB theories of knowledge. More broadly, Gettier cases also show (and it is clear from some of the essays in this volume that internalists would not disagree) that no strictly internalist account of warrant can be successful. But I think their significance extends further. It is not uncommon to dismiss concern with Gettier problems as so much scholastic niggling; and perhaps the long line of circumventions and countercircumventions, the complicated "fourth conditions" together with their more complicated refutations and the counterrefutations, the cycles and epicycles—perhaps these do give that impression. But I believe we can still learn something interesting about the structure of knowledge by thinking about Gettier problems. In particular, we can learn something by thinking further about another and oft-noted feature of these Gettier situations: in these Gettier cases, *S*'s justified true belief does not constitute knowledge because, given the circumstances, it is only accidentally, or by serendipity, or by just dumb luck that *S* forms a true belief in the situation.

Mea Culpa

Now my own response to Gettier is off the mark, as Klein and Feldman point out. The chief problem is that (given my understanding of the environmental condition) what I said handles only *some* Gettier problems, leaving others untouched. Let me begin by recalling what I said.

By way of general comment, I noted that Gettier examples involve something like mild cognitive environmental pollution; in each of these cases the cognitive environment, I said, diverges in some small or subtle way from the paradigm or standard sort of environment for which our faculties are designed.[5] Clocks seldom stop precisely twelve hours before you look at them, people don't ordinarily take the trouble to erect phony barns, it's most unusual to develop just this kind of tinnitus after a lifetime of monitoring wind speed by listening to wind chimes, and so on. This still seems to me correct. Gettier examples involve relatively minor failures of fit between cognitive capacities and cognitive environment; as a consequence it is only by happy cognitive accident that a true belief is formed in the circumstance in question. Of course if just *any* example that shows justification and truth insufficient for knowledge is a Gettier example, then there will be Gettier examples that involve not just a bit of retail lack of fit between cognitive capacities and environment, but wholesale lack of fit. A madman, for example, or the victim of a Cartesian evil genius, or someone who has been envatted by Alpha Centaurian cognitive scientists might well be completely justified (in any of the ordinary ways of understanding justification), and nevertheless display not minor but monumental failure of fit between cognitive capacities and cognitive environment. These examples are indeed counterexamples to a JTB theory, but they seem out of the spirit of Gettier examples—perhaps because (as it is plausible to think) JTB theories implicitly presuppose something like a proper function condition.[6]

Well, this seems right, but how is it supposed to handle Gettier problems? I went on to call attention to misleading cognitive responses of a certain sort: Müller-Lyer examples, straight sticks that look bent in water, mirages, dry North Dakota roads that look wet on a hot summer's day, airplanes high in the sky that look small, and so on. In these cases there is no cognitive malfunction (no failure to conform to the design plan); still the cognitive responses are misleading. (I can remember the astonishment with which I learned, as a child, that airplanes are actually large enough to contain people.) What is the explanation of these responses? Why are they in our cognitive repertoire? If the perceptual system is designed to produce true beliefs, why are these misleading responses part of it? The answer, I said, lay in the area of tradeoffs and compromises. We can imagine that the designer (God or evolution) aims to have a creature of our general style: made of flesh and blood and bone rather than plastic and steel, of roughly our size, in a world with our regularities, with a cognitive system mediated by brain and nervous system. Now of course the designer also aims at producing a cognitive system that furnishes us with true beliefs, and the more accurate the better. But perhaps a maximally excellent cognitive system of this sort would require too large a brain, so large we would have to hold up our heads with both hands, thus being unable to play the piano or go rock climbing (or fight off predators). So tradeoffs and compromises are necessary: trade a bit of cognitive excellence for reasonable brain size and mobility, for example.

Müller-Lyer *et al.*, therefore, are present, not because they serve the general function of providing true beliefs (they don't), but because they are a locus of a best or satisfactory compromise between these competing desiderata. Of course in a way they *do* serve that general function, by way of being part of a best compromise. But this, I said, is to serve it *indirectly* rather than *directly*: "the thing to say is that *R* [the cognitive response member of the relevant triple of the design plan] is joined with *M* [the circumstance member] not in order to *directly* serve the main purpose of providing true beliefs (it doesn't do that) but to do so *indirectly* . . ." (WPF p. 40). But then consider any of these misleading responses (*there is an oasis near by* or *it must have rained on the road recently*): a belief produced in this way can happen, by virtue of cognitive good luck, to be true. If so, the belief is *accidentally* true, and we have a Gettier example. By way of stating a general clause or condition to deal with Gettier problems, I put it like this:

> Take a perceptual illusion or false testimony case and add that the belief produced is true (but by accident): then what you have is a quasi-Gettier case. The belief in question has little warrant and, though true, does not constitute knowledge; *for a belief has warrant for you only when it is produced by a segment of the design plan directly aimed at truth.* (WPF p. 40, italics added)

Now Klein has more than one objection. He suggests that my view is committed to the possibility that a false belief *f* should have warrant sufficient for knowledge; if so (as in Gettier's original example) *S* could disjoin a true belief with *f*, thus deducing from *f* a true belief. This belief should have as much warrant as f, so that (according to my view) the belief should constitute knowledge: but of course in fact it wouldn't.[7] This objection isn't conclusive. There is more than one reason, but chief among them is just the fact that my account isn't committed to the possibility that a false belief should have warrant sufficient for knowledge. (I'll argue below, p. 329, that a false belief *can't* have that degree of warrant.)

He has another objection, however, that reveals a defect in the above clause.[8] Here is his example. I own a Chevrolet van, drive to school one afternoon, park the van, and go to my office. As it turns out, my van is demolished by a runaway gravel truck or (Shope's example) a wayward meteorite. By an astonishing stroke of good fortune, however, I had entered and just won the win-a-van (a Chevrolet) contest sponsored by the local Varsity Club, although I haven't yet heard the good news. You ask me what sort of automobile I own, and I reply cheerfully (and truthfully), "a Chevy van."

This is a classic Gettier case: my belief is true and justified but doesn't constitute knowledge (it is true 'just by accident'; had I not won the win-a-van contest it would have been false). But it also eludes my proposed condition for fending off quasi-Gettier cases. For consider a situation just like the one in the example up to the time where my van is destroyed—perhaps the gravel truck takes an alternate route or the meteorite is deflected by a collision with another and disintegrates before it hits the ground. Had this happened, my van would have suffered no damage, my belief that I own a Chevrolet van would have been formed in just the way it is in the example, and the belief *would* have constituted knowledge. The belief is produced in just the same way (by the same processes governed by the same parts of the design plan) in the two situations; but then the fact that the belief constitutes knowledge in the one situation but not the other cannot be attributed to the belief-producing processes being aimed "directly" at the production of true belief in the one case but "indirectly" in the other. The same bit of the cognitive system, governed by the same bit of the design plan produces the same belief in the two situations; if the process in question is governed by a bit of the design plan aimed directly at the truth in the one case, the same goes in the other. Hence the proposed clause designed to cover Gettier cases doesn't distinguish the two cases.

We can see the same thing even more simply. Consider the Russell-Gettier example: you form the true belief that it is now noon by looking at a clock that happened to stop last night at midnight. The processes that produce this belief in you are the very ones that would have produced the same belief had the clock not stopped at midnight but continued to keep proper time. If in the one case the processes involved are only indirectly aimed at producing true belief, the same is true in the other case. But in the first case you lack knowledge and in the second you have it. So the proposed clause doesn't do the job.

The Resolution Problem

Consider the Russell-Gettier case, the van case, and the other cases my clause doesn't properly deal with, and consider the cognitive processes that produce the relevant beliefs in those cases: these processes don't do well in those cases. The process of telling time by glancing at the clock won't ordinarily lead to false belief: but in situations where the clock has stopped, it ordinarily *will* lead to false beliefs. (In *those* situations, if the belief produced is true, it will be only by accident, by pure dumb luck.) If your van has been destroyed by a meteorite but you haven't yet heard the bad news, you will ordinarily hold a false belief; your belief will be true only if something very unusual happens—you win the win-a-van lottery, or your grandmother unexpectedly dies and leaves you her Chevy van.

In WPF I spoke of our *cognitive environment*, and I added that a belief has warrant only if it is formed in an *appropriate* cognitive environment. For the most part I was thinking of our cognitive environment as the one we enjoy right here on earth,[9] the one for which we were designed by God or evolution. This environment would include such features as the presence and properties of light and air, the presence of visible objects, of other objects detectable by our kind of cognitive system, of some objects not so detectable, of the regularities of nature, the existence of other people, and so on. Call this our "maxi-environment"; in stating the environmental condition, what I (mostly) had in mind was a maxi-environment. Our cognitive faculties are designed to function in *this* maxi-environment, the one in which we find ourselves, or one like it. They are not designed for a maxi-environment in which, e.g., the only food available contains a substance that seriously inhibits memory, or where there is constant darkness, or where there aren't any distinguishable objects, or where there is little or no regularity, at least of a kind we can detect, or where everything is in a state of constant random flux.

But there is also a much less global cognitive environment. For any belief B and (more relevantly) the exercise E of my cognitive powers issuing in *B*, there is also a much more specific and detailed state of affairs we might call its "cognitive mini-environment."[10] For example, there is the cognitive mini-environment of the van case, the Gettier-Russell mini-environment in which I happen to look at a clock that has stopped, and the fake barn environment. On the other hand, there are also the cognitive mini-environments in which the clock I glance at is keeping proper time, the ones in which my van remains unmolested in the place I parked it, and the ones where there are only real barns. We can think of a cognitive mini-environment of a given exercise of cognitive powers *E* as a *state of affairs* (or proposition)—one that includes all the relevant epistemic circumstances obtaining when that belief is formed. Consider any current belief *B* I hold and the exercise *E* of cognitive powers producing it: the mini-environment *M* for *E* (call it "MBE") includes the state of affairs specified by my cognitive maxi-environment, but also much more specific features of my epistemic situation. It will include, for example, the presence or absence of fake barns, of my van's being destroyed in unforeseen ways (if it is), of Paul's brother Peter being in the neighborhood, and any other relevant epistemic circumstance. To be on the safe side, let *MBE* be as full as you please, as large a fragment of the actual world as you like. (No doubt elegance would counsel cutting *MBE* back to epistemically relevant features; that, however, would set us the laborious task of giving an account of relevance, thus perversely sacrificing ease to elegance.)

In any event, we must note that a given exercise of (properly functioning) cognitive faculties can be counted on to produce a true belief in *some* mini-environments but not in others. In the ones where my van remains unharmed where I parked it, the processes that ordinarily produce in me the belief that I now own a van will produce a true belief; not so if the van is destroyed in some quirky fashion I could not have anticipated. You form an opinion as to what time it is by glancing at a clock; this exercise of cognitive powers can be counted on to produce true belief in the usual mini-environments (in which the clock is keeping reasonable time); not so for ones in which it has stopped. I form a belief as to the identity of the person standing in Paul's doorway by taking a quick look from across the street; this exercise of cognitive faculties can be counted on to produce a true belief in a mini-environment where Paul is the only person in the neighborhood that looks at all like Paul; not so for one in which Paul's look-alike twin brother Peter is (unbeknownst to me) staying in Paul's house.

Note the relativity to the specific belief-producing exercise of cognitive powers. I take a quick look from across the road: then I am as likely as not to form a false belief about the identity of that person of Pauline appearance standing in the doorway. But if I go right up to him and look closely I could tell that it wasn't Paul. I form a false belief (that my van remained undamaged right where I parked it) in the van example, but I wouldn't have, had I called on other cognitive processes; if I had hired a detective to watch my van, I would have received the bad news. I glance at a stopped clock and form a false belief as to the time; not so if I watch it for a period of ten minutes and see that the minute hand doesn't move. We are therefore thinking here of a specific exercise of properly functioning cognitive faculties: such an exercise can be counted on to produce a true belief with respect to some cognitive mini-environments but not with respect to others.

A possible hitch: *MBE*, of course, is a state of affairs including the circumstances in which a belief *B* is formed by *E*. But does the fact, if it is a fact, that *E produces a true belief* get included in *MBE*? Does the mini-environment of the van case include the proposition that (owing to my luck with the lottery) I *do* in fact own a van and also believe that I do, so that *MBE* includes my forming a true belief with respect to whether I own a van? If so, then of course with respect to *that* situation the exercise of cognitive powers in question can be counted on to produce a true belief. But we want to *ask* whether a certain exercise of cognitive powers is or isn't to be counted on to provide true belief in its cognitive mini-environment; *MBE* must therefore be specified in such a way that it doesn't include *E*'s producing a true belief and also doesn't include *E*'s producing a false belief. The proposition that *S* forms a true belief will be neither true nor false[11] in *MBE*. But of course an actual situation in which someone forms a belief will be maximally specific, and *will* include that *S* forms a true belief, if in fact *S* does so. So let's say that *MBE is* maximally specific except for the truth or falsehood of the proposition that *S* forms a true belief by way of *E*. A cognitive mini-environment will be a state of affairs *diminished with respect to* that proposition—a state of affairs as much as possible like the actual maximally specific situation, given that *MBE* includes neither the proposition that *S* forms a true belief nor its denial.

An exercise of my cognitive powers, therefore, even when those powers are functioning properly (perfectly in accord with my design plan) in the maxi-environment for which they are designed, can be counted on to produce a true belief with respect to *some* cognitive mini-environments but not with respect to others. Some mini-environments are *favorable* for a given exercise of cognitive powers; others are *misleading*, even when my faculties are functioning properly. These mini-environments, we might say, are such that my faculties are not designed to produce a true belief in or with respect to them— even though they include the maxi-environment for which my faculties have indeed been designed (by God or evolution). The cognitive processes involved in the van case and Russell-Gettier examples are unreliable in the van and Russell-Gettier mini-environments; in *those* circumstances the processes in question, even when functioning properly, are more likely to lead to false beliefs than to true.[12] These mini-environments are misleading with respect to those cognitive exercises; we might also say that in these misleading mini-environments our faculties (more exactly, specific exercises of them) display a certain deplorable *lack of resolution*. Even when my cognitive powers are subject to no dysfunction, I am unable (by a quick glance) to distinguish Peter from Paul, or the case where the clock is keeping good time and shows 12:00 noon from the case where it stopped at midnight. In phony barn country my cognitive faculties don't (by way of a casual look from the road) provide the resolution needed to enable me to distinguish the genuine article from the *papier mâché* mockups. And when the cognitive mini-environment is misleading, when it is one within which the relevant exercise of cognitive powers suffers from this lack of resolution, then if I form a *true* belief, it will be just by accident, just by way of dumb luck. It will not be because the situation is one for which my faculties (or this kind of exercise of them) are designed to produce true belief.

This is the resolution problem. It isn't, of course, a problem for a *knower*; it's a problem for an epistemologist. It's a problem for my account, at least if we neglect cognitive mini-environments in stating the environmental condition. It isn't enough for warrant that the *maxi*-environment be one for which the faculties in question are designed to produce true belief; that is the lesson of the Notre Dame van case and others like it—indeed, of Gettier cases more generally.

The resolution problem is a problem for other accounts as well. Consider justificationism: since the usual Gettier cases fall within the area of insufficient resolution, a satisfactory statement of the elusive "fourth condition" will have to include a solution to the resolution problem. It also afflicts reliabilisms. William Alston thinks of knowledge (minus a bell or whistle or two) as true belief produced by a reliable belief-producing process or mechanism—i.e., a process that (in our maxi-environment) ordinarily produces true beliefs. But clearly a true belief can meet this condition and fail to have warrant, and that in two quite different ways. First, it can fail to do so by way of failure of proper function. My vision is reliable; I've passed all the tests with flying colors. But if I get drunk and see snakes in my bedroom, my belief has little or no warrant; and even if there happens to be a snake or two lurking in the corner, I certainly don't know that there is. But second, it isn't implausible to suppose that Alston was implicitly presupposing a proper function condition. If so, his view is affected by the resolution problem: the clock stopped at midnight, the van case, Paul's look-alike twin Peter—they and their ilk all lurk in the wings. In these cases the belief in question is produced by reliable processes functioning properly, all right, but in a situation where those processes display insufficient resolution. Things are less clear with coherentism (partly because coherentism itself is less clear), but given any plausible conception of coherence, it certainly seems that a belief could be appropriately coherent with its significant others even when its production falls into the area of irresolution. But then there will be situations where a belief is true and meets the coherence condition, but is nonetheless unwarranted.

Defeasibility to the Rescue?

In WCD I said that internalists take it that some quality—justification of one sort or another, perhaps—gives us the basic structure and form of warrant, with a fillip of some sort needed to evade Gettier. Several contributors—BonJour, Feldman, Swain—quite properly took me to task for this unduly flip way of stating the matter; there is no call for speaking thus disrespectfully of that fourth condition, calling it a mere fillip. Let me put it instead like this: justificationists think of justification as giving the basic structure of warrant; it takes up most but not all of the conceptual space between true belief and knowledge, so that a fourth condition is needed to occupy the rest of the space. But of course an internalist might reply that the fourth condition is every bit as important as the third, and takes up just as much conceptual space. Well, given the lack of a metric for conceptual space, there's not a lot of sense arguing about how much of it is taken up by what here; let's suppose that the internalists are the experts on what it is they think. In any event this fourth condition, whatever exactly the internalist proposes to propose, will have to solve the resolution problem.

Enter defeasibility. A defeasibility clause is not of itself an entire theory of warrant, of course; it requires a base clause. Defeasibility clauses are essentially ways of grappling with the resolution problem, but they don't themselves provide a base or operative step. Thus they have often (early Klein, Swain, Pollock, others) been grafted onto a *justificationist* account of one sort or another: a true belief constitutes knowledge if it is justified and undefeated. But (as Swain in effect points out) a defeasibility account can in principle be added to any of several *different* base accounts of warrant. Swain says he accepts a defeasibility account in which it is justification[13] that is the base property; but it could also be employed where the base step is *being reliably produced* or *being produced by properly functioning cognitive faculties . . .* , or *being (appropriately) coherent*. In accounts of this sort a defeasibility clause rides on the back of some specification of the base clause for warrant.

A really good first question, clearly enough, is whether some defeasibility account—some defeasibility clause grafted onto a base clause—actually succeeds in resolving the resolution problem. There are several such proposals, but Peter Klein's is as good as any: I shall take a careful look at it. Now Klein cunningly sneaks up on what he takes to be the right account; I'll refer you to the text to see just how he does it, but the final product is something like

(K) S knows p if and only if

   (1) p is properly grounded: either justified or reliably produced,

and

   (2) there is no defeater d such that either (a) if p is justified for S, adding d to S's beliefs is such that p is not justified, or (b) if p is not justified for S and the belief state containing p is reliably produced, then adding d to S's beliefs moves p's justificatory status too far from p's being justified.

First, what does Klein mean by 'justification'? As he is thinking of it (I take it), a belief is justified for me only if I have *evidence* for it; and I think by 'evidence' he means *propositional* evidence, evidence from other propositions I believe. So a belief p is justified for me only if I accept it on the evidential basis of other propositions, and only if those others do in fact evidentially support it. A belief that I accept in the basic way—for example, the belief that I am being appeared to redly, or that $2 + 1 = 3$, or that I had an orange for breakfast—is not justified.

Second, note that clause (1) means that the base or operative step in

Klein's account of warrant is a sort of hybrid (which is of course nothing against it): a belief meets that base condition just if it is either justified or reliably produced. This is the "general" theory; as it stands, Klein thinks, it won't quite do the job because the second clause is too strong. It is too strong, because there are certain kinds of defeaters that shouldn't count. For example, you see Tom in Tom's doorway, forming the belief that it is Tom you see; unbeknownst to you, Tom's grandmother is telling a neighbor that Tom has a look-alike brother, Don, indistinguishable from Tom from more than 10 feet away. This is a defeater for your belief that you see Tom. As it happens, however, Tom's grandmother is senile, and in fact Tom has no siblings at all. The defeater, therefore, is a *misleading* defeater, and doesn't relieve your belief of warrant. By way of repair, he proposes that the defeaters whose absence (2) requires be *genuine* ("a defeater is genuine just in case it defeats without depending on a false proposition," p. 117). This rough and ready characterization of genuineness gives way to a more official characterization (p. 117):

> . . . a proposition, d, is an *initiating defeater of S's belief that p* and d* is an *effective defeater of S's belief that p* iff d is the first proposition in an inference chain C, such that the last member of C, call it d*, is such that when d* is added to S's beliefs, p is not justified. . . . So, we can say that an initiating defeater, d, is *genuine* just in case it is true and there is some inference chain, C, to an effective defeater, d*, and there are no false propositions in C.

He then adds that a belief *p* is warranted for *S* just if *p* is properly grounded for *S* and there is no genuine defeater of it.

Will (K) do the trick? We might think, first, that this account suffers from undue vagueness: "*too far* from being justified"? Well, this vagueness does make it harder to assess the theory (to come up with counterexamples, e.g.), but I doubt the complaint is justified. Any satisfactory account will have to be vague. Suppose phony barn country starts a quarter-mile away from where you're looking at barns? Do you know then? Or a half-mile, or a mile, or 30 miles? Suppose those fake barns were there yesterday (or ten minutes ago) but have since been destroyed, or suppose they will be there within ten minutes? Suppose there's only one (or two, or *n*) phony barn(s) in the county, or within a mile, or a half-mile, or within eyeshot of where you are? Suppose they decided at the town meeting not to erect any fake barns, but it was a really close decision, and some people planned to erect some anyway? There is certainly a substantial and ineliminable area of vagueness here, and it's not clear that (K) displays more of it than the notion of warrant itself.

1. False Beliefs in My Noetic Structure

So the vagueness isn't a problem; in fact it's a virtue. Nevertheless this account does suffer from grave difficulties. First, it seems to have the implication that if I hold a false belief, then any belief I have that is properly grounded but not justified is (or easily can be) defeated. Before I give the argument, however, we must be clear about just how an effective defeater works. According to Klein, a defeater d^*, for p, "is such that when d* is added to S's beliefs, p is not justified." Here I gather that Klein is thinking as follows: consider the set A of S's beliefs, and add the defeater d^*, thus moving to a new set A^*; then check to see whether p is justified with respect to A^*. I gather he's also thinking that when we add d^* to A, we delete p; otherwise, obviously, p will automatically be justified with respect to A^*, being a member of A^*. And of course we must delete not only p, but also any conjunctions of which p is a conjunct and more generally, any proposition that entails p. Still further, for any pair of propositions that together entail p, we must delete one or the other; the same for triples, quadruples, etc. From a rough and ready point of view, however, perhaps we could put it like this: to reach A^*, move first from A to A *diminished with respect to p* (a set of propositions maximally similar to A that does not entail p); then add d^*. This is *very* rough and ready (for one thing it won't really work when p is noncontingent— it's not really *entailment* we want, but a more epistemic notion of some kind), but stating this condition exactly is a project for some other occasion.

Now for the argument that if I hold a false belief, then any belief I have that is properly grounded but not justified is (or easily can be) defeated. Suppose I (mistakenly) believe

(A) Glasgow is larger than Chicago,

and suppose I also hold the properly grounded (by way of memory, say) belief

(B) I had an orange for breakfast.

From (A) I deduce (and add to my beliefs)

(C) If $-A$, then $-B$ (material implication).

Then $-A$, the denial of (A), is both a genuine initiating and an effective defeater for (B), the inference chain in question being just $-A$ itself (or the unit set of $-A$). The only member of this chain is true; $-A$ is an *effective* defeater because the result of adding it to my beliefs (diminished with respect to (B)) entails the denial of (B); hence (B) is "too far" from being justified with respect to that set of beliefs. So, on this account, if I believe any false proposition A, I won't know any proposition B that isn't justified for me; I won't know any propositions in the basic way. And the fact is we don't really need that basicality condition—won't the argument work just as well for a proposition B that is *justified* for me?[14]

The same problem, so it seems to me, afflicts the more elaborate account of defeater-genuineness in Klein's carefully crafted book *Certainty: A Refutation of Scepticism*.[15] The idea is that a genuine defeater is an initiating defeater that isn't misleading; and a *misleading* initiating defeater (again) is one such that the inference chain to the effective defeater depends upon some false proposition. The problem is to explain this lack of dependence. Klein puts it like this:

> Let us suppose, then, that an initiating defeater, d_1, is *misleading* if and only if there is some false proposition, f, in *every* D-chain between d_1 and an effective defeater, d_n, and f occurs in a link in the d-chain prior to every link in which a false proposition in E occurs. (*Certainty* p. 148)

I refer the reader to the text for details; but a *D*-chain is an evidential chain going from d_1 to the effective defeater; this chain can contain propositions from E, which is the set of S's beliefs (actually, the subset she can properly take as evidence, but this complication won't be relevant here). And the account stipulates that a defeater is misleading only if there is no *d*-chain in which the first false proposition is a member of E. The idea (see note 16) is that a defeater is really misleading only if its defeating power, so to speak, does not depend upon any falsehoods in S's beliefs, but does depend upon falsehood in the initiating defeater itself. Then we can say that you know p only if there are no genuine initiating defeaters for p for you, i.e., only if all the defeaters of p for you are misleading.

But I'm sorry to say this fails to do the job in the same way as the

condition in Klein's paper. Suppose I am a mathematical neophyte; on
David Hilbert's authority I mistakenly believe the denial of Gödel's
first theorem (GT). Where the arrow expresses material implication,

(H) $(-(GT) \rightarrow ((GT) \rightarrow -(2 + 1 = 3))) \, \& \, (GT)$

is now a genuine defeater for the proposition $2 + 1 = 3$ for me. For a
defeater is genuine if there is at least one D-chain such that the first
false proposition in it is a member of my set of beliefs. Here (H) is the
initiating defeater and $-(2 + 1 = 3)$ the effective defeater; one D-
chain will begin with the two conjuncts of (H), the third item being
$-(GT)$. In this case, of course, there won't be any false proposition
prior to $-(GT)$, which is one of my beliefs. If so, however, then on
Klein's account of knowledge I have a genuine defeater for my belief
that $2 + 1 = 3$ and thus do not know this proposition. Clearly the
example can be generalized: if there is any false proposition I believe,
I won't know anything at all. But that's unduly demanding.

The problem here is the highly articulate and complex nature of our
design plan. False beliefs can indeed *sometimes* prevent a proposition
from achieving the status of knowledge, thus depriving it of a status it
would otherwise have;[16] but it is also possible to have knowledge that
p even if (because of false beliefs I hold) there are true propositions
not themselves rendering plausible any falsehood which, if added to
my evidence, would bring it about that *p* is not justified for me. One
sort of condition where this can happen is if *p* has a great deal of
warrant in the basic way.

2. Insufficient Generic Flexibility

Second, Klein's account suffers from two kinds of unhappy inflexi-
bility. First, an account of knowledge ought not to be tied to the
human design plan: if it is really an account of *knowledge* (as opposed
to *human* knowledge) it ought to apply to all the kinds of knowledge
there are or could be. But obviously there could be creatures (God
could create creatures) with cognitive styles very different from ours.
For example, there could be creatures who had knowledge, but whose
design plan did not involve justification in Klein's sense at all; these
creatures' cognitive architecture doesn't allow for accepting a belief
on the evidential basis of other beliefs. For such creatures, all beliefs
would be held in the basic way; none would be accepted on the
evidential basis of others, and none would be justified. Such creatures

could be either more impressive than we are, from a cognitive point of view (presumably God's knowledge is of this sort), or less impressive. Suppose we think about such a hypothetical creature: call him Sam. Suppose further that Sam's cognitive faculties sometimes display insufficient resolution; it is therefore possible that a belief *p* of Sam's should be true by accident. According to (K), *p* constitutes knowledge only if it satisfies the second clause of (K): there are no genuine defeaters for it. But how can this clause apply to Sam, given that his design plan is such that none of his beliefs is ever justified? Wouldn't they all always be "too far" from being justified?

Perhaps Klein could think of it like this: there is an objective *is-a-good-reason-for* relation (see Klein p. 117). This is a relation that holds among *propositions*; it does not involve reference to a noetic structure or system of cognitive powers; it makes no reference to knowers and their quirks, idiosyncrasies, and limitations.[17] (Perhaps it involves entailment and objective probability.) Then we can still raise the question whether there is a defeater for Sam's belief *p*: the question is whether there is some true proposition in the neighborhood such that the result of adding it to the propositions Sam does in fact believe is "too far" from standing in that objective relation to *p*.

Suppose there is that relationship. It is still possible that God (or evolution) has designed Sam in such a way that it *doesn't matter* whether there are true propositions which, when added to what Sam believes, yield a set of propositions with respect to which Sam's belief *p* is far from being justified. We can see how this could be the case with respect to us. Suppose I am in phony barn country, but the fact is I'm not able to look at any of the phony barns. Maybe I have a guardian angel who prevents me from ever doing so, or maybe those phony barns are made from a certain substance that causes my eyes to water when I look in the direction of one, thus preventing me from seeing it. Then when I look at a barn and judge that it is a barn, I will be right; furthermore, I will know that I see a barn, even though there is a (Kleinian) defeater for this belief. In the same way, perhaps Sam's cognitive system is designed in such a way that he always or nearly always forms true beliefs, despite the fact that these defeaters are present. And if so, then even though there are genuine defeaters lurking in the neighborhood, Sam doesn't believe the truth just by accident; he believes the truth because of the way he's designed. To put it another way, Klein's implicit characterization of accidentality is too parochial; it depends upon universalizing what are in fact specific features of the human cognitive design plan, not features that every cognitive design plan will have to display.

3. Insufficient Specific Flexibility

But even if we confine ourselves to our own design plan, (K) is still too inflexible. (K) confers the title of knowledge upon some beliefs that are accepted in the basic way: for example, those that Descartes and Locke were especially enthusiastic about, such as self-evident propositions and beliefs appropriately about my own mental life (*I'm being appeared to redly*), as well as other beliefs that are reliably produced. But (K) fails to take account of the fact that warrant comes in degrees, and thus fails to accommodate the fact that some basic beliefs get an enormous amount of warrant in the basic way, enough to overwhelm propositional evidence against them. They can constitute knowledge even if, *so far as available propositional evidence goes*, there is a balance of evidence against them. For example, suppose I am appeared to redly, take note of my phenomenal field, and form the belief

(R) I am being appeared to redly.

(R) is not justified for me in Klein's sense, because I don't believe it on the basis of any other propositions at all. We may assume (at least for purposes of argument) that (R) is reliably produced; it therefore meets the first of (K)'s conditions. But it could run afoul of the second and still constitute knowledge. For the fact is

(B) I display a certain brain structure such that 6 out of 10 people who display that structure are never appeared to redly.

If (B) were added to my beliefs (of course deleting (R), any proposition that entails it, etc.), then, with respect to that set of beliefs, it would be more likely than not that I am not being appeared to redly. (R), then, would be a long way from being justified—adding this proposition would move its justificatory status "too far" (I'd guess) "from *p*'s being justified." (B) is therefore a defeater for (R). But of course the fact is I would know (R); in fact I would know it even if I also knew or believed (B).

Clearly there are many different sorts of examples of this general sort. The problem with (K), here, is that it fails to match the complex, highly articulated architecture of our design plan. It can happen that a given belief p gets a great deal of warrant in the basic way: beliefs about my own mental life, to be sure, but also perceptual beliefs, memory beliefs, simple *a priori* beliefs, perhaps religious beliefs or beliefs about God, and the like. It could also happen that there is a genuine (in Klein's sense) defeater d for p; that fact needn't be sufficient for denying that p constitutes knowledge. Indeed, something stronger is true: it could be both that I know p and that I *believe d*. It is possible, that is, that I believe p in the basic way, that p be very far from being justified for me by virtue of the fact that I believe d, and that p nonetheless constitutes knowledge.[18]

4. Problems Inherited from Reliabilism

In his version of defeasibility theory (as opposed, e.g., to Swain's), Klein helps himself to a reliabilist notion: p is properly grounded just if either it is justified or it is *reliably produced*. But beware of reliabilists bringing gifts: in helping himself to this reliabilist theme, Klein inherits reliabilist problems. I don't have the space to go into this properly,[19] but I think we can see briefly that there will be real problems. For how is Klein understanding 'reliably produced'? Suppose he takes it as in Alstonian generic reliabilism:[20] 'produced by a reliable belief-producing process or faculty'—a *concrete* process or faculty (so far no truck with Goldmanian types). Well, suppose my (reliable) perceptual faculties malfunction (due to drink or drugs) and I think I see pink rats, forming the belief that indeed there are pink rats in the room; and suppose as it happens there are some (in the closet, perhaps). Then this belief is properly grounded (the belief is reliably produced). Furthermore, there need be no defeater—no true proposition which, when added to my beliefs, yields a set with respect to which the belief in question is "too far" from being justified.[21] But then, on this account, I would know that there are pink rats in the room—which I don't.

Suppose instead we take 'reliably produced' in terms of Goldmanian types. Out of the frying pan into the fire. For, for any necessary proposition I believe—that there is such a person as God, if there is, that there is not, if there is not—there will be a reliable type of which that belief will be a product, no matter *how* I actually came to the belief (see WPF pp. 205–208). And again, there need be no true proposition which, when added to my beliefs, makes p "too far" from being justified. So on this way of taking 'reliably produced', any

necessary proposition I believe will automatically constitute knowledge for me—even if I can't see that the proposition is necessary,
know of no arguments for it, and come to the belief in a totally
outrageous way. And while I can't take the space to show this here,[22]
beliefs of necessary truths will present the same problem if we take
'reliably produced' in such a way as to satisfy the reliabilist conditions
laid down by the early Dretske,[23] the later Dretske,[24] Robert Nozick,[25]
or Fred Suppe.[26]

5. An Unnecessary Difficulty

I am halfhearted about this final difficulty, because I think it is a
problem Klein unnecessarily creates for himself. As Klein thinks of
justification (personal communication), it isn't necessary, for me to be
justified in believing p on the evidential basis of q, that I see the
connection between q and p, see that the former really does offer
evidential support for the latter. All that is required is that I believe
the former, accept the former on the basis of the latter, and the former
actually support the latter. But this leads to real difficulties. Suppose I
believe, say, Gödel's second theorem, not because I see that it is true,
or have followed a proof, or have been told by someone in the know,
but because of some cognitive glitch: my favorite comic book character
asserts it, and I always believe anything my favorite comic book
character asserts. But suppose also the fact is I believe propositions
from which Gödel's theorem deductively follows, by an argument that
is easy for a normal human being to follow. Furthermore, there is no
true proposition p that can be added to my beliefs, such that Gödel's
theorem isn't justified with respect to the resulting set of propositions.
Then my belief in Gödel's theorem satisfies the conditions for knowledge laid down in (K); but surely it doesn't constitute knowledge. I
say I am halfhearted about this objection, because I can't see why
Klein doesn't simply require that I am justified in believing p on the
basis of q only if I (at least implicitly and dimly) see that p does in fact
support q. He fears an infinite regress here, but I fail to discern it.

The Environmental Condition Revisited

But of course none of this helps me with the resolution problem. All
well enough to complain that *Klein* hasn't really solved it: do I have
anything better to offer?

Our problem is that a true belief B can fail to be knowledge by way of being 'accidentally true'—i.e., it can be just by accident that I form a true belief on this occasion—even though *B* is produced in an appropriate maxi-environment and the other conditions of warrant are met. The problem is that there is a certain retail lack of fit between a particular exercise of cognitive powers and a particular cognitive mini-environment. I can't visually distinguish a real barn from a barn facade—that is, I can't do so from the highway and given a certain angle of vision. (Of course I can tell it's a real barn if I walk around behind it, or if it is a barn we are building.) In the van case, the processes that lead me to and sustain the belief that I own a Chevy van don't enable me to distinguish between the situation where I do in fact own a van, and the sort of situation where my van is destroyed by that meteorite or errant gravel truck. As I pointed out above (p. 314), some mini-environments are favorable for a given exercise of cognitive capacities, and others are unfavorable, misleading, for a given exercise of cognitive capacities.

But then the solution to the resolution problem (and hence also the Gettier problem) is simple enough: the conditions for warrant as I stated them include an environmental condition; and that condition must be understood in such a way that it specifies an appropriate cognitive mini-environment (as well as an appropriate maxi-environment). A belief *B* has warrant only if *MBE* is favorable for the exercise of cognitive powers *E* by which *B* was produced, is the sort of mini-environment for which the powers of which *E* is an exercise are designed (by God or evolution), the sort of mini-environment in which *E* can be counted on to produce a true belief. Together with the other conditions of warrant, this clarification or amplification of the environmental condition will enable us to solve the resolution problem and elude Gettier without resort to the distinction between processes directly aimed at producing true belief and those that are not directly so aimed.[27]

But can we say anything more precise than 'can be counted on'? Perhaps not; perhaps that sort of precision isn't attainable or necessary here. Still, it won't hurt to give it a try. Shall we construe 'can be counted on' probabilistically, for example? There may be possibilities along this line; however, I'd like to explore a slightly different direction, a direction which will also display connections with some other views.

In some of his very early work Fred Dretske suggested that we think about *counterfactuals* in this context, a thought later taken up and amplified by Robert Nozick. According to Nozick, *S* knows *p* if and only if (1) *S* believes *p*, (2) *p* is true, (3) if *p* were false, *S* would not believe p, and (4) if p were true S would believe p. (Nozick adds an epicycle involving methods of knowledge that won't concern us here.) Taken as an attempt to explicate warrant, these conditions have foundered. First, as Richard Fumerton shows, they encounter crippling difficulty when it comes to knowledge of necessary truths.[28] They also come to grief because of various possibilities of cognitive malfunction, for knowledge of contingent as well as of necessary truths.[29] Still further, that third clause seems to have the consequence that we can't know (for example) that our cognitive faculties are functioning properly (if they weren't, we might still believe that they are); but surely we (sometimes) can. Taken as a total account of warrant, then, these counterfactuals won't do the job.

In "Postscript to 'Proper Functionalism and Virtue Epistemology' " (pp. 275–77), Ernest Sosa offers an alternative to Nozickian tracking— "Cartesian tracking," as he calls it—as a naturalistic account of proper function. So taken, Cartesian tracking too, I believe, has serious problems (see pp. 369–70). Still, something in this general neighborhood could perhaps serve to explain what it is for an exercise of cognitive powers to be such that it can be counted on to deliver a true belief. So consider a given belief B, the exercise E of cognitive powers that produces B, and the cognitive mini-environment MBE in which it is formed. Then

(F) MBE is *favorable* for E, if and only if, if S were to form a belief by way of E, S would form a true belief.

Then we can say that

(Resolution Condition) A belief B produced by an exercise E of cognitive powers has warrant only if MBE is favorable for E.

We may add that a belief has warrant if and only if it meets the conditions of warrant as I stated them in WPF, the environmental condition understood to include favorability on the part of the relevant mini-environment as well as suitability of the maxi-environment.

A couple of comments. First, of course, we aren't to suppose that my forming a true belief B by way of E is sufficient for the favorability of MBE; the truth of p and q is not sufficient for the truth of the counterfactual *if* p *then* q. This is a point on which the usual (Lewisian, Stalnakerian) semantics for counterfactuals is inadequate. Consider quantum effects: perhaps in fact the photon went through the right slit rather than the left; that is not enough to entail that if it had gone through either slit, it would have gone through the right. I toss the die; it comes up 5. That is not sufficient to entail that if I had tossed the die, it would have come up 5. The truth of a counterfactual requires not just that *p and* $-q$ be false in fact; it is also necessary that even if things had been moderately different, it still wouldn't have been the case that *p* and $-q$. To put it in familiar semantical terms, the counterfactual is true only if there is no *sufficiently close* possible world in which *p* is true but *q* is not. How close is sufficiently close? That is of course a question without an answer; counterfactuals are in this way quite properly vague.

Second: note that (RC) guarantees that no false belief has warrant: if in fact my belief that *p* is false, then the counterfactual specified in (RC) has a true antecedent and a false consequent.

(RC) rules out many cases where the other warrant conditions are met but the belief doesn't constitute knowledge—many, but perhaps not all. For suppose you have a box in which there is a vase. If I open the box, however, I don't directly see the vase—what I see is its reflection in a cleverly placed mirror. I open the box, take a quick look, and form the firm belief that there is a vase inside. The warrant conditions are met, and so is (RC): if I were to form a belief on the topic of the focal proposition of this mini-environment by way of an exercise of those cognitive powers, I would form a true belief. The situation is one in which that exercise of cognitive powers can be counted on to produce a true belief. But does this true belief really constitute knowledge? If I *know* about the arrangement (maybe I'm inspecting boxes of this sort to find the few in which the vase has been left out), then perhaps I do—just as I know that Mount Hood is conical by seeing a photograph of it or by seeing it on TV. But suppose I *don't* know about the arrangement, have no idea about any mirrors in that box. *Then* do I know? The 'causal chain' by way of which I come to form the belief, some might say, is somewhat 'deviant'. Perhaps that's true, but does it destroy knowledge? Not all deviant causal chains do; does this one? The answer isn't clear. It isn't *obvious* that I know; in fact one is a bit less strongly inclined to think so than to think not. But it also isn't obvious that I *don't* know; furthermore, it isn't obvious that this case falls into one of those areas of vagueness in the penumbra of the concept of knowledge. So perhaps it isn't really clear whether or not we have a counterexample here. Even if we do, however, we may still rest reasonably satisfied, for the moment anyway, with the vaguer formulation of the environmental condition.

II: Replies to Individual Authors

Ad Lycan

William Lycan chides me for failing to address the sort of explanationist coherentism made famous by Nelson Goodman, W. V. Quine,
Wilfrid Sellars—and Lycan himself.[30] Of course he's right; this version
of coherentism does indeed deserve close attention. (I can only plead
human frailty and insufficient space-time.) He puts his "typical"
explanationism as follows:

> (EXP) . . . s/he holds that a hypothesis is warranted by its ability to
> explain a particular set of data better than any other available
> hypothesis. . . . (p. 4)

This leaves us wondering about those data: how do *they* get warrant?
Here Lycan appeals to what he calls "the Principle of Credulity,"
which is "Accept at the outset each of those things that seems to be
true" (p. 5). He claims further that this principle is a consequence of
the "more general characteristically explanationist claim that *conservativeness . . .* is a theoretical virtue" (p. 6); and he argues that
"whatever epistemic or justifying status inheres in the other standard
pragmatic theoretical virtues (simplicity, testability, fruitfulness,
power, and the like), conservativeness shares that same status" (p. 6).
His suggestion seems to be that one of my beliefs can acquire warrant
just by virtue of seeming to me to be true.[31] A belief doesn't get *much*
warrant in this way ("A belief is justified by the bare fact of our holding
it, I maintain, but only to the smallest degree," p. 7), but it does get
a smidgen.

Here I have a question and a problem. First, the question: theoretical
virtues are ordinarily thought of as characteristic of *hypotheses*, or
explanations, or *scientific theories*; how then do other sorts of beliefs—for example, "spontaneous beliefs" (p. 5) such as those produced by memory and perception—get in on the largess? That's the
question; the problem is this. Although in (EXP) Lycan uses the term
'warrant', he soon starts focusing his attention on *justification*. It
sounds as if he thinks my belief or I myself might be *justified* just by
virtue of the belief's seeming to me to be true. Agreed: at least for
deontological and responsibility-related construals of justification. If a
belief simply seems right to me, perhaps *obviously* right, perhaps as
obviously right as any belief I have, how can I be irresponsible or go
contrary to duty in holding it? So perhaps I'm *justified* by a belief's

simply seeming to me to be true; but of course the belief in question might have no warrant. Lycan mentions (pp. 14–15) the Cartesian madmen who think they are gourds—summer squash, perhaps, or pumpkins. Such beliefs might be *justified* (better, the believer might be justified in holding them) just by virtue of the fact that they seem true to him, but of course in this way it doesn't follow that they have or thus acquire any degree of *warrant*.

This problem with ambivalence (I hesitate to say "equivocation") between justification and warrant persists and reappears at other points in Lycan's paper. Some of my objections to coherentism, as he points out, involve the possibility of a person's forming a mad belief, his other beliefs then settling into a coherent pattern around it. Lycan's comment:

> Plantinga's examples are . . . cases of someone's starting with one or more weird ideas that have no foundation in the real world, and then constructing a coherent system of beliefs that surround and support those ideas. . . . I say the weirdo *is* justified in accepting the wild belief and the system that goes with it. (pp. 18–19)

Elsewhere (note 20):

> I take the position that a smoothly and globally deceived victim [e.g., a brain in a vat] is not only conceptually possible, but is exactly as well justified as is a comparable, counterpart subject whose experience is similar but veridical.

Well, I think so too. If we take justification in anything like its original deontological sense, it is hard to disagree: the weirdo is indeed justified, as is the smoothly and globally deceived victim. But their beliefs might nonetheless have no *warrant* at all: mad beliefs don't acquire warrant just by way of seeming true, or even by way of being integrated into a coherent system of some sort.

So perhaps Lycan is really thinking throughout of *justification*, not warrant; perhaps he thinks a certain kind of coherence is necessary and sufficient for justification, with some further fourth condition (a condition designed to deal with Gettier or the resolution problem) required for warrant. If so, he and I, I think, still have a disagreement, in fact a pair of disagreements. First, it seems quite clear that justification—at least if taken as responsibility or in some other way fairly close to its original deontological sense—does not require explanatory coherence. Jimmie G., Oliver Sacks's Lost Mariner (Lycan pp. 14–16), had a noetic structure that displayed minimal explanatory coherence; nevertheless he might have been as responsible as you please; he might have been doing his level best; he might have been wholly justified.[32] Whether my beliefs display coherence might not be up to me; if it isn't, my failure to be coherent will not reflect on my responsibility.

But what if Lycan isn't thinking of justification in this way—what if he just *defines* 'justification' in terms of coherence? Then of course coherence will be necessary for justification; and Lycan's overall view would simply be that explanatory coherence is necessary for warrant, along with another and so far unspecified condition to deal with Gettier or the resolution problem. This view also seems to me mistaken. Just as coherence is clearly *insufficient* for warrant, so it is also *unnecessary*. Or rather (as it seems to me), no more coherence is necessary than is required for proper function. Noetic structures such as ours must display a certain degree of coherence in order to satisfy that condition; although I can't go into the matter here, it is clear that various kinds and degrees of incoherence are incompatible with a belief's being produced under the conditions of warrant. But why think warrant requires more coherence than is required by proper function? In particular, why think that much by way of *explanatory* coherence is required? I believe the corresponding conditional of *modus ponens*; I also believe that it is wrong to lie about one's colleagues in order to advance one's career. I believe both with great, near maximal firmness. But neither of these propositions, as far as I can see, is in any straightforward sense an *explanation* of other propositions I believe; nor is either *explained by* any other propositions I believe. And yet they have, I should judge, maximal or near maximal warrant.

Following Sosa, BonJour (p. 60) distinguishes reflective knowledge from *animal* knowledge, the sort of knowledge an animal or small child can have; and he claims that a certain kind and degree of coherence is required for the former, even if not for the latter. Perhaps he is right; and perhaps there is also an important variety of knowledge for which explanatory coherence is crucial. We can be grateful to Lycan and explanatory coherentists for calling our attention to this variety of knowledge,[33] even if their comments do not apply to knowledge as such.

Ad Lehrer

Keith Lehrer's characteristically acute and penetrating essay contains much by way of sound philosophy; I'd like to begin by noting a couple of important points where we agree. First, each of us hopes to play Elisha to Thomas Reid's Elijah, thus inheriting Reid's mantle (II Kings 2:11–15). In particular, each of us sees crucial significance in Reid's First Principle 7:

> Another first principle is—*That the natural faculties, by which we distin-guish truth from error, are not fallacious.* If any man should demand a proof of this, it is impossible to satisfy him . . . because, to judge of a demonstration, a man must trust his faculties, and take for granted the very thing in question. If a man's honesty were called in question, it would be ridiculous to refer it to the man's own work, whether he be honest or not.[34]

Lehrer's esteem for Principle 7 is unveiled in his (T) (p. 41); mine is displayed in the contention (WPF chap. 12) that acquiring an unde-feated defeater for this principle wreaks unholy havoc with one's entire noetic system, perhaps even bringing it about that whatever else you believe, you believe irrationally. Lehrer also seems to me approxi-mately right in his diagnosis of Mr. Truetemp's predicament (p. 32–33). As I see it, Truetemp has a defeater for his belief in the fact that (as he no doubt thinks) he is constructed like other human beings and none of *them* has this ability; furthermore, everyone he meets scoffs or smiles at his claim that he does have it. Truetemp's defeater means that his belief does not meet the conditions for warrant; hence (contra Lehrer) he doesn't constitute a counterexample to my analysis of warrant. (If Truetemp doesn't have a defeater here, he also lacks warrant, since proper function, in his situation, requires that he *have* a defeating belief.)

Still further, I agree with Lehrer in holding that at least certain kinds of knowledge demand the sort of coherence of which he speaks. And even further yet, I believe we agree that Gettier problems depend essentially on the resolution problem, i.e., on the fallibility of our cognitive faculties even when they are functioning properly (and even if we disagree about how to resolve the resolution problem).

Still, there remain several interesting points of disagreement. Al-though I very much admire Lehrer's *Theory of Knowledge* (as other of his works) I am disinclined to believe that his account of knowledge there is successful; but I can't take the space here to explain why.[35] Instead, I'd like to respond to his comments on my evolutionary argument against naturalism (WPF chap. 12), and on his suggestion that my account of warrant is incompatible with the idea that God could cause me to know a proposition by specially causing me to believe it.

Turning to the first topic, Lehrer represents me as arguing that naturalism and evolution taken together cannot supply us with any reason for thinking that our cognitive faculties function reliably (in such a way as to provide us with mostly true beliefs), agrees that this is in fact so, but then taxes me with inferring from this "the much stronger conclusion that our beliefs are likely to be false if evolutionary theory is correct" (p. 27). That would indeed be a miserable inference, but I plead not guilty. What I did argue is as follows. Consider philosophical naturalism (N)—as van Fraassen says (this volume p. 172), a view not easy to characterize, but at any rate including the idea that neither theism nor any view similar to it is true; consider the view (E) that our cognitive faculties have come to be by way of the sorts of mechanisms to which contemporary evolutionary theory directs our attention; and consider

(R) My cognitive faculties are reliable.

P(R/N&E), the objective conditional probability of (R) on N&E, I argued, is either low or inscrutable—such that we can't even make a decent estimate of it. Now (R) is really a version of Reid's first principle; I agree with Reid and, I hope, Lehrer in holding that (R) has a great deal of warrant in itself, in the basic way. Like other beliefs that get warrant in the basic way, however, (R) can be defeated, and my claim is that the low or inscrutable probability of (R) on N&E furnishes one who accepts N&E with a defeater for (R)—a defeater that can't be itself defeated. One who has a defeater for (R), furthermore, has a reason for rejecting, withholding, being agnostic with respect to any belief she holds, including, of course, N&E itself. The latter, therefore, is in a certain crucial sense self-defeating and hence (for someone aware of the argument) can't rationally be held.

Obviously many questions can be (and have been[36]) raised about this argument, but it wasn't at all a matter of making the inference Lehrer mentions. Still, what Lehrer says at a neighboring juncture raises an extremely interesting point about the argument. He suggests that

it may be that, though our justification or warrant for the things we believe does not depend on an argument concerning God, the existence of God does supply a better philosophical explanation for why the proper functioning of our faculties yields true beliefs or has a trustworthy if fallible tendency to do so. (p. 28)

He then argues that in fact this isn't so: the existence of God does not supply a better explanation. Why not? Here he neatly turns the tables. I've argued in various places that the existence of evil doesn't provide a strong (probabilistic) argument for the nonexistence of God; Lehrer argues, correspondingly, that the existence of God doesn't provide the materials for a strong (probabilistic) argument that our cognitive faculties are reliable. Now in one way this is obvious; as Reid notes in Principle 7 (quoted above), one can't sensibly give any argument at all for the reliability of our cognitive faculties. But Lehrer really has something different up his sleeve:

> Compare, finally,
>
> S. Satan and his cohorts produce incredible deceps of error
>
> with
>
> E. Evolutionary processes produce incredible deceps of error.
>
> I find little to choose between them. A naturalist wishing to assign a high probability to the conclusion that the proper functioning of our faculties yields truth because they are the result of evolution must assign a low probability to E, while a supernaturalist wishing to assign a high probability to the conclusion that the proper functioning of our faculties yields truth because they are designed by God must assign a low probability to S. (pp. 29–30)

This is relevant to the evolutionary argument against naturalism as follows. I argued that P(R/N&E) is low or inscrutable, and I claimed that this gives the devotee of N&E a defeater for R. But Lehrer gives us a reason for supposing that something similar goes for the theist. P(R/Theism), we can take him as suggesting, is also low or inscrutable: for even if we have been created by God, it is possible that God allows Satan to deceive us massively (just as it is possible that God allows both us and Satan to create other kinds of havoc); furthermore, we can't make a decent estimate of the probability that God *would* allow us to be thus deceived. But then P(R/T) is inscrutable for the theist, like P(R/N&E) for the evolutionary naturalist; the former, therefore, is in the same boat as the latter, having the same sort of defeater for (R).

Very clever! This is a *tu quoque* (you're another) objection; it resembles an objection brought by Carl Ginet in the piece mentioned in note 36. Consider austere theism, the view that we have been created by a very powerful and knowledgeable being. Austere theism (call it "A") is obviously and immediately entailed by theism *simpliciter*; it differs from the latter in not including the proposition that we human beings have been created in the image of God, part of which involves our resembling God by way of our ability to form true beliefs and have knowledge. Ginet pointed out that P(R/A) is low or inscrutable; but any theist who isn't deductively challenged believes A; so any such theist has a defeater for R—just like the evolutionary naturalist! My reply was that the low or inscrutable value of P(R/A) doesn't give the theist a defeater for R. The reason is that he knows or believes that the warrant A has for him is derivative from the warrant T has for him; it is T, not A, that he knows by way of the *Sensus Divinitatis* or by way of faith and the "Internal Testimony of the Holy Spirit." But if I rationally believe that the warrant, for me, of a proposition Q is derivative from that of a proposition P, for me, then for any proposition R, if I don't believe that P is a defeater, for me, of R, then Q is not a defeater, for me, of R.[37] So, for example, I know that

N You have an old Nissan;

acting on the principle that it is always nice to believe an extra truth or two, I infer:

J You have a Japanese car

and

O You own an old car.

I then note that P(J/O) is low (most people who own an old car do not own a Japanese car), and conclude (in considerable puzzlement) that I have a defeater for J. But of course I am mistaken: P(J/O) may be low, but O is not a defeater for J. The reason is just that the warrant of both O and J is derivative, for me, from that of N; since N is not a defeater, for me, of J, neither is O. Lehrer's objection is similar to Ginet's, but stronger; its beauty lies in the fact that it concedes creation in the image of God but still produces a defeater. Granted, that's how we were created, but there is also (at least on Christian theism) the fall into sin and the possibility of deceit by Satan (that father of lies) and his cohorts. According to Christian doctrine, furthermore, the fall into sin has indeed damaged the image of God in us, and has damaged our cognitive faculties: were it not for sin and the fall, we human beings would find the existence of God as obvious and uncontroversial as that of trees and horses. To put it in terms of John Calvin's way of looking at the matter, sin has damaged and compromised the *Sensus Divinitatis*, and also to some degree corrupted our apprehension of moral truth. So the probability of R on T plus this Christian teaching is either low or inscrutable. And doesn't this provide the Christian with a defeater for R, and hence for everything else she believes, including Christianity?

But there is a reply, and substantially the same reply as to Ginet. The Christian believes she knows these central Christian truths— creation and fall into sin—by way of divine revelation. This can be construed in more than one way; for simplicity, take it Calvin's way. Very much oversimplified, the idea is that the Christian knows these truths by way of the Internal Testimony of the Holy Spirit, which prompts acceptance of what the Bible teaches; more exactly, what God intends to teach in the Bible. Part of what the Christian thus learns is that divine grace *restores* the image of God in the believer; part of the effect of the work of the Holy Spirit is for the doleful effects of sin to be increasingly mitigated. (In particular, this restoration cures, repairs the damage to the *Sensus Divinitatis*; it removes our blindness to the existence of God and enables us to see, once more, some of his glory and majestic beauty.) As a Christian sees it, then, she is a person in whom the image of God has been partly restored, so that once more she resembles God with respect to the ability to form true beliefs and have knowledge.

If so, however, she needn't after all have a defeater for (R). For what she thinks has warrant for her is the *whole* message of Christianity, the *whole* of what the Holy Spirit testifies to. What she knows by way of Revelation and the Internal Testimony of the Holy Spirit isn't just T (theism), but the whole Christian story, including fall, redemption, and restoration of the image of God. But then (by the principle enunciated three paragraphs back) the fact that the probability of R with respect to some *part* of that whole is low or inscrutable doesn't give her a defeater for R, unless R is also unlikely with respect to that whole; and of course it isn't. More generally, if S rationally believes that the warrant, for him, of a belief B is derivative from that of a belief A, then B won't be a defeater, for him, for any belief C if he doesn't believe that A is a defeater for C.

Finally and briefly, I'd like to comment on Lehrer's argument that if God specially *causes* me to believe something or other, then, on my view of warrant, that belief does not constitute knowledge. I hope this isn't correct, because in *Warranted Christian Belief*, the third and (I devoutly hope) last in the Warrant series, I follow John Calvin and much of the rest of the Christian tradition in arguing that Christian faith is produced by way of the Internal Testimony of the Holy Spirit;

I also mean to hold, of course, that Christian faith so produced can constitute knowledge. And in fact it *isn't* correct. What happens in this case, we can suppose, is that there is a smallish revision in the design plan governing the relevant parts of my cognitive architecture, as well as the architecture of will and what Jonathan Edwards calls "affections," in particular the *religious* affections.[38] The relevant cognitive powers are, so to say, mildly redesigned, and they work properly according to this new design plan.

Lehrer's case is a little different, however: there isn't any alteration in the design plan, but God simply, directly, and specially causes a belief to well up within you. But can't I take this to be a special limiting case of cognitive faculties or belief-producing processes functioning properly? God instills a true belief in you, intending in so doing to instill in you a true belief. Why can't I think of his doing that as itself a belief-producing process, especially since that is precisely what it is? True, this belief isn't exactly produced by a cognitive *faculty*, or at least by one of *my* cognitive faculties; but it is produced by a properly functioning cognitive *process*, and I think that's sufficient.

Ad BonJour

Laurence BonJour's paper is lucid and thoughtful; it also enters deep waters. I don't have the space to pursue nearly all the important topics he broaches; I shall have to content myself with commenting on just two.

1. Justification Not Even Necessary for Warrant?

BonJour points out that my way with justificationists was a bit quick. I argued that justification, taken either deontologically or in terms of having a reason or evidence, isn't *nearly* sufficient for warrant.[39] He replies, substantially, that there are no near misses in logic; an analysis is either correct or it isn't (there's no such thing as being *nearly* correct); we've known since Gettier that we need a fourth condition; fourth conditions can't be said to vary in size or significance; and there isn't any metric for conceptual space. Of course I realize that distance is a metaphor here, and that it isn't possible to quantify distance, so taken. Nonetheless, I think it is a metaphor we understand and can usefully employ, and that in fact justification *isn't* anywhere nearly sufficient for warrant—contrary to what I took BonJour to mean when he said that the justified true belief account is substantially correct.

But suppose the internalists (BonJour, Feldman) insist that they mean no such thing: justification, they say, is *one* condition needed for warrant, and a fourth condition is *also* needed; neither is more sizable or important than the other, and they never intended to suggest anything to the contrary. Well, the internalists are presumably the authorities on what they do and did mean. What I shall argue instead, then, is that justification isn't even a *necessary* condition for warrant. (If that's right, then internalists don't have so much as a *third* condition, let alone a fourth.)

First, take justification in the sense of evidence, or reason, or ground—the way BonJour seems to take it.[40] Clearly one can know many propositions without having evidence or a reason for them: obvious truths of arithmetic and logic, for example, such as $2 + 1 = 3$ are not accepted on the basis of reasons or grounds (see WPF p. 188), but can nonetheless constitute knowledge.[41] The same goes for memory beliefs (see WPF pp. 188–89).

As for justification taken deontologically (in terms of duty or obligation), things are a bit more complicated. Here the idea would be that you don't really know some proposition *p* unless you have been *responsible* in forming and sustaining the belief that *p*, and you have satisfied the relevant duties or obligations. Now clearly there are *some* duties such that one can't know *p* without satisfying them: for example, the duty not to destroy your cognitive capacities by taking mind-altering drugs. But presumably that isn't the sort of duty the deontological internalist has in mind. If he were satisfied to stop here, he could argue in the same way that justification is a necessary condition of, say, *digestion*. You won't digest properly if you don't conform to the duty not to commit suicide, as well as the duty not to destroy your digestive system in thoughtless and ill-conceived experimentation with ground glass or sword swallowing. So what duties or obligations, with respect to a belief, *are* the ones satisfaction of which is relevantly required by warrant? In WCD (p. 45) I argued that one could know much even if violating the epistemic duties Roderick Chisholm suggests. Of course other deontological internalists might suggest other duties; perhaps there are other good candidates for the relevant epistemic duty. If there are, however, it is exceedingly hard to see what they might be. True, there might be specific beliefs *B* such that in fact *B* won't constitute knowledge unless some duty has been satisfied; but of course that isn't sufficient. What is needed is some duty such that satisfaction of *that* duty is required for any belief to enjoy warrant—or perhaps the idea would have to be (less demandingly) that for each belief *B*, there is some duty such that satisfaction of that duty is necessary for *B* to have warrant. But what could such duties be? No matter how undutiful I am, no matter what relevant duties and obligations I flagrantly flout, won't I still be able to know that $3 + 1 = 4$ and that I am being appeared to redly? It is up to the deontological internalist to specify the duty or duties she has in mind; but it is at the least exceedingly difficult to see what they might be. The fact is, I don't believe there are any such duties.

But if this is true, then justification is neither anywhere nearly sufficient for knowledge, nor even necessary for it; it isn't even a third condition.[42]

2. Skepticism?

BonJour asks (p. 63), "Why isn't Plantinga's view itself a deep and troubling version of skepticism?" By way of reply: first, the claim that we *do* have knowledge is no part of my official account of warrant; that account says only what conditions are necessary and sufficient[43] for a belief's having it, not that any of our beliefs meet those conditions. But of course I do think we have a good deal of knowledge, and depend on that opinion in presenting counterexamples to various alleged necessary conditions for knowledge; I should therefore be distressed if it turned out that my conditions for warrant guarantee skepticism. Why does BonJour think they do so? His basic reason, I think, is contained in the following:

> On his [i.e., my] view, while we may have "warrant" and even knowledge *if* the right conditions are satisfied, we apparently have no way to tell from the inside whether those conditions are ever satisfied, nor any reason at all to think that they are (though we might still, of course, be "warranted" in believing and even know that they are satisfied, if the belief that they are satisfied should itself happen to satisfy Plantinga's conditions). If a particular belief is called into question, either theoretically or as a possible basis for action, we are apparently helpless to resolve the resulting issue in any way that we can understand to be adequate, as helpless as the dumbest, least reflective animal. (p. 63)

And of course BonJour thinks that if we *are* thus helpless, in these ways, then we don't in fact have knowledge.

Now, first, it seems to me wholly mistaken to say that if a belief is called into question, then, on my view, we are helpless to resolve the resulting issue: if you claim that Newark is in New Jersey and I that it is in New York, a quick look at a map ought to settle the issue, and there is nothing in my account of warrant to suggest otherwise. But of course this isn't the sort of "settling" BonJour has in mind; what he means is that on my view we can't provide a certain kind of ultimate answer to the skeptic. We can't satisfy the skeptical demand that we be able to tell "from the inside" that the conditions of warrant are in fact satisfied. But what is it to tell "from the inside that *p*"? And wouldn't the same skeptical questions arise about whatever it was that one appealed to in settling this from the inside? You will believe such things as that you are appeared to thus and so: but don't you then, on BonJour's showing, need some reason to think that you really *are* appeared to in the way you think you are? And what about the answers to *those* questions, and so on, world without end? I *think* BonJour believes that *a priori* knowledge will fend off the looming regress; and I think he means to say that we can tell from the inside that the conditions of warrant are satisfied only if we can tell *a priori* that they are. (As he says in a slightly different connection (p. 54), "An empirical argument would seem to be obviously question-begging in relation to the larger problem of whether all of our perceptual experiences might be caused in some aberrant way.")

But again: don't the same questions arise about *a priori* belief and alleged knowledge? Can't we raise the same skeptical problems? I believe the corresponding conditional of *modus ponens* and that $2 + 1 = 3$; indeed, I believe each necessarily true. These beliefs seem wholly obvious; I find myself utterly convinced. They have about them, furthermore, the peculiar feel that *a priori* beliefs have—that feel that somehow they just couldn't possibly be false. But of course such a feel could be misleading. A *false* belief, obviously enough, could have that sort of feel for me: I could be mad, or a victim of an Alpha Centaurian cognitive scientist, or a brain in a vat, or a victim of a Cartesian evil demon. Indeed, it was in this very context of *a priori* knowledge that Descartes turned to that evil demon scenario. So obviously I can be wrong, even when it seems *a priori* for all the world that the belief is true. As a matter of fact, this isn't merely an abstract possibility: some propositions that have that *a priori* feel about them *are* false, as is shown by certain versions of the Russell paradox (see WCD pp. 104–5). So do I have any reason to think that $2 + 1$ really does equal 3? Of course it *seems* to me that it does and indeed necessarily does; but how much is that worth? BonJour complains that on my accounts of induction and our knowledge of other minds, we *just find* ourselves believing, under certain circumstances, that the sun will rise tomorrow or that Sally is angry, without any real insight into how it is that the sun's having risen lo! these many days makes it likely that it will rise tomorrow. But are we any better off in the *a priori* case? When we contemplate the corresponding conditional of *modus ponens*, we just find ourselves with this powerful inclination to believe that this proposition is true, and indeed couldn't be false. But (as we also know) such inclinations are by no means infallible. We really don't have any reasons or grounds for this belief; we simply, so to say, *start* with it.

But then the question for BonJour is this: why are simple *a priori* beliefs exempt from this demand that we must have a good reason for thinking a belief true, if it is to constitute knowledge? He seems to me to face a dilemma at this point. If he treats *a priori* belief differently from perceptual belief, belief about other minds, inductive beliefs, and the like, then he's guilty of a sort of arbitrariness. As Reid says,

> Reason, says the skeptic, is the only judge of truth, and you ought to throw off every opinion and every belief that is not grounded on reason. Why, sir, should I believe the faculty of reason more than that of perception? They came both out of the same shop, and were made by the same artist; and if he puts one piece of false ware into my hands, what should hinder him from putting another?[44]

On the other hand, if BonJour insists that *all* beliefs, *a priori* beliefs as well as others, must meet this condition, then he insists on a condition for knowledge that cannot possibly be met, at least by finite beings like us, beings with only finitely many beliefs. Indeed, can it be met by God himself, essentially, yea, necessarily omniscient as he is? Would God have an answer to the question 'What is your reason for believing that $2 + 1 = 3$?' I doubt it. He knows that $2 + 1 = 3$ and that's that; he doesn't know it by way of some infinite chain of propositions, each his reason for the succeeding one. But however things stand with God, it is clear that you and I do not have a reason for believing such elementary truths of logic and arithmetic; and yet we do know them, and know that we know them.

So does my account of warrant entail skepticism? Only if we add this further condition BonJour insists on—and given that condition, *every* account of warrant will entail skepticism. For let the conditions of warrant be whatever you like: if we insist that knowledge of p requires knowledge that the conditions of warrant with respect to p be satisfied, we immediately start something we can't finish, embark upon a regress we can't complete. In other words, it isn't my account of warrant that guarantees skepticism: it is this condition BonJour adds.

Ad Foley

In an uncharacteristic display of intolerance, Richard Foley declares a pox on all our houses. Justification, reliability, proper function, causal connection between belief and its object, fit between cognitive powers and cognitive environment—none is either necessary or sufficient for warrant. What counts, rather, is *accuracy* and *comprehensiveness*: knowledge is sufficiently accurate, comprehensive belief. It doesn't matter how you acquire that splendid set of beliefs. It could be by the sheerest chance; perhaps, by lucky happenstance, it happens when your brain is scrambled by a stroke or an errant bolt of lightning. It doesn't matter whether your beliefs are justified in the deontological sense: you could be a real epistemic villain and nonetheless know an enormous amount. It doesn't matter whether you have evidence for any or all of these beliefs. It doesn't matter whether your cognitive faculties are reliable: they can be as unreliable as you please, but if by dumb luck they happen on some occasion to produce such a fine upstanding set of beliefs, you have knowledge.

Now I don't believe that accuracy and comprehensiveness by themselves are sufficient for knowledge. (Foley and I first had this conversation some ten years ago; apparently neither has succeeded in convincing the other.) Let me explain why I'm doubtful. Note first that Foley's suggestion flies in the face of one of the strongest intuitions (as it seems to me) that we have in this area: the intuition that if I know p, then it can't be just by accident that I form the true belief that p.[45] On Foley's account, this can be as accidental as you please. Second, knowledge requires a certain degree of stability. Suppose I am captured by Alpha Centaurian super scientists, or am a victim of a Cartesian evil demon: my tormentors run a nasty experiment in which my beliefs alternate between two-second periods where I have very accurate and comprehensive true belief, and two-second periods in which my beliefs are pitiably confused and mistaken. Do I have knowledge during the two-second periods when I have accurate and comprehensive true belief? I doubt it, just as I would my mechanic's claim that my van works just fine seven-eighths of the time (and who can sensibly ask for more?), since it is only one of the eight cylinders that refuses to fire. Foley tries to justify himself by claiming that "it is not impossible to have fleeting moments of insight" (p. 92); that's true, but it doesn't follow that just any amount of instability is compatible with knowledge.

There is another problem here, one of which Foley is doubtless aware. Clearly the account needs an addition: that the belief system in question is accurate and comprehensive *in the neighborhood*, so to speak, of *p*, the belief that putatively constitutes knowledge. For suppose that I am magnificently knowledgeable, knowing as much science, even, as Carl Sagan. I drive through that phony barn country in Wisconsin, having no idea about what those sly Wisconsinites have been up to. Then couldn't my (true) belief that I see a barn (it stands in the middle of a clump of four fake barns) be an element of an accurate and comprehensive system of beliefs about barns (their history, characteristic employment, construction, etc.) but still fail to constitute knowledge? We'd have to construe 'accurate and comprehensive' in such a way that it somehow guarantees that I wouldn't or couldn't drive through phony barn country without believing that it was indeed phony barn country. Similarly for the van case (pp. 312 ff.) 'accurate and comprehensive' would have to be construed, somehow, in such a way that it precludes either my failing to learn that my van has been destroyed, or my failing to learn that I've won the Varsity Club win-a-van lottery. We'd also have to construe this condition in such a way that it eludes the original Gettier case. But how can we do that? Couldn't I have a very accurate and comprehensive system of beliefs that nonetheless contained a false belief *p*? Maybe I know an enormous amount about Napoleon, but am mistaken about the birthplace of his maternal grandfather, thinking he was born in X, a village three miles from his actual birthplace. If so, couldn't I disjoin some belief *q* with *p*, which was such that while it was true, I have no reason to think it is? Maybe I have no idea what his maternal grandfather's name was (that fact has been obscured by the mists of time); but I idly deduce *Napoleon was born in X or his maternal grandfather's name was Pierre* (and as it happens, his name was indeed Pierre) from my belief about his birthplace. We'd have to construe 'accurate and comprehensive' in such a way that it precludes this possibility too. In general, we'd have to construe this condition in such a way that its satisfaction doesn't permit an area of lack of resolution, or else doesn't permit my having true beliefs in that area. But how can we do this, short of insisting on omniscience or near omniscience in the vicinity of *p*?

This condition of accuracy and comprehensiveness, therefore, is going to have to be *very* strong. (When Foley is arguing that nothing beyond accuracy and completeness is necessary, he speaks of a set of beliefs much more accurate and comprehensive than yours or mine.) But won't that lead to an opposite problem? Can't I know something even if I don't enjoy much by way of accurate and comprehensive belief? As my grandmother aged, she knew less and less. Eventually she didn't know much at all—but she still knew her name, that the man living with her was her husband, that she had four children, and that she didn't have a dog. My problem with Foley's account is that I don't see how he can sail between Scylla and Charybdis. I don't see how his account can simultaneously meet two conditions: first that 'accurate and comprehensive' be so construed that Gettier problems with *sufficiency* can't arise, and second, that it be so construed that I can know *p* even if I don't know (or believe) a great deal more.

Ad Klein

I've already had my say about much of Peter Klein's paper; here I want to add just one brief point. Klein proposes the Garden of Eden Case (pp. 109–110) to show that even if I am in fact designed and created by God, it could be that I should come to know something God didn't intend me to know: "My story shows that we can pull apart our having knowledge from the intentions of our maker—if there were one. Were our maker to intend that we remain ignorant and design us with that plan in mind, we could rebel and gain knowledge. In other words, I think the root notion of proper function is such that we *can* gain knowledge, even though doing so would not be to function properly" (p. 110).[46]

But here we need a distinction. God didn't intend that Cain kill Abel; when Cain did so, however, it wasn't that his limbs (or other systems or organs) were malfunctioning. It was rather that he was using the powers God gave him for a wicked purpose, a purpose contrary to what God intended. In fact, if his arms (e.g.) *had* malfunctioned at the crucial moment, *then* he would not have been able to kill Abel. We must distinguish proper function of system or organ (function in accord with design plan) from our using the power in question in a way God intends us to. The former is required for warrant, not the latter.

Ad Swain

Marshall Swain argues that "the theory that knowledge is ultimately undefeated justified true belief (the defeasibility theory, hereafter) is superior to Plantinga's version of the warranted true belief view . . . as an account of knowledge." He adds that the former is also superior to the latter in that "the defeasibility theory does not commit us, or even threaten to commit us, to the idea that our faculties must function in accordance with some design plan, which is the feature of Plantinga's view of warrant that leads to supernaturalism" (p. 132). Swain has two main claims: first, that the defeasibility theory is superior to my account of warrant, just as an account of warrant (its proposal as to the necessary and sufficient conditions of warrant is closer to the truth than mine); and second, that it is also superior in that it doesn't have the supernaturalistic implications my theory is alleged to have. I have two brief comments.

First, Swain says he prefers the view according to which warrant is "ultimately undefeated justified true belief." But what does he mean by 'justified'? He doesn't tell us; but if we take it in either of the most common ways—either in terms of epistemic responsibility or in terms of evidence—it doesn't seem to be necessary (see pp. 317–18). Taken the second way, justification seems clearly unnecessary; as I argued in WPF (pp. 186 ff.) many beliefs constitute knowledge without having either propositional evidence or phenomenological evidence. Perhaps they must have what I called impulsional evidence, this feeling that the belief in question is indeed true (WPF pp. 190 ff.), but this is really an inevitable accompaniment of belief and isn't a further condition in addition to believing p.[47] On the other hand, I've already argued (p. 330–31) that there doesn't seem to be any epistemic duty the satisfaction of which is a necessary condition of knowledge; I can be as undutiful as you please and nevertheless know, e.g., that I am being appeared to redly or that $2 + 1 = 3$. (That is not to say that there are no specific kinds of knowledge such that having knowledge of that kind requires conformity to some duty or other.) As I see it, then, Swain's account doesn't succeed in providing a necessary condition of warrant (unless he has some quite unusual account of justification up his sleeve).

As to sufficiency, that would depend upon just how Swain proposes to gloss 'undefeated'. Peter Klein's proposed condition doesn't seem sufficient, and it's about as good as defeasibility accounts get. I therefore persist in believing that my account (with the amplified environmental condition) does better than any defeasibility account currently on offer.[48] Indeed, a defeasibility theory can't be successful without adding a clause involving proper function. For clearly there are beliefs that achieve warrant in the basic way; as far as I can see, however, any successful attempt to specify *how* they receive warrant in the basic way will require the notion of proper function. The only plausible alternative would be to follow Klein and appeal to reliability; as we saw in thinking about Klein's proposal, however, appeal to reliability without proper function is bootless.

This leads directly to Swain's second contention; a defeasibility account of warrant, he says, is superior to mine in that it doesn't threaten to commit us to supernaturalism. But that is at best a dubious advantage. In WPF, I do indeed argue that there is no way to give a naturalistic account of the notion of proper function. More exactly, what I argue is that there is no way to give an account of proper function that doesn't involve the activity of conscious, intelligent agents; anything that functions properly or improperly is in this respect like an artifact. That means that on my account, if we human beings have knowledge, then we have been designed by one or more conscious intelligent agents. In my own view this agent would of course be God; but it is also at least abstractly possible that it be an agent or agents of some other sort.

But first, my claim that proper function can't be analyzed or explained naturalistically isn't really part of the account of warrant; it isn't itself an *epistemological* claim at all. Someone could share my epistemological views even if he added that he was agnostic as to whether there is a decent naturalistic analysis of proper function, or even if he went on to endorse some naturalistic analysis of it. And second, if I am right about proper function, it will be a lot more than warrant or knowledge that carries an apparent commitment to supernaturalism. The same will go, for example, for the notions of sanity and health. Medical science is full of descriptions of how organs or systems work when they function properly, as well as descriptions of what happens when they fail to function properly. A naturalist *already* has the problem of deciding what to do with this absolutely pervasive concept; he'll need some *general* way of accommodating or dealing with proper function. Perhaps he will deny my suggestion that it implies design by a conscious and intelligent agent; or perhaps he will take refuge in some form of fictionalism, suggesting that we can adopt the "functional stance" even if in reality there is no such thing as proper (or improper) function; or perhaps he will try something else. The point is only this: whatever problem he has with my account of warrant is a problem he *already* has; hence he need not reject this account because of that problem.

Ad van Fraassen

Bas van Fraassen's subtle picture of science is powerfully drawn, presented with irony, force, passion. To echo Jonathan Edwards in another connection, "I could not but stand and admire"—as indeed with all van Fraassen's work. (As with some of his work, however, I also find my admiration deeper than my understanding.) Much in his paper cries out for comment. His topics differ considerably from everyone else's, however; a proper comment would require much by way of stage setting and considerable shifting of gears; furthermore I hope to write elsewhere on the topics he takes up. I shall therefore restrict myself to a brief comment on just one of the many hares he starts.

As arresting as any theme in the paper is the claim that materialism, that venerable and widely revered piece of metaphysics, really isn't a *claim* or a *view* at all, but instead an *attitude*:

> I propose the following diagnosis of materialism: it is not identifiable with a theory about what there is, but only with an attitude or cluster of attitudes. These attitudes include strong deference to science in matters of opinion about what there is, and the inclination to accept (approximative) completeness claims for science as actually constituted at any given time. Given this diagnosis, the apparent knowledge of what is and what is not material among newly hypothesized entities is mere appearance. The ability to adjust the content of the thesis that all is matter again and again is then explained instead by a *knowing-how* to retrench which derives from invariant attitudes. (p. 170)

Here van Fraassen harks back to an old empiricist or positivist theme: much of what you are initially inclined to take to be a claim about the world, a position, an opinion as to what there is, is really no such thing. (Carnap suggested that metaphysics is perhaps a form of *music*: *bad* music no doubt—nothing to rival Mozart or maybe even Madonna—but music nonetheless.) But while the positivists were crude, wholesale, disdainful, and dismissive in their assaults on metaphysics, theology, ethical views, and the like, van Fraassen is subtle, piecemeal, and non-dismissive—though a certain disdain remains. In claiming that materialism is an attitude rather than a view, he is only, he says, giving the straight story about materialism, not attacking or dismissing it: "This does not reflect badly on materialism; on the contrary, it gives materialism its due" (p. 170).[49] Indeed, van Fraassen regards his own *empiricism* as an attitude rather than a claim. But while there is no condemnation as such in calling materialism an attitude rather than a thesis, the materialist still has a problem: false consciousness. She often confuses "theses held with attitudes expressed" (p. 170). In declaring "matter is all," says van Fraassen, she is really expressing an attitude rather than (as she confusedly sees herself) stating a view as to what there is.

This is a fascinating thesis, presenting a powerful challenge to *soi-disant* materialists. Of course questions arise about attitudes: what sort of things *are* they? That's not wholly clear, but at any rate they can include "strong deferences," e.g., to science in matters of opinion, and "inclinations to accept" certain factual claims; they can also include commitments—e.g., to form one's opinions in terms of contemporary science—as well as judgments of worth or value. The heart of van Fraassen's claim is that there is more to materialism than factual judgment: there is also this cluster of attitudes. In fact materialism, as he thinks of it, doesn't include, just as such, any factual judgment at all. At any given time it is, so to say, embodied in opinion of one sort or another ("Its incarnation at any moment will be some position distinguished by certain empirical consequences, and these will either stand or fall as science evolves," p. 170). But the opinions associated with materialism at a moment are not essential to it; one can be a materialist without accepting those opinions; at bottom materialism is a cluster of attitudes rather than a factual opinion or judgment. Materialism may include an "inclination to accept" certain factual judgments, but there is no factual judgment such that accepting that judgment is necessary to being a materialist. For first, the inclination may be to accept different opinions in response to different circumstances: if science says at t that matter is particulate, then at t the materialist will be inclined to believe that all is particulate or made of particles; but if at t^* science says matter is *not* particulate, then at t^* the proper materialist will be inclined to reject the previous opinion. And second, of course, the attitude includes a *tendency* to accept certain factual opinions; but (I should think) the tendency isn't necessarily realized within the breast of any given materialist.

This suggestion is at the least insouciant; the materialist may have stronger terms for it. But what leads van Fraassen to make the suggestion? That the materialist always knows how to retrench in the face of new scientific developments and hypotheses. Perhaps first she thinks that matter consists just in elementary particles and things made of them; but then science posits forces, which are not particles; her reaction, of course, is not to *give up* materialism, but instead *amend* it. As science marches (or sashays) along, positing its enormous variety of entities of ever-stranger sorts, she always knows how to retrench. And that is because, says van Fraassen, her materialism really consists, not in a view as to what there is, but in a cluster of attitudes including a commitment to endorse whatever science comes up with.

This is indeed a striking feature of materialism. But here I find in myself a wholly unfamiliar inclination to defend the materialist, or at any rate her self-understanding; this knowing how to retrench is compatible with a view of materialism that departs less from her own idea as to what she is up to. It is indeed hard to say precisely what matter is; but perhaps this is due, not to the term's having no cognitive content at all, but to more than usual vagueness. Perhaps the materialist, at any given time, says something like this: all is matter, and matter is what current science says there is, *together with anything sufficiently similar* to what current science says there is. What constitutes *sufficient* similarity is of course unstated; that is the source of the vagueness. The crucial respects of similarity are also unstated; perhaps there is in fact no way to make them wholly explicit, and perhaps they change with changes in science. But materialism could then still be an opinion, a claim, even if a bit nebulous and inspecific, a little like the claim that the truth is whatever is sufficiently similar to what the pope or the Synod of the Christian Reformed Church says. So taken, materialism would still have the reflexive character van Fraassen mentions: what is sufficiently similar to what science *now* says there is may not be sufficiently similar to what it will say one hundred years from now—more likely, what *isn't* sufficiently similar to what it now says there is may be sufficiently similar to what it will then say there is. (So materialism may be less a specific opinion than an evolving group of opinions.) But (provided science doesn't change too rapidly) at any given time the materialist may know how to retrench: perhaps current science says there are things of kind k but none of kind k^*; the materialist then denies that there are things of kind k^*; but then science moves on and says there are indeed things of kind k^*; provided k^* isn't too different from k, the materialist can easily retrench. She thought there were no things of that kind, but now thinks there are—while remaining a materialist.

Materialism thus thought of has or may have "cognitive content"; it needn't be so vague as not to eliminate *anything*. Perhaps there are no explicitly stateable and reasonably precise necessary and sufficient conditions for something's being material, but there may be necessary conditions. If materialism is true, for example, there won't be any such person as the God of traditional theism: no all-knowing, everlasting, all-powerful, and wholly good being who has created the world. (If the materialist could retrench as far as all *that*, then materialism would indeed be contentless.) Still further, perhaps (but this is only a guess) an entity could be a material entity only if it had a spatial location of some sort. Perhaps it need not be any distance from *us*; but perhaps it will have to be at some distance from *something*, if only itself. This condition isn't wholly vacuous, at least for those of us who adopt more or less traditional views as to the nature of numbers, propositions, states of affairs, possible worlds, and the like; these things exist but have no spatial location. Furthermore *God* isn't at any distance from anything, not even himself. I'm not sure the materialist ought to prefer this diagnosis of his condition to van Fraassen's but it is at any rate an additional option.

Now van Fraassen adopts the same line with respect to *naturalism*. ("Yet I venture to assert: we see here too a position that only purports to be a factual thesis," p. 172). It too, he suggests, is an attitude or a congeries of attitudes—perhaps overlapping or even identical with materialism ("Perhaps it is just the materialism I have been discussing here, under a different name," p. 172). And this means that the evolutionary argument I gave against naturalism in chapter 12 of WPF can't possibly be successful: that argument is stated as turning on the probability that our cognitive faculties are reliable, given a certain proposition that includes naturalism as a conjunct. But if naturalism is an *attitude* rather than an opinion, then, of course, there *is* no proposition that includes naturalism as a conjunct. The best my argument could do would be to refute "some temporary tradeable asset of the position" (p. 172), leaving the central core, the constituting attitude, untouched.

Well, perhaps a modest philosopher ought to be content with refuting the current assets of the position, even if those assets are tradeable; its subsequent assets can be left to the attention of subsequent modest philosophers. More fundamentally, however, I propose the same claim here as with materialism (which won't be hard if indeed naturalism, as van Fraassen suggests or at any rate entertains, is indeed the very same thing as materialism). Perhaps naturalism too is a view, all right, but also an unusually vague view. Perhaps it is the view that there is no such person as God, or anything sufficiently similar to God. As van Fraassen suggests, it is exceedingly hard to see precisely what naturalism—or worse, naturalistic epistemology—is supposed to be (see pp. 172 ff.). But surely you can't consistently be both a naturalist and a traditional theist, i.e., someone who believes there is an all-powerful, all-knowing, wholly good person who has created the heavens and the earth. Perhaps it is also not possible to be (consistently) both a naturalist and, say, an absolute idealist in the style of Hegel or Bradley (as the saying goes, absolute Idealism is really a continuation of Protestantism by other means), or a believer in Plato's Idea of the Good, or a Neo-Platonic emanationist, or a believer in the Stoic's *Nous*, or in Spinoza's *Deus sive Natura*, or Tillich's Ground of Being, or angels. Some of these may not be coherently characterizable; assuming that they are, however, some seem to fall clearly outside what a naturalist can admit, and others (Spinoza, Tillich) seem to fall into that area of vagueness. If this is right, then naturalism is a view after all, even if only a hazy view; naturalism is a saying, even if a dark saying. If so, my argument against naturalism doesn't fail for this reason, at any rate, whatever its other blemishes.

Ad Conee

Earl Conee is scandalized by my claim that proper functionalism, with what he sees as its ultimate reference to God, is a brand of *naturalistic* epistemology.[50]

> Thus Plantinga's theory of warrant—"proper functionalism" for short— invokes God, the epitome of a supernatural entity. Amazingly, Plantinga nonetheless regards his theory of warrant as a naturalistic proposal. He is quite open about this. He explicitly advocates a supernatural ontology for a naturalistic epistemology. (p. 183)

He goes on to make an impassioned argument that my epistemological views are about as unnaturalistic as you can get. But here what we really face is an illustration of van Fraassen's point about the elusiveness of naturalism, or more exactly, of the project of naturalizing epistemology. Conee himself seems to recognize this:

> Perhaps in the end Plantinga does not intend to be taken completely seriously in arguing in the ways that we have reviewed that his theory of warrant is a naturalistic theory. After counting his theory as a radical naturalism, he makes the following lighthearted comment: "[S]triking the naturalistic pose is all the rage these days, and it's a great pleasure to be able to join the fun." (p. 195)

"I take no pleasure in spoiling anyone's fun," he says, but then he goes on to scold me for undue frivolity:

> But it would be too costly to allow this recreational endeavor to go unchallenged. Stretching our interpretation to accommodate proper func-

tionalism in the category of "naturalistic epistemology" would so distort the meaning of the phrase as to ruin it for those who are earnestly trying to mean something natural by it. (p. 195)

Earnestly trying, no doubt, but so far without much success, which was really my point in claiming that my account of warrant is naturalistic. The advocates of naturalism and more particularly naturalistic epistemology clearly suppose the latter a very good thing; beyond that things are wide open. To illustrate this fact, I argued that my account of warrant, despite its supernaturalistic setting, is really naturalistic according to at least some current accounts. Jaegwon Kim and Hilary Kornblith, for example, see the essence of naturalistic epistemology as a matter of rejecting normativity in epistemology. Kornblith asks us to consider the questions

(1) How ought we to arrive at our beliefs?

and

(2) How do we arrive at our beliefs?

and then characterizes naturalism in epistemology as follows:

I take the naturalistic approach in epistemology to consist in this: question 1 cannot be answered independently of question 2. Questions about how we actually arrive at our beliefs are thus relevant to questions about how we ought to arrive at our beliefs. Descriptive questions about belief acquisition have an important bearing on normative questions about belief acquisition.[51]

Well, this leaves quite a lot of leeway. What is meant by the first question—what kind of normativity is it that is at issue, what is the force of the 'ought'? Is Kornblith thinking of duty, obligation, requirement, deontology? What he says elsewhere makes it clear that he isn't. There is a use of 'ought', however, that might be relevant: its use when we say such things as that your blood pressure ought to be fairly close to 120/80, that when you press the starter button, the engine ought to turn over, and that a 60-year-old man ought to be able to run a mile in 10 minutes. This is the 'ought' of proper function. And of course (as I argued in WPF, p. 46) how we ought to arrive at our beliefs in this sense of 'ought' is indeed relevant to how we actually arrive at our beliefs, at least if we construe the latter as how we arrive at them when there is no cognitive malfunction; indeed, so taken, questions (1) and (2) are identical. Furthermore, it seems likely (though he doesn't say) that Kornblith *is* construing 'actually arrive at' as 'actually arrive at when there is no dysfunction'; how we arrive at our beliefs when there is cognitive malfunction, or madness, or insanity, I take it, will not be of much relevance to the question how we *ought* to arrive at them, no matter how we construe the latter. So on this way of understanding naturalistic epistemology, my account of warrant qualifies. Conee demurs (p. 187), but his demurral depends, as far as I can see, upon confusing the normativity that goes with warrant with warrant itself. It is indeed true, as he claims, that the latter involves more than proper function; it doesn't follow, of course, that the same goes for the former. I therefore persist in thinking that my account of warrant passes Kornblith's test for being naturalistic. If this be heresy, I invite Kornblith to shoulder some of the blame.

I distinguished three grades of normative involvement, suggesting that there are three corresponding grades of naturalism in epistemology: the first renounces deontology in epistemology; the second is the one outlined by Kornblith; and the third, inspired by Quine, eschews any kind of normativity not invoked in science. I've just argued that my account is a naturalism of the second grade; it is obviously one of the first grade as well. But it is also a naturalism of the third grade, in that medical science, psychology, biology, and other sciences employ, explicitly or implicitly, the notion of proper function, and thus employ the only sort of normativity involved in my account of warrant. True, the teleology involved in proper function is a source of a certain embarrassment for those who think science shouldn't or doesn't involve any such thing, perhaps taking refuge in the pious if unfounded[52] hope that teleology can be reduced, somehow, to notions more naturalistically antiseptic. Whether science should or shouldn't involve teleology, however, it does.[53]

Again, Conee demurs, claiming that what I see as the notion of proper function in the sciences I mention is really no such thing. He points out first that this notion isn't involved in physics and chemistry, apparently inferring (p. 191) that this means it isn't really involved in other sciences (such as medicine, biology, and psychology) either. I fail to follow the inference. *Pliotropy* and *gross national product* aren't to be found in physics and chemistry; does it follow that they aren't to be found in biology or economics either? (Or that the latter aren't sciences?) He next suggests that what is really involved in science is something quite different from the proper function I profess to find there:

> . . . accurate psychological generalizations say no more than what must happen in sentient organisms when the distinct kind ["level," "scale"] of causal process that is governed by psychological forces is operative. . . . The intended qualification of psychological laws just sets aside other potential influences, nonpsychological factors that must be at least controllable in their impact if theoretical psychology is to be practicable. (p. 191)

I'm a bit in the dark about this claim: what, for example, are "psychological forces"? Be that as it may (and no doubt it will), this seems to me to be inaccurate. What is to be ruled out, in the functional generalizations in question, is more than just potential influences from outside the 'level' under consideration. A hungry cat confronted by a plump mouse will give chase—unless she is suffering from congestive heart failure, or is paralyzed, or . . . —or is *insane*. Psychological malfunction need not involve invasion from some other level.

Finally, Conee's own characterization of naturalism in epistemology (a little softly focused, he admits) seems to me to let in my account of warrant. "Using broad and blurry terms," he says, "the theme can be said to be that of locating the epistemic within nature, and finding epistemic topics to be suitable for investigation by scientific methods" (pp. 183–84). Once more, I'm not sure how to take this: what it is to locate the epistemic within nature? Part of epistemology, presumably, would be to say what knowledge or warrant is: but what would it be for such an account to locate them within nature? Further, why can't my account of knowledge meet these conditions? On my view, human beings are to be found, naturally enough, within nature: is this sufficient for locating the epistemic within nature? I should also think, furthermore, that at least some epistemic topics are "suitable for investigation by scientific methods." One such epistemic topic would involve description of how human cognitive faculties function when they function properly—or improperly. Under the latter heading would come such topics as the cognitive disturbances involved in schizophrenia, the way in which cognitive faculties are impaired by dementia praecox, and many more; these topics not only can be but have been investigated scientifically.

But I am afraid this will not satisfy Conee. What he really means, I think, is given in the following:

> He [i.e., I] begins to support it by making the stunning assertion that naturalistic epistemology is "quite compatible with supernaturalistic theism" (p. 46). This seems quite doubtful. If naturalistic epistemology is what it appears to be—an application of a naturalistic world view and methodology to epistemic topics—then it is incompatible with any sort of supernaturalism. (p. 184)

So it looks as if a naturalistic epistemology, by Conee's lights, must as such entail, e.g., that there is no such person as God, whom Conee rightly sees as paradigmatically supernatural. (It might have to entail more, at any rate if atheism and naturalism do not coincide; perhaps it would have to entail that Bradley's metaphysics is false (if coherent) and that there is no such thing as Plato's idea of the Good.) Alvin Goldman's reliabilism, then, would not be a naturalistic epistemology, since it is clearly compatible with the existence of God (assuming the latter self-consistent). The same would go for Fred Dretske's epistemology. The same would also go for Conee's own evidentialism: it too is clearly compatible with the existence of God. (Not that Conee claims that his own epistemology *is* naturalistic—so far as I know, he doesn't.) Quine's suggestions are ordinarily taken as definitive or at least paradigmatic of naturalistic epistemology; but clearly a theist could consistently share Quine's opinion that there is nothing to epistemology except empirical psychology, at least if neither theism nor this opinion is itself necessarily false. So by this standard, no one we know, not even Quine, the old master himself, is a naturalistic epistemologist. Indeed, is naturalistic epistemology thus conceived even possible? How could you have an epistemology that entails the nonexistence of God? Of course you could say: "Here is my epistemology: first there is no such person as God, second, . . ."; but would the first conjunct really be *epistemology* as opposed to an irrelevant theological addition? Could you have an evolutionary epistemology just by proclaiming, as its first tenet, that Darwinism is indeed true? (If so, could you also have, e.g., a *vegetarian* epistemology?) This standard for naturalistic epistemology seems a bit high. I don't doubt there can be an epistemology that fits naturally (to use some more softly focused terminology) with philosophical naturalism or atheism, but the relation between it and naturalism will be subtler than entailment.

A more moderate suggestion is embodied in the passage I quoted at the beginning of this section. Perhaps what Conee really means is something like this: "Whatever exactly naturalistic epistemology is (and it may be hard to say just what), at any rate it can't entail the existence of God.'' That seems initially sensible. Of course if traditional theism is true, God is a necessary being, so that every proposition entails the existence of God; but perhaps we can bracket that difficulty, or at any rate ignore it and hope for the best. But *does* my account entail (in the relevant sense, whatever precisely that is) the existence of God? I don't think so. The account does, of course, invoke the notion of proper function; and as a matter of fact I also argue (see WPF chap. 11) that there is no correct naturalistic analysis of proper function. But the latter claim, as I said in response to Swain, is not really part of the epistemology. Someone else could have the same epistemological views as mine even if he thought there *is* an accurate naturalistic analysis of proper function, or was agnostic about whether there is. I also believe that the existence of matter entails the existence of God (and not just by way of the latter's being a necessary being); but I wouldn't think of this claim as part of physics. Suppose I agree with Quine: the content of epistemology is really empirical psychology; but suppose I also believe, e.g., that there couldn't be any living beings unless there were such a person as God: would that mean that my epistemology wasn't naturalistic after all?

There is much more to be said here, and the topic, despite the lightheartedness Conee notes at the end of his paper, seems to me really important. It is of a piece with the question whether there can be such a thing as Christian or theistic philosophy, science, literary criticism, art, and the like. Newton thought God had created the world and instituted the scientific laws and regularities; he also thought gravity was, or was a manifestation of, divine activity; does that make Newtonian physics theistic? If not, what more would be required? Suppose you accept one of the inflationary cosmologies presently on offer because you think they avoid singularities that suggest divine creation, and you think no such suggestions should emanate from science: does that make your physics naturalistic? Van Fraassen addresses some of these questions in his paper. These are excellent questions, but will have to await another occasion.

Ad Feldman

Richard Feldman's penetrating comment makes three claims: (1) that I erred in thinking those whom I called internalists are internalists with respect to *warrant* (they are rather internalists with respect to *justification*, taken one way or another), (2) that my objections to internalistic views are wanting, and (3) that my own view is deficient in that it doesn't properly handle certain Gettier cases. He's right on (3); the deficiency, I hope, is remedied by the amplification of the environmental clause in Part I.

As to (1), I took internalists to be saying that the "basic shape" of warrant is given by an internalist notion (ordinarily justification of one or another variety), together with what I called a codicil or fillip to appease Gettier. Feldman demurs, claiming that internalists don't think of the additional condition needed to evade Gettier as a fillip, or a codicil, or a smallish addition, or anything else of the sort; they don't think of any internalist notion as nearly sufficient for warrant; and while they are internalists about justification, they are not internalists about the fourth condition. Well, as I said above, there is nothing to be gained by arguing about how close to sufficiency internalists think justification is; we must give them the last word about that. So let's agree that internalists think justification is necessary for warrant, but are not prepared to claim that it is anywhere nearly sufficient for it. (Of course, insofar as they are internalists about justification and also think it necessary for warrant, they are internalists about warrant in the sense that they are internalists about (what they see as) a necessary condition of warrant.)

But *is* justification necessary for warrant? The real question, as it seems to me, is whether internalists really succeed in stating even a *third* condition of knowledge, a condition that is both necessary for warrant or knowledge and independent of belief. I argued this above with respect to justification taken deontologically, as a matter of doxastic or epistemic responsibility. But the same goes, I think, for the other main branch of the justification tradition: the idea that justification is a matter of forming and sustaining belief only on the basis of evidence. I should like to illustrate this problem for internalists with reference to Feldman's own internalist view, *evidentialism*.[54] This is an important view, and one with a long and distinguished history. On Feldman's version, a belief is justified for S if and only if it fits S's evidence. I criticized evidentialism in WCD; Feldman responded in "Proper Functionalism," *Nous* XXVII, 1 (March 1993); my riposte, involving a further criticism of evidentialism, was in "Why We Need Proper Function" (*loc. cit.*); and here we have Feldman's reply to *that*. Feldman's present response, however, involves misunderstanding, no doubt due as much to expository ineptness on my part as hermeneutical inadequacy on his. Let me try again.

My criticism went as follows. First, concede that the evidentialist internalist is making only the limited claim that justification is necessary for warrant and that S's belief B is justified just if it fits S's evidence. To evaluate this claim, of course, we must know what is to count as evidence. My claim was that the evidentialist faces a dilemma (or possibly a trilemma); no matter how he construes *evidence*, he winds up in hot water. More specifically, either he winds up with a condition that isn't necessary, or he winds up with one that isn't independent of belief (and thus isn't even a third condition). We can see this as follows. What are the possibilities for construing this notion of evidence? First, there is *propositional* evidence: my propositional evidence for one of my beliefs is one or more other beliefs on the evidential basis of which I hold the belief in question.[55] Although most twentieth-century discussions have tended to limit evidence to propositional evidence, the Feldmanian evidentialist can't sensibly do so. The reason is familiar: we know (for example) simple arithmetical truths as well as certain propositions about our own mental life, neither of which are accepted on the evidential basis of other propositions; propositional evidence is not necessary for knowledge. Second, then, there is *sensuous* evidence, for example, sensuous imagery of the sort involved in visual (and other sorts of) perception. What we have in these cases is 'the evidence of the senses'—the phenomenological sensuous evidence furnished by way of being appeared to in those characteristic ways involved in perception. Can the evidentialist rest here, i.e., can he sensibly hold that evidence is exhausted in propositional and sensuous evidence? I don't think so; fitting the evidence thus construed isn't necessary for warrant. Consider my knowledge that $2 + 1 = 3$ or any other obvious mathematical or logical truth. I don't believe this proposition on the evidential basis of any other proposition, but I also don't believe it on the basis of sensuous imagery.[56] So it doesn't fit my evidence;[57] but it is obviously warranted for me. If evidence is construed in either of these two ways, or as their disjunction, justification (fitting the evidence) isn't necessary for warrant or knowledge.

There is one further possibility: what in WPF and "Why We Need Proper Function" I called "impulsional" evidence. That sensuous imagery I mentioned isn't the only kind of phenomenology that can be thought of as evidence. Consider again the belief that $2 + 1 = 3$; in addition to the sensuous imagery there is also something like a certain *felt attractiveness* of the belief; it *feels* right, somehow, and other beliefs you might consider in its place ($2 + 1 = 5$?) feel wrong, weird, absurd, eminently rejectable. $2 + 1 = 3$ has about it a sense of rightness, or fittingness, or appropriateness. Perhaps the thing to say is that there is a sort of felt inclination, or impulse, to accept this proposition as opposed to others; indeed, perhaps impulsional evidence is no more than the phenomenal reflection of the fact that you do in fact believe the proposition in question. In any event, this kind of phenomenology is involved in *a priori* belief, but in all other sorts of belief as well. In the *a priori* case, then, there are really two quite different sorts of experience or phenomenology: the fleeting, fragmentary, indistinct, unstable, sometimes random sensuous imagery, on the one hand, and on the other, the felt inclination or impulse to believe *that* proposition, as opposed to others that might suggest themselves. Many other kinds of beliefs involve both these kinds of phenomenal experience and, as far as I can see, all beliefs involve impulsional evidence.

Now return to the Feldmanian evidentialist, who holds that a necessary condition of *p*'s having warrant for *S* is that *p* fits *S*'s evidence. As we saw, if he means by 'evidence' just propositional evidence, or propositional evidence together with sensuous evidence, then he is mistaken: a belief can be warranted without enjoying the benefit of either of those kinds of evidence. But perhaps he can construe 'evidence' very broadly, including under that rubric this felt impulse to believe, this sense of the proposition's being true or right. If he takes 'evidence' in *that* way, then, I think, he's right in claiming that evidence is a necessary condition of warrant (and knowledge). But then he has *another* problem. For the evidentialist, clearly enough, means to assert that justification is a necessary condition of warrant, and a necessary condition *in addition* to the truth and belief conditions. But taken this way the evidential condition adds nothing to the belief condition. You have impulsional evidence for *p* just by virtue of *believing p*; *p* fits *this* kind of evidence just if you believe it. It isn't even possible that you believe *p* but lack impulsional evidence for it: how could it be that you believe *p* although *p* doesn't seem to you to be true?[58] If so, however, what the evidentialist really needs is not a *fourth* condition, but a *third*. For evidential justification (construed thus broadly) guarantees only belief and a necessary accompaniment of belief: the nonsensuous phenomenal counterpart of the belief, the sense that the proposition believed is indeed true. So the proposition that *S*'s belief that *p* fits *S*'s evidence, on this construal of 'evidence', is satisfied by *S*'s merely believing *p*.

My point, then, was (and is) that the evidentialist faces a dilemma. If he takes the notion of evidence *narrowly*, so that it includes propositional evidence together with sensuous phenomenal evidence, but does not include impulsional evidence, then he is mistaken in claiming that justification is necessary for warrant (knowledge): in many cases of warranted belief—many cases of memory and *a priori* belief, for example—the belief need fit neither phenomenal nor propositional evidence. On the other hand, if he takes 'evidence' broadly (so that it includes impulsional evidence) then justification is indeed necessary for warrant—but only because it is necessary for belief itself. If so, however, the evidentialist isn't proposing a further condition of warrant independent of truth and belief; what he proposes is only a necessary condition of belief. Given that the evidentialist intends one or the other of these construals of evidence (and he certainly hasn't suggested any others), his evidential condition is either not necessary or not independent of the belief condition. In either case he fails to state a further necessary condition of warrant; so the fact is he hasn't so far stated a necessary condition of knowledge independent of the belief condition.

I hope this clarifies the point.

Ad Markie

Peter Markie concludes (1) that my account of degrees is not well developed, (2) that a certain conditional which on my account would have to be necessarily true is in fact contingent if true at all, and (3) that my account, as it stands, has no place for epistemically inappropriate degrees of warranted belief. As to (1), he is of course right, and I thank him for helping me think about the matter to a bit better effect.

Things are less clear with respect to (2) and (3), however. Begin with (3):

> Plantinga's theory does not allow for cases of warranted belief in which the degree of belief is epistemically inappropriate. Consider first the cases in which our confidence is too low, those in which we are warranted in believing p but believe p with less intensity than is called for by its degree of warrant. According to Plantinga's theory, since our degree of belief is inappropriate, our belief is not the result of a properly functioning cognitive faculty aimed at the truth, in which case our belief is unwarranted and our degree of belief is not epistemically insufficient after all. . . . Now consider the cases in which our confidence is inappropriately high, those in which we are warranted in believing p but believe p with more intensity than is called for by its degree of warrant. Once again, according to Plantinga's theory, since our level of belief is inappropriate,

our belief is . . . unwarranted and our degree of belief is excessive, not because it is more than the belief's positive degree of warrant deserves, but because the belief has no warrant at all. Plantinga's theory thus precludes the existence of warranted beliefs in which the belief level is too high. (p. 231)

As it stands, this criticism is question begging. I proposed that degree of warrant (given the satisfaction of the conditions of warrant) is proportional to degree of belief (or is at least a monotonic, increasing function of the latter); but this quotation from Markie presupposes that degree of warrant is *not* such a function of degree of belief. So suppose we restate the objection: the claim is that there are some cases where someone's belief is warranted for her, but she holds the belief in question with too little firmness, and others where her belief is warranted for her, but she holds it with too *much* firmness. An example of the first would be the sort of case in which I have a great deal of evidence for some proposition *p*—that my mother's name is 'Lettie' or that it is likely that I will die within the next couple of years—but for one reason or another do not believe *p* with the firmness it deserves. I do indeed *believe p* (I don't merely think it probable) but I don't believe it firmly. In that case, says Markie, the fact is the belief obviously has a great deal of warrant for me. This is a problem for me, in that the firmness of the belief diverges from that dictated by the design plan: hence there is cognitive malfunction, in which case on my view the belief has little or no warrant.

But *does* this belief have much by way of warrant for me? If I don't believe it firmly, then surely I *don't know* it, no matter how much evidence I have for it. That seems to me to be a pretty obvious feature of our concept of knowledge. Someone might say that a diffident student really knows the answers to the exam questions, even if (due to lack of self-confidence) he is quite unconfident of them. But this (I think) is an analogical extension of the central concept: he *should* know (he has evidence sufficient for knowing) and he *would* know if it weren't for that lack of self-confidence; but the fact is (in the literal and central use) he *doesn't* know; he isn't convinced of the answer, or he isn't firmly enough convinced. So I doubt that there is a real problem here.

The other sort of case—the case where someone has enough evidence for knowledge, but believes too firmly—worries me more. To think about these cases to good effect, we must think about the degrees of belief compatible with knowledge. First, to know one must of course believe *simpliciter*; this is distinct from being willing to bestow some degree of probability—even a probability of 1—on the proposition in question (see WPF p. 8). Second, there are degrees of belief, and also degrees of belief compatible with knowledge; that is, there are propositions p and q such that I know both, but believe p more firmly than q. So suppose I know (and hence believe) both that I went to the beach yesterday (I clearly remember doing so) and that $2 + 1 = 3$. The design plan dictates (so I say) that someone in my position should believe these two to different degrees: the second should be believed with maximum firmness, but the first to some degree a bit short of that. But suppose (contrary to the design plan) I believe both first and second to the max. Then don't I still know the first, even though I believe it to a degree different from that specified by the design plan, so that my faculties are malfunctioning (to at least a moderate degree) in producing in me a belief as firm as all that? Well, it is clear, first, that this belief doesn't have as much warrant for me as $2 + 1 = 3$, even though I believe it as firmly as the latter. But doesn't it have *some* warrant, and indeed enough warrant for knowledge? You and my other friends will indulgently concede that I do know that I went to the beach yesterday, even if my belief on that head is a little too enthusiastic.

The answer, I think, is that while there is a *bit* of malfunction here, it isn't significant enough to destroy warrant.[59] For my faculties to be functioning properly, in the relevant sense, it isn't necessary that they be functioning *perfectly* (see WPF pp. 10–11). I can know a lot by virtue of vision, even if my vision isn't 20–20; I can know much by way of memory even if (as with other people my age) it doesn't work quite up to the specifications of the design plan. I'd say the same here: warrant is determined by the degree of belief specified in the design plan, given that the conditions of warrant are met. But the proper function condition can be met even if it isn't met perfectly, and I think that is what is going on in this case.

Finally, and perhaps most worrisome, Markie argues that what he calls the Degrees of Warrant Principle,

(DW) Under the conditions of warrant, degree of warrant is an increasing function of degree of belief,

contrary to what my view requires, is a contingent truth if true at all. He suggests that the crucial premise in the most plausible argument I could give for the necessity of (DW) would be the necessity of his (3) (p. 227):

> (3) The degrees of belief dictated by the design plan for any faculty, insofar as the design plan is aimed at producing true beliefs, are proportional to the degrees of warrant the beliefs formed by the faculty will have if warranted. (p. 227)

Couldn't we (as Markie argues) have been designed by an incompetent designer,[60] one who assigns the wrong degrees of belief to a given belief in a given situation? (3) does seem contingent, at least within the parameters of this inquiry.

But my account does not require that (3) *be* necessary. According to (DW), *under the conditions of warrant*, degree of warrant is a monotonically increasing function of degree of belief. (That is compatible with different degrees of belief being mapped to the same degree of warrant and indeed, strictly speaking, with all degrees of belief being mapped to the same degree of warrant; it is not compatible, of course, with the same degree of belief being mapped to different degrees of warrant.) But among the conditions of warrant is that of the design plan's being a *good* one; so what I am committed to is the claim that if the design plan in question is a *good* one, then it will mandate that degree of warrant be an increasing function of degree of belief.

Of course that doesn't automatically get me out of trouble; it all depends upon what goodness for a design plan requires. I explained goodness in terms of reliability: if a belief has warrant, then "the module of the design plan governing its production must be such that it is objectively highly probable that a belief produced by cognitive faculties functioning properly according to that module (in a congenial environment) will be true or verisimilitudinous" (WPF p. 18). I was thinking of this reliability condition as an *explication* of goodness for a design plan; but Markie's points incline me to think that it should instead be thought of as just one of the conditions entailed by goodness for a design plan. Perhaps another condition is that the design plan be such that degree of warrant be a monotonically increasing function of degree of belief. This condition is (trivially) satisfied by such a being as God, all of whose beliefs (presumably) are held to the same degree and enjoy the same (maximal) degree of warrant; it is also met by any other knowers all of whose beliefs have the same degree of warrant. But for creatures like us, creatures with beliefs of differing degrees of warrant, it requires differing degrees of belief, and requires that where belief *A* has more warrant than *B*, then *A* will be believed more firmly than *B*. It isn't hard to see how this would go. Indeed, perhaps degree of warrant is correlated both with degree of firmness of belief and also with degree of reliability. For example, consider *a priori* belief. This faculty or power produces belief of maximal firmness with respect to simple logical and arithmetical truths. These beliefs are also the ones with maximal warrant; and no doubt they are also the ones (so we think, anyway) where the faculty in question is most reliable, most likely to produce true belief.

Ad Pappas

"Ad Pappas" is a misnomer: since all of what George Pappas says seems eminently sensible, I have nothing to say in reply. I have perhaps one question. Pappas suggests that people who have learned how to reason in accord with a rule like *modus ponens* do not now but at one time had to reason by way of paying explicit attention to the rule:

> . . . they have reached a stage at which they achieve new knowledge in this domain—for example, that this sequence admits of modus ponens detachment—without the need to rely on rules which describe permissible moves when formulas have specific structures. No doubt when they first learned elementary logic they needed to fall back on the rule, perhaps recalling to mind what the rule was and then carefully noting that a given sequence falls under the rule. But now. . . . (p. 245)

He goes on to compare such a reasoner with a person whose job it is to classify buttons according to a rule: at first she must constantly consult the rule, but later on the rule becomes internalized and she follows it automatically.

Perhaps this is right if we are thinking of exercises in formal logic. There we have sentential or propositional variables (or schematic letters) and formalized patterns of "inference"; and we have to check carefully to see whether a pair of sentences do in fact meet the conditions for being the premises of *modus ponens*. But if we are thinking of actual reasoning (and perhaps this is not what Pappas is thinking of), the sort we all do unselfconsciously in ordinary life and more self-consciously and explicitly in philosophy, then, so it seems to me, this description wouldn't be accurate. I doubt that there is ever a stage in our learning to reason in which we explicitly reason by way of applying the rule *modus ponens*. Rather, even as very young children we see, with respect to a specific conditional proposition, that it must be the case that if its antecedent is true, then so is its consequent; if we also believe or learn the antecedent, we automatically draw the conclusion. Following Aristotle, I conjecture we first see these relations in specific cases and then later on derive or (more likely) hear the rule from others. But of course Pappas may not have intended anything to the contrary.

Ad Sosa

Ernest Sosa is widely and rightly known as a fine epistemologist, but also as a person of generous spirit. This generosity is made manifest in his writing *two* essays for this volume! I have a brief comment on each. In the first, "Plantinga on Epistemic Internalism," Sosa reflects on my suggestion that we can understand current internalism about justification (and warrant) if we note that justification is conceived *deontologically*, in terms of epistemic duty, obligation, requirement.[61] My idea was that there is a certain internal connection (or congeries of connections) between internalism and justificationism taken deontologically.

Now Sosa distinguishes three grades of justificatory involvement and suggests that the one relevant to my discussion ("Let us focus on epistemic justification of the third degree—the sort of epistemic justification used by Plantinga to defend deontologism as a route to epistemic internalism," p. 81) goes like this:

> (Sosa Justification) S is *justified$_3$* (justified to the third degree) in ∅'ing iff in ∅'ing S abides by an objective duty through a knowledgeable choice or at least through a choice based on a correct belief as to what one ought then to do. . . . (p. 77)

Sosa then argues that deontologism falls into an infinite regress here (p. 8): you are justified in believing a proposition P_1 only if you justifiably believe

P2 Believing P1 is right;

but of course you are justified in believing P2 only if you justifiably believe

P3 Believing P2 is right;

and so on. So you would be justified in believing any proposition P1 only if you believe infinitely many propositions, a feat most of us can't manage.

But is the requisite sense of justification really as demanding as (Sosa Justification)? The analogy, of course, is with justified actions, permissible actions, actions with respect to which I am within my rights. But can't I be justified, in taking such an action, even if I do not explicitly hold the belief that the action in question *is* right? I am within my rights in crossing my right leg over my left; no doubt I was within my rights on every occasion when I performed that maneuver; but I doubt that I ever formed the belief that this was indeed permissible. The question never really came up. Is it really required, for me to be within my rights, that I raise the question whether this *is* the right thing to do? I'm inclined to think not. So I'm inclined to think the regress never begins: what objective justification requires is that the action in question be in fact in accord with the right rule; what subjective justification requires is that I be nonculpable in not believing that the action in question is wrong; neither requires that I have formed the belief that it is in fact right.

But if the regress *does* begin, it ends almost as quickly as it begins. For suppose I am wrong: suppose it *is* required, somehow, that I believe, perhaps in some implicit and *sub tabula* way, that the action in question is justified. And suppose furthermore I do indeed believe that it is. I don't, it seems to me, have to raise the *further* question whether I am (deontologically) justified in believing that the action is justified, in order to be within my rights in believing that it *is* justified. For in many or most cases it simply isn't up to me whether or not I believe this. It's as obvious as $7 + 5 = 12$ that there is nothing wrong with drawing a breath, or crossing my right leg over my left (rather than *vice versa*). I am certainly within my rights in believing the former, if only because I can't believe anything else; the same goes, I think, for the latter. But then I will be within my rights in believing that I may cross my right leg over my left, no matter what else I believe; in particular, it isn't required that I raise the question whether I *am* within my rights in believing that.

As it looks to me, then, the regress doesn't get started at all, or else it ends after the first step.

Sosa's other contribution, "Postscript to 'Proper Functionalism and Virtue Epistemology,' " is a continuation of a discussion which began with his "Proper Functionalism and Virtue Epistemology" in a *Nous* symposium on my Warrant books and continued with my reply,

"Why We Need Proper Function."[62] Sosa argues that his own "virtue epistemology" is simpler and more plausible than mine, inasmuch as mine involves the notions of proper function and design plan. He and I agree that a belief is warranted only if it is produced by an ability, or faculty, or power; we also agree that faculties are the sorts of things that have functions, and that they can function properly or improperly. Where we disagree, though, is over my suggestion that the notion of proper function involves that of design: "And the notion of 'functioning *properly*' is not far to seek. In none of that, however, do I see a need to import any notion of design, either theological or merely teleological" (p. 273).

Well, at the level of *epistemology*, I'm not sure we disagree. I say the notion of warrant involves the notion of proper function; Sosa apparently agrees. I go on to say that it isn't possible to give a 'naturalistic' account or explanation or analysis on the notion of proper function; here apparently Sosa disagrees. But the latter claim isn't really part of the epistemology, as I see it; I should have thought it's a *metaphysical* claim, not an epistemological claim.[63] Sosa's *epistemology*, as far as I can see, involves the notions of faculties having functions (including that of furnishing us with true beliefs), of their functioning properly (and surely here he'd want to note the relativity of the latter to the right kind of environment), and of their being 'well designed'—i.e., such that when they do function properly, they do furnish us with true beliefs. But these are also the basic elements of my account of warrant, which can be expressed in just those terms: a belief has warrant for *S*, so I say, if and only if it is produced by cognitive faculties that (a) are functioning properly in the right kind of (maxi- and mini-) environment, (b) have the production of true beliefs as their function, and (c) are 'well designed' in the sense that there is a high objective probability that a belief meeting the two preceding conditions will be true. So I can't see that Sosa's *epistemology* is simpler and more streamlined than mine, although his *metaphysics* might be. Of course if I am right and the notion of proper function *entails* that of design, then his metaphysics will be simpler only at the cost of failing to include an important truth, or, worse, embracing necessary falsehood.

In "Proper Functionalism and Virtue Epistemology" Sosa argues that proper function (cognitive proper function, anyway) doesn't entail design by offering an account of what it is for a cognitive faculty to function properly (an account that doesn't involve intelligent design): it does so if it "tracks the truth." I mistakenly took him to intend this in *Nozick's* sense and offered objections; in "Postscript to 'Proper Functionalism and Virtue Epistemology' '' he now points out that he *wasn't* following Nozick here. What he did and does intend is

> *S*'s cognitive faculty *F* tracks the truth (and functions properly) if and only if, (1) if *P* were true *F* would produce (in *S*) the belief *P*, and (2) if *F* were to produce (in *S*) the belief that *P*, *P* would be true. (p. 276)

He then goes on to point out that this account of tracking has several advantages over Nozick's.

Now this isn't a *general* ('naturalistic') account of proper function; it applies only to belief-producing faculties or processes. Of course that's no problem in the present context. If (contrary to expectations) Sosa can give a 'naturalistic' account of proper function for cognitive faculties, more power to him—whether or not it is possible to give such an account of proper function generally. And his account *does* seem superior to Nozick's. But it still won't do the trick. A cognitive faculty can meet this condition without functioning properly; this account (like the more general naturalistic accounts of proper function[64]) isn't sufficient. Consider, first, necessary truths, e.g., Gödel's First Theorem, or the Fundamental Theorem of the Calculus. Note that the instantiations of the first of the two tracking conditions with such a necessary truth yield a conditional that has a necessary antecedent and a contingent consequent; instantiations of the second condition with a necessary truth yield a conditional with a necessary consequent and a contingent antecedent. Both are problematic. Take the second:

> If faculty *F* were to produce belief in Gödel's theorem (i.e., produce a belief whose content was Gödel's theorem) Gödel's theorem would be true.

Well, no doubt; and also, if F were to produce belief in the *denial* of the theorem, it would be true. I suppose the plausible thing to think here is that a faculty automatically meets this condition for any necessary truth; this conditional is a necessary truth.

Not so, of course, for the first condition:

> If Gödel's theorem were true, *F* would produce belief in it.

What does this *mean,* and when or how would it be true? It's not wholly clear. Suppose we think about it from the perspective of possible worlds: this conditional will be true if and only if, in the nearby worlds in which Gödel's theorem is true, F produces belief in it. Of course the theorem is true in all the nearby possible worlds (as well as those afar off); this condition, therefore, reduces to the claim that in the nearby possible worlds, *F* produces belief (in *S*) in Gödel's theorem. But that is quite compatible with *F*'s malfunctioning. Perhaps *S* believes the theorem, not because he can see or prove that it is true, but because he suffers from a malady which causes him to believe any mathematical proposition whose name in English begins with 'G', or perhaps any mathematical statement of a certain level of complexity; or because he is obsessed with German mathematicians and automatically believes any mathematical claim he thinks put forward by any German mathematician. (Sadly enough, he also believes that arithmetic is complete, thinking that this claim was put forward by Hilbert.) Then his cognitive faculties, at least the ones involved in producing the belief in question, are not functioning properly, despite their meeting this tracking condition. And of course if I'm right about this case, the same will go for nearly any other necessary truth. Thus (as I see it) the existence of God is a necessary truth. Now while of course I don't for a moment agree with those sociologists of religion who think any belief in God a matter of cognitive malfunction, I should think it would be *possible* that belief in the existence of God be produced by malfunctioning cognitive faculties. If so, however, those beliefs would meet Sosa's tracking conditions but result from cognitive malfunction (and would therefore lack warrant).

The same problem will arise for very many contingent truths—they too will be such that a malfunctioning faculty can meet Sosa's tracking conditions in producing belief in them. Any proposition true in all the nearby possible worlds will be of that sort. This would include propositions stating physical regularities (the velocity of light, the values for the force of gravity and for the weak and strong nuclear forces, the fact that the earth is very old, the distance from the earth to the sun, and the like). Each automatically is such that if I were to believe it, it would be true; each also meets the converse condition if in fact I believe it in all the nearby possible worlds—no matter what the source of the belief, and even if the source is in some kind of cognitive dysfunction. So I doubt that Sosa's naturalistic account of cognitive proper function is successful.

Ad Kvanvig

Jonathan Kvanvig pleads for more breadth, more scope. We should see warrant (the property or quantity enough of which distinguishes knowledge from mere true belief) as a special case of something broader—indeed, of *two* things broader. On the one hand, he proposes that we think of warrant not just as a property of *beliefs*, but also as a property of (or relation among) propositions just as such, regardless of believers or knowers and their idiosyncrasies. On the other hand, there are many propositional attitudes in addition to belief: doubt, withholding, assuming, hope, fear, desire, disgust, and the like. Kvanvig thinks that warrant (as a property of beliefs) is just a special case of a property that can attach to these other propositional attitudes as well: he laments the fact that I don't provide an account of this more general property.[65] He also claims that I am an Aristotelian in epistemology. In his use, this is not a compliment: "Aristotelianism in epistemology offers a distinctive answer to the question of where to begin, an answer I will argue is incorrect" (p. 282).

As to the suggestion that there is a great deal more to epistemology than an exploration of warrant, I enthusiastically agree. First, warrant is only one kind among others of positive epistemic status that can be enjoyed by beliefs: there is an additional whole litany of epistemic values that can be enjoyed by beliefs (WPF p. 2). And second, Kvanvig is quite right in pointing to all those other propositional attitudes and their importance.[66] By way of self-exculpation, I suppose I might offer a couple of bromides: we have to start somewhere, and warrant is as good a place as any; we can't do everything, and hence can't be faulted for picking one worthwhile project as opposed to all the others. At bottom, I think this has to be my defense; but I am prepared to concede that possibility that one can't do a really proper job on warrant without exploring the analogically related properties of these other propositional attitudes.

Indeed, the fact is work of this kind is very much needed. Since Descartes, Locke, and the Enlightenment, the standard view (among intellectuals at any rate) has been that one can never go wrong by withholding belief.[67] The mark of the wise person is a certain chariness about belief, a certain doxastic standoffishness, reluctance, restraint. What is required is temperance. You can never go wrong by withholding, but you can easily go wrong by believing. You can easily make a fool of yourself by believing unwisely, but not by abstaining from belief. Belief is a little like alcohol, and the standard view concurs with the attitude of the WCTU towards the latter: possibly it's acceptable in moderation, but it can be very dangerous, and all things considered, perhaps abstinence is the only completely safe stance. But of course this can't really be correct for belief; the standard view is mistaken

here. A person who fails to believe that there are other people or that
there has been a past is not an epistemic saint whose virtues far exceed
that of the run of humanity; she is more like an epistemic invalid
suffering from a cognitive disorder. Obviously there is such a thing
as undue fastidiousness with respect to belief. One can go wrong
(epistemically speaking) by failing to believe just as well as by believing; there is no safe haven. This has important application in philosophy of religion: we aren't just given in advance that agnosticism is a
safe and secure epistemic haven, with belief in God a somewhat risky
and speculative epistemic venture.

So I applaud Kvanvig's desire for a broader look; certainly there is
at least an analogue of warrant for other propositional attitudes, and I
have no doubt that a careful look at these analogues would throw light
on warrant (for beliefs). But this is a task for someone else: I commend
it to Kvanvig himself.

On the other hand, I am less happy with his (anti-Aristotelian, he
says) suggestions about an analogue of warrant for *propositions* (as
opposed to beliefs). In part this is because I don't really understand
him. Sufficient for being an Aristotelian, he seems to say, is thinking
that (according to the central and paradigmatic core of our notion of
warrant) it is fundamentally *beliefs* that have warrant (though by
extension we can speak of a proposition p's having warrant for a
person when her belief that p does). But is there an alternative?
Warrant is (roughly) whatever must be added to true belief to get
knowledge; that is, it is a property or quantity had by *beliefs*. So how
could the basic notion of warrant fail to attach initially to beliefs? How
could it be that the basic notion here is warrant as had by *propositions*?

Kvanvig also says that "for the Aristotelian epistemologist, doxastic
warrant has primacy over propositional support" (p. 283). This and
other things he says suggest that what he is really interested in is a
supports relation that holds between (among) propositions—an *evidential* relation that holds between p and q whether or not anyone
recognizes or responds to its holding. Perhaps he is thinking of either
logical or objective conditional probability (including entailment as a
special case) (see WPF pp. 140–42, 144–51); or perhaps he is thinking
of conditional epistemic probability (WPF chap. 8 and 9). (The difference would be that conditional epistemic probability is independent of
individual believers but does involve a reference to the human (or
other) design plan, while objective conditional probability does not.)
What leads me to doubt that these are what Kvanvig has in mind is

that in fact I did say a fair amount about these notions, and Kvanvig says I didn't deal with the property or relation *he's* interested in.

Kvanvig's main concern, however, is in the question whether 'propositional support' can be defined in terms of what he calls 'propositional warrant'—the sort of warrant a belief *p* can receive by being accepted on the evidential basis of another belief *q* that evidentially supports it. Put in his terms, this is the question whether 'propositional support' can be understood in terms of what he calls 'psychological support'. The former is (apparently) just a relation among propositions; the latter is a relation among propositions and people. (*That the butler did it* has psychological support for Holmes, who sees how the evidence bears on the question; it has only propositional support for Watson, who has the same evidence (believes those propositions that in fact support the proposition that the butler did it) but doesn't see the evidential connection and believes just on a hunch.) Kvanvig argues—convincingly, I think—that it is at any rate extremely difficult to see how propositional support could be defined or explained in terms of psychological support.

As I say, I am not entirely confident of my understanding of Kvanvig here. Insofar as I do understand him, I take him to be claiming that (to put things in my terminology) neither objective nor logical (conditional) probability can be defined or explained in terms of epistemic probability (WPF chap. 8 and 9). This seems right, and the account of epistemic conditional probability I gave makes an essential reference to logical probability. (On the other hand, epistemic probability is not *just* a special case of logical or objective probability. The logical probability of *p* on *q* can be very high when the epistemic probability of *p* on *q* is not—if, for example, no human being could grasp or understand the propositions or see the relevant relationships.) So neither is explicitly definable just in terms of the other, but epistemic probability is to be explained partly in terms of objective probability. But doesn't that make me an *anti-Aristotelian*, rather than an Aristotelian, as Kvanvig claims?

There is much more to be said about Kvanvig's contribution, as indeed about all the others. Sufficient unto the day is the discussion therein, however, and I am obliged to stop here—though not without thanking the contributors once more for these fine essays.

Notes

I'm extremely grateful for penetrating criticism and wise counsel to Mike Bergmann, Andrew Koehl, Kevin Meeker, Trenton Merricks, and Mike Rea.

1. "Is Justified True Belief Knowledge?" *Analysis* 23 (1963) pp. 121–23.

2. See WCD pp. 6–8.

3. For a fuller explanation of these examples see WCD pp. 31 ff.

4. Though often attributed to Alvin Goldman, this example was first used by Ginet; see G. C. Stine, "Skepticism and Relevant Alternatives," *Philosophical Studies* 29, 1976, p. 254. Stine also reports that Goldman attributes the example to Ginet.

5. Designed, whether by God or evolution. In what follows, I'll understand this qualification but not constantly repeat it.

6. More exactly (in view of the case of the aging forest ranger), proper function of cognitive powers and processes *internal* to the epistemic agent.

7. See Trenton Merricks, "Warrant Entails Truth," *Philosophy and Phenomenological Research* 55 (1995), 841–55.

8. Feldman proposes a similar example on pp. 217–18, as does Robert Shope in "Gettier Problems" (*Routledge Encyclopedia of Philosophy*), and his forthcoming book *Knowledge as Power*. Like Klein's, Shope's example is automotive.

9. Although of course there could be similar environments elsewhere in the universe, and environments sufficiently similar to permit us to have knowledge, were we somehow transported to them.

10. In WPF I wasn't clear about the distinction between cognitive maxi- and mini-environments; Swain (esp. p. 140) asks penetrating questions about my treatment of cognitive environments.

11. A proposition p is true (false) in a situation S just if necessarily, if S had been actual, p would have been true (false). So what I mean here, of course, is not that the proposition S *forms a true belief* has the property of being neither true nor false in the cognitive mini-environment in question, but only that it doesn't have the property of being true in that situation, and also doesn't have the property of being false in it.

12. We must therefore say that a cognitive faculty—vision, say—can be unreliable in a given mini-environment M even though it is reliable in the maxi-environment included in M.

13. Though I am unable to tell what he means by 'justification': see p. 346.

14. Furthermore, the official account was supposed to explicate the rough and ready genuineness condition according to which "a defeater is genuine just in case it defeats without depending upon a false proposition"; $-A$, in the example, meets the official condition for genuineness, but it obviously *does* depend upon a false proposition—my mistaken belief (C). What has gone awry? Klein's meaning, I think, is that a *misleading* defeater is one such that the falsehood upon which its defeating force depends, attaches to the defeater *itself*, not to one of my beliefs. (Clearly I could acquire a genuine defeater for one of my beliefs by coming to believe something false.)

15. (Minneapolis: University of Minnesota Press, 1981), pp. 137–50.

16. The issues here are relevant to philosophy of religion. Suppose theism

is true and there is such a thing as the *Sensus Divinitatis* (perhaps restored and extended by what Calvin calls "the internal testimony of the Holy Spirit") and suppose my belief (G) that there is such a person as God is properly based on these sources, thus constituting knowledge. But then I reflect on the evil the world contains and come to believe that the probability of (G) given the existence of (e.g.) suffering on the part of innocent children is low. Even if this probability belief is in fact mistaken, and even if I continue to believe (G), it could be that I no longer *know* (G).

17. For strictures on this suggestion, see WPF p. 164.

18. For example, it could be that the existence of evil together with the rest of what I believe is such that belief in God is not justified for me (in Klein's sense); it doesn't follow that I don't know that there is such a person as God. For perhaps the nonpropositional warrant theistic belief gets (e.g., from Calvin's *Sensus Divinitatis*) is strong enough to counterbalance the weakness of the propositional evidence.

19. But see "Reliabilism, Analyses and Defeaters," pp. 427–34, for hints.

20. *Ibid.*, p. 428.

21. In particular the proposition *I am drunk and my faculties are malfunctioning* won't be such a defeater. Adding it to a set of propositions standing in the is-a-good-reason-for relation to another doesn't yield a set that doesn't stand in that relation to that other.

22. See "Reliabilism, Analyses and Defeaters," pp. 429–34.

23. "Epistemic Operators," *Journal of Philosophy* vol. 67, 1970, pp. 1007 ff., and "Conclusive Reason," *Australasian Journal of Philosophy* vol. 49, 1971, pp. 1 ff.

24. In *Knowledge and the Flow of Information* (Cambridge, Mass.: MIT Press, 1981), pp. 172–178.

25. In *Philosophical Explanations* (Cambridge, Mass.: Harvard University Press, 1981). (Nozick's account is very similar to the early Dretske's.)

26. *The Semantic Conception of Theories and Scientific Realism* (Chicago: University of Illinois Press, 1989), p. 368.

27. There is such a distinction, and it is important; but it isn't needed to evade Gettier.

28. See his *Metaepistemology and Skepticism* (Lanham, Md., and London: 1995), p. 123.

29. See my "Positive Epistemic Status and Proper Function" in *Philosophical Perspectives 2, Epistemology*, 1988, ed. James Tomberlin (Atascadero, Calif.: Ridgeview, 1988), pp. 15–18.

30. *Judgement and Justification* (Cambridge: Cambridge University Press, 1987).

31. Compare my "impulsional evidence" (WPF pp. 192–93). In my view, however, a belief produced by cognitive malfunction—e.g., the belief that I am Napoleon—need have no warrant at all, despite the fact that it enjoys impulsional evidence.

32. And if you think that his beliefs really *were* fairly coherent, think about a person whose beliefs (by virtue of cognitive malfunction, say) are not.

33. But what about beliefs like the two I just mentioned? Do they constitute reflective knowledge or animal knowledge? If the former, then not all reflective knowledge requires explanatory coherence; if the latter, then animal knowledge is necessary for reflective knowledge, so that the latter is not reflective all the way down.

34. *Inquiries and Essays,* ed. by Ronald Beanblossom and Keith Lehrer (Indianapolis: Hackett, 1983), pp. 275–76.

35. Briefly, I think it requires too much; for example, it isn't necessary, for knowledge, to believe or accept that you aren't isolated in his sense; you might know much, even if this thought has never occurred to you.

36. Among published and semipublished objections are William Alston's comments on the paper, presented at a conference at Santa Clara University in the spring of 1992, Carl Ginet's "Comment's on Plantinga's Two Volume Work on Warrant" *Philosophy and Phenomenological Research* (Vol. LV, No. 2), June 1995, pp. 403 ff., Timothy O'Connor's "An Evolutionary Argument Against Naturalism?" *Canadian Journal of Philosophy* (Vol. 24, No. 4) Dec. 1994, pp. 527 ff., Richard Otte's comments on the paper, presented at the same symposium as Alston's, Glenn Ross's "Undefeated Naturalism" and David Hunt's "Is Metaphysical Naturalism Self-Defeating?" presented at the Pacific Division meetings of the APA in March 1994, Leopold Stubenberg's "Is Naturalism Really Defeated?" presented at a colloquium at the University of Notre Dame in 1994, Wesley Robbins's "Is Naturalism Irrational?" *Faith and Philosophy* (Vol. 11, No. 2) April 1994, pp. 255 ff., and a paper by Evan Fales presented at the Central Division meetings of the APA in April 1995. In "Naturalism Defeated" (presently unpublished but copies available) I consider these and other objections to the argument, concluding that they are inconclusive, and that the argument stands.

37. In "Naturalism Defeated," this is the "Second Principle of Defeat" (I owe this principle to Steven Wykstra). For more detail on this principle, and on defeaters generally, see that paper.

38. See his *A Treatise Concerning the Religious Affections,* ed. by John E. Smith (New Haven: Yale University Press, 1959), pp. 95 ff.

39. BonJour thinks my stipulative notion of warrant "unfortunate"; his reason is that what is required in addition to true belief are perhaps *two* conditions (not just one) and furthermore two conditions that are "incommensurable." I agree with the latter (modulo a bit of a puzzlement about incommensurability) but don't see the problem. As a matter of fact I take warrant to be something like the conjunction of *four* conditions: proper function, appropriate (mini- and maxi-) environment, relevant part of the design plan both *aimed* at truth, and *successfully* aimed at truth. I don't know whether or not these conditions are incommensurable in BonJour's sense, but they *are* incommensurable in the sense that no amount or degree of one of them can make up for absence of another.

40. "The *third* condition, for which the term 'justification' is most standardly employed, has to do with the presence of something like a reason or ground for the truth or likely truth of the belief" (p. 49); he's clearly thinking, furthermore, that the ground has to be something of which the epistemic agent is aware.

41. I return to this point on pp. 343 ff. Bonjour says: "I think that his [my] account of *a priori* knowledge as being based merely on a distinctive sort of phenomenology (see *WPF* Ch. 6) is highly misleading at best" (note 16). But here I think he has uncharacteristically erred: my claim was that *a priori* belief is *not* based on evidence, phenomenological or otherwise. See WPF pp. 104, 191–92.

42. See my reply to Feldman, pp. 357–61.

43. BonJour suggests that I was proposing my conditions as an account of *justification* or the third condition. That wasn't what I had in mind: I was intending to give necessary and sufficient conditions for warrant, and that is how I also intend the revised statement in Part I (The Resolution Problem).

44. *An Inquiry into the Human Mind*, in *Inquiries and Essays*, ed. Ronald Beanblossom and Keith Lehrer (Indianapolis: Hackett, 1983), pp. 84–85.

45. See Klein, p. 98.

46. See also Michael Shope's forthcoming *Knowledge as Power*, draft pp. 28–29.

47. For more detail, see pp. 359–60.

48. Swain also refers (pp. 143–45) to some examples of BonJour's involving Norman the clairvoyant; these examples, he says, show that my account isn't sufficient for warrant. I don't find these examples convincing. What makes them initially *seem* convincing, I think, is that we think of Norman as knowing and believing the same sorts of things the rest of us know and believe. If so, he has a defeater for his suddenly and inexplicably acquired belief that the president is in New York. On the other hand, if we *all* had these clairvoyant powers, if there was nothing special about them, then he wouldn't have a defeater and would indeed know.

49. But then what is the force of the 'but only' in the second line of the above quotation?

50. Rather as I am when theologians like Paul Tillich and Gordon Kaufmann advertise their theological views as more sophisticated and satisfactory varieties of theism.

51. *Naturalizing Epistemology* (Cambridge: MIT Press, 1987) p. 3.

52. See WPF chap. 11.

53. As J. B. S. Haldane once quipped, teleology is like a mistress to a biologist: he can't live without her, but he is unwilling to be seen with her in public.

54. Feldman and Conee, "Evidentialism," *Philosophical Studies* 48, pp. 15 ff.

55. Perhaps other conditions should be added; I don't have the space here to go into the matter.

56. There *is* sensuous imagery connected with the belief (I am appeared to as with a fleeting and partial glimpse of a blackboard on which the English sentence $2 + 1 = 3$ is written), but I don't believe the proposition on the basis of that imagery (as I argue on pp. 104 ff. of WPF).

57. Unless we stipulate that a proposition for which I have no evidence automatically fits my evidence, in which case, obviously, of course even worse problems rear their ugly heads.

58. It is of course possible that in some sense *p* seems to you to be true, when the fact is you don't believe *p*. I still find in myself an inclination to believe the proposition *every property has a complement and there is such a property as non-self-exemplification*, even though I also believe that proposition false. But here the question is whether one can believe a proposition when it doesn't so much as seem to you to be true; that's what I am inclined to think is impossible.

59. This response also applies to the first case.

60. It might be argued that God is a necessary being, is essentially omniscient, and in every possible world designs the faculties of cognitive beings; if that were so (and something like it has been a part of much traditional thought about God) then it isn't possible that there be an incompetent designer of cognitive faculties.

61. See WCD chap. 1.

62. Both in *Nous* Vol. XXVII, No. 1 (March 1993).

63. See my replies to Swain and Conee.

64. See WPF chap. 11.

65. "Unfortunately, we do not find in Plantinga's two-volume work any discussion of this further property" (p. 285).

66. See van Fraassen's paper for the suggestion that *materialism* and *naturalism* are not really beliefs but another kind of propositional attitude.

67. According to Descartes (at least as he is ordinarily understood: but see note 29 on p. 13 of WCD) the central epistemic duty is to refrain from believing what is not clear and distinct for you. Since it is not possible, according to him, to refrain from believing what *is* clear and distinct, you can never go wrong by abstaining from belief.

Index

About the Contributors

Laurence BonJour is professor of philosophy at the University of Washington. He is the author of *The Structure of Empirical Knowledge* (Harvard, 1985) and of many articles on epistemolgy and related topics.

Earl Conee is associate professor of philosophy at the University of Rochester. His research includes work in ethics, the philosophy of mind, and epistemology. His publications include "Evidentialism" (*Philosophical Studies,* 1985) with Richard Feldman, and "Evident But Rationally Unacceptable" (*Australasian Journal of Philosophy,* 1987).

Richard Feldman is professor of philosophy and chair of the department at the University of Rochester. His main areas of publication include epistemology, philosophy of mind, and philosophy of language. His publications include "Evidentialism" (*Philosophical Studies,* 1985), "Reliability and Justification" (*Monist,* 1985), "Proper Functionalism" (*Noûs,* 1993), "Good Arguments," in *Knowledge and the Social,* ed. by Fred Schmitt, (Rowman and Littlefield, 1994), "In Defense of Closure" (*Philosophical Quarterly,* 1995), and *Reason and Argument* (Prentice Hall, 1993).

Richard Foley is professor of philosophy and Dean of Arts and Sciences at Rutgers University. He is the author of *The Theory of Epistemic Rationality* (Harvard, 1987) and *Working Without a Net: A Study of Egocentric Epistemology* (Oxford, 1993).

Peter Klein is professor of philosophy at Rutgers University. In a series of papers, beginning with "A Proposed Definition of Propositional Knowlege" (*Journal of Philosophy,* 1971) and continuing through the paper in this volume, he has developed and defended versions of the defeasibility theory of knowledge. In addition, beginning with his book, *Certainty: A Refutation of Scepticism* (Minnesota, 1984) and a series of subsequent articles, he has sought to clarify the various forms of scepticism and to show that no form can ultimately be defended by cogent arguments.

Jonathan L. Kvanvig is professor of philosophy at Texas A&M University. He has published in epistemology, philosophy of religion, and philosophy of language. Among his publications are *The Possibility of an All-Knowing God* (Macmillan, 1986), *The Intellectual Virtues and the Life of the Mind* (Rowman and Littlefield, 1992), and *The Problem of Hell* (Oxford, 1993).

Keith Lehrer is Regents Professor at the University of Arizona and Honorary Professor at Karl-Franzens University of Graz. He is the author of several books, including *Knowledge* (Oxford, 1974), *Rational Consensus in Science and Society* with Carl Wagner (Reidel, 1981), *Thomas Reid* (Routledge, 1989), *Metamind* (Oxford, 1990), *Theory of Knowledge* (Westview and Routledge, 1990). His philosophy is the subject matter of three books edited by others: *Keith Lehrer*, edited by Radu Bogdan (Reidel, 1980), *The Current State of the Coherence Theory: Critical Essays on the Epistemic Theories of Keith Lehrer and Laurence Bonjour*, edited by John W. Bender (Kluwer, 1989), and *Metamind, Knowledge, and Coherence: Essays on the Philosophy of Keith Lehrer*, edited by Johannes Brandl, W. Gomboez, and Christian Piller (Rodopi, 1991). He is past president of the Pacific Division and chair of the Board of Officers of the America Philosophical Association.

William G. Lycan is William Rand Kenan, Jr. Professor of Philosophy at the University of North Carolina. His principal areas of research are the philosophy of language, the philosophy of mind, and epistemology. He is the author of *Logical Form in Natural Language* (MIT, 1984), *Knowing Who* (with Stephen Boër) (MIT, 1986), *Consciousness* (MIT, 1987), *Judgement and Justification* (Cambridge, 1988), *Modality and Meaning* (Kluwer, 1994), and *Consciousness and Experience* (MIT, 1996).

Peter J. Markie is professor of philosophy at the University of Missouri-Columbia. He received his Ph.D. from the University of Massachusetts-Amherst. His publications include *Descartes's Gambit* (Cornell, 1986), *A Professor's Duties* (Rowman and Littlefield, 1995), and numerous articles in the history of philosophy, ethics and, most recently, epistemology.

George S. Pappas is professor of philosophy at Ohio State University. He has also taught at Western Ontario, Texas, Western Washington, and Dalhousie. He is the editor of *Justification and Knowledge* (Reidel, 1979), coeditor (with Marshall Swain) of *Essays on Knowledge and Justification* (Cornell, 1978), and coauthor (with James Cornman and Keith Lehrer) of the 4th edition of *Philosophical Problems and Arguments* (Hackett, 1993).

Alvin Plantinga is O'Brien Professor of Philosophy at the University of Notre Dame. He is well known for his work in philosophy of religion, metaphysics, and epistemology. His major works include *God and Other Minds* (Cornell, 1967), *God, Freedom, and Evil* (Harper & Row, 1974), *The Nature of Necessity* (Oxford, 1974), and the two volumes on warrant, *Warrant: The Current Debate* and *Warrant and Proper Function* (Oxford, 1993).

Ernest Sosa is professor of philosophy and Romeo Elton Professor of Natural Theology at Brown University. He has published papers in metaphysics and epistemology, and some of his work in epistemology has been collected in *Knowledge in Perspective* (Cambridge, 1991).

Marshall Swain is professor of philosophy at Ohio State University. He is the editor of *Induction, Acceptance, and Rational Belief* (Reidel, 1970), coeditor with George Pappas of *Essays on Knowledge and Justification* (Cornell, 1978) and author of *Reasons and Knowledge* (Cornell, 1981).

Bas C. van Fraassen is professor of philosophy at Princeton University. His interests include philosophy of science (especially issues related to probability theory and to the foundations of physics) and philosophical logic. He is the author of *An Introduction to the Philosophy of Time and Space* (Random House, 1970), *Formal Semantics and Logic* (Macmillan, 1971), *The Scientific Image* (Oxford, 1980), *Laws and Symmetry* (Oxford, 1989), and *Quantum Mechanics: An Empiricist View* (Oxford, 1991).